The
Book
of

WISDOM

Multnomah Books *Sisters, Oregon*

THE BOOK OF WISDOM
published by Multnomah Books
Multnomah Publishers, Inc.

© 1997 by Multnomah Publishers, Inc.
International Standard Book Number: 1-57673-176-6
Printed in the United States of America

Unless otherwise indicated, Bible quotations are from
the King James Version (KJV).

Also quoted:
The New International Version (NIV) © 1973, 1984 by International Bible Society, used by permission of Zondervan Publishing House

The Living Bible (TLB) © 1971 by Tyndale House Publishers

The New Testament in Modern English, Revised Student Edition © by J.B. Phillips, 1972,
Macmillan Publishing Company

For information:
Multnomah Publishers, Inc.•Post Office Box 1720•Sisters, Oregon 97759

97 98 99 00 01 02 03 04 — 10 9 8 7 6 5 4 3 2 1

CONTENTS

Selections in this book are
reprinted according to the punctuation,
capitalization, and spelling styles of their original sources.

INTRODUCTION

Shortly after World War II, General Omar Bradley observed, "The world has achieved brilliance without wisdom, power without conscience. Ours is a world of nuclear giants and ethical infants."

Indeed, we live and raise our families in an age when truth and values seem to have unraveled. Ethics have become more situational than steadfast; the road most traveled is often the path of least resistance. When faced with tough situations and choices, we often find it easier to settle for the convenient, the expedient, the less accountable.

Nuclear giants, ethical infants. As years have passed and we have become even more "enlightened," some observers have termed us a culture without a compass, in which people not only are wondering what is the right thing to do, but are also questioning, "Is there a right thing *at all?*"

But recently we've seen encouraging signs of hope—signs that perhaps the infant is waking up and grasping for a compass. One example is the heartening success of William Bennett's *Book of Virtues* among secular and religious audiences alike. Bennett's book seems to have roused the innate desire within people's souls for a moral compass to consult during life's unpredictable journey.

Which brings us, quite naturally, to *The Book of Wisdom*. Whenever we reach that proverbial fork in the road and find ourselves wondering, "What should I do in this situation? Which path should I choose?" we are seeking *wisdom*—the assurance that we're traveling life with compass in hand. Wisdom empowers us to cease wandering situational pathways, to view life's journey from a higher perspective. It gives us the ability to make better choices. To say and do the right thing. To choose character over convenience. To truly enjoy life—because we've chosen the paths that lead to a deeper sense of fulfillment and peace.

If these are your desires, you're going to enjoy—and benefit greatly from— *The Book of Wisdom*.

Within these pages you will find a wealth of practical wisdom through the ages, from classic to contemporary writers. Entries have been carefully selected to provide insight and guidance in fifteen key areas of your life:

- handling adversity
- succeeding with your money
- enjoying and succeeding at your work

- coping with life's hurts
- learning to love
- enjoying a good marriage
- being a good parent
- being a good friend
- being a good citizen
- saying and doing the right thing
- finding peace and fulfillment
- enjoying life to the full
- enjoying your relationship with God
- growing older
- ending well.

Enjoy *The Book of Wisdom* any way you like—in brief glimpses or for hours at a time…as a conversation starter with family or friends…for a relaxing read at hearthside or at bedtime…for help in preparing a talk or presentation…or whenever you reach a fork in the road. You may or may not agree with everything you read (a risk inherent in any anthology from a spectrum of religious and secular writers), but if this book stimulates your thinking or advances your journey toward truth, it will be time well spent. Our hope is that you will realize the wonderful promise written by a very wise man almost 3,000 years ago:

> Turn your ear to wisdom and apply your heart to understanding…then you will find the knowledge of God…you will understand what is right and just and fair—*every good path*. For wisdom will enter your heart, and knowledge will be pleasant to your soul. Discretion will protect you, and understanding will guard you.
>
> Adapted from Proverbs 2:2-3, 5, 9-11 (NIV)

We also wish to extend our grateful thanks and acknowledgment to the outstanding team who prepared this book: Candace McMahan, managing editor; Debbie Gowensmith, Jan Kershner, Lisa Baba Lauffer, and Amy Simpson, contributing editors; and DeAnne Trujillo and Kerri Loesche, assistant editors. To each of you, thank you for your labor of love and for your commitment to excellence. It shows. Many thousands of readers will reap the benefits for years to come.

THE PUBLISHERS

Handling

ADVERSITY

CHAPTER ONE

HANDLING ADVERSITY

—⁓⁓⁓—

Life is difficult.

This is a great truth, one of the greatest truths. It is a great truth because once we truly see this truth, we transcend it. Once we truly know that life is difficult—once we truly understand and accept it—then life is no longer difficult. Because once it is accepted, the fact that life is difficult no longer matters.

> M. Scott Peck, M.D.
> *The Road Less Traveled*

There are occasions when I talk to a man who is riding high on some recent insight or triumph, and for the moment life probably seems to him to have no problems. But I just don't believe that most people are living the smooth, controlled, trouble-free existence that their careful countenances and bland words suggest. Today never hands me the same thing twice and I believe that for most everyone else life is also a mixture of unsolved problems, ambiguous victories and vague defeats—with very few moments of clear peace. I never do seem to quite get on top of it. My struggle with today is worthwhile, but it is a struggle nonetheless and one I will never finish.

> Hugh Prather
> *Notes to Myself*

We must not hope to be mowers,
And to gather the ripe gold ears,
Unless we have first been sowers
And watered the furrows with tears.

It is not just as we take it,
This mystical world of ours,
Life's field will yield as we make it
A harvest of thorns or of flowers.

Johann Wolfgang von Goethe
"Perseverance"

Life doesn't always work the way we'd like it to. If we had our way, it would be easier, consistently fair, and more fun. There'd be no pain and suffering, we wouldn't have to work, and we wouldn't have to die. We'd be happy all the time. Unfortunately, we don't get our way. We get reality instead. But reality is an excellent teacher. It helps us learn, although often slowly and painfully, some of life's greatest lessons. One of them is this: *the world will not devote itself to making us happy.*

Whether we like it or not, this is one of life's great truths. Philosophers have argued for thousands of years about why life works the way it does, but that's not our concern. Our concern is *how* it works. If we don't understand and accept life as it is, we'll keep wishing for something else and never get it. We'll keep complaining and whining about the way things should be but never will be. Once we understand that the world won't devote itself to making us happy, we begin to accept that responsibility for ourselves.

Hal Urban
20 Things I Want My Kids to Know

Pain is inevitable. Suffering is optional.

anonymous

One of the most common and naive sentences in the English language is perhaps the following: "If I can just get through this problem, then everything will be all right." There comes a time, and it may well be the birth of maturity, when we realize that once we get through our present problem there will be another one, slightly larger and a little more intense, waiting to take its place.

Problems are the litmus paper of the human story. How we respond to them may well be a measure of our health. All of us feel overwhelmed at some time or another. But problems in and of themselves are not necessarily bad. In fact, the root of the word *problem* means "to throw or to drive forward." A life without problems would be meaningless and empty.

Tim Hansel
You Gotta Keep Dancin'

The beauty remains; the pain passes.

Auguste Renoir
(his answer when asked why he continued to paint
despite debilitating arthritis)

For the word crisis, the Chinese use a combination of two characters. These two characters are those which designate "danger" and "opportunity." This disjunction seems to be true of every crisis. It is a turning point, and, depending on how one makes the turn, he can find danger or opportunity. The forks in the road of human life that demand decisions of us are always crossroads of danger and opportunity. As in the medical usage of this term, when a patient is pronounced "critical," the implication is that he can move either towards life or death.

In the process of faith, doubts and crises must occur. Paul Tillich points out that only through crises can faith mature. Doubt eats away the old relationship with God, but only so that a new one may be born. The same thing is true of our human, interpersonal relationships...One thing is certain, that passage through the darkness of doubts and crises, however painful they may be, is essential to growth in the process of faith.

John Powell
A Reason to Live! A Reason to Die!

Consider it pure joy, my brothers, whenever you face trials of many kinds, because you know that the testing of your faith develops perseverance. Perseverance must finish its work so that you may be mature and complete, not lacking anything.

James 1:2-4 (NIV)

However mean your life is, meet it and live it; do not shun it and call it hard names. It is not so bad as you are. It looks poorest when you are richest. The faultfinder will find faults even in paradise. Love your life, poor as it is. You may perhaps have some pleasant, thrilling, glorious hours, even in a poorhouse. The setting sun is reflected from the windows of the almshouse as brightly as from the rich man's abode; the snow melts before its door as early in the spring.

Henry David Thoreau
Walden

Just before he died on June 2, 1941, Lou [Gehrig] called me from his office. Mayor LaGuardia had appointed him to the New York City Parole Board to work with and encourage youthful lawbreakers. Gehrig threw himself into the work with everything he had, or had left. He also kept up a lively interest in research into the disease that had driven him out of baseball.

It was a note about the latter that prompted his phone call.

"I've got some good news for you," he said. "Looks like the boys in the labs might have come up with a real breakthrough. They've got some new serum that they've tried on ten of us who have the same problem. And, you know something? It seems to be working on nine out of the ten. How about that?" He was elated.

I tried not to ask the question, but it came out anyway, after a bit.

"How about *you*, Lou?"

Lou said, "Well, it didn't work on me. But how about that for an average?— nine out of ten! Isn't that great!"

I said yes, it was great.

So was he.

Bob Considine
They Rose Above It

When it is dark enough, you can see the stars.

Charles A. Beard

…only one danger can arise from adversity. And that is mistaking your failures for yourself. In other words, if you identify yourself with your failures, problems, and disappointments, you will probably become a failure.

Denis Waitley
Being the Best

Do you know one of life's greatest ways of making us grateful? Overcoming adversity. Grateful people often had a difficult childhood, suffered troubling losses, or had to compete against the odds. And they succeeded. But in doing so, they realized they could just as easily have failed. Although they worked hard, they know that "success" was a gift.

Charlie Hedges
Getting the Right Things Right

An Oak, which hung over the bank of a river, was blown down by a violent storm of wind, and as it was carried along by the stream, some of its boughs brushed against a Reed which grew near the shore. This struck the Oak with a thought of admiration, and he could not forbear asking the Reed how he came to stand so secure and unhurt, in a tempest which had been furious enough to tear up an Oak by the roots? Why, says the Reed, I secure myself by a conduct the reverse of yours: instead of being stubborn and stiff, and confiding in my strength, I yield and bend to the blast, and let it go over me, knowing how vain and fruitless it would be to resist.

Æsop
Fables

As an artist I enjoy watching other artists at work—not just painters, but anyone with an artistic bent.

I recall visiting a sculptor's studio. She was working on several designs, large lumps of clay in various stages of completion. Each piece sat on a turnstile, covered with damp cheesecloth, in a shaded section of her studio. The sculptor moved from one design to another, assured that each piece would remain soft, pliable, and supple until she returned.

The clay could readily harden if the humidity or temperatures in her studio changed even slightly. But not so with the wax my sculptor friend used in designing pieces for reproduction. It remained soft and pliable, easy to work with. Whenever she wanted to create a work of art, she would warm the wax with a hair dryer and it was immediately ready for work.

Hardened clay is brittle, easily damaged. If dropped, it can fracture into a thousand pieces. Dropped wax, however, only bends from the pressure of the fall. Impressionable and pliable, it can be quickly remolded.

People are like that. People who are hardened in their resolve against God are brittle, their emotions are easily damaged. But those who bend to the will of God find perfect expression in however God molds them.

Joni Eareckson Tada
Secret Strength

There is no path
so dark,
nor road so steep,
nor hill so slippery
that other people have
not been there
before me
and survived.
May my dark times
teach me to help
the people I love
on similar journeys.

Maggie Bedrosian
"No Road Too Steep"

Cancer is so limited—
It cannot cripple love
It cannot shatter hope
It cannot corrode faith
It cannot destroy peace
It cannot kill friendship
It cannot suppress memories
It cannot silence courage
It cannot invade the soul
It cannot steal eternal life
It cannot conquer the spirit.

anonymous
"What Cancer Cannot Do"

If you are turning 16, you stand in front of the mirror scrutinizing every inch of your face. You agonize that your nose is too big and you're getting another pimple—on top of which you are feeling dumb, your hair isn't blonde and that boy in your English class has not noticed you yet.

Alison never had those problems. Two years ago, she was a beautiful, popular and smart eleventh-grader, not to mention a varsity lacrosse goalie and an ocean lifeguard. With her tall slender body, pool-blue eyes and thick blonde hair, she looked more like a swimsuit model than a high school student. But during that summer, something changed.

After a day of lifeguarding, Alison couldn't wait to get home, rinse the salt-water out of her hair and comb through the tangles. She flipped her sun-bleached mane forward. "Ali!" her mother cried. "What did you do?" She had discovered a bare patch of skin on the top of her daughter's scalp. "Did you shave it? Could someone else have done it when you were sleeping?" Quickly, they solved the mystery—Alison must have wrapped the elastic band too tightly around her pony tail. The incident was soon forgotten.

Three months later, another bald spot was found, then another. Soon, Alison's scalp was dotted with peculiar quarter-sized bare patches. After diagnoses of "It's just stress" to remedies of topical ointments, a specialist began to administer injections of cortisone, 50 in each spot to be exact, every two weeks. To mask her scalp, bloody from the shots, Alison was granted permission to wear a baseball hat to school, normally a violation of the strict uniform code. Little strands of hair would push through the scabs, only to fall out two weeks later. She was suffering from a condition of hair loss known as alopecia, and nothing would stop it.

Alison's sunny spirit and supportive friends kept her going, but there were some low points. Like the time when her little sister came into her bedroom with a towel wrapped around her head to have her hair combed. When her mother untwisted the towel, Alison watched the tousled thick hair bounce around her sister's shoulders. Gripping all of her limp hair between two fingers, she burst into tears. It was the first time she had cried since the whole experience began.

As time went on, a bandanna replaced the hat, which could no longer conceal her balding scalp. With only a handful of wispy strands left, the time had come to buy a wig. Instead of trying to resurrect her once long blonde hair, pretending like nothing was ever lost, she opted for an auburn shoulder-length one.

Why not? People cut and dye their hair all the time. With her new look, Alison's confidence strengthened. Even when the wig blew off from an open window of her friend's car, they could all share in the humor.

As summer approached, Alison began to worry. If she couldn't wear a wig in the water, how could she lifeguard again? "Why, did you forget how to swim?" her father asked. She got the message.

And after wearing an uncomfortable bathing cap for only one day, she mustered up the courage to go completely bald. Despite the stares and occasional comments from less than polite beachcombers—"Why do you crazy punk kids shave your heads?"—Alison adjusted to her new look.

She arrived back at school that fall, no hair, no eyebrows, no eyelashes, with her wig tucked away somewhere at the back of her closet. As she had always planned, she would run for school president—changing her campaign speech only slightly. Presenting a slide show on famous bald leaders from Gandhi to Mr. Clean, Alison had the students and faculty rolling in the aisles.

In her first speech as the elected president, Alison addressed her condition, quite comfortable answering questions. Dressed in a tee shirt with the words "Bad Hair Day" printed across the front, she pointed to her shirt and said, "When most of you wake up in the morning and don't like how you look, you may put on this tee shirt." Putting on another tee shirt over the other, she continued. "When I wake up in the morning, I put on this one." It read, "No Hair Day." Everybody cheered and applauded. And Alison, beautiful, popular and smart, not to mention varsity goalie, ocean lifeguard and now school president with the pool-blue eyes, smiled back from the podium.

Alison Lambert with Jennifer Rosenfeld
"No Hair Day"

The world breaks everyone and afterwards many are strong at the broken places.
Ernest Hemingway
A Farewell to Arms

The modern technology which has brought us so many helpful new products, plastics, insecticides, and preservatives looms like a deadly curse for a friend of mine.

Linda has been chemically poisoned. As a result, she's lost the ability to tolerate this synthetic world of ours.

I went to see her last week at her little place tucked back in the Santa Barbara hills. For two weeks prior, I had to go through a total "detoxification" of my clothes, my body, and my hair. I couldn't use perfumes, deodorants, or soaps. I couldn't even eat garlic or onion or anything spicy.

As we ate together in her home, Linda described an incident from the previous week. She was forced to endure a lengthy confinement in her bedroom simply because the neighbors down the road were having a barbecue. One whiff of wind-blown lighter fluid can cause her to lose consciousness.

Because of her disability, Linda is mostly alone. She is isolated from friends and family. Yet her solitude is often disturbed by a persistent visitor at her door. This unwelcome acquaintance knocks and knocks, whining and pleading to get in.

His name is Self-Pity.

It's certainly easy to understand why Linda feels tempted to let this unrelenting visitor in. It would be easy to feel sorry for herself when she has to use an old-style metal telephone with ancient, deteriorating parts that can't be replaced. Her shouted conversations over that phone leave her frustrated and exhausted.

Does she have it rough? Don't you think she deserves some time off for a few hours' visit with Self-Pity? Some people would say yes—and understandably so.

But Linda? Listen to what she told me:

"No, Joni, suffering and sickness and pain don't rank high on my list of best possible options for a happy life. But God alone can determine what's best for me. Only He sees the beginning from the end. He's the only One who knows what it's going to take to conform me to the image of His Son. And He spares no pain in accomplishing His will in my life. I don't need pity; and what I need even less is my own pity."

We all find days when Self-Pity, like an obnoxious salesman, keeps ringing the bell and pounding on our door. Days when we feel as though nobody has it as tough as we do. You know those days: a dish clatters to the floor, the phone rings, the garbage disposal chokes to death, the automatic garage door opener goes on strike, and the bank informs you that another check just bounced.

Ah, poor me! you think to yourself.

Before you offer hospitality to old Self-Pity, remember Linda in the Santa Barbara hills. Linda who endures so much aloneness, but surrounds herself with the prayers of caring Christian friends…and refuses to allow that persistent knocker entrance.

If she can keep that door closed and latched, so can you.

Joni Eareckson Tada
Glorious Intruder

God uses chronic pain and weakness, along with other afflictions, as his chisel for sculpting our lives. Felt weakness deepens dependence on Christ for strength each day. The weaker we feel, the harder we lean. And the harder we lean, the stronger we grow spiritually, even while our bodies waste away. To live with your "thorn" uncomplainingly—that is, sweet, patient, and free in heart to love and help others, even though every day you feel weak—is *true* sanctification. It is true healing for the spirit. It is a supreme victory of grace. The healing of your sinful person thus goes forward, even though the healing of your mortal body does not. And the healing of persons is the name of the game so far as God is concerned.

Dr. J. I. Packer
Hot Tub Religion

"W. T., how did you like your heart attack?"

"It scared me to death, almost."

"Would you like to do it again?"

"No!"

"Would you recommend it?"

"Definitely not."

"Does your life mean more to you than it did before?"

"Well, yes."

"You and Nell have always had a beautiful marriage, but now are you closer than ever?"

"Yes."

"How about that new granddaughter?"

"Yes. Did I show you her picture?"

"Do you have a new compassion for people—a deep understanding and sympathy?"

"Yes."

"Do you know the Lord in a richer, deeper fellowship than you had ever realized could be possible?"

"Yes."

"How'd you like your heart attack?"

Silence was his answer.

Bob Benson
Something's Going on Here

Not only so, but we also rejoice in our sufferings, because we know that suffering produces perseverance; perseverance, character; and character, hope. And hope does not disappoint us, because God has poured out his love into our hearts by the Holy Spirit, whom he has given us.

Romans 5:3-5 (NIV)

We do not first get all the answers and then live in light of our understanding. We must rather plunge into life—meeting what we have to meet and experiencing what we have to experience—and in the light of living try to understand. If insight comes at all, it will not be before, but only through and after experience.

John Claypool
Tracks of a Fellow Struggler

And so they made themselves comfortable; but the poor duckling, who had crept out of his shell last of all, and looked so ugly, was bitten and pushed and made fun of, not only by the ducks, but by all the poultry. "He is too big," they all said, and the turkey cock, who had been born into the world with spurs, and fancied himself really an emperor, puffed himself out like a vessel in full sail, and flew at the duckling, and became quite red in the head with passion, so that the poor little thing did not know where to go, and was quite miserable because he was so ugly and laughed at by the whole farmyard. So it went on from day to day till it got worse and worse. The poor duckling was driven about by every one; even his brothers and sisters were unkind to him, and would say, "Ah, you ugly creature, I wish the cat would get you," and his mother said she wished he had never been born. The ducks pecked him, the chickens beat him, and the girl who fed the poultry kicked him with her feet. So at last he ran away, frightening the little birds in the hedge as he flew over the palings…

It would be very sad, were I to relate all the misery and privations which the poor little duckling endured during the hard winter; but when it had passed, he found himself lying one morning in a moor, amongst the rushes. He felt the warm sun shining, and heard the lark singing, and saw that all around was beautiful spring. Then the young bird felt that his wings were strong, as he flapped them against his sides, and rose high into the air. They bore him onwards, until he found himself in a large garden, before he well knew how it had happened. The apple-trees were in full blossom, and the fragrant elders bent their long green branches down to the stream which wound round a smooth lawn. Everything looked beautiful, in the freshness of early spring. From a thicket close by came three beautiful white swans, rustling their feathers, and swimming lightly over the smooth water. The duckling remembered the lovely birds, and felt more strangely unhappy than ever.

"I will fly to those royal birds," he exclaimed, "and they will kill me, because I am so ugly, and dare to approach them; but it does not matter: better be killed by them than pecked by the ducks, beaten by the hens, pushed about by the maiden who feeds the poultry, or starved with hunger in the winter."

Then he flew to the water, and swam towards the beautiful swans. The moment they espied the stranger, they rushed to meet him with outstretched wings.

"Kill me," said the poor bird; and he bent his head down to the surface of the water, and awaited death.

But what did he see in the clear stream below? His own image; no longer a dark, gray bird, ugly and disagreeable to look at, but a graceful and beautiful swan. To be born in a duck's nest, in a farmyard, is of no consequence to a bird, if it is hatched from a swan's egg. He now felt glad at having suffered sorrow and trouble, because it enabled him to enjoy so much better all the pleasure and happiness around him; for the great swans swam round the new-comer, and stroked his neck with their beaks, as a welcome.

Into the garden presently came some little children, and threw bread and cake into the water.

"See," cried the youngest, "there is a new one," and the rest were delighted, and ran to their father and mother, dancing and clapping their hands, and shouting joyously, "There is another swan come; a new one has arrived."

Then they threw more bread and cake into the water, and said, "The new one is the most beautiful of all; he is so young and pretty." And the old swans bowed their heads before him.

Then he felt quite ashamed, and hid his head under his wing; for he did not know what to do, he was so happy, and yet not at all proud. He had been perse-cuted and despised for his ugliness, and now he heard them say he was the most beautiful of all the birds. Even the elder-tree bent down its bows into the water before him, and the sun shone warm and bright. Then he rustled his feathers, curved his slender neck, and cried joyfully, from the depths of his heart, "I never dreamed of such happiness as this, while I was an ugly duckling."

Hans Christian Andersen
"The Ugly Duckling"

Character cannot be developed in ease and quiet. Only through experience of trial and suffering can the soul be strengthened, vision cleared, ambition inspired, and success achieved.

Helen Keller
Helen Keller's Journal

Batter my heart, three personed God; for you
As yet but knock, breathe, shine, and seek to mend;
That I may rise and stand, o'erthrow me and bend
Your force to break, blow, burn and make me new.
I, like an usurped town, to another due,
Labour to admit you, but Oh, to no end;
Reason, your viceroy in me, me should defend,
But is captived and proves weak or untrue.

Yet dearly I love you and would be loved fain,
But am betrothed unto your enemy:
Divorce me, untie or break that knot again,
Take me to you, imprison me, for I
Except you enthrall me, never shall be free,
Nor ever chaste, except you ravish me.

John Donne
"Batter My Heart"

Adversity introduces a man to himself.

anonymous

God created man something on the order of a rubber band. A rubber band is made to stretch. When it is not being stretched, it is small and relaxed; but as long as it remains in that shape, it is not doing what it was made to do. When it stretches, it is enlarged; it becomes tense and dynamic, and it does what it was made to do. God created *you* to stretch.

Charles Paul Conn
Making It Happen

I asked the Lord that I might grow
In faith and love and every grace—
Might more of His salvation know,
And seek more earnestly His face.

'Twas He who taught me thus to pray,
And He, I trust, has answered prayer;
But it has been in such a way
As almost drove me to despair.

I hoped that in some favored hour
At once He'd answer my request;
And, by His love's consuming power,
Subdue my sins, and give me rest.

Instead of this, He made me feel
The hidden evils of my heart,
And let the angry powers of hell
Assault my soul in every part.

Yes, more, with His own hand He seemed
Intent to aggravate my woe;
Crossed all the fair designs I schemed,
Blasted my gourds, and laid them low.

"Lord, why is this?" I trembling cried:
"Wilt Thou pursue Thy worm to death?"
"'Tis in this way," the Lord replied,
"I answer prayer for grace and faith.

"These inward trials I employ,
From self and pride to set thee free
And break the schemes of earthly joy,
That thou mayest seek thy all in Me."

anonymous
"The Lord's Way"

The more rain, the more rest,
Fine weather's not always best.

Mother Goose

I'll never forget the night in 1946 when disaster and challenge visited our home.

My brother George came home from football practice and collapsed with a 104-degree temperature. After an examination, the doctor informed us it was polio. This was before the days of Dr. Salk; polio was well-known in Webster, Missouri, having killed and crippled many children and teenagers.

After the crisis had passed, the doctor felt it was his duty to inform George of the horrible truth. "I hate to tell you this, son," he said, "but the polio has taken such a toll that you'll probably never walk again without a limp, and your left arm will be useless."

...The next day the nurse walked into his room to find him lying flat on his face on the floor.

"What's going on?" asked the shocked nurse.

"I'm walking," George calmly replied.

He refused the use of any braces or even a crutch. Sometimes it would take him 20 minutes to get out of the chair, but he refused any offers of aid.

I remember seeing him lift a tennis ball with as much effort as a healthy man would lift a 100-pound barbell.

I also remember seeing him step out on the mat as captain of the wrestling team.

But the story doesn't stop there. The following year, after being named to start for Missouri Valley College in one of the first football games to be televised locally, he came down with mononucleosis.

It was my brother Bob who helped reinforce George's already strong philosophy of never giving up.

The family was sitting in his room at the hospital when Valley's quarterback completed a 12-yard pass to the tight end and the announcer said, "And George Schlatter makes the first catch of the game."

Shocked, we all looked at the bed to make sure George was still there. Then we realized what had happened. Bob, who had also made the starting line-up, had worn George's number so George could spend the afternoon hearing himself catching six passes and making countless tackles.

As he overcame mono, he did it with the lesson Bob taught him that day—there is always a way!

George was destined to spend the next three falls in the hospital. In 1948, it was after he stepped on a rusty nail. In 1949, it was tonsillitis, just before he was to sing in an audition for Phil Harris. And in 1950, it was third-degree burns over 40 percent of his body and collapsed lungs. His life had been saved by my brother Alan who, after an explosion had set George's body on fire, put the flames out by throwing himself on George. He received serious burns himself.

But after each challenge, George came back stronger and more sure of his own ability to overcome any obstacle. He had read that if one looks at the roadblocks, he isn't looking at the goal.

Armed with these gifts of the spirit and the laughter of the soul, he entered the world of show business and revolutionized television by creating and producing such innovative shows as "Laugh In" and "American Comedy Awards," and has won an Emmy for his special on Sammy Davis Jr.

He had literally been through the furnace and had come out of it with a soul as strong as steel, and used it to strengthen and entertain a nation.

John Wayne Schlatter
"The Finest Steel Gets Sent Through the Hottest Furnace"

Pain that cannot forget
falls drop by drop
upon the heart

until in our despair there comes wisdom
through the awful
grace of God.

Æschylus

I asked God for strength, that I might achieve.
I was made weak, that I might learn humbly to obey...

I asked for health, that I might do great things.
I was given infirmity, that I might do better things...

I asked for riches, that I might be happy.
I was given poverty, that I might be wise...

I asked for power, that I might have the praise of men.
I was given weakness, that I might feel the need of God...

I asked for all things, that I might enjoy life.
I was given life, that I might enjoy all things...

I got nothing I asked for—but everything I had hoped for.

Almost despite myself, my unspoken prayers were answered.

I am, among men, most richly blessed!

an unknown Confederate soldier
"A Creed for Those Who Have Suffered"

Others decide to leave their troubles to God and then get well. Let the problems in your life be your teachers. Always describe your difficulties with words that express your feelings. Then look at the things in your life that fit the description and heal them. Your life will improve and you will derive physical benefits, too. Remember, life is a labor pain but the pains are not inflicted by someone else. You decide what you go through to give birth to yourself.

Bernie S. Siegel, M.D.
Foreword: Chicken Soup for the Surviving Soul

Nothing about being human amazes me more than this capacity for revival.

How dull and meaningless and hopeless life can seem—only to become exciting, vibrant, and filled with hope the next day. Whole nations come back from destruction and oppressions—when great problems get addressed and resolved.

All our exits may become entrances.

The human capacity to take whatever life dishes out and to come back is never to be underestimated. How amazing it is, knowing we are all going to die anyhow, that we are so determined to live as well as we can, no matter what. For all our little deaths, we defy our fate and come to life again and again, and yet again.

Robert Fulghum
From Beginning to End

'Tis a lesson you should heed,
Try, try again.
If at first you don't succeed,
Try, try again.

W. E. Hickson
Try and Try Again

These are the times that try men's souls. The summer soldier and the sunshine patriot will, in this crisis, shrink from the service of their country; but he that stands it *now*, deserves the love and thanks of man and woman. Tyranny, like hell, is not easily conquered; yet we have this consolation with us, that the harder the conflict, the more glorious the triumph. What we obtain too cheap, we esteem too lightly: it is dearness only that gives every thing its value. Heaven knows how to put a proper price upon its goods; and it would be strange indeed if so celestial an article as FREEDOM should not be highly rated...

I love the man that can smile in trouble, that can gather strength from distress, and grow brave by reflection. 'Tis the business of little minds to shrink; but he whose heart is firm, and whose conscience approves his conduct, will pursue his principles unto death.

Thomas Paine
Speech to American revolutionary troops
facing a crisis of morale

If you're trying to achieve, there will be roadblocks. I've had them; everybody has had them.

But obstacles don't have to stop you. If you run into a wall, don't turn around and give up. Figure out how to climb it, go through it, or work around it.

Michael Jordan
I Can't Accept Not Trying

Had an old neighbor when I was growing up named Doctor Gibbs. He didn't look like any doctor I'd ever known. Every time I saw him, he was wearing denim overalls and a straw hat, the front brim of which was green sunglass plastic. He smiled a lot, a smile that matched his hat—old and crinkly and well-worn. He never yelled at us for playing in his yard. I remember him as someone who was a lot nicer than circumstances warranted.

When Doctor Gibbs wasn't saving lives, he was planting trees. His house sat on ten acres, and his life-goal was to make it a forest. The good doctor had some interesting theories concerning plant husbandry. He came from the "No pain, no gain" school of horticulture. He never watered his new trees, which flew in the face of conventional wisdom. Once I asked why. He said that watering plants spoiled them, and that if you water them, each successive tree generation will grow weaker and weaker. So you have to make things rough for them and weed out the weenie trees early on.

He talked about how watering trees made for shallow roots, and how trees that weren't watered had to grow deep roots in search of moisture. I took him to mean that deep roots were to be treasured.

So he never watered his trees. He'd plant an oak and, instead of watering it every morning, he'd beat it with a rolled up newspaper. Smack! Slap! Pow! I asked him why he did that, and he said it was to get the tree's attention.

Doctor Gibbs went to glory a couple years after I left home. Every now and again, I walk by his house and look at the trees that I'd watched him plant some twenty-five years ago. They're granite strong now. Big and robust. Those trees wake up in the morning and beat their chests and drink their coffee black.

I planted a couple trees a few years back. Carried water to them for a solid summer. Sprayed them. Prayed over them. The whole nine yards. Two years of coddling has resulted in trees that expect to be waited on hand and foot. Whenever a cold wind blows in, they tremble and chatter their branches. Sissy trees.

Funny thing about those trees of Doctor Gibbs. Adversity and deprivation seemed to benefit them in ways comfort and ease never could.

Every night before I go to bed, I go check on my two sons. I stand over them and watch their little bodies, the rising and falling of life within. I often pray for them. Mostly I pray that their lives will be easy. "Lord, spare them from hardship." But lately I've been thinking that it's time to change my prayer.

Has to do with the inevitability of cold winds that hit us at the core. I know my children are going to encounter hardship, and my praying they won't is naive. There's always a cold wind blowing somewhere.

So I'm changing my eventide prayer. Because life is tough, whether we want it to be or not. Instead, I'm going to pray that my sons' roots grow deep, so they can draw strength from the hidden sources of the eternal God.

Too many times we pray for ease, but that's a prayer seldom met. What we need to do is pray for roots that reach deep into the Eternal, so when the rains fall and the winds blow, we won't be swept asunder.

Philip Gulley
Front Porch Tales

When life hands us difficult circumstances and dangerous situations, we all need safe hiding places. When you face the fire, where do you go to seek rescue?

A whole host of dangers lie in life's path, and at any time those dangers can threaten to overtake us. Many say we have a *multitude* of places to seek safety from life's challenges, but truly we have only one—Jesus Christ.

Consider the early pioneers who traveled across the vast plains of America. As they crossed the country, they often found themselves in a sea of grass for miles on end. In autumn, the grass turned brown and dry from exposure to the sun and lack of water. This condition caused a huge fire hazard, and the pioneers greatly feared seeing a wall of fire coming their way! They feared that they would have no escape as the wind blew the fire toward them faster than they could run. But the pioneers devised a way to survive this hazard. When they saw a wall of fire coming toward them, they ignited the grass behind them. The wind bringing the fire toward them also blew out the fire behind them, leaving a safe firebreak. The pioneers simply moved into the center of the blackened area, and when the larger wall of fire approached them, it went around them, leaving them unscathed. The pioneers' only safe haven in the midst of the fire was where the fire had already been.

We read in 2 Peter that "the day of the Lord will come…and the elements will melt with fervent heat; both the earth and the works that are in it will be burned up." Even as we read, the fire of God's wrath comes upon this world, and we have only one safe hiding place. When that fire comes, we need to run to the place where the fire has already been—the cross of Christ. Through faith in Christ we realize that the fire that fell upon Him should have fallen upon us, and we find the one place of escape.

Perhaps you face a wall of fire today. If so, seek the One who has endured the fire, for you'll find safety only in His presence.

D. James Kennedy and Jerry Newcombe
New Every Morning

Four score and seven years ago, our fathers brought forth on this continent a new nation, conceived in liberty, and dedicated to the proposition that all men are created equal.

Now we are engaged in a great civil war, testing whether that nation, or any nation so conceived and so dedicated, can long endure. We are met on a great battlefield of that war. We have come to dedicate a portion of that field as a final resting place for those who here gave their lives that that nation might live. It is altogether fitting and proper that we should do this.

But in a larger sense we cannot dedicate, we cannot consecrate, we cannot hallow this ground. The brave men, living and dead, who struggled here, have consecrated it far above our poor power to add or detract. The world will little note, nor long remember, what we say here, but it can never forget what they did here. It is for us the living, rather, to be dedicated here to the unfinished work which they who fought here have thus far so nobly advanced. It is rather for us to be here dedicated to the great task remaining before us—that from these honored dead we take increased devotion to that cause for which they gave the last full measure of devotion, that we here highly resolve that these dead shall not have died in vain, that this nation, under God, shall have a new birth of freedom, and that government of the people, by the people, for the people, shall not perish from the earth.

Abraham Lincoln
"The Gettysburg Address"

Little strokes fell great oaks.

Benjamin Franklin
Poor Richard's Almanac

As disasters go, this one was terrible, but not unique, certainly not among the worst on the roster of U. S. air crashes. There was the unusual element of the bridge, of course, and the fact that the plane clipped it at a moment of high traffic, one routine thus intersecting another and disrupting both. Then, too, there was the location of the event. Washington, the city of form and regulations, turned chaotic, deregulated, by a blast of real winter and a single slap of metal on metal. The jets from Washington National Airport that normally swoop around the presidential monuments like famished gulls are, for the moment, emblemized by the one that fell; so there is that detail. And there was the aesthetic clash as well—blue-and-green Air Florida, the name a flying garden, sunk down among gray chunks in a black river. All that was worth noticing, to be sure. Still, there was nothing very special in any of it, except death, which, while always special, does not necessarily bring millions to tears or to attention. Why, then, the shock here?

Perhaps because the nation saw in this disaster something more than a mechanical failure. Perhaps because people saw in it no failure at all, but rather something successful about their makeup. Here, after all, were two forms of nature in collision: the elements and human character. Last Wednesday, the elements, indifferent as ever, brought down Flight 90. And on that same afternoon, human nature—groping and flailing in mysteries of its own—rose to the occasion.

Of the four acknowledged heroes of the event, three are able to account for their behavior. Donald Usher and Eugene Windsor, a park police helicopter team, risked their lives every time they dipped the skids into the water to pick up survivors. On television, side by side in bright blue jumpsuits, they described their courage as all in the line of duty. Lenny Skutnik, a 28-year-old employee of the Congressional Budget Office, said: "It's something I never thought I would do"—referring to his jumping into the water to drag an injured woman to shore. Skutnik added that "somebody had to go in the water," delivering every hero's line that is no less admirable for its repetitions. In fact, nobody had to go into the water. That somebody actually did so is part of the reason this particular tragedy sticks in the mind.

But the person most responsible for the emotional impact of the disaster is the one known at first simply as "the man in the water." (Balding, probably in his 50s, an extravagant mustache.) He was seen clinging with five other survivors to the tail section of the airplane. This man was described by Usher and Windsor as appearing alert and in control. Every time they lowered a lifeline and flotation ring to him, he passed it on to another of the passengers. "In a mass casualty, you'll find people like him," said Windsor. "But I've never seen one with that commitment." When the helicopter came back for him, the man had gone under. His selflessness was one reason the story held national attention; his anonymity another. The fact that he went unidentified invested him with a universal character. For a while he was Everyman, and thus proof (as if one needed it) that no man is ordinary.

Still, he could never have imagined such a capacity in himself. Only minutes before his character was tested, he was sitting in the ordinary plane among the ordinary passengers, dutifully listening to the stewardess telling him to fasten his seat belt and saying something about the "no smoking sign." So our man relaxed with the others, some of whom would owe their lives to him. Perhaps he started to read, or to doze, or to regret some harsh remark made in the office that morning. Then suddenly he knew that the trip would not be ordinary. Like every other person on that flight, he was desperate to live, which makes his final act so stunning.

For at some moment in the water he must have realized that he would not live if he continued to hand over the rope and ring to others. He *had* to know it, no matter how gradual the effect of the cold. In his judgment he had no choice. When the helicopter took off with what was to be the last survivor, he watched everything in the world move away from him, and he deliberately let it happen.

Yet there was something else about the man that kept our thoughts on him, and which keeps our thoughts on him still. He was *there,* in the essential, classic circumstance. Man in nature. The man in the water. For its part, nature cared nothing about the five passengers. Our man, on the other hand, cared totally. So the timeless battle commenced in the Potomac. For as long as that man could last, they went at each other, nature and man; the one making no distinctions of good and evil, acting on no principles, offering no lifelines; the other acting wholly on distinctions, principles and, one supposes, on faith.

Since it was he who lost the fight, we ought to come again to the conclusion that people are powerless in the world. In reality, we believe the reverse, and it takes the act of the man in the water to remind us of our true feelings in this matter. It is not to say that everyone would have acted as he did, or as Usher, Windsor and Skutnik. Yet whatever moved these men to challenge death on behalf of their fellows is not peculiar to them. Everyone feels the possibility in himself. That is the abiding wonder of the story. That is why we would not let go of it. If the man in the water gave a lifeline to the people gasping for survival, he was likewise giving a lifeline to those who observed him.

The odd thing is that we do not even really believe that the man in the water lost his fight. "Everything in Nature contains all the powers of Nature," said Emerson. Exactly. So the man in the water had his own natural powers. He could not make ice storms, or freeze the water until it froze the blood. But he could hand life over to a stranger, and that is a power of nature too. The man in the water pitted himself against an implacable, impersonal enemy; he fought it with charity; and he held it to a standoff. He was the best we can do.

Roger Rosenblatt
"The Man in the Water," Time, January 25, 1982

When I consider how my light is spent,
Ere half my days in this dark world and wide,
And that one talent which is death to hide
Lodged with me useless, though my soul more bent
To serve therewith my Maker, and present
My true account, lest He returning chide;
"Doth God exact day-labor, light denied?"
I fondly ask. But Patience, to prevent
That murmur, soon replies, "God doth not need
Either man's work or His own gifts. Who best
Bear His mild yoke, they serve Him best. His state
Is kingly: thousands at His bidding speed,
And post o'er land and ocean without rest;
They also serve who only stand and wait."

John Milton
"When I Consider How My Light Is Spent"
(written after this poet had become blind)

One of my joys and passions is my voice. I love to perform in our local community theaters. My throat became very sore during a particularly grueling show run. It was my first time performing an operatic piece, and I was terrified I had actually done damage to my vocal cords. I was a lead and we were about to open. So I made an appointment with my family doctor where I waited for an hour. I finally left in a huff, went back to work, grabbed a phone book and found a throat specialist close by. Once more I made an appointment and off I went.

The nurse showed me in and I sat down to wait for the doctor. I was feeling very disgruntled. I rarely get sick and here I was sick when I needed to be healthy. Besides, I had to take time out of my workday to go to two different doctors, both of whom kept me waiting. It was very frustrating. Why do these things have to happen? A moment later the nurse came back in and said, "May I ask you something personal?"

This seemed odd; what else do they ask you but personal questions in a doctor's office? But I looked at the nurse and replied, "Yes, of course."

"I noticed your hand," she said a bit hesitantly.

I lost half of my left hand in a forklift accident when I was 11. I think it is one of the reasons I didn't follow my dream of performing in theater, although everyone says, "Gee, I never noticed! You are so natural." In the back of my mind I thought that they only wanted to see perfect people on stage. No one would want to see me. Besides, I'm too tall, overweight, not really talented…no, they don't want to see me. But I love musical comedies and I do have a good voice. So one day I tried out at our local community theater. I was the first one they cast! That was three years ago. Since then, I have been cast in almost everything I tried out for.

The nurse continued, "What I need to know is how it has affected your life."

Never in the 25 years since it happened has someone asked me this. Maybe they'll say, "Does it bother you?" but never anything as sweeping as, "How has it affected your life?"

After an awkward pause, she said, "You see I just had a baby, and her hand is like yours. I, well, I need to know how it has affected your life."

"How has it affected my life?" I thought about it a bit so I could think of the right words to say. Finally, I said, "It has affected my life, but not in a bad way—I do many things that people with two normal hands find difficult. I type about 75 words a minute, I play guitar, I have ridden and shown horses for years, I even have a Horsemaster Degree. I'm involved in musical theater and I am a professional speaker, I'm constantly in front of a crowd. I do television shows four or five times a year. I think it was never 'difficult' because of the love and encouragement of my family. They always talked about all the great notoriety I would get because I would learn how to do things with one hand that most people had trouble doing with two. We were all very excited about that. That was the main focus, not the handicap.

"Your daughter does not have a problem. She is normal. You are the one who will teach her to think of herself as anything else. She will come to know she is 'different,' but you will teach her that *different* is wonderful. Normal means you are average. What's fun about that?"

She was silent for a while. Then she simply said, "Thank you" and walked out.

I sat there thinking, "Why do these things have to happen?" Everything happens for a reason—even that forklift falling on my hand. All the circumstances leading up to me being at this doctor's office and this moment in time happened for a reason.

The doctor came in, looked at my throat and said he wanted to anesthetize and put a probe down it to examine it. Well, singers are very paranoid about putting medical instruments down their throats, especially ones so rough they need to be anesthetized! I said, "No thanks," and walked out.

The next day, my throat was completely better.

Why do these things have to happen?

Lilly Walters
"Why Do These Things Have to Happen?"

To keep me from becoming conceited because of these surpassingly great revelations, there was given me a thorn in my flesh, a messenger of Satan, to torment me. Three times I pleaded with the Lord to take it away from me. But he said to me, "My grace is sufficient for you, for my power is made perfect in weakness." Therefore I will boast all the more gladly about my weaknesses, so that Christ's power may rest on me. That is why, for Christ's sake, I delight in weaknesses, in insults, in hardships, in persecutions, in difficulties. For when I am weak, then I am strong.

2 Corinthians 12:7-10 (NIV)

The Chinese believe that before you can conquer a beast, you must first make it beautiful. It may sound contradictory, but for all the losses we incur in illness, we also have an opportunity to gain. You may mourn your losses, but you do not allow these losses to obscure your sense of what you can become. You may curse your fate, but you must also count your possibilities.

...One of the things that has so impressed me as I talk to people with life-threatening illnesses is the fact that they often say the sickness is worth what they learned from it, about themselves and about God. I'm sure not every ill person feels that way, but if not, they are missing one of the great blessings of life.

Few things focus the mind like being diagnosed with a deadly disease. Being a minister for forty years has given me the awesome privilege of standing by the bedside of many a saint as they have gone to meet God. I've talked to many businessmen as they lay dying. And do you know what? None have ever said to me, "Oh, Pastor, I wish I had spent more time at the office." You know what they say? "Oh, Pastor, I wish I had spent more time with my family."

I remember that after my mother had been diagnosed with cancer, she talked to me about noticing the leaf on a tree, how green a blade of grass was, the shape of clouds, the song of a bird, and the design on a rose. Her senses were tremendously heightened. Often only after being confronted with a life-threatening illness, do we realize the price tags *have truly* been switched and that most of our labor has been in the junk business.

Recovery may not be possible in every case but renewal is. The opportunity for reexamination and reevaluation of the life you have been living and the values you have lived for offers you the chance to choose the new life you will lead, rather than simply living out the one you have accumulated over the years. In short, you answer the question, "Is what I have been living for worth dying for?" Even for terminal patients, whatever time may be left to them can be spent living out a renewed life. Renewal comes from a fresh encounter with God, a new appreciation of His Work and His grace, a higher regard for friends and fellowship.

...As much as I appreciate good health, if I make it a requirement for a happy life, then I am enslaved to the fickleness of life and the unpredictability of my body. If in the growth process I have been brought up to believe that "prosperity" is the norm and my right, I will be flattened when I slam into the wall of reality. It takes time to recover from this surprising assault on my beliefs. Then gradually I begin to recover, learning that real life doesn't require "prosperity."

I must ask myself the question: Does my happiness, my joy, my feeling of worth depend upon being healthy? We are free when we no longer require health, however much we prefer it, to be happy and at peace.

...Let's face it, most of us will not trust God until we have to. As long as we have one more dollar in the bank, one more how-to book to read, one more seminar to attend, one more trick up our sleeve, we will not trust God.

...it is not the praises of prosperity that impress me, but the praises that come from adversity...For it is as we discover and embrace the work God is intending to do in us, that we can also accept His method of reaching us—and experience deeper faith, stronger courage, and even more genuine joy in the midst of suffering.

Ron Dunn
Will God Heal Me?

At this moment, America, the finest, most loving nation on Earth, is at war, at war against the oldest enemy of the human spirit: evil that threatens world peace.

At this moment, men and women of courage and endurance stand on the harsh desert and sail the seas of the Gulf. By their presence they're bearing witness to the fact that the triumph of the moral order is the vision that compels us. At this moment, those of us here at home are thinking of them and of the future of our world. I recall Abraham Lincoln and his anguish during the Civil War. He turned to prayer, saying: "I've been driven many times to my knees by the overwhelming conviction that I have nowhere else to go."

So many of us, compelled by a deep need for God's wisdom in all we do, turn to prayer. We pray for God's protection in all we undertake, for God's love to fill all hearts, and for God's peace to be the moral North Star that guides us. So, I have proclaimed Sunday, February 3d, National Day of Prayer. In this moment of crisis, may Americans of every creed turn to our greatest power and unite together in prayer.

Let us pray for the safety of the troops, these men and women who have put their lives and dreams on hold because they understand the threat our world faces.

Let us pray for those who make the supreme sacrifice. In our terrible grief, we pray that they leave the fields of battle for finer fields where there is no danger, only tranquillity; where there is no fear, only peace; and where there is no evil, only the love of the greatest Father of all.

Let us pray for those who are held prisoner, that God will protect these, his special children, and will enlighten the minds and soften the hearts of their captors.

Let us pray for the families of those who serve. Let us reach out to them with caring, to make them part of a greater family filled with love and support.

Let us pray for the innocents caught up in this war, all of them, wherever they may be. And let us remember deep in our hearts the value of all human life, everywhere in the world.

Let us pray for our nation. We ask God to bless us, to help us, and to guide us through whatever dark nights may still lay ahead.

And above all, let us pray for peace, "peace…which passeth all understanding."

On this National Day of Prayer and always, may God bless the United States of America.

George Bush
Radio address to the nation on the National Day of Prayer

But when it comes to putting broken lives back together…the human best tends to be at odds with the holy best. To do for yourself the best that you have it in you to do—to grit your teeth and clench your fists in order to survive the world at its harshest and worst—is, by that very act, to be unable to let something be done for you and in you that is more wonderful still. The trouble with steeling yourself against the harshness of reality is that the same steel that secures your life against being destroyed secures your life also against being opened up and transformed by the holy power that life itself comes from. You can survive on your own. You can grow strong on your own. You can even prevail on your own. But you cannot become human on your own. Surely that is why, in Jesus' sad joke, the rich man has as hard a time getting into Paradise as that camel through the needle's eye because with his credit card in his pocket, the rich man is so effective at getting for himself everything else he needs that he does not see that what he needs more than anything else in the world can be had only as a gift. He does not see that the one thing a clenched fist cannot do is accept, even from le bon Dieu himself, a helping hand.

Frederick Buechner
The Sacred Journey

We commend to thy fatherly goodness all those, who are any ways afflicted, or distressed, in mind, body, or estate; that it may please thee to comfort and relieve them, according to their several necessities, giving them patience under their sufferings, and a happy issue out of all their afflictions.

Prayer Book
"Collect or Prayer for All Conditions of Men"

Weeks later, as I looked back, I began to see how my responses to my sister's illness were like the flowers I harvest from my garden. When a bloom is cut from the plant, the stem seals the severed area to preserve the moisture it contains. This self-protective action prevents the flower from taking in any additional water. So while the sealing is an attempt to preserve life, it also keeps the plant from receiving sustenance from sources such as water in a vase. For this reason, florists instruct buyers to make a fresh cut in the stem and immediately place it in water to extend its life.

When I first received word about Elizabeth, I, like the flower, felt as though I had to seal my resources within myself to survive. I had just come through an emotionally and physically draining season of my life that had left me feeling incapable of dealing with this crisis.

But when Les suggested God could somehow speak through me even though I felt so fragile, it was as if someone had made a fresh cut and placed me in water. Deciding I could go to Utah and survive—whatever the outcome—gave me a quiet strength. That strength grew every day.

I wasn't strong because of any special wisdom or stamina within myself, but because I had been plunged into the water of the Great Sustainer.

Patsy Clairmont
Normal Is Just a Setting on Your Dryer

I am the man who has seen affliction by the rod of his wrath. He has driven me away and made me walk in darkness rather than light; indeed, he has turned his hand against me again and again, all day long.

He has made my skin and my flesh grow old and has broken my bones. He has besieged me and surrounded me with bitterness and hardship. He has made me dwell in darkness like those long dead.

He has walled me in so I cannot escape; he has weighed me down with chains. Even when I call out or cry for help, he shuts out my prayer. He has barred my way with blocks of stone; he has made my paths crooked.

Like a bear lying in wait, like a lion in hiding, he dragged me from the path and mangled me and left me without help. He drew his bow and made me the target for his arrows.

He pierced my heart with arrows from his quiver. I became the laughingstock of all my people; they mock me in song all day long. He has filled me with bitter herbs and sated me with gall.

He has broken my teeth with gravel; he has trampled me in the dust. I have been deprived of peace; I have forgotten what prosperity is. So I say, "My splendor is gone and all that I had hoped from the LORD."

I remember my affliction and my wandering, the bitterness and the gall. I well remember them, and my soul is downcast within me. Yet this I call to mind and therefore I have hope: Because of the LORD's great love we are not consumed, for his compassions never fail. They are new every morning; great is your faithfulness. I say to myself, "The LORD is my portion; therefore I will wait for him."

The LORD is good to those whose hope is in him, to the one who seeks him; it is good to wait quietly for the salvation of the LORD. It is good for a man to bear the yoke while he is young.

Let him sit alone in silence, for the LORD has laid it on him. Let him bury his face in the dust—there may yet be hope. Let him offer his cheek to one who would strike him, and let him be filled with disgrace.

For men are not cast off by the Lord forever. Though he brings grief, he will show compassion, so great is his unfailing love. For he does not willingly bring affliction or grief to the children of men.

Lamentations 3:1-33 (NIV)

CHAPTER TWO

Succeeding With My

MONEY

SUCCEEDING WITH MY MONEY

We ought to change the legend on our money from "In God We Trust" to "In Money We Trust." Because, as a nation, we've got far more faith in money these days than we do in God.

Arthur Hoppe
Quoted in *Way*, June 1963

A man is never so on trial as in the moment of excessive good fortune.

Lew Wallace
Ben-Hur

Men may not get all they pay for in this world, but they must certainly pay for all they get.

Frederick Douglass
Life and Times of Frederick Douglass

We forget what gives money its value—that someone exchanged work for it.

Neal O'Hara
Quoted in *Reader's Digest*, March 1961

"My lady"…had yet to learn that money cannot buy refinement of nature, that rank does not always confer nobility, and that true breeding makes itself felt in spite of external drawbacks.

Louisa May Alcott
Little Women

Whilst the rights of all as persons are equal, in virtue of their access to reason, their rights in property are very unequal. One man owns his clothes, and another owns a county.

Ralph Waldo Emerson
Politics

The U. S. Treasury Department has a "conscience fund," set up by President James Madison in 1811. Any time an American citizen sends "conscience" money to the government (to make up for equipment taken while in the army, for underpaying taxes, etc.) it goes into this fund. About a quarter of a million dollars is added to the fund each year.

Barbara Seuling
You Can't Count a Billion Dollars

Almost any man knows how to earn money, but not one in a million knows how to spend it. If he had known so much as this, he would never have earned it.

Henry David Thoreau
Journal

You say, 'I am rich; I have acquired wealth and do not need a thing.' But you do not realize that you are wretched, pitiful, poor, blind and naked.

Revelation 3:17 (NIV)

A mutual fund is a large pool of investment money from lots and lots of people. When you invest in a fund, you buy shares and become a *shareholder* of the fund. A fund manager and his or her team of assistants figure out which specific securities (for example, stocks, bonds, money market securities) they should invest the shareholders' money in to accomplish the objectives of the fund and keep you as a happy customer.

Because good mutual funds take most of the hassle and cost out of figuring out which companies to invest in, they are one of the best investment vehicles, if not the best, ever created. They allow you to diversify your investments—that is, invest in many different industries and companies instead of in just one or two. Funds enable you to give your money to the best money managers in the country—some of the same folks who manage money for the already rich and famous. And they are the ultimate couch potato investment! But, unlike when you're watching *Hard Copy* or playing Nintendo, you'll be doing yourself a big favor by investing in mutual funds...

What's really cool about mutual funds is that—once you understand them—you realize that they can help you meet a bunch of different financial goals.

Eric Tyson
Mutual Funds for Dummies

Nothing can we call our own but death
And that small model of the barren earth
Which serves as paste and cover to our bones.

William Shakespeare
Richard II

There was a time when a fool and his money were soon parted, but now it happens to everybody.

Adlai E. Stevenson
The Stevenson Wit

Farmer. In times like these, when wishes soar but power fails, I contemplate the steady comfort found in gold: gold you can spend on guests; gold you can pay the doctor when you get sick. But a small crumb of gold will buy our daily bread, and when a man has eaten that, you cannot really tell the rich and poor apart.

Euripides
Electra

If you pick up a starving dog and make him prosperous, he will not bite you. This is the principal difference between a dog and a man.

Mark Twain
Pudd'nhead Wilson's Calendar

Money has never appeared to me as valuable as it is generally considered. More than that, it has never even appeared to me particularly convenient. It is good for nothing in itself; it has to be changed before it can be enjoyed; one is obliged to buy, to bargain, to be often cheated, to pay dearly, to be badly served. I should like something which is good in quality; with my money I am sure to get it bad.

Jean Jacques Rousseau
Confessions

At the Pacific Union Club in San Francisco the kitchen staff scours all the coins brought into the building by members tainted with the commerce of the streets. Only after the coins have been thoroughly polished do the waiters presume to offer them as change on silver trays.

Rituals similarly devout obtain in every quarter of American society—not only in the better banks, where the tellers always present new currency, but also in every financial institution subtle enough to disguise the provenance of the numbers so primly arranged on balance sheets and computer screens. The laundering of money is a large and profitable industry, employing hundreds of thousands of workers (accountants, lawyers, investment managers, etc.) who, like their colleagues in the criminal trades, send millions of dollars every day to the purifying baths in Switzerland, Grand Cayman and the Bahamas.

I cannot think of any other people as obsessive as the Americans about the ritual washing of money. It is as if we know, somewhere in the attic of our Puritan memory, that money is a vile substance—ungodly and depraved.

Lewis H. Lapham
Money and Class in America

For the love of money is a root of all kinds of evil.

I Timothy 6:10 (NIV)

Let me tell you about the very rich. They are different from you and me. They possess and enjoy early, and it does something to them, makes them soft where we are hard, and cynical where we are trustful, in a way that, unless you were born rich, it is very difficult to understand.

F. Scott Fitzgerald
"The Rich Boy"

Money has become the grand test of virtue.

George Orwell
Down and Out in Paris and London

It is wrong to assume that men of immense wealth are always happy.

John D. Rockefeller, Sr.
Quoted in *The Age of the Moguls*

There was another thing that did not exist in these islands; that was money. The swans would never have permitted anything so low and degrading to enter their domain. Gold they tolerated, but merely for ornamentation, where it could light up some dull surface. But to traffic with money, and to bargain, and barter—that was unheard of.

Carmen Sylva
"The Swan Lake"

Men make counterfeit money; in many more cases, money makes counterfeit men.

Sydney J. Harris
Quoted in *Reader's Digest*, April 1968

When you let money speak for you, it drowns out anything else you meant to say.

Mignon McLaughlin
The Second Neurotic's Notebook

The devil was piqu'd such saintship to behold,
And longed to tempt him like good Job of old;
But Satan now is wiser than of yore.
And tempts by making rich, not making poor.

Alexander Pope
Moral Essays

Money destroys human roots wherever it is able to penetrate, by turning desire for gain into the sole motive. It easily manages to outweigh all other motives, because the effort it demands of the mind is so very much less. Nothing is *so* clear and *so* simple as a row of figures.

Simone Weil
The Need for Roots

In America, the land of the permanent revolution, ulcers and cancer often become, for the men at the top, the contemporary equivalent of the guillotine.

Ted Morgan
Quoted in the *New York Times,* July 13, 1986

Affluence separates people. Poverty knits 'em together.

Ray Charles
Brother Ray

Among the most boring jobs in the country, those of bank guards and highway toll collectors—both of whom are surrounded by money—rank in the top ten.

Barbara Seuling
You Can't Count a Billion Dollars

What I know about money, I learned the hard way—by having had it.

Margaret Halsey
The Folks at Home

Where there is money, there is fighting.

Marian Anderson
Marian Anderson, A Portrait

The praises of poverty need once more to be boldly sung. We have grown literally afraid to be poor. We despise anyone who elects to be poor in order to simplify and save his inner life. If he does not join the general scramble and pant with the money-making street, we deem him spiritless and lacking in ambition. We have lost the power even of imagining what the ancient idealization of poverty could have meant: the liberation from material attachments, the unbribed soul, the manlier indifference, the paying our way by what we are or do and not by what we have, the right to fling away our life at any moment irresponsibly—the more athletic trim, in short, the moral fighting shape.

William James
Varieties of Religious Experience

You, O money, are the cause of a restless life! Because of you we journey toward a premature death; you provide cruel nourishment for the evils of men; the seed of our cares sprouts from your head.

Sextus Propertius
Elegies

When I have any money I get rid of it as quickly as possible, lest it find a way into my heart.

John Wesley

The Americans have little faith. They rely on the power of the dollar.

Ralph Waldo Emerson
Nature, Addresses and Lectures

May your money perish with you, because you thought you could buy the gift of God with money!

Acts 8:20 (NIV)

If you would know what the Lord God thinks of money, you have only to look at those to whom he gives it.

Maurice Baring
Quoted by Dorothy Parker in
Writers at Work: First Series

The world is too much with us; late and soon,
Getting and spending, we lay waste our powers:
Little we see in Nature that is ours;
We have given our hearts away, a sordid boon!
This sea that bares her bosom to the moon;
The winds that will be howling at all hours,
And are up-gathered now like sleeping flowers;
For this, for everything, we are out of tune;
It moves us not. I'd rather be
A Pagan suckled in a creed outworn;
So might I, standing on this pleasant lea,
Have glimpses that would make me less forlorn;
Have sight of Proteus, rising from the sea;
Or hear old Triton blow his wreathèd horn.

William Wordsworth
"The World Is Too Much With Us"

The ways by which you may get money almost without exception lead downward.

Henry David Thoreau
Life Without Principle

Be not penny-wise; riches have wings, and sometimes they fly away of themselves, sometimes they must be set flying to bring in more.

Francis Bacon
Of Riches

Again, it will be like a man going on a journey, who called his servants and entrusted his property to them. To one he gave five talents of money, to another two talents, and to another one talent, each according to his ability. Then he went on his journey. The man who had received the five talents went at once and put his money to work and gained five more. So also, the one with the two talents gained two more. But the man who had received the one talent went off, dug a hole in the ground and hid his master's money.

After a long time the master of those servants returned and settled accounts with them. The man who had received the five talents brought the other five. "Master," he said, "you entrusted me with five talents. See, I have gained five more."

His master replied, "Well done, good and faithful servant! You have been faithful with a few things; I will put you in charge of many things. Come and share your master's happiness!"

The man with the two talents also came. "Master," he said, "you entrusted me with two talents; see, I have gained two more."

His master replied, "Well done, good and faithful servant! You have been faithful with a few things; I will put you in charge of many things. Come and share your master's happiness!"

Then the man who had received the one talent came. "Master," he said, "I knew that you are a hard man, harvesting where you have not sown and gathering where you have not scattered seed. So I was afraid and went out and hid your talent in the ground. See, here is what belongs to you."

His master replied, "You wicked, lazy servant! So you knew that I harvest where I have not sown and gather where I have not scattered seed? Well then, you should have put my money on deposit with the bankers, so that when I returned I would have received it back with interest."

Matthew 25:14-27 (NIV)

Money is an article which may be used as a universal passport to everywhere except heaven, and as a universal provider of everything except happiness.

anonymous

A man and his Wife had the good fortune to possess a Goose which laid a Golden Egg every day. Lucky though they were, they soon began to think they were not getting rich fast enough, and, imagining the bird must be made of gold inside, they decided to kill it in order to secure the whole store of precious metal at once. But when they cut it open they found it was just like any other goose. Thus, they neither got rich all at once, as they had hoped, nor enjoyed any longer the daily addition to their wealth.

Æsop
Fables

Of course, no discussion of investing is complete without including the potential risks involved in making an investment. There is one fundamental rule that you should never, ever, *ever*, forget…

…the greater the potential reward being offered, the greater the risk involved in making that investment. Let me say that again. The greater the potential reward being offered, the greater the risk involved in making that investment. Say it with me this time. *The greater the potential reward being offered, the greater the risk involved in making that investment.* Or, in everyday plain English, *There's no free lunch.*

What I just did to make my point might strike you as silly, but there's nothing silly (or funny) about the experiences of countless people who have learned this simple lesson only after losing thousands (and often hundreds of thousands) of dollars in an investment that was "just as safe" as a money market account but offered a higher return. The truth is that the link between risk and reward is as certain as the link between sowing and reaping. It's inescapable. Anyone who tells you differently is either self-deceived or is trying to deceive you.

Austin Pryor
Sound Mind Investing

The love of money is a form of infantilism. The man who loves money is the man who has never grown up. He has never passed from the world of fairy tales into the world of philosophy.

Robert Lynd
Searchlights and Nightingales

We are money-mad. Greed and wealth have chained the beast of power.

William Edward Burghardt Du Bois
"What Is Wrong with the United States?"

In all well-instituted Commonwealths, Care has been taken to limit Men's Possessions; which is done for many Reasons, and among the rest, for one which perhaps is not often considered, That when Bounds are set to Men's Desires, after they have acquired as much as the Laws will permit them, their private Interest is at an End, and they have nothing to do but to take care of the Publick.

Jonathan Swift
Thoughts on Various Subjects

All the wants which disturb human life, which make us uneasy to ourselves, quarrelsome with others, and unthankful to God, which weary us in vain labors and foolish anxieties, which carry us from project to project, from place to place in a poor pursuit of we don't know what, are the wants which neither God, nor nature, nor reason hath subjected us to, but are solely infused into us by pride, envy, ambition, and covetousness.

William Law
A Serious Call to a Devout and Holy Life

Money is everything in this world to some people, and more than the next to other poor souls.

Augusta Evans
Beulah

Hetty Howland Green, considered the greatest woman financier in history at the time of her death in 1916, left an estate estimated at around $100 million. The stories about her unwillingness to part with her money are hair-raising, including one account that her son went without medical treatment while she looked for a free clinic, resulting in the loss of his leg.

Barbara Seuling
You Can't Count a Billion Dollars

To the covetous man life is a nightmare, and God lets him wrestle with it as best he may.

Henry Ward Beecher
Sermons

The soul of the covetous is far removed from God, as far as his memory, understanding and will are concerned. He forgets God as though He were not his God, owing to the fact that he has fashioned for himself a god of Mammon and of temporal possessions.

Saint John of the Cross
The Dark Night of the Soul

It is not the man who has too little who is poor, but the one who hankers after more. What difference does it make how much there is laid away in a man's safe or in his barns, how many head of stock he grazes or how much capital he puts out at interest, if he is always after what is another's and only counts what he has yet to get, never what he has already. You ask what is the proper limit to a person's wealth? First, having what is essential, and second, having what is enough.

Lucius Annaeus Seneca
Letters to Lucilius

Beware of an inordinate desire for wealth. Nothing is so revealing of narrowness and littleness of soul than love for money. Conversely, there is nothing more honorable or noble than indifference to money, if one doesn't have any; or than genuine altruism and well-doing if one does have it.

Marcus Tullius Cicero
De Officiis

If you make money your God, 'twill plague you like a Devil.

Thomas Fuller
Gnomologia

Some men make money not for the sake of living, but ache
In the blindness of greed and live just for their fortune's sake.

Juvenal
Satires

Before the invention of signs to represent riches, wealth could hardly consist in anything but lands and cattle, the only real possessions men can have. But, when inheritances so increased in number and extent as to occupy the whole of the land, and to border on one another, one man could aggrandise himself only at the expense of another; at the same time the supernumeraries, who had been too weak or too indolent to make such acquisitions, and had grown poor without sustaining any loss, because, while they saw everything change around them, they remained still the same, were obliged to receive their subsistence, or steal it, from the rich; and this soon bred, according to their different characters, dominion and slavery, or violence and rapine. The wealthy, on their part, had no sooner begun to taste the pleasure of command, than they disdained all others, and, using their old slaves to acquire new, thought of nothing but subduing and enslaving their neighbors; like ravenous wolves, which, having once tasted human flesh, despise every other food and thenceforth seek only men to devour.

Thus, as the most powerful or the most miserable considered their might or misery as a kind of right to the possessions of others, equivalent, in their opinion, to that of property, the destruction of equality was attended by the most terrible disorders. Usurpations by the rich, robbery by the poor, and the unbridled passions of both, suppressed the cries of natural compassion and the still feeble voice of justice, and filled men with avarice, ambition and vice.

Jean Jacques Rousseau
Origin of Inequality

You can't take it with you.

anonymous

The love of money, if unjustly gained, is impious, and, if justly, shameful; for it is unseemly to be merely parsimonious even with justice on one's side.

Epicurus
Fragments, Vatican Collection

A faithful man will be richly blessed, but one eager to get rich will not go unpunished.

Proverbs 28:20 (NIV)

It is my opinion that a man's soul may be buried and perish under a dungheap, or in a furrow of the field, just as well as under a pile of money.

Nathaniel Hawthorne

Debt, grinding debt, whose iron face the widow, the orphan, and the sons of genius fear and hate—debt, which consumes so much time, which so cripples and disheartens a great spirit with cares that seem so base, is a preceptor whose lessons cannot be foregone, and is needed most by those who suffer from it most.

Ralph Waldo Emerson
Nature

Imagine for a moment some of the incredible benefits you're going to experience when you are free of consumer debt.

First, you're going to be in control of your cash flow. When you no longer have to service those debilitating monthly debt payments, you have more money to enjoy life, handle emergencies, give to your church or favorite charity, build your savings reserve, and invest for future dreams.

Second, you'll stop the drain of compound interest working *against* you and get it working *for* you. Instead of paying 16, 18, 20 percent on the money you owe, you'll be earning 5-15 percent (sometimes more) on those funds as you redirect them toward savings and investments. Eliminate the pay-out, add the earnings, and in effect you're earning 21 to 35 percent on those dollars!

Third, you'll feel financially free. No longer will you feel like a "slave to the lender," making endless payments on depreciating or already-consumed purchases. Peace of mind is one of the best investments you'll ever make.

Fourth, you'll be able to make future purchases with cash. When there's a genuine need or you just want to do something for the fun of it, you'll pay with cash instead of plastic. With your rejuvenated savings program, the funds will be there for you, designated for just such an event. You won't spend months or years and countless interest dollars paying for your purchase. You'll be in charge instead of the lender charging you. It makes financial sense, and it's a wonderful place to be.

Dan Benson
21 Days to Financial Freedom

Why do we, in fact, almost all of us, desire to increase our incomes? It may seem, at first sight, as though material goods were what we desire. But, in fact, we desire these mainly in order to impress our neighbours. When a man moves into a larger house in a more genteel quarter, he reflects that "better" people will call on his wife, and some unprosperous cronies of former days can be dropped. When he sends his son to a good school or an expensive university, he consoles himself for the heavy fees by thoughts of the social kudos to be gained. In every big city, whether of Europe or of America, houses in some districts are more expensive than equally good houses in other districts, merely because they are more fashionable. One of the most powerful of all our passions is the desire to be admired and respected. As things stand, admiration and respect are given to the man who seems to be rich. This is the chief reason why people wish to be rich. The actual goods purchased by their money play quite a secondary part.

John Russell
Sceptical Essays

Ah! if the rich were rich as the poor fancy riches!

Ralph Waldo Emerson
Nature

As riches grow, care follows, and a thirst
For more and more.

Horace
Odes

The sleep of a laborer is sweet, whether he eats little or much, but the abundance of a rich man permits him no sleep.

Ecclesiastes 5:12 (NIV)

Resolve not to be poor: whatever you have, spend less.

Samuel Johnson

Before borrowing money from a friend, decide which you need more.

Addison H. Hallock
Quoted in *Reader's Digest*, September 1962

Money: a blessing that is of no advantage to us excepting when we part with it.

Ambrose Bierce
The Devil's Dictionary

What your house is worth, frankly, is of no financial significance whatsoever if you have no intention of ever selling it. That's why many financial experts have noted that home ownership should, in most cases, be part of a financial plan but it shouldn't be the entire financial plan. On its own, such a plan can't survive. You can't spend your house! Even if you do plan on selling your house later in life and renting or buying a lower-cost accommodation, you certainly don't want to be forced to do so in case you change your mind later. Home ownership must work in conjunction with saving ten percent, building a retirement fund, and being properly insured...

I would argue that the real costs of home ownership, even without a mortgage, come close to the cost of renting an adequate apartment. Property tax, insurance, utilities, upkeep, and let us not forget time, add up to a hefty annual cost—an often underestimated hefty annual cost.

I don't want to belabor this point. I do think home ownership is an excellent investment—one of the best. But excellent and perfect are not synonymous. I just want to inform our young friends here, especially the single ones, that renting is not throwing your money away.

David Chilton
The Wealthy Barber

Humanly speaking, it is only when the hair is white, when...life is almost over, that men begin to realize how hopelessly elusive is the happiness promised by wealth and fame.

Joseph McSorley
Be of Good Heart

Funny how a dollar can look so big when you take it to church, and so small when you take it to the store.

Frank A. Clark
Quoted in *Register and Tribune Syndicate,* October 1970

Socrates. I do nothing but go about persuading you all, old and young alike, not to take thought for your persons or your properties, but first and chiefly to care about the greatest improvement of the soul.

Plato
Apology

Dollars cannot buy yesterday.

Admiral Harold R. Stark
Quoted in *Time,* December 16, 1940

He who serves God with what costs him nothing, will do very little service, you may depend on it.

Susan Warner
What She Could

I was born into it and there was nothing I could do about it. It was there, like air or food or any other element...The only question with wealth is what you do with it.

John D. Rockefeller, Jr.
Quoted in *Time,* September 24, 1956

Just as an ex-smoker courts disaster if she keeps packs of cigarettes around the house, so you risk blowing it if you carry too many credit cards. The average couple owns seven or eight cards, often running up one to make payments on the other. Each card comes with a credit limit of a few hundred to several thousand dollars. Lurking behind each card is a financial institution dedicated to convincing you to charge everything from Nassau junkets to nose jobs. They don't care whether you're dogpaddling in debt—they just want you to build as much debt as possible so they can earn heaps of interest on what they hope is a v-e-r-y s-l-o-w payback.

Truth is, you don't want or need much of this type of credit. Why? Because the sum of your available credit is actually held against you when it's time to apply for good credit, such as a home mortgage, equity line of credit, or business loan. Mortgage lenders assume you will max out every cent of credit that is available to you, so they add up all the *credit limits* (not what you actually owe) from every account you have and count this total as a liability on your balance sheet.

In addition, multiple cards are a bad idea because you simply do not need either the motive or the means to accrue tens of thousands of dollars in consumer debt. Let's face it: the temptation is just too great. Whether you max out one card or spread your charges among several, it's far too easy to justify excessive spending: *It's okay, we have the credit.*

Reduce temptation by narrowing the sum total of your credit cards to one. Not one *handful,* one *card.* Select the all-purpose card (MasterCard, VISA, Discover) with the lowest interest rate. This is the one (and only) card you'll keep for check-writing identification, car rental, or a genuine stuck-out-in-the-boonies emergency. Then—are you ready for some fun?—take the others, insert between scissors, and turn those cards into confetti. Once you pay off the ones you've slashed to bits, you're going to write those companies requesting that (1) they close your account, and (2) they confirm *in writing* that they have done so *at your request*.

Meanwhile, as you progress on your journey to financial freedom, resist all enticements for additional consumer credit. Yes, you're going to receive more warm, fuzzy letters from bank presidents. You'll see tempting signs as you enter department stores: "Apply Now for Instant Credit and Receive 10% Off Today's Purchases!" Don't. Instead, think *debt-free*.

Dan Benson
21 Days to Financial Freedom

Dug from the mountainside, washed from the glen,
Servant am I or master of men.
Steal me, I curse you;
Earn me, I bless you;
Grasp me and hoard me, a fiend shall possess you;
Live for me, die for me,
Covet me, take me,
Angel or devil, I am what you make me.

anonymous

Money is only money, beans tonight and steak tomorrow. So long as you can look yourself in the eye.

Meridel Le Sueur
Crusaders

...money isn't so hot, after all. What with incipient heart attacks, lots of bottles of little pills you have to take all the time, and losing your temper over the food or the service in hotels. Most of the rich people I've known have been fairly miserable.

Agatha Christie
Endless Night

Theirs is an endless road, a hopeless maze, who seek for goods before they seek God.

Saint Bernard of Clairvaux
On the Love of God

A good name is more desirable than great riches; to be esteemed is better than silver or gold.

Proverbs 22:1 (NIV)

I have been asked many times what is the biggest financial mistake I see, and the answer is easy—*a consumptive lifestyle.* A consumptive lifestyle is simply spending more than you can afford, or spending more than you should, given your other goals and priorities. Almost everyone in America falls victim to living a consumptive lifestyle...

We are, as a society, bombarded with a hedonistic philosophy. "Enjoy it now." "You only go around once." "Live it up." "You owe it to yourself."

Incidentally, I have observed—not at all scientifically proven, but still observed—that the more television a person watches, the higher lifestyle the person is apt to desire. Television advertising is extremely sophisticated and effective. In a similar way, the more time you spend in shopping malls, the higher lifestyle you are apt to want because you are surrounding yourself with temptation. It is much like going to the grocery store just before mealtime to do your weekly shopping. Chances are that you will spend substantially more than if you went after a meal and with a specific list in hand.

Ron Blue
Master Your Money

Man enters the world with closed hands, as if to say: "The world is mine." He leaves it with open hands, as if to say: "Behold, I take nothing with me."

The Midrash

One must choose, in life, between making money and spending it. There's no time to do both.

Edouard Bourdet
Les Temps difficiles

No one can serve two masters. Either he will hate the one and love the other, or he will be devoted to the one and despise the other. You cannot serve both God and Money.

Therefore I tell you, do not worry about your life, what you will eat or drink;

or about your body, what you will wear. Is not life more important than food, and the body more important than clothes? Look at the birds of the air; they do not sow or reap or store away in barns, and yet your heavenly Father feeds them. Are you not much more valuable than they? Who of you by worrying can add a single hour to his life?

And why do you worry about clothes? See how the lilies of the field grow. They do not labor or spin. Yet I tell you that not even Solomon in all his splendor was dressed like one of these. If that is how God clothes the grass of the field, which is here today and tomorrow is thrown into the fire, will he not much more clothe you, O you of little faith? So do not worry, saying, "What shall we eat?" or "What shall we drink?" or "What shall we wear?" For the pagans run after all these things, and your heavenly Father knows that you need them. But seek first his kingdom and his righteousness, and all these things will be given to you as well. Therefore do not worry about tomorrow, for tomorrow will worry about itself. Each day has enough trouble of its own.

Matthew 6:24-34 (NIV)

Money, like dung, does no good till 'tis spread.

Thomas Fuller
Gnomologia

Money is an amoral instrument, and like science serves good and evil alike. There's no such thing as dirty money; the stain is only on the hand that holds it as giver or taker.

A. M. Sullivan
Dun's Review

Imagine, for a moment, that you're offered a chance to buy insurance that reimburses you for the cost of a magazine subscription in the event the magazine folds and you don't get all the issues you paid for. Because a magazine subscription doesn't cost much, I don't think you would buy that insurance.

What if you could buy insurance that pays for the cost of a restaurant meal if you get food poisoning? Even if you're splurging at a fancy restaurant, you don't have a lot of money at stake, so you'd probably decline that coverage as well.

The point of insurance is to protect against losses that would be financially catastrophic to you, not to smooth out the bumps of everyday life. The examples above are silly, but some people buy equally silly policies without knowing it.

Eric Tyson
Personal Finance for Dummies, 2nd Edition

It is not earthly riches which make us or our sons happy; for they must either be lost by us in our lifetime, or be possessed when we are dead, by whom we know not, or perhaps by whom we would not.

Saint Augustine
The City of God

Better to go to heaven in rags, than to hell in embroidery.

English proverb

Let's assume you've been careful not to get into a financial sand trap. You pay your bills on time, you make a good living, your credit cards are under control. So how come you don't have anything left at the end of the month? Probably because you have not made a conscious effort to save.

The best way to increase your savings: Start saving. Easy for us to say, you think. Here's how. When you're buying something for 79 cents, don't dig through your change purse and find 79 cents. Break a dollar. Do this with all your purchases. Then, as your pocket or purse starts to get heavy with accumulated change, or every night when you get home from work, take your change out and put it in a coin jar. As soon as it's filled up, roll it, take it to the bank and deposit it in your savings account. You can't get rich on $57 a month, but it's more than a lot of people save. It's a start.

Next, along with your other bills, pay yourself every month. When you write your checks for the electric bill, gas bill, phone bill, etc., write one to your savings account, too. Maybe it's 10 percent of your monthly take-home income. If you can do more, do more. What you're gradually building up to is a six-month nest egg. That means you want to have enough money in the bank to pay your absolute necessities for six months. Add up your monthly mortgage, insurance premiums, car payments, food, utilities, and minimum payments on credit cards. Multiply by six. Scary, isn't it? But this is your goal.

Ken and Daria Dolan
Straight Talk on Money

Do not store up for yourselves treasures on earth, where moth and rust destroy, and where thieves break in and steal. But store up for yourselves treasures in heaven, where moth and rust do not destroy, and where thieves do not break in and steal. For where your treasure is, there your heart will be also.

Matthew 6:19-21 (NIV)

Money, material though it be, does lie at the base of the most useful work you do. In itself nothing, it is the basis of much of the best effort which can be made for spiritual purposes.

Arthur J. Balfour, Earl of Balfour
Quoted in *The Mind of A. J. Balfour*

Don't go around saying the world owes you a living. The world owes you nothing. It was here first.

Mark Twain
Quoted in *Reader's Digest*, March 1963

There is no dignity quite so impressive, and no independence quite so important, as living within your means.

Calvin Coolidge
Quoted in *Reader's Digest*, August 1953

Johnson. (to Edwards,) "From your having practised the law long, Sir, I presume you must be rich." *Edwards.* "No, Sir; I got a good deal of money; but I had a number of poor relations to whom I gave a great part of it." *Johnson.* "Sir, you have been rich in the most valuable sense of the word." *Edwards.* "But I shall not die rich." *Johnson.* "Nay, sure, Sir, it is better to *live* rich than to *die* rich."

James Boswell
The Life of Samuel Johnson

All the money in the world will not buy you a kid who will do homework, or maturity for a kid who needs it. It may buy a kid who knows how to buy.

Bill Cosby

All the money in the world doesn't mean a thing if you don't have time to enjoy it.

Oprah Winfrey
Quoted in *Ladies' Home Journal*, December 1988

Command those who are rich in this present world not to be arrogant nor to put their hope in wealth, which is so uncertain, but to put their hope in God, who richly provides us with everything for our enjoyment.

1 Timothy 6:17 (NIV)

However mean your life is, meet it and live it; do not shun it and call it hard names. It is not so bad as you are. It looks poorest when you are richest. The faultfinder will find faults even in paradise. Love your life, poor as it is. You may perhaps have some pleasant, thrilling, glorious hours, even in a poor-house. The setting sun is reflected from the windows of the almshouse as brightly as from the rich man's abode; the snow melts before its door as early in the spring. I do not see but a quiet mind may live as contentedly there, and have as cheering thoughts, as in a palace. The town's poor seem to me often to live the most independent lives of any. Maybe they are simply great enough to receive without misgiving. Most think that they are above being supported by the town; but it oftener happens that they are not above supporting themselves by dishonest means, which should be more disreputable. Cultivate poverty like a garden herb, like sage. Do not trouble yourself much to get new things, whether clothes or friends. Turn the old; return to them. Things do not change; we change. Sell your clothes and keep your thoughts. God will see that you do not want society. If I were confined to a corner of a garret all my days, like a spider, the world would be just as large to me while I had my thoughts about me. The philosopher said: 'From an army of three divisions one can take away its general, and put it in disorder; from the man the most abject and vulgar one cannot take away his thought.' Do not seek so anxiously to be developed, to subject yourself to many influences to be played on; it is all dissipation. Humility like darkness reveals the heavenly lights. The shadows of poverty and meanness gather around us, 'and lo! creation widens to our view.' We are often reminded that if there were bestowed on us the wealth of Crœsus, our aims must still be the same, and our means essentially the same. Moreover, if you are restricted in your range by poverty, if you cannot buy books and newspapers, for instance, you are but confined to the most significant and vital experiences; you are compelled to deal with the material which yields the most sugar and the most starch. It is life near the bone where it is sweetest. You are defended from being a trifler. No man loses ever on a lower level by magnanimity on a higher. Superfluous wealth can buy superfluities only. Money is not required to buy one necessary of the soul.

Henry David Thoreau
Walden

If you want to know whether you are destined to be a success or a failure in life, you can easily find out. The test is simple and it is infallible. Are you able to save money? If not, drop out. You will lose. You may think not, but you will lose, as sure as you live. The seed of success is not in you.

James J. Hill
Quoted in Reader's Digest, June 1922

Most of us have, at one time or another, lived from paycheck to paycheck—and lots of us still do. This may seem normal to people who've recently entered the work force, but it shouldn't be shrugged off casually.

Not having any money in reserve is a bad habit to start. And, like many bad habits, it can influence lots of other decisions that you have to make later on.

The best solution for preventing this bad habit—or breaking it, if you're already there—is adopt the discipline of making and living within a budget.

I hope that my argument for living under a budget is more than the lecture you've heard from parents and teachers a thousand times before. Budgeting is the only scientific tool any of us has for taking control of our finances. Working people do it. So do millionaires—especially ones with the dreaded liquidity problems. Just ask Donald Trump. Even corporations do it. And these guys budget for more than just the thrill of filling in blanks on a sheet of paper. They do it because the process itself can be helpful in figuring out how we live and spend our money.

It's tempting to say, "I can't afford to save money now, but I'm definitely going to start saving as soon as I'm making more money." You may be surprised to learn that you could be comfortably living within your means and still have enough to put money aside for the things you want.

Even if you just save a few dollars a month, using a system for analyzing your finances gives you the perspective to make informed decisions. If trouble—or better times—come along at some point in the future, you'll be able to adjust your spending accordingly. This helps make bad times not so bad and good times last longer.

More than anything else, the discipline of a budget gives you a feeling of control over some part of your life. If you hate not having enough money to pay your bills, or buy a new car or even a house, you have to start finding your hidden money right now.

Cornelius P. McCarthy
The Under 40 Financial Planning Guide

When reason rules, money is a blessing.

Publilius Syrus
Moral Sayings

When the urge for unplanned credit card spending rears its seductive head (and it will), ask yourself some tough questions to see if this purchase is really necessary. Start with "Why do I want this? Is it a whim I'll regret in a week?" Then ask yourself, "Will I want this item as badly in thirty days when the bill comes?" Several smart people I know actually make themselves walk out of a store to discuss, think about, pray, and "sleep on" an unplanned purchase before committing to it (good advice, even when you intend to pay with cash). It's amazing how much something back at the mall decreases in importance after a night's sleep.

Dan Benson
21 Days to Financial Freedom

It's good to have money and the things that money can buy, but it's good, too, to check up once in a while and make sure that you haven't lost the things that money can't buy.

George Horace Lorimer

Go into the street, and give one man a lecture on morality, and another a shilling, and see which will respect you most.

Samuel Johnson
Quoted in *The Life of Samuel Johnson*

Food to eat! Clothes to wear! A house to live in! These are things everyone needs. Is there any money left? When a family has extra money, there are many ways to use it. Many families like to use some of this money to help others. Peter's father sends a check to help. We like to share. Money is a handy thing to have. There are presents to buy for friends, and happy vacation trips, and parties to enjoy. You may buy nice things for your house—beautiful pictures and more books. Peter buys flowers for his mother. Money is to use. Use it well!

Jene Barr
What Can Money Do?

Those...who know the true use of money, and regulate the measure of wealth according to their needs, live contented with few things.

Baruch Spinoza
Ethics

Now let's move on to our second area of smarter spending: luxuries. Do you have three movie channels on your cable TV bill every month, rather than just one? C'mon, do you really need more than one? How many movies have you watched lately? How about that new VCR with automatic hocus-pocus programming? Not only does your old VCR work just fine, but it will probably take you two years to figure out how to work the newfangled machine, assuming that you have mastered the one you now own.

On the other hand, if your VCR or camera breaks, nowadays it may be cheaper to buy a new one than to fix the old one. We hate to replace rather than fix, but the bottom line is the bottom line. With technology changing rapidly, often you really can buy for less.

Maybe you're a taxi taker. That's a luxury you'll never miss if there's good public transportation in your area. How about the bus? The subway? A nice walk? Try it and you might like it! And you sure will save a bundle of change—just leave for work a few minutes early.

Take five minutes to go through the coupons in your Sunday paper. Here's the way to use coupons: Clip only the ones you know you'll use—products you regularly buy, name brands you can't substitute. Don't buy products you wouldn't ordinarily buy just because you've got a coupon. That's not going to save you money! In fact, in many cases you can do better with the regular price on a less expensive brand. But if you will buy only one brand of peanut butter, why not get a discount when it's offered?

Ken and Daria Dolan
Straight Talk on Money

There is no wealth but life. That country is the richest which nourishes the greatest number of noble and happy human beings; that man is richest who, having perfected the functions of his own life to the utmost, has also the widest helpful influence, both personal, and by means of his possessions, over the lives of others.

John Ruskin
Unto This Last

Why, you may ask, do you need a financial plan at all?

The answer is quite simple.

There is only one sure way to achieve financial security: You must identify your goals, then adopt strategies to meet them.

True, if you're like most people—the vast majority of Americans, in fact—you seem to get by from year to year without a financial plan. You collect your salary, pay your bills, and keep yourself and your family housed, clothed, and fed.

But what happens if a financial crisis occurs? You may find yourself lacking the funds or insurance to cover mounting bills.

And what about those luxuries you've always longed for—an ocean-going sailboat, perhaps, or a mountain hideaway? Do they seem always to dangle just beyond your financial grasp? And how will you pay for your child's education? Or support yourself adequately in your retirement?

If you talk with the people who are most comfortable in their lives—the people who have achieved true financial security—you'll find they took an organized approach to financial management early on. Some did the work themselves. Others hired competent advisers to help them. But, somehow, they made sure the job was done.

The bottom line to financial security: You can get what you want only with an organized financial plan and the discipline to make it work.

And the best time to start planning is now.

Stanley H. Breitbard and Donna Sammons Carpenter
The Price Waterhouse Book of Personal Financial Planning

Receive wealth or prosperity without arrogance; and be ready to let it go.

Marcus Aurelius

Meditations

A friend of mine tells a story about his grandfather, a prominent small-town businessman in the 1950s and 1960s, who dismissed credit cards as a device that would bankrupt working people not accustomed to managing revolving debt. "If you really have credit, you don't need a piece of plastic to prove it," the old man said. And there is a kernel of truth to this argument.

People's reactions to credit cards can be extreme. Just about everyone knows someone who's managed to load up on credit card debt that they'll be paying off for years. On the other hand, an investment banker I know—who's as rich as anyone under 40 who doesn't play professional baseball—can't stand using the things. He only carries one or two (as opposed to other, far less wealthy, people who carry six or eight) and uses them as infrequently as possible.

Credit cards are one of the best and worst conveniences of modern life. Like most good things, they are best enjoyed in moderation. The credit available through most credit cards is more expensive than any other kind of loan you can have. That's why the investment banker I know hates plastic.

On the practical level, credit cards are essential for certain activities of modern life: renting a car, staying at most hotels, or paying for things over the phone. Plus, having a credit card is one of the first steps you take in building the kind of credit you need to buy bigger things—like a car or a house...

Credit habits have a lot to do with the way people feel about themselves and their place in life. Like many people in their twenties and thirties, you may think of credit cards as a way to borrow against money you'll make in the future. Don't. When you start thinking that you can borrow now against the future, remember that credit card companies are making money—between 12 and 20 percent a year—on that hope.

The interest you'll have to pay between now and when you're making more money in the future can diminish the impact of any raises or promotions.

Cornelius P. McCarthy

The Under 40 Financial Planning Guide

Without doubt, the highest privilege of wealth is the opportunity it affords for doing good, without giving up one's fortune.

Marcus Tullius Cicero
De Officiis

As he looked up, Jesus saw the rich putting their gifts into the temple treasury. He also saw a poor widow put in two very small copper coins. "I tell you the truth," he said, "this poor widow has put in more than all the others. All these people gave their gifts out of their wealth; but she out of her poverty put in all she had to live on."

Luke 21:1-4 (NIV)

Succeeding at My

WORK

CHAPTER THREE

SUCCEEDING AT MY WORK

—⁊⁊⁊—

He that can work is a born king of something.

Thomas Carlyle
Chartism

My art instructor, an excellent craftsman, told me a compelling story about the benefits of diligent work.

Many years ago there was a famous Japanese artist named Hokusai, whose paintings were coveted by royalty. One day a nobleman requested a special painting of his prized bird. He left the bird with Hokusai, and the artist told the nobleman to return in a week.

The master missed his beautiful bird, and was anxious to return at the end of the week not only to secure his favorite pet, but his painting as well. When the nobleman arrived, however, the artist humbly requested a two-week postponement.

The two-week delay stretched into two months—and then six.

A year later, the nobleman stormed into Hokusai's studio. He refused to wait any longer and demanded both his bird and his painting. Hokusai, in the Japanese way, bowed to the nobleman, turned to his workshop table, and picked up a brush and large sheet of rice paper. Within moments he had effortlessly painted an exact likeness of the lovely bird.

The bird's owner was stunned by the painting.

And then he was angry. "Why did you keep me waiting for a year if you could have done the painting in such a short time?"

"You don't understand," Hokusai replied. Then he escorted the nobleman into a room where the walls were covered with paintings of the same bird. None of them, however, matched the grace and the beauty of the final rendering. Yet, out of such hard work and painstaking effort came the mastery of Hokusai's art.

My art instructor's point was clear. Nothing of real worth or lasting value comes easy.

That's certainly true with my painting. As a Christian, I feel compelled to produce quality, the best I can do "as unto Him." To others it may appear that I sit in front of an easel and with a bit of quick inspiration render an effortless drawing. Let me tell you, behind what looks like spontaneous creativity and raw talent are hours of research, experiments, sketches, and color tests.

This must also be true of the canvas of our lives. Behind every attractive Christian life are things like discipline, prayer in the secret place, diligent study of God's Word, discreet acts of generosity, and obedience when nobody's looking.

We can't copy the world's slipshod way of looking at art—or life. If we want to have something of real worth and lasting value in our character, it won't come easy.

It never does.

Joni Eareckson Tada
Glorious Intruder

He who does nothing renders himself incapable of doing any thing: but while we are executing any work, we are preparing and qualifying ourselves to undertake another.

William Hazlitt
The Plain Speaker

Love labor: for if thou dost not want it for food, thou mayest for physic. It is wholesome for thy body and good for thy mind.

William Penn
Some Fruits of Solitude

A commonwealth of Ants, having, after a busy summer, provided every thing for their wants in the winter, were about shutting themselves up for that dreary season, when a Grasshopper in great distress, and in dread of perishing with cold and hunger, approached their avenues, and with great humility begged they would relieve his wants, and permit him to take shelter in any corner of their comfortable mansion. One of the Ants asked him how he had disposed of his time in summer, had he not taken pains and laid in a stock, as they had done? Alas! my friends, says he, I passed away the time merrily and pleasantly, in drinking, singing, and dancing, and never once thought of winter. If that be the case, replied the Ant, all I have to say is this: that they who drink, sing, and dance in the summer, run a great risk of starving in the winter.

Æsop
Fables

No race can prosper till it learns there is as much dignity in tilling a field as in writing a poem.

Booker T. Washington
Address, Atlanta Exposition,
September 18, 1895

To work is to pray.

Saint Benedict of Nursia
Motto

We make a mistake in setting up a sharp division between the work which earns our "living" and the "living" that is earned. We are living all the time we are earning, and if we want to live well or happily must live well or happily then. And it is equally true that we are earning all the time we are living—though it be only the devil's wages of boredom and disillusion. Earning and living are not two separate departments or operations in life. They are two names for a continuous process looked at from opposite ends.

Lawrence Pearsall Jacks
"Breadwinning and Soulsaving"

Work is something that engages the heart and the mind as well as the hand, something that involves the surmounting of difficulties for results that are deemed important by the worker.

Jacques Barzun
Address to 39th Annual Conference of Eastern College Personnel Officers,
October 4, 1965

The most common problem caused by defining yourself in terms of your vocation derives from implicit personality theories…Simply stated, the person who is successful in one realm—business, medicine, law—who defines himself in terms of his career will experience inordinate conflict if he is not comparably successful in all other domains. In essence, being a successful butcher, baker, or candlestick maker imposes a restriction on a person's freedom to perform related activities at less-than-superior levels.

The most problematic aspect of this circumstance—which is similar to problems brought on by encore expectations—is that self-imposed performance demands are not limited to areas of known success. Whereas a successful individual could diversify his business pursuits or take up a new hobby as a means of developing a rewarding sideline, his own burdensome expectations can force him to keep on doing only what he does best. Such a victim of The Success Syndrome thus confines his behavior only to "safe" activities for fear of risking his reputation and self-esteem in "uncharted waters."

Dr. Steven Berglas
The Success Syndrome

Five principles of persuasion:
1. Approach the situation with positive expectations…
…Have you ever approached someone with a proposal while inside you were thinking, "This is a waste of time. They'll never approve this." If *you* don't believe your suggestion stands a chance, how can they?…
2. Anticipate and voice their objections…
Determine why they might turn you down, and then state their arguments first. If you don't preface your points with their objections, they won't even be listening to you; they'll be waiting for their turn to talk so they can tell you why your recommendation won't work…

3. Number and document each point...

The easiest and quickest way to lend legitimacy to points is to number them. Enumerating evidence makes material sound like facts rather than opinion so it carries more weight...

4. Meet their needs and speak their language...

People won't do things for *your* reasons; they'll do them for their own...

Ask yourself what's most important to the person you're trying to persuade... Figure out how your proposal will benefit him and then address those advantages...

5. Motivate them to "try on" your ideas...

The goal is to actively involve them with questions and stories so they *see* what you're *saying*. As soon as they picture what is being proposed, they're out of the passive, resistive mode and imagining your idea as if it were a done deal.

Sam Horn
Tongue Fu!

It's one thing to be open to new ideas; it's quite another to go on the offensive and actively hunt for them. I encourage you to be a "hunter" and search for ideas outside your area...

Where do you hunt for ideas?...

I've asked many people this question. Here are some of their ideas...

Family Trips. Whenever our family goes on vacation, I have made it a practice to take them on a tour through an operating plant to see how things are made and what procedures are used...

Junk Yards. Going to a junk yard is a sobering experience. There you can see the ultimate destination of almost everything we desire...

Daydreaming to a Sound Effects Record. It really sets my mind free.

*Flea Markets...*If you want to know what a free economy is all about, go to a flea market. There you can see what values people place on things.

Old Science Magazines. I get ideas from reading old popular science magazines from the early twentieth century. There were many good ideas proposed then which couldn't be implemented because the materials weren't available then...

Want Ads. The want ad section of the newspaper is what people are all about—not the front page...

Studying a Subject on a Shallow Level. I get more ideas from a $2.98 basic introductory paperback than a $20 text.

Roger Von Oech
A Whack on the Side of the Head

Let us consider the way in which we spend our lives.

This world is a place of business. What an infinite bustle! I am awaked almost every night by the panting of the locomotive. It interrupts my dreams. There is no sabbath. It would be glorious to see mankind at leisure for once. It is nothing but work, work, work.

If a man walks in the woods for love of them half of each day, he is in danger of being regarded as a loafer; but if he spends his whole day as a speculator, shearing off those woods and making earth bald before her time, he is esteemed an industrious and enterprising citizen.

The ways by which you may get money almost without exception lead downward. To have done anything by which you earned money *merely* is to have been truly idle or worse. If the laborer gets no more than the wages which his employer pays him, he is cheated, he cheats himself...

The aim of the laborer should be, not to get his living, to get "a good job," but to perform well a certain work; and, even in a pecuniary sense, it would be economy for a town to pay its laborers so well that they would not feel that they were working for low ends, as for a livelihood merely, but for scientific, or even moral ends. Do not hire a man who does your work for money, but him who does it for love of it.

Henry David Thoreau
Life Without Principle

"Inside-out" means to start first with self; even more fundamentally, to start with the most *inside* part of self—with your paradigms, your character, and your motives.

It says if you want to *have* a happy marriage, *be* the kind of person who generates positive energy and sidesteps negative energy rather than empowering it. If you want to *have* a more pleasant, cooperative teenager, *be* a more understanding, empathetic, consistent, loving parent. If you want to *have* more freedom, more latitude in your job, *be* a more responsible, a more helpful, a more contributing employee. If you want to be trusted, *be* trustworthy. If you want the secondary greatness of recognized talent, focus first on primary greatness of character.

The inside-out approach says that private victories precede public victories, that making and keeping promises to ourselves precedes making and keeping promises to others. It says it is futile to put personality ahead of character, to try to improve relationships with others before improving ourselves.

Inside-out is a process—a continuing process of renewal based on the natural laws that govern human growth and progress.

Stephen R. Covey
The Seven Habits of Highly Effective People

Children, you must remember something. A man without ambition is dead. A man with ambition but no love is dead. A man with ambition and love for his blessings here on earth is ever so alive. Having been alive, it won't be hard in the end to lie down and rest.

Pearl Bailey
Talking to Myself

Lazy hands make a man poor, but diligent hands bring wealth. He who gathers crops in summer is a wise son, but he who sleeps during harvest is a disgraceful son.

Proverbs 10:4-5 (NIV)

A man is not idle because he is absorbed in thought. There is a visible labour and there is an invisible labour.

Victor Hugo
Les Misérables

I like work: it fascinates me. I can sit and look at it for hours. I love to keep it by me: the idea of getting rid of it nearly breaks my heart.

Jerome K. Jerome
Three Men in a Boat

You don't have to feel passionate about your job to feel passionate about your life. Enthusiasm is catching. Let it begin anywhere, and watch in amazement as even the most resistant timber catches fire.

Where to begin? Sing in the bathtub. Tap-dance while the computer prints out. Treat yourself to the rarest cheese on the shelf. Take every opportunity to jump out of yourself and into humor, openness, perspective, and faith.

When your passion is reignited, follow it wherever it may lead. If you are not ready to hand in your resignation and leap into a void, you can—at least—take a class on the subject, or maybe an after-hours internship, join the professional association, or be on the lookout for a mentor.

Use your very life as fuel, and trust that while the fire in your heart is transforming your inner experience, the heat and warmth you are producing will be attracting new opportunities to you beyond your wildest dreams.

Carol Orsborn
How Would Confucius Ask for a Raise?

The world is sown with good; but unless I turn my glad thoughts into practical living and till my own field, I cannot reap a kernel of the good.

Helen Keller
Optimism

Therefore, my beloved brethren, be ye steadfast, unmoveable, always abounding in the work of the Lord, forasmuch as ye know that your labour is not in vain in the Lord.

1 Corinthians 15:58

Work consists of whatever a body is *obliged* to do, and Play consists of whatever a body is not obliged to do.

Mark Twain
Tom Sawyer

The one thing that's saving me—saving me, I mean, not from any melodramatic issues but just from sheer unhappiness—is lots and lots of work.

Dylan Thomas
Letters to Vernon Watkins

Far and away the best prize that life offers is the chance to work hard at work worth doing.

Theodore Roosevelt
Labor Day address, Syracuse, New York, 1903

Work is needed to express what is true: also to receive what is true. We can express and receive what is false, or at least what is superficial, without any work.

Simone Weil
Gravity and Grace

Be thankful for the troubles of your job. They provide you with about half of your income. If it were not for the things that go wrong, the difficult people you have to deal with, the problems and unpleasantness of your working day, someone could be found to handle your job for about half of what you are being paid. It takes intelligence, resourcefulness, patience, tact, and courage to meet the troubles of any job. That is why you hold your present job. And it may be the reason why you aren't holding down an even bigger one. If all of us would start to look for more troubles and learn to handle them cheerfully, with good judgment, as opportunities rather than irritations, we would find ourselves getting ahead at a surprising rate. For it is a fact that there are plenty of jobs waiting for men and women who aren't afraid of the troubles connected with them.

Harvey Mackay
Sharkproof

Work spares us from three great evils: boredom, vice, and need.

François Voltaire
Candide

Whatever you do, work at it with all your heart, as working for the Lord, not for men, since you know that you will receive an inheritance from the Lord as a reward. It is the Lord Christ you are serving.

Colossians 3:23-24 (NIV)

Children don't know what a hard day's work is. Until we adults tell them.

One afternoon not long ago, we were baby-sitting our three-year-old nephew and one-year-old niece. Wanting their parents to return home to extra happy children, we filled the afternoon with fun activities. What could a toddler enjoy better than an afternoon of Popsicles, Winnie the Pooh videos, and kickball? We were proud of how sweetly the little cousins played together and looked forward to giving a happy, no-tears report about a fun afternoon.

But late in the afternoon, I ruined it all. I decided to mow the lawn.

While the children were playing happily inside with my wife, I decided to slip out and cut the grass before dusk. I had put off the dreaded chore all week. It was getting dark and the meteorologist predicted rain the next day. If I procrastinated another day, I'd have to machete the lawn before mowing it. So I cranked up the push mower and began the unpleasant task, dripping in the late summer, North Carolina humidity.

When I mow the lawn, I have one thought on my mind: getting done. With that consuming focus, I didn't notice that my nephew had come out of the house. Little Jake was standing on the sidewalk crying out to me. I shut off the lawn mower to hear him.

"Uncle Alan, I want to mow the lawn with you."

I smiled, crouched down, and told my little buddy that only Uncle Alan could use the big mower and reassured him I'd be done shortly.

I resumed mowing. But after two more passes over the lawn, Jake was still standing there. His call was louder. He was pleading, begging, bargaining with me. In an attempt to appease him, I fetched a broom and asked him to "help" by sweeping the sidewalk.

It didn't work. As I cut two more swaths of grass, Jake laid down his broom, broke into tears, and sobbed. He wept with his whole heart at full volume. When I went to comfort him, he was inconsolable.

"I just wanted to help you mow the lawn, Uncle Alan," Jake cried out repeatedly. "I just wanted to help you."

As my attempts at consolation failed (along with various bribes), I thought to myself, "*What is wrong with this picture?*"

I thought about asking him, "Let me get this straight. Inside the house there are toys and playmates. In the back yard there is a swing set and slide. But you would rather push a heavy mower through shin-high grass in the July sun? You would rather be shoving this mower, with ragweed flying up your nose and yellow jackets nipping at your ankles?

"You're mixed up," I was tempted to say. "Mowing isn't fun. It's work. Don't you know the difference between work and play?!"

But there was no need to ask. Jake's desire to mow the lawn was no different from the desires of any other young child. All toddlers beg to do the chores their parents dread. They don't just covet mowing. They want to rake, bake, and vacuum. My two-year-old considers it a great treat when he gets to help me take out the trash or pull weeds.

Thankfully, I held my tongue. Jake will be told to hate work soon enough. The whole world will teach him. He'll learn it from commuters' faces on Monday morning. He'll learn that when people say, "Thank God it's Friday," they're not really thanking the Lord but cursing their work. He'll hear people gripe about their jobs and will listen to country musicians sing about taking this job and shoving it.

So I just hugged little Jake and longed for a heart that draws no boundaries between work and play. And I thought how great would a country be if its people worked with the joy of a child at play? How much better built would our buildings be if all the workers had the fervor of a child with Lego blocks? How soon would we discover a cure for cancer if every science student worked with the determination of a child with a jigsaw puzzle? How much less crime would we have if, as a child, everyone received as much love and attention as a toddler's baby doll?

I realized that Jake isn't mixed up about work. I am.

During a recent stay at a nice hotel, I was excited about the sophisticated exercise room boasting five different stepping machines. But it perturbed me that the elevator was broken and I had to take the stairs to get there. Likewise, people who go to the mall to get out of the house and walk will, nonetheless, spend fifteen minutes driving around the parking lot to get a space twenty feet closer to the entrance.

It's strange. Children can't wait to grow up and do the work of adults. Adults can't wait to retire and quit doing the work they once longed to do. Children spend their early years pretending to be firemen and nurses and truck drivers. Real firemen and nurses and truck drivers spend their adulthood thinking about collecting a pension and getting out of the rat race.

It makes you wonder. Where did we go wrong? When did work start feeling so much like work?

You don't have to turn far in your Bible to find the answer. Work was cursed at the same time that every other curse entered the world: when Adam and Eve disobeyed God's simple command.

The woman brought a curse upon the fruitfulness of her womb: "I will greatly increase your pains in childbearing; with pain you will give birth to children" (Genesis 3:16).

The man brought a curse upon the fruitfulness of his hands: "Cursed is the ground because of you; through painful toil you will eat of it all the days of your life. It will produce thorns and thistles for you, and you will eat the plants of the field. By the sweat of your brow you will eat your food" (v. 17-19).

If the above verses were all you read, you might think that work was a curse that God put upon humanity. Such thinking leads to the conclusion that man and woman's disobedience made God so angry that he invented work to oppress the creatures.

That's the way most people view work. As a curse. An oppressive necessity. Hence, getting off work is better than going to work. Friday is better than Monday. If work is a curse, then we should do only what is necessary to get what we want in return.

I once imagined that Adam and Eve just lounged around their lush garden before the Fall. No weeds. No in-season or out-of-season. No planting or harvesting. No pits in their apricots. No worms in their corn. Surely paradise was like a great cruise-ship getaway. Plenty of sweets, swimming pools, and smorgasbords.

But, oddly, in Adam and Eve's paradise there is no mention of midnight buffets or freshly prepared salad bars. There are no waiters serving the couple frosty drinks with little, floating umbrellas. It appears that Adam and Eve had to pluck their own fruit. They had to crack their own coconuts, peel their own bananas, and squeeze their own orange juice. God was not dropping food in their mouths like a mother bird to her wide-beaked babies.

There was work to do before the Fall. Adam had a vocation before he ate his apple. The Scripture says it plainly: "The LORD God took the man and put him in the Garden of Eden *to work it and take care of it*" (Genesis 2:15).

The Hebrew word for work means "to till" the ground. Adam didn't have a gas-powered tiller or tractor. He probably didn't have much of a hoe. God put the man in the garden to work it with his hands. Adam had a strenuous, time-consuming job. And he loved it—until he sinned.

Adam had changed. There was tilling of soil before the Fall and tilling of soil after it. But Adam's attitude changed totally. The Hebrew word for "painful toil" usually refers to emotional pain, not physical pain. All of a sudden, work felt like work.

What began as a vocation to be enjoyed became a job to get done. The calling that was a gift and blessing to Adam suddenly felt like a tyrannical task hanging over him. He perspired before the Fall, but now he noticed the sweat. His hands were in the dirt before the sin, but now they felt dirty.

Like everything else, sin made work a selfish endeavor. Adam quit working as unto the Lord and started working as unto himself. After sin, there was no more caring for the garden. It became all about *taking* from the garden. Before, the soil in his hands was a reminder of God's magnificent provision. Afterwards, it was only a necessary means of gain.

How do you see your work? A calling, or a paycheck? How do you view your chores? An opportunity to bless your family, or an aggravating necessity?

Author Sue Bender lived a hurried, chaotic life. Around five o-clock each morning, she began her busy, driven days with an ambitious "Things to Do" list. Maybe you can identify with her when she writes, "I valued accomplishments. I valued being special. I valued results."

But, feeling unsatisfied with her busy life, Sue Bender decided to do something quite unusual. She moved in with an Amish family in Brimfield, Iowa.

The Amish are a simple people stereotyped for their shunning of electricity and automobiles. They are recognized by their simple black-and-white attire and their horse-and-buggy travel. While their religious separatism may be misguided in some ways, the Amish people remind America of a time when life was a lot slower, and the line between work and play a lot fuzzier.

The busy, fast-paced author was surprised to watch the Amish women at work, cooking, canning, and cleaning. "No one rushed," Bender observed [in her book, *Plain and Simple: A Woman's Journey to the Amish*]. "Each step was done with care. The women moved through the day unhurried. There was no rushing to finish so they could get on to the 'important things.' For them, it was all important."

And she watched Eli, the father of the family, work the fields.

"Caring for the land, every day, is my way to be close to God. His land must be honored," she heard Eli say. And watching the Amish farm their land, Bender learned:

> Their intention is to make things grow and do work that is useful. I couldn't say exactly what the difference is, but I felt a difference. They work to work. Their work time isn't spent "in order to do something else"—to have free time on weekends, go to a restaurant, or save for a vacation or retirement. They do not expect to find satisfaction in that vague "something out there" but in the daily mastery of whatever they are doing.

In summary, Bender noted that the Amish do not just value the product of their work. They also value the process.

That's what little children do.

Children don't build sand castles in order to take pictures of them or in hopes of winning a cash award. They build sand castles just for the pleasure of the process. My little nephew Jake didn't want to mow the lawn so he could stand back and observe a manicured yard. He just wanted the pleasure of pushing the mower.

Adults value the results. Children value the means. Before the Fall, Adam valued the process of tilling the soil. Afterwards, he mainly valued the product of tilling the soil.

For a chance at childhood again, we must learn to value the process of work as well as the product. Our work, like our lives, must be redeemed.

Work needn't be drudgery. The curse can be broken.

Paul, one of the hardest working men in history, had a simple prescription: "Whatever you do, work at it with all your heart, as working for the Lord, not for men, since you know that you will receive an inheritance from the Lord as a reward. It is the Lord Christ you are serving" (Colossians 3:23-24).

You don't wash dishes for the family. You wash them for the Lord. When you change a diaper, you don't just serve your child, you serve Christ. You don't sell real estate for a commission, you sell it for the Lord. You don't argue a case for a jury's decision, you argue for the Lord.

Imagine if your work became God-centered rather than me-centered. Imagine if the process became as important as the product. Wouldn't it take the pressure off? Wouldn't it bring back the fun?

There was work in paradise before the Fall. There surely will be work in Heaven. But you'll forget to call it "work." In even the most challenging tasks, you'll feel like a child at play. Who knows, I may beg an angel to let me take a turn mowing some celestial lawn.

But while you're waiting to get to work in Heaven, why not get a little more of Heaven in your work now? Ask God to change your attitude about your work. Ask Him to help you work like a child. It may not happen overnight, but be patient. God is still *working* on you. And God loves His work.

Alan D. Wright
A Chance at Childhood Again

Originality and the feeling of one's own dignity are achieved only through work and struggle.

Fyodor Dostoevsky
A Diary of a Writer

Have you ever sensed a lack of purpose in your work? Have you struggled to see the reward for all your effort? Is it all getting a little wearisome?

Why go the extra mile for this company? They'll never reward me for it.

Why put fabric softener on his shirt? He'll never notice anyway.

He never says anything about my new recipes. Why do I keep trying?

Why should I put myself out on this English assignment? It'll be graded by some graduate assistant, anyway. The prof will never see it.

Maybe—just maybe—you've been doing your work for the notice and praise of men. Maybe you've been laboring for your own personal gratification. Talk about tiresome! That kind of service can get very old and stale. Fast.

It's the motive that counts. Doing your work wholeheartedly "as for the Lord" can transform virtually any task you're called on to perform...whether it's counting widgets in a widget factory, writing a term paper in economics, cleaning the kitchen for the umpteenth time, or giving loving care to someone who fails to acknowledge or appreciate you.

The Lord Jesus will neither overlook nor forget the tasks you perform in His name. Nor will He fail to reward you.

Joni Eareckson Tada
Secret Strength

Vocations which we wanted to pursue, but didn't, bleed, like colors, on the whole of our existence.

Honoré de Balzac
La Maison Nucingen

Some time ago I was in a room with twenty-plus corporate staffers whose tenure with the company ranged from five to twenty-five years. As an icebreaker for our daylong session, I asked the participants to answer three questions about themselves for the rest of the group: Who are you? Who were you? Who do you want to be? Most notable were the responses I heard to the third question.

Several people disclosed admirable goals such as "I want to be a good father" and "I want to continue to grow and learn."

About a third of the group, however, candidly told their peers, "I like my job OK, but it's not fulfilling. I want to work with kids" or "I want to help addicts." In short, "I want a chance to *make a difference*. I want a more significant life."

The desires of these corporate staffers are in no way unique. I've spoken with management and workers all over the world—from the high-rise office buildings in San Francisco to the North Sea of the UK to the rain forest of Papua New Guinea to the deserts of Saudi Arabia. It's amazing the number of people I find who have devoted years to pursuing their "ideal life" by means of a dream career, only to fall short of what they *really* want.

You, too, want your life to make a difference. You want a chance in life to carve your own mark and leave a tiny, yet meaningful piece of yourself behind. These desires reflect a deep and soulful drive for significance that is common to all people.

Let's be very clear at the onset: The issue is not about getting a better career (although career *can* play a major role). The issue at stake goes far beyond "what people do at work" to "what people do with their lives"! It's about making a *life* that counts.

I've led a rather eclectic life. After leaving college I was in manufacturing for twelve years, then went to seminary and was a pastor for six years. Today I'm a forty-six-year-old, self-employed management consultant, racking up frequent-flyer miles, while trying to be a good husband and father. I tend to keep busy, and as a result, over the last five years I have come to a life-changing realization: There are a lot of things I will do in my life, but in the end, only a few of them will really matter. Those will be the *right things*.

An effective adage is used in management development to describe the distinctive of a good leader. It is said that while managers concentrate on *doing things right*, leaders concentrate on *doing the right things*. In business you can do hordes of things right, such as accounting, marketing, manufacturing, and customer service. But, if you do not do *the right things*, like develop the right product for the right market and get it to the customer at the right time, you'll be out of business in a heartbeat.

The same principle is true for life in general. You are probably doing scores of things right, but are they *the right things?* Are they the kinds of things that contribute to the life you really want?

Charlie Hedges
Getting the Right Things Right

The same man cannot well be skilled in everything; each has his special excellence.

Euripides
Rhesus

From a very early age, perhaps the age of five or six, I knew that when I grew up I should be a writer. Between the ages of about seventeen and twenty-four I tried to abandon this idea, but I did so with the consciousness that I was outraging my true nature and that sooner or later I should have to settle down and write books.

George Orwell
"Why I Write"

Look always on an idea with interest, deep humility as well; for this may be the fingertip of something waiting to be born, and coming from a sphere you know not of, but touching you, and awakening you to try.

Phylos
The Growth of a Soul

Talent is like a call, for it draws us to a vocation or at least an expression of an art that not only uplifts us, but finds its fullness in being shared. It could be a gift for relations to children or for crafting a loving household or for working with persons who are physically or mentally challenged. Having such a gift becomes a call that summons us to special relationships and creates open spaces in which others may grow and thrive.

Responsibilities and commitments may be calls, drawing us out when we prefer to be left alone or go in a different direction. I have worked with people whose relationships have wandered into dry and dusty places. In these deserts of the heart, it is easy to look to other people and other places where sweet water seems to flow; but there is part of us that has the power to cross these deserts and, by so doing, make them bloom again. It is the power of love, integrity and even sacrifice, and it is our commitment that can call it forth from within us.

Our lives are woven from a melody of such calls that help us to define ourselves.

David Spangler
The Call

Every calling is great when greatly pursued.

Oliver Wendell Holmes, Jr.
Speech, Suffolk Bar Association, February 8, 1885

The artisan or scientist or the follower of whatever discipline who has the habit of comparing himself not with other followers but with the discipline itself will have a lower opinion of himself, the more excellent he is.

Giacomo Leopardi
Pensieri

My first conscious memory dates from when I was four. I was being taken for a walk by the nursemaid. I was dressed in knickerbockers, with a fawn-coloured coat, and on my head was a red tam-o'-shanter—you know, the round cap with a little tail protruding from its centre, like the remains of a cut umbilical cord. And then out of the hawthorn hedge there hopped a fat toad. What a creature, with warty skin, its big eyes bulging up, and its awkward movements! That comic toad helped to determine my career as a scientific naturalist.

Julian Huxley
Memories

The most gifted natures are perhaps also the most trembling.

André Gide
Journals

Every natural power exhilarates; a true talent delights the possessor first.

Ralph Waldo Emerson
The Scholar

Only God knows what is one's real work.

Anton Chekhov
Uncle Vanya

Looking at the masses of humanity, driven this way and that way, the Christian teaching is apt to be forgotten that for each individual soul there is a vocation as real as if that soul were alone upon the planet. Yet it is a fact.

Mark Rutherford
The Deliverance of Mark Rutherford

Every man has his own vocation. The talent is the call.

Ralph Waldo Emerson
Essays: First Series

Everyone must row with the oars he has.

English proverb

An aspiration is a joy for ever, a possession as solid as a landed estate, a fortune which we can never exhaust and which gives us year by year a revenue of pleasurable activity.

Robert Louis Stevenson
Virginibus Puerisque

There is one social skill that can serve as your strongest asset in a job interview...in business, it helps more than any other single qualification, with the possible exception of being the owner's eldest child. That is enthusiasm. A look of vitality and happiness, an interest in the world and an eagerness to participate in life, is what is called charm in the social milieu; but in the working world it is called competence.

Judith Martin
Miss Manners' Guide to Excruciatingly Correct Behavior

If you would hit the mark, you must aim a little above it;
Every arrow that flies feels the attraction of earth.

Henry Wadsworth Longfellow
"Elegiac Verse"

A thought which does not result in an action is nothing much, and an action which does not proceed from a thought is nothing at all.

Georges Bernanos
The Last Essays of Georges Bernanos

I know I can write if I can just get my study really together, really functional. When I finish that wall with the new, longer boards, and I space those boards out rather than having books two deep on the shelves, I know I'll be ready. I just need to file those copies of other stories, poems, notes, ideas. I know that when I get them in the file cabinet, I'll be that much closer to being ready. If I just clear my desk, organize the top so there's room to write, put some new ballpoints in my favorite pens, wipe the dust, start a new notebook, I'll be ready. Right after I scrape the paint from the windowpanes behind my desk.

If I just finish that touch-up painting on the hallway leading to my study, all will be in readiness. If I patch the crack in the bedroom, get more water pressure to the shower, clean the toilet, I'll have time to write. I just have to wash the stairs to the secret hallway once more and I think I'll finally have that plaster dust under control. If I finish building that spaceship in the secret hallway, I know I'll be inspired to write. If I just had two comfortable couches in the den.

If I could be assured that my fourteen-year-old cat is thin because it's so hot and not because she's dying, if I had a dining room set, I'd be ready to write. If I caulked that stairway leading to the basement, if I swept the basement, if I moved the barbecue pit back to the garage, if I hung those tools in the garage, and put up a new back fence, then I could really write.

If my vegetable garden and flowers survive better next year, I know I'll just blossom as a writer. If I could just get to the grocery store. If I could just stop worrying about this sudden hair loss I'm having, I know I could concentrate, focus, and write. If I just had clean hair.

If I could compose at the typewriter instead of having to write in longhand first, if I had a computer, if my teeth were cleaned, if my bowels were regular, I know I could write.

If I were a better cook I'd be a better writer. Organization in the kitchen begets organization in the study...If my ankle would heal, if only I could jog again, then I'd be in good shape to write. If I lost ten pounds I'd be confident enough.

If I were just a little happier, I know I could write. If I were just a little taller, that would do it for sure. If I could just have a little equilibrium, a little hope, a little serenity. If I could just have one year of total harmony, I know I'd be at peace enough to write. If I could just get over my past, I'd be able to write about it. If I just felt secure, if I knew my mother really loved me, if I were pretty, I know I could write. If I could just finish therapy, I know I'd be ready.

If I can just get through this one lifetime, I know I'll be ready and able to write.

Jane Ellen Ibur
"If Only"

We were not idle when we were with you, nor did we eat anyone's food without paying for it. On the contrary, we worked night and day, laboring and toiling so that we would not be a burden to any of you. We did this, not because we do not have the right to such help, but in order to make ourselves a model for you to follow. For even when we were with you, we gave you this rule: "If a man will not work, he shall not eat." We hear that some among you are idle. They are not busy, they are busybodies. Such people we command and urge in the Lord Jesus Christ to settle down and earn the bread they eat.

2 Thessalonians 3:7-12 (NIV)

To know a man, observe how he wins his object, rather than how he loses it; for when we fail our pride supports us, when we succeed, it betrays us.

Charles Caleb Colton
Lacon

The house praises the carpenter.

Ralph Waldo Emerson
Journals

In order that people may be happy in their work, these three things are needed: They must be fit for it: they must not do too much of it: and they must have a sense of success in it.

John Ruskin
Pre-Raphaelitism

Do the work that's nearest,
Though it's dull at whiles,
Helping, when you meet them,
Lame dogs over stiles.

Charles Kingsley
The Invitation

To be well prepared for productive work, we also must clearly understand that *people are important.* This statement—people are important—is so simple, it borders on the sentimental and yet in our busy world of increased emphasis on technology, of pressures and problems on every side, of almost hourly crises, one of our most difficult tasks still remains—that of dealing humanely with one another...

Somehow we must understand that regardless of vocation the focus of our work ultimately will touch the lives of people.

Ernest L. Boyer
Commencement Address, Westmont College, 1980

Wealth stays with us a little moment if at all; only our characters are steadfast, not our gold.

Euripides
Electra

Most people would succeed in small things, if they were not troubled with great ambitions.

Henry Wadsworth Longfellow
Driftwood

The men who run corporate America are people-watchers. However, watching is not the main difference between the good and poor communicators. The great communicators are all listeners. They listen carefully, patiently, even kindly to their subordinates. They encourage people to speak to them. They hardly ever step on a man's ego or a woman's sentence. Even if they don't like a suggestion, they treat it with respect and they treat the people coming to them with respect. The really great communicators are great receivers as well as great senders of messages.

John T. Molloy
Live for Success

One becomes more interested in a job of work after the first impulse to drop it has been overcome.

Fulton J. Sheen
Way to Happiness

Next to courage, honesty is the most precious virtue. Your honesty might be the most memorable part of any successful job interview and what wins you the job.

Even if it doesn't an employer is likely to remember you. Because of your candor, you'll be the first to hear about another opening at the XYZ organization...

Honesty gives you an instant name and organizational visibility. In an interview, honesty can be charming and memorable, and your job is to make an impression—even if you don't get the job. (The guy who remembers you is going to call about a job you *do* fit.)

So don't bluff...

To discover the truth, many employers ask the same question in different ways. Much like a trial lawyer who questions a witness. Be prepared to tell about a spotty work record, five relocations in three years, and a patchy education. Most job-search problems are attitudinal: We believe our work record is spotty when, in fact, it's in the nature of our work; our relocations might be necessary to our jobs or personal life; and our education (or lack of it) might have nothing to do with our work.

Richard K. Irish
Go Hire Yourself an Employer

If a man has a talent and cannot use it, he has failed. If he has a talent and uses only half of it, he has partly failed. If he has a talent and learns somehow to use the whole of it, he has gloriously succeeded, and won a satisfaction and a triumph that few men ever know.

Thomas Wolfe
The Web and the Rock

If a great thing can be done at all, it can be done easily. But it is that kind of ease with which a tree blossoms after long years of gathering strength.

John Ruskin
Quoted in *The Author's Kalendar*

He who works his land will have abundant food, but he who chases fantasies lacks judgment. Diligent hands will rule, but laziness ends in slave labor. The sluggard craves and gets nothing, but the desires of the diligent are fully satisfied.

Proverbs 12:11, 24; 13:4 (NIV)

Interviewers like:
• People who are prepared...
• "Hokey as it sounds, I like someone with a firm handshake. I don't want to arm wrestle with them but an immediate, firm handshake gets the interview started off in the right direction."
• "I like a person who asks questions about us, as well as answers our questions about him..."
• "Self confidence..."
• "I make it a point to address people I've just met by their first names and I'm impressed when they respond by using my first name..."

Interviewers don't like:

• "I hate 'Nervous Nellies.' When I see someone squirm and fidget I feel like they're hiding something. Maybe they're lying to me."

• "Braggers! I expect a potential new-hire to tell me the best about him or herself, but I'm suspicious of the ones who claim to have run the last company they worked at single-handedly."

• Inappropriate dress…

• Lack of eye contact…

• Poor posture. "Maybe you'd call it 'body language' but I can tell a lot by how a person sits or stands. Some people hunch over like they're in pain and others sprawl all over the place. I like people who sit up, look alert and relaxed."

While a nice appearance and good manners won't substitute for skills and experience, they certainly can make you the one who is chosen from a group of similarly qualified individuals!

Paul D. Davis
When Your Corporate Umbrella Begins to Leak

If you want to hit a bird on the wing you must have all your will in focus, you must not be thinking about yourself, and, equally, you must not be thinking about your neighbor; you must be living in your eye on that bird. Every achievement is a bird on the wing.

Oliver Wendell Holmes, Jr.
The Mind and Faith of Justice Holmes

We may judge a man's ability by three things: by what he has done (including the impression he has made on others), by what he himself appears to believe he can do, by our own dramatic imagination, based on his immediate personality, of what he might do. If these do not agree it is prudent to observe him further.

Charles Horton Cooley
Life and the Student

Somewhere back in the dark ages, someone, probably a mother, said, "If it's worth doing, it's worth doing well." There is a corollary. Lots of things *aren't* worth doing well and even more aren't worth doing at all!

Learn to prioritize and get results from only those efforts which are really important. Carry a little notebook…for several days and jot down everything that *really* worries, frustrates, and makes you angry. This could be anything from the crowded traffic to and from work, your teenager's messy room,…unwanted phone calls, or dirty dishes in the sink. What you will find is that many of the things we worry about are little details not worth a minute of our concern.

Having gathered your list of things that bug you, apply the Will-it-matter-in-two-weeks? test. Starting with the easiest to let go, decide to eliminate that one item from being a bother in your life. Things like your son's strange haircut or messy room simply will not pass the test. Let go of them one after another. Then you begin to focus on the items on your list that really deserve your attention, such as making sure the computer program you write works, remembering your wife or husband's birthday, or selling up to your monthly quota. In other words, pick out the important items in your life and control only them while letting the others go…

When in doubt, laugh. It's good for you!

Eleanor Baldwin
300 New Ways to Get a Better Job

He was a strong man, which is almost the same…as to say a man with little time for kindness. For if you stop to be kind, you must swerve often from your path. So when folk tell me of this great man and that great man, I think to myself, Who was stinted of joy for his glory? How many old folk and children did his coach wheels go over? What bridal lacked his song, and what mourner his tears that he found time to climb so high?

Mary Webb
Precious Bane

By their fruits ye shall know them.

Matthew 7:20

Men may suffer terribly from the death of a loved one, the breakup of a marriage, or some other personal tragedy. But what brings them to the point of immobilization most often is the loss of their job.

Myron Brenton
The American Male

It's easy to understand why people want to stay with good boss-parents. What's hard to believe is how many people find it tough to leave the bad ones. Personnel experts are now beginning to discover what psychologists have always known: bad parents often inspire more blind loyalty than good ones.

The complex relationships between bad bosses and their subordinates are often an extension of ancient childhood struggles…Here are some examples…

1. If you felt abandoned or afraid a parent would leave when you were young…you might be afraid it will happen again. So you try to be very, very good and work very, very hard to please your bosses—no matter how belittling they are.

2. If a parent didn't help you resolve your teen-age rebellion…you might just shift that rebellion onto the workplace, self-destructively lashing out at your boss or refusing to obey company rules.

3. If you have an unresolved need for a loving, caring parent…you might blindly idealize your bosses—even if they are mean or cruel.

4. If your parents were constantly criticizing your behavior…you might not only identify with critical bosses, but continually try to placate them and win their approval…

Just as children from alcoholic families often marry alcoholics in an attempt to resolve old wounds, so do children with unresolved family tensions seek out bad bosses time and again. They are determined to triumph this time and set the problem right.

Jacqueline Horner Plumez, Ph.D.
Divorcing a Corporation

Whether it is given or received, criticism often stirs anger in the workplace. Many times, criticism is motivated by anger, and then is typically responded to in a defensive, if not overtly angry, manner. Yet productive criticism is a crucial skill for anger management because it becomes the means by which you can help somebody improve or change a vexing behavior.

The problem, of course, is that only a few know how to give or take criticism productively. Immediately begin to make criticism an anger management communication skill by doing two things:

1. Change your perception of criticism. Think of it as a TASK—to Teach Appropriate Skills and Knowledge. This definition of criticism will keep your anger away because it will remind you that the goal of the criticism is to help you

develop, motivate, educate, and improve...Remember, it is always better to direct your anger than to disguise it as "I'm telling you this for your own good," a common preface for criticism...

2. Always protect self-esteem. Criticism that threatens self-esteem—"This is terrible work"; "That was a stupid idea"—is sure to arouse anger. Criticism that protects self-esteem has a better chance of being acted upon and helps build a better relationship between you and the recipient...

Some helpful tips to protect self-esteem when criticizing are:

- Use "I" statements instead of accusatory "you" statements.
- Avoid destructive labeling statements.
- Focus on how the person can improve rather than on what he did wrong.

Hendrie Weisinger, Ph.D.
Anger at Work

Make it your ambition to lead a quiet life, to mind your own business and to work with your hands, just as we told you, so that your daily life may win the respect of outsiders and so that you will not be dependent on anybody.

1 Thessalonians 4:11-12 (NIV)

The tallest trees are most in the power of the winds, and ambitious men of the blasts of fortune.

William Penn
Some Fruits of Solitude

Workaholic organizations leap from crisis to crisis. The crisis infuses a false energy into the people...

They pull together, they are selfless, and they expend effort. They also get a high from getting through the experience...This is called peak performance.

I call it a prescription for burnout. Any stress expert can tell us the rudimentary facts of burnout...

Ordinarily, stress-management is a training workshop in which employees...are introduced to theories of stress; taught relaxation techniques; and counseled about the importance of nutrition and exercise in reducing stress...Never do stress workshops point to the origins of stress in the organization: management and the workaholic corporate culture. Subtly, stress workshops imply that the employee is to blame for being stressed out. Yet a large amount of stress actually comes from management policy, style, and climate...

Why is it that people must be pumped up to do their work? Why isn't the mission of the organization...enough?...

In healthy organizations the challenge of their mission and the integrity of their process is enough. They don't need techniques for interesting people in work. The environment provides sufficient real events (some of them crisis) that there isn't a need to make artificial ones.

Workaholic organizations are crisis-ridden and crisis creators. This is because the addictive process is a process of confusion. The crisis serves to keep everyone busy and away from asking those deeper questions that could lead to recovery and healing.

Diane Fassel, Ph.D.
Working Ourselves to Death

All work and no play makes Jack a dull boy.

James Howell
Proverbs

Thou, O God, dost sell us all good things at the price of labor.

Leonardo da Vinci
Notebooks

When an organization is moving closer to your removal, people send inconsistent signals...Some questions you should ask yourself are:

Is your boss spending less time with you?

Is the interaction less relaxed? More formal?

Are you not being brought in on things as much as you used to or should expect to be?

Has the boss started turning to other people to get things done that were usually in your purview?

Has the boss started to build the organization around you—in effect acting as though you were already gone?

Is the boss or are others in the organization directly accessing your subordinates? Is this a departure from past practice?

Is there a freeze on your decisions, with requests frequently denied or pre-rogatives challenged?

Are you precluded from making major changes—be it organizational, hiring, or starting new projects? Do you seem to be in a holding pattern, pending you don't know what?

Have people in the organization become increasingly resistant to your ideas and actions?

Do you sense that your influence on your own staff has seriously dimin-ished—much like a lame duck?

Listen carefully to what is being said and what is not being said. Don't ignore your instincts…

Don't become overly suspicious, looking for demons behind every desk. However, if you're in an unstable situation, give due consideration to the danger signals. You want to be able to deal effectively with the realities of the situation and move to your advantage.

Richard Gould
Sacked! Why Good People Get Fired
and How to Avoid It

Six days you shall labor, but on the seventh day you shall rest; even during the plowing season and harvest you must rest.

Exodus 34:31 (NIV)

Feeling discontent…is the career equivalent of going through a midlife crisis. You probably didn't expect it, and no one plans for it. But it's been brewing for a while. You've made a heavy investment in your career only to find yourself blocked or trapped in mid-path. You're no longer a rookie and the stakes are high. You feel frustrated, bored, and ready for a change. But if you're like most people, you don't have a clue as to what to do next…

The problem, of course, is that you don't yet know whether a change will really solve the crisis. So the trick is not to move quickly; it's to move insightfully.

Ask yourself what you really want from your career and what's possible. Write your answers in a notebook. Wait a week and write new answers. Are they the same? Different? Discuss your answers with a friend or mentor. Keep in mind your own complexity and hidden needs. Your answers don't have to be terse bullet points on a page. Simplify later.

This is also the time to confront yourself with a second set of critical questions:

- What am I willing to settle for?
- What do I feel I deserve in my career, in life?
- What will I feel like in five years if nothing changes?

Your evolving answers to these questions will begin to shape and define your vision for change.

Dory Hollander, Ph.D.
The Doom Loop System

Of all words connected to the process of change, "no" carries more trepidation than any other. We tend to fear hearing or saying this word, believing something terrible will happen. Some of you will avoid confrontation of any sort—you won't ask for a raise you deserve; you won't make an important contact call; you won't go on an interview because the answer might be *no*. This fear of rejection is the greatest dilemma of all...

In truth, *no* has two real advantages:

First, a firm *no* completes an event and kicks off a new beginning. When someone says, "Sorry, we've chosen someone else," and even, "You're fired," it may not feel good, but it creates *closure* and opens a space for the next endeavor. *No* can be a release from the past and a relief—now you can go on unencumbered. It is a simple statistic: You will get a certain number of nos to every yes. And no is often preferable to maybe. Being strung along with false hope can be time wasting, manipulative, and counterproductive. "No" can be more painless than a falsely polite "maybe." You need to be astute, though, to listen for a "moving maybe"—genuine deliberation that leads to a *yes*.

Second, when someone says *no*, you can question why. This can be valuable information to you. You can learn under which conditions they would say yes, or what specifically you need to do to come back, or go forward elsewhere, with new strength.

Carole Hyatt
Shifting Gears

She gets up while it is still dark; she provides food for her family and portions for her servant girls. She considers a field and buys it; out of her earnings she plants a vineyard. She sets about her work vigorously; her arms are strong for her tasks. She sees that her trading is profitable, and her lamp does not go out at night...She watches over the affairs of her household and does not eat the bread of idleness.

Proverbs 31:15-17, 27 (NIV)

March 1961. I was twenty-one; my sixth-grade teacher would have said, "Gloria, you're much too old to cry." Nevertheless, three-week-old F. Scott and I had been crying nonstop for three weeks with no sign of a letup.

To make matters worse, my husband, Sid, cried too. In his last semester of a two-year junior college degree program, he was on the brink—no, actually, there was no brink to it—he was flunking. Flunking in school and in his door-to-door vacuum cleaner sales job. He was bringing in the equivalent of ten cents an hour after we paid fifty cents each for the "free" knife sets he and I (plural-pregnant tense) gave to potential customers to get his size fourteen feet inside their doors. Banging our own door, we shouted out our frustration with each other, our screaming child, and life in general. Finally, exhausted, we decided that the sales job must go before we were bankrupt and ungraduated.

No straws had to be drawn to know that it was I who must get the job. With two years of college and experience in an insurance company calculating policy loans, we figured that I shouldn't have any trouble getting a job. Wrong! First of all, I did not drive, having promised the driver's training teacher in high school that I wouldn't.

Secondly, we didn't have a car anyway. Even in 1961 a ten-cents-an-hour job would not buy much twenty-five-cents-a-gallon gasoline.

Until then we hadn't needed a car. We lived across the street from the college in the former Seminary Residence. Even though the building had been converted to apartments, everyone continued to refer to it as the Seminary Residence. That title in itself meant a lot to us in righteousness status. And for fifty dollars a month, we could make do with a kitchen and a bedroom, and a shared bath down the hall, especially as the single students began moving out about the same time that Screaming F. Scott arrived. Soon we had the entire floor to ourselves.

For all practical purposes I figured the job needed to be within walking distance and should have night hours since child care was expensive, more so I assumed, for a child who cried constantly. I reasoned that Sid could cry with F. Scott at night as he studied and I worked. I could then be free to cry with our baby during the day while Sid was in classes.

Fortunately, on the highway only four blocks away was the Hideaway Inn, in need of a waitress. Unfortunately, the job paid only forty cents an hour. "Thirty cents better than your recent job," I reminded Sid as he rocked an even more protesting F. Scott. "One of the other waitresses," I added, already including myself as a group member even though I had no previous experience, "got on the list to get hired down at Bombs for nothing per hour, zero!" Bombs was the classiest restaurant around Des Moines at the time. "It's the tips, up to fifty a day down there if you're good."

Tips turned out to be the key word, especially after I found out that the first check would be delayed for two weeks, and the cost of my uniform, twenty-five dollars, would be deducted, leaving me, if I didn't eat anything on the job, seven dollars! So, wiping away three weeks' worth of tears, I turned on a smile to rival neon flashing. "Smile for F. Scott's milk" became my motto.

I approached each of my assigned tables with the enthusiasm of a hockey fan, intent upon winning the customers over to me forever or for the rest of my waitressing career, whichever came first. Just as soon as I asked my patrons if they wanted coffee, I started a conversation. Eventually I explained that I had just had a baby and that I needed money for his milk. Then, before I asked them if they wanted dessert, I always served up a sticky, sweet compliment.

By the second night the pockets of my rose-colored, unpaid-for pinafore filled up to a clinking, and by seven the next morning they jingled happily as I pranced home to the Seminary Residence. F. Scott screamed his greeting, and Sid grinned sleepily as I dumped the change on our unmade bed. We counted the quarters and dimes into stacks, finally touching noses, cooing, "Ten dollars."

That initial ten dollar drop gradually swelled into a torrent of tip money for me, but with it an aridity developed around the edges of the Hideaway dining room, mummifying the experienced waitresses, especially Judy. Judy rolled her eyes up to her bleached, back-combed beehive when customers began requesting my tables.

"Well, jeesee-peesee!" she mumbled her favorite expression under her breath as she directed me toward the new arrivals with her top-heavy hairdo. I always thanked her while practically skipping a circle around her to get to my guests who couldn't wait to hear all about how "little F. is doin'" and to offer more advice on how to cure colic. Out of respect for customers, I always wrote their advice down on the back cardboard of my pad, no matter how ridiculous the ritual was that they suggested.

Soon Judy had more to think about. She was moving up on the list for Bombs. "I'm up to seven now," Judy said the night after Pinkie and Birdie quit in anticipation of being called; they were numbers one and two on the Bombs list. "I'll be number two in a couple of weeks," she said loud enough for Jim, the manager, to hear.

"I got news for you. You're already number two," he mumbled. I didn't know how Jim found out, but I'm sure Judy didn't hear him. Later, when I saw Judy, I forgot all about telling her because in the meantime Jim called me into his office to let me know what a great job I was doing and could I possibly work a double shift on the weekends once in a while on account of a couple more waitresses on days as well as two more cooks were also quitting. I told him I would have to consult with Sid since I wasn't sure about his schedule. Then, to stay on his good side, I added, "I don't know how much of F. Scott Sid can take even if he is an English major." I laughed but Jim didn't. I don't think he got the joke. Maybe he hadn't ever taken American Lit.

When Sid said that I could work for one or two double shifts, I didn't know whether to be happy for the chance to make more in tips or sad because of being dead tired. All that smiling was wearing me out along with not getting much sleep during the day with F. Scott still raging, despite doctor and customer "cures."

With my mind zeroing in on all the money I would be earning, I rushed into Jim's office with "Yes!" practically falling off my lips, ready to agree to whatever he asked me to do. "You'll work Saturday night and stay on to work all day Sunday then?" Jim beamed.

Consenting to Jim's schedule was actually my second mistake. My first was not checking the calendar ahead of time. Sunday was Mother's Day.

F. Scott and I cried a more poignant duet than usual when we discovered at the same moment that I would be smiling, serving, slaving for other mothers and their children on my first Mother's Day as a mother. "I don't see what the big deal is," Sid said. I cried harder. F. Scott cried harder.

Luckily, my own mother who lived in Austin sent me a glittery rhinestone pin that spelled MOTHER in big letters. As I attached MOTHER to my pinafore Saturday night before I went into action, I felt better. At least all the patrons, even the ones I could not wait on, would know the sacrifice I was making, especially on Sunday, by being there with them.

By seven with the sun shining the way it should on Mother's Day, I was more exhausted than I could ever remember being. When Jim motioned me into his office, my heart did a joyful flip, hoping he would tell me to go on home. Instead, he pointed at my MOTHER pin. "I won't fine you this time, Gloria, but didn't you remember that jewelry is not to be worn on the uniform?"

As I removed the MOTHER pin and put it in my pocket with the tips, I could feel the tears gathering for a storm inside my body. I walked out with no words. And no smile. No matter how hard I tried that morning to smile, I could not force it back to my face…

"What's the matter with you, Smiley?" Judy was actually joking with me as she poured maple syrup into glass pitchers on a tray…"You'll perk up in about a half an hour. Just wait…Busiest day in the restaurant business…"

Judy was right. But as wise as I began to see she was in her predictions, she could never have prepared either one of us for what happened in the busiest hour of the busiest of all restaurant days.

Mother's Day at twelve noon, May 1961. With every table surrounded by occupied chairs and a waiting area stuffed with hungry children and frazzled parents, suddenly, without warning, the cook ripped off his white hat and apron. Screaming "I quit!" he ran out the back door…

Shocked, I stared at Judy. "What are we going to do?"

"Do?" She smiled at me. "Looks like we're gonna be doin' some cookin'." She bounded over to the grill and grabbed the tongs. "Let's see. My fillets…these must be your strips…"

I gulped. "Well, nobody told me that cooks can't wear jewelry." I rescued MOTHER from my pocket of tips and stuck it back on the pinafore. Suddenly, I felt one hundred percent better. "Might as well tell 'em the truth…Sympathy will be with us. It'll be a great tip-maker. Please bear with us. Since the cook just quit, we'll be cooking your meal as well as serving it, just like home, huh?"

Judy laughed. I laughed, a sincere laugh, my first sincere anything at the Hideaway.

If it hadn't been for Judy, I don't think I ever would have survived that afternoon. She even made me a waffle "For free!" and soaked it in strawberry syrup. "Eat it," she demanded when I protested about my customers, my tips. "Gloria, you're much too skinny! You're beginning to look like a tip!" She sounded a lot like my sixth-grade teacher, who hadn't taught me nearly as much about life and work, humor and honesty in a year as Judy had in a few hours.

Actually, Mother's Day weekend was my last at the Hideaway. With splotches of strawberry syrup and MOTHER glaring across my chest, I planted myself in front of Jim at the end of my shift. "I quit! I'm going to learn how to drive."

As I walked out of the Hideaway for the last time, Judy honked. "Want a lift?" Happy to get home to Sid and F. Scott quicker with my news, I hopped into Judy's '54 Chevy...

That Mother's Day turned out perfectly after all. When I got home and picked F. Scott up from his crib, he smiled at me for the first time. And, come to think of it, most of his life since, he's been smiling sincere smiles; so have I.

Virginia Rudasill Mortenson

"Hideaway Inn"

Contrary to popular opinion, work is not the result of the curse. Adam was given the task of cultivating and keeping the Garden before sin ever entered (Genesis 2:15).

Then what was the curse? It was the addition of "thorns and thistles" that turned work into a "toil" and made the whole thing a sweaty hassle. But work itself is a privilege, a high calling, a God-appointed assignment to be carried out for His greater glory.

Today, it isn't literal briars and stinging nettles that give us fits; it's thorny people whose thistlelike attitudes add just enough irritation to make the job...well, just a job. It's the little things, the small yet persistent stings, that foul up the work and turn a potential thing full of wonder into a sweaty curse.

The difference is people. No, let's get specific. The difference is you.

The place you work will never be better than you make it.

Charles R. Swindoll

The Finishing Touch

"Be strong, all you people of the land," declares the LORD, "and work. For I am with you," declares the LORD Almighty. "This is what I covenanted with you when you came out of Egypt. And my Spirit remains among you. Do not fear."

Haggai 2:4-5 (NIV)

If you want to be successful, it's just this simple:
  Know what you're doing.
    Love what you're doing.
      And believe in what you're doing.

Will Rogers

CHAPTER FOUR

Coping With

LIFE'S HURTS

COPING WITH LIFE'S HURTS

—⟳—

There is no man in this world without some manner of tribulation or anguish, though he be king or pope.

Thomas à Kempis
The Imitation of Christ

People don't ever seem to realize that doing what's right's no guarantee against misfortune.

William McFee
Casuals of the Sea

"Why not you?"

Those three words changed my life.

One day I was talking with a friend on the telephone about her husband, who had suffered a stroke two years earlier. She had been bothered, she told me, that every day, as he sat at the kitchen table, he would ask, "Why me?" Finally, tired of hearing it, she asked, "Why not you?"

After our conversation ended, I knew I would always carry with me the message behind the words. I had just had my second surgery within the year for metastatic malignant melanoma. I could not look toward the future without crying. I was enraged because I was a cancer victim. After all, I was a good person; I taught health classes and lived by my teaching. How could this possibly happen to me?

At that moment, I turned from looking at my disease as a curse and turned it into a challenge. I had to get my head out of the sand, past the anger, the *"Why me?"* and look toward the future positively. I would learn to participate in my recovery and I looked forward to the challenge.

Peggy Maddox
On the Edge

Pursue, keep up with, circle round and round your life, as a dog does his master's chaise. Do what you love. Know your own bone, gnaw at it, bury it, unearth it, and gnaw it still.

However mean your life is, meet it and live it; do not shun it and call it hard names. It is not so bad as you are. It looks poorest when you are richest. The faultfinder will find faults even in paradise. Love your life, poor as it is.

Henry David Thoreau
Walden

Badness you can get easily, in quantity: the road is smooth, and lies close by. But in front of excellence the immortal gods have put sweat, and long and steep is the way to it, and rough at first. But when you come to the top, then it is easy, even though it is hard.

Hesiod
Works and Days

The softest things in the world overcome the hardest things in the world.

Lao-tzu
The Way of the Lao-tzu

There are three modes of bearing the ills of life: by indifference, by philosophy, and by religion.

Charles Caleb Colton
Lacon

Perhaps nothing causes more people to stumble in their faith than the problem of suffering. None of us is exempt from tribulation. We all face it at one time or another. And in our pain and desperation, we often ask, "Why, Lord?"

Have those words ever echoed through the chambers of your soul in the middle of some dark and starless night?

We can't get rid of all pain, trouble, hurt, injury, and sorrow. People fall off things and hurt themselves. Shall we then do away with the law of gravity? People have accidents in cars, planes, trains, and boats. Shall we then get rid of all forms of transportation? Suffering is a part of our world, and if Christians were exempt from all trouble and pain, everyone would immediately recognize the payoffs. If all Christians had an abundance of money, health, and happiness, our characters would never develop. Christianity would degenerate to a mere commercial venture.

So while we would avoid adversity if we could, it serves important purposes in our lives. First, trouble and sorrow equip us to help others by making us compassionate and willing to reach out to those in need. Second, trouble and sorrow draw us to God and drive us to our knees; they make us long for our real home, heaven. The third and greatest purpose of trouble is to make us Christlike. If we are to become like Jesus, we will, like Him, have to pass through the valley of the shadows. Although unpleasant at the moment, often out of the greatest suffering comes the greatest love and beauty.

D. James Kennedy and Jerry Newcombe
New Every Morning

Sweet are the uses of adversity,
Which, like the toad, ugly and venomous,
Wears yet a precious jewel in his head;
And this our life exempt from public haunt
Finds tongues in trees, books in the running brooks,
Sermons in stones and good in everything.

William Shakespeare
As You Like It

Many are the afflictions of the righteous: but the LORD delivereth him out of them all.

Psalm 34:19

O God! who is able and willing to assist me, what grounds have I not to place my whole confidence in you, to throw myself into the arms of your providence, and wait the effects of your bounty? You have care of all. I will therefore give myself up entirely to you, live always in your presence, and ever guide myself by your fear and love. It is this grace I now ask of you, the God of my heart, and my portion forever. Grant me to weigh well and to follow your admonition: "Be not solicitous, for your heavenly Father knoweth that you have need of all these things." Amen.

The Book of Common Prayer

God is our final refuge and strength, a very present help in trouble. Therefore will not we fear, though the earth be removed, and though the mountains be carried into the midst of the sea; Though the waters thereof roar and be troubled, though the mountains shake with the swelling thereof. Selah. There is a river, the streams whereof shall make glad the city of God, the holy place of the tabernacles of the most High. God is in the midst of her; she shall not be moved: God shall help her, and that right early. The heathen raged, the kingdoms were moved: he uttered his voice, the earth melted. The LORD of hosts is with us; the God of Jacob is our refuge. Selah. Come, behold the works of the LORD, what desolations he hath made in the earth. He maketh wars to cease unto the end of the earth; he breaketh the bow, and cutteth the spear in sunder; he burneth the chariot in the fire. Be still, and know that I am God: I will be exalted among the heathen, I will be exalted in the earth. The LORD of hosts is with us; the God of Jacob is our refuge. Selah.

Psalm 46

Why does God bring thunderclouds and disasters when we want green pastures and still waters? Bit by bit we find, behind the clouds, the Father's feet; behind the lightning, an abiding day that has no night; behind the thunder, "a still small voice" that comforts with a comfort that is unspeakable.

The whole claim of the redemption of Jesus is that He can satisfy the last aching abyss of the human soul, not only hereafter, but here and now.

Oswald Chambers
In the Presence of His Majesty

And is this Power benevolent or malevolent? I see it as purely benevolent. For I can see that in the midst of death life persists, in the midst of untruth truth persists, in the midst of darkness light persists. Hence I gather that God is Life, Truth, Light. He is Love. He is the Supreme God.

Mohandas K. Gandhi
All Men Are Brothers

I should know by this time that just because I feel that everything is useless and going to pieces and badly done and futile, it is not really that way at all. Everything is all right. It is in the hands of God. Let us abandon everything to Divine Providence.

And I must remember, too, that often beautiful scenery or a perfect symphony leaves me cold and dreary. There is nothing the matter with either the scenery or the music—it is myself. I have endured other miseries cheerfully at times. So I must be calm, patient, enduring, and meditate on the gifts of the Holy Spirit.

I am writing this for my consolation and courage some future day when God sees fit and thinks me strong enough to bear longer-continued crosses.

It is to remind myself so that maybe I will be stronger.

Dorothy Day
Quoted in *By Little and By Little:*
The Selected Writings of Dorothy Day

Often, problems are knots with many strands, and looking at those strands can make a problem seem different.

Fred Rogers
You Are Special

You want a better position than you now have in business, a better and fuller place in life? All right, think of that better place and you in it as already existing. Form the mental image. Keep on thinking of that higher position, keep the image constantly before you and…no, you will not suddenly be transported into the higher job, but you will find that you are preparing yourself to occupy the better position in life…your body, your energy, your understanding, your heart will all grow up to the job…and when you are ready, after hard work, perhaps after years of preparation, you will get the job and the higher place in life.

Joseph Appel

When Samahria and I started working with our autistic son, our program to help him cure himself was condemned as silly, based on an impossible dream. I have witnessed, firsthand, many wonderful people making the impossible possible in their own lives. Nothing has moved me more than watching the birth of happiness and love and seeing the fruits that come from living in happiness and love. If we can bring that alive in our lives, then certainly nothing is impossible.

Barry Neil Kaufman
Happiness Is a Choice

It is not the critic who counts, not the man who points out how the strong man stumbles or where the doers of deeds could have done them better. The credit belongs to the man who is actually in the arena, whose face is marred by dust and sweat and blood, who strives valiantly, who errs and comes short again and again because there is no effort without error and shortcomings, who knows the great devotion, who spends himself in a worthy cause, who at best knows in the end the high achievement of triumph and who at worst, if he fails while daring greatly, knows his place shall never be with those timid and cold souls who know neither victory nor defeat.

Theodore Roosevelt
Speech, April 10, 1899

They can because they think they can.

Virgil

In reading my teacher's lips I was wholly dependent on my fingers: I had to use the sense of touch in catching the vibrations of the throat, the movements of the mouth and the expression of the face; and often the sense was at fault. In such cases I was forced to repeat the words or sentences, sometimes for hours, until I felt the proper ring in my own voice. My work was practice, practice, practice. Discouragement and weariness cast me down frequently; but the next moment the thought that I should soon be at home and show my loved ones what I had accomplished, spurred me on, and I eagerly looked forward to their pleasure in my achievement.

"My little sister will understand me now," was a thought stronger than all obstacles. I used to repeat ecstatically, "I am not dumb now." I could not be despondent while I anticipated the delight of talking to my mother and reading her responses from her lips.

Helen Keller
The Story of My Life

In the everyday language of the drug addict, we see the "Great Lie" exposed...The "getting high" is another way of saying, "I am not good enough."

Being a recovering alcoholic, I know the real feelings behind this fantasy language. I know what it is to search for meaning in a drug...seek an answer in a drink...crave for happiness in a buzz. It is but an escape from reality...

The healing rests in the belief and confidence we have in ourselves. Do you believe that you can move mountains? Your belief will be dependent upon your seeing that such power is not located in the physical moving of mountains, but in knowing that you were created to create...

To know that I have a purpose in this world; to know in every fiber of my being that I am important and unique; to know that without me the world would not be the same; to actually know that I make that much difference: *That* is walking on water.

Father Leo Booth
Spirituality and Recovery

They said first-degree life, you know: "We sentence you to natural life at Walpole State Prison." And I had never been arrested before in my life...I thought I was goin' to just fall apart when it happened to me. And that's when the faith, you know, came into my heart. I said, Wait a minute: I can't just fall apart here. I said, I didn't do nothin' to be here; I didn't do a thing. But I said, I'm goin' to keep my faith; I'm goin' to keep my spirit high and somehow I'm goin' to beat this...somehow, you know.

Bobby Joe Leaster
(wrongly imprisoned for fifteen years and then acquitted)
Quoted in *The Search for Meaning:*
Americans Talk About What They Believe and Why

Let me do my work each day; and if the darkened hours of despair overcome me, may I not forget the strength that comforted me in the desolation of other times.

Max Ehrmann
A Prayer

Be of good courage, and he shall strengthen your heart, all ye that hope in the LORD.

Psalm 31:24

Courage is the strength to face pain, act under pressure, and maintain one's values in the face of opposition. You gain strength, courage and confidence by every experience in which you really stop to look fear in the face. You are able to say to yourself, "I lived through this horror. I can take the next thing that comes along."

Eleanor Roosevelt
You Learn by Living

I had returned home from college for summer vacation. It was a hot, humid summer day, typical weather for Iowa that time of year. The air was so close and thick that I felt as though I was going to suffocate.

I longed for relief from the heat, or at least a fresh breeze to stir up the air. The sky grew black. A warm wind blew in through the fields. It rustled its way through the rows of corn, rattled the barn doors, and blew dust through the open windows of the old farmhouse. The barn doors trembled on their hinges. The curtains flapped hauntingly. There was no doubt about it. A storm was brewing.

Dad said simply, "It looks like hail."

Nothing was more threatening to roses. Delicate leaves and petals are no match against on onslaught of icy pellets. We got out the old buckets to cover the rose plants. Suddenly the air grew deathly still.

The sudden change startled us. We lifted our heads to the sky and saw it— an ominous dark cloud stretched into the shape of a long, slithering black snake. It dropped its poisonous head to the earth and struck in a cloud of dust! It moved across the land with alarming speed. We had no way to defend ourselves against a tornado. Our only chance was to run away, hopefully fast enough.

We leaped into the car and fled in a cloud of dust down the old gravel road. Then, as quickly as it appeared, the black, serpentine cloud periscoped its way back into the sky and disappeared.

We were safe! We could go back home. The old Chevy rumbled up the dirt road and approached the hill that hid our farm home. We always knew we were close to home when we reached this hill because you could see the tip of the old red barn peeking over the top of the hill. But that day there was no sign of the barn rising above the hill. Dad kept his foot to the pedal, hoping his eyes would see what his heart feared was gone. At the crest of the hill we saw the devastating damage. The monster cloud had devoured the entire farm. Every building was gone.

The tornado had swept up the house, the barn and all the other buildings. Like some monstrous vacuum cleaner, it had sucked them away and dropped them in an unwelcomed heap on the neighbor's farm.

All of Dad's years of hard work had been leveled, destroyed in one fell swoop. He gripped the steering wheel with his well-worn hands. The gnarled knuckles turned white with rage. This silent, gentle man began to beat the steering wheel. Bitter tears crept across his stubby cheeks. "It's all gone, Jenny!" he cried. "It's all gone!"

IT WAS ALL GONE! What a devastating blow! I looked at my father. What a bitter disappointment! Disappointed? Yes! Discouraged? Definitely not. Disappointments are life's realities. Discouragement is a human reaction.

Dad was not about to take this set-back lying down. He refused to be discouraged. Instead, he chose to be challenged. He still had fight left in him. Sure, it was all gone. ALL GONE! But we were not done in! We still had recovery power within us.

We managed to find shelter that night with relatives. Then we heard about a house in town that was being demolished. It was being cleared away to make way for a new one. The owners said we could have the materials if we would take the house apart and clear the lot for the new building. What a deal! No ball and chain for us! We carefully pried one board from another. We peeled off the wood siding, one plank at a time. The studs and beams were carefully saved, and then we extracted and straightened every nail. Those salvaged supplies built a new house on the same farm where the original house had stood.

ALL GONE! BUT NOT DONE IN! The new house served Mom and Dad well until my older brother Henry got married. Then, as is the custom in those parts, my parents moved to town to allow Henry and his wife a chance to take over the farm. The newlyweds lived in that house for forty years!

ALL GONE? Perhaps! BUT NOT DONE IN! DISAPPOINTED? Absolutely! BUT NOT DEFEATED!

Thinking back on my parents' experience in the tornado, I can say of them, Disappointed? Yes. Defeated? Never! In the face of what looked like defeat, he turned his experience into a challenge.

Robert H. Schuller
Life's Not Fair, but God Is Good

That which does not kill me makes me stronger.

Friedrich Nietzsche
"Maxims and Missiles," Twilight of the Idols

Forbearing one another, and forgiving one another, if any man have a quarrel against any: even as Christ forgave you, so also do ye.

Colossians 3:13

In retrospect, I feel about my life the way some people feel about war. If you survive, then it becomes a good war. Danger makes you active, it makes you alter, it forces you to experience and thus to learn...Yet even here I see a gift, for in place of my narrow, pragmatic world of cause and effect and matter moving to immutable laws, I have burst into an infinite world full of wonder. The whole mystery of the universe has my reverence. Nothing is sure but nothing can be dismissed. I pay attention.

All of us are haunted by the failed hopes and undigested deeds of our forebears...My toughest lesson was to renounce my own sense of specialness, to let the princess die along with the guilt-ridden child in my closet, to see instead the specialness of the world around me.

Always I was traveling from darkness into the light. In such journeys, time is our ally, not our enemy. We can grow wise. As the arteries harden the spirit can lighten. As the legs fail, the soul can take wing. Things do add up. Life does have shape and maybe even purpose. Or so it seems to me.

Sylvia Fraser
My Father's House: A Memoir of Incest and of Healing

Anger is a signal, and one worth listening to. Our anger may be a message that we are being hurt, that our rights are being violated, that our needs or wants are not being adequately met, or simply that something is not right. Our anger may tell us that we are not addressing an important emotional issue in our lives, or that too much of our self—our beliefs, values, desires, or ambitions—is being compromised in a relationship. Our anger may be a signal that we are doing more and giving more than we can comfortably do or give. Or our anger may warn us that others are doing too much for us, at the expense of our own competence and growth. Just as physical pain tells us to take our hand off the hot stove, the pain of our anger preserves the very integrity of our self. Our anger can motivate us to say "no" to the ways in which we are defined by others and "yes" to the dictates of our inner self.

Harriet Goldhor Lerner, Ph.D.
The Dance of Anger

"Don't give up." That's the best thing I could tell somebody who just remembered she was a survivor [of sexual abuse]. That's the most important thing right in the beginning. There are people who have lived through it, and as trite, and as stupid, and as irrelevant as it sounds to you right now, you will not be in so much pain later. Even not so far in the future. If you made it this far, you've got some pretty good stuff in you. So just trust it, no matter what outside messages you get. You're the only person who can tell yourself what you need to do to heal. *Don't give up on yourself.*

Ellen Bass and Laura Davis
The Courage to Heal:
A Guide for Women Survivors of Child Sexual Abuse

We who lived in the concentration camps can remember the men who walked through the huts comforting others, giving away their last piece of bread. They may have been few in number, but they offer sufficient proof that everything can be taken from a man but one thing: The last of his freedoms—to choose one's attitude in any given set of circumstances, to choose one's own way.

Viktor E. Frankl
Man's Search for Meaning

Many of us have had the attitude that life is something that happens to us and that all we can do is make the best of it. It is basically a victim's position, giving power to people and things outside of ourselves. We are beginning to realize that the power rests in us, that we can choose to create our life the way we want it to be.

Shakti Gawain
Reflections in the Light

Then came Peter to him, and said, Lord, how oft shall my brother sin against me, and I forgive him? till seven times? Jesus saith unto him, I say not unto thee, Until seven times: but, Until seventy times seven.

Matthew 18:21-22

When everything seems gray, look for color.

Cherry Hartman
Be-Good-to-Yourself Therapy

"To listen"—in faith—to find one's way and have the feeling that, under God, one is really finding it again.

This is like playing blindman's buff: deprived of sight, I have, in compensation, to sharpen all my other senses, to grope my way and recognize myself as I pass my fingers over the faces of my friends, and thus find what was mine already and had been there all the time. What I would have known all the time was there, had I not blindfolded myself.

Dag Hammarskjöld
Markings

A man who suffers before it is necessary suffers more than is necessary.

Lucius Annaeus Seneca
Letters to Lucilius

There is a tradition, that in the planting of New-England, the first settlers met with many difficulties and hardships, as is generally the case when a civilized people attempt establishing themselves in a wilderness country. Being piously disposed, they sought relief from heaven, by laying their wants and distresses before the Lord in frequent set days of Fasting and Prayer. Constant meditation and discourse on these subjects kept their minds gloomy and discontented; and, like the children of Israel, there were many disposed to return to that Egypt, which persecution had induced them to abandon. At length, when it was purposed in the Assembly to proclaim another fast, a farmer of plain sense rose, and remarked that the inconveniences they suffered, and concerning which they had so often wearied heaven with their complaints, were not so great as they might have expected, and were diminishing every day as the colony strengthened; that the earth began to reward their labour, and to furnish liberally for their subsistence; that the seas and rivers were found full of fish, the air sweet, the climate healthy; and above all, that they were there in the full enjoyment of liberty, civil and religious: He therefore thought that reflecting and conversing on these subjects would be more comfortable, as tending more to make them contented with their situation; and that it would be more becoming the gratitude they owed to the divine being, if, *instead of* a FAST, *they should proclaim a* THANKSGIVING. His advice was taken, and from that day to this, they have in every year observed circumstances of public felicity sufficient to furnish employment for a THANKSGIVING DAY, which is therefore constantly ordered and religiously observed.

Benjamin Franklin
"The Internal State of America"

Let us be contented with what has happened to us and thankful for all we have been spared. Let us accept the natural order in which we move. Let us reconcile ourselves to the mysterious rhythm of our destinies, such as they must be in this world of space and time. Let us treasure our joys but not bewail our sorrows. The glory of light cannot exist without its shadows. Life is a whole, and good and ill must be accepted together.

Winston S. Churchill
Amid These Storms: Thoughts and Adventures

I feel my life ebbing away and I don't know what to do about it. I can't seem to get control of myself right now. I make resolutions, one after another...but can't keep them. I'm still in a funk, desperate, restless, tired, incommunicable.

I guess I realize my life *is* ebbing away. It's an hour later than it was, or a day. I know I have that much less time. I am, and am not, at the mercy of time. It plagues me, even when I understand best how time does not limit or imprison me.

Life is out there, *there*, on the street where the sun is shining. The air is stirring against people's legs, arms and faces. And life is *here*. If I were to open a window, could *there* become *here*, and *here* become *there*?

I ask myself: If I were to die today—and had just four hours' notice—what would I really want to do?

I would really want to go from *here* to *there*. I would want to celebrate life by sharing it.

I can do this now.

Malcolm Boyd
Malcolm Boyd's Book of Days

Suffering is like the seed of an herb when planted in the earth. The seed remembers itself and endures in the darkness so that it can grow up into the sunlight one day as an entirely transformed flower. When you understand the suffering and the forces of darkness, you can end suffering and bring light to the people.

Ginevee
Quoted in *Walk in Balance*

It's easy to get bogged down in the circumstantial and mundane, but if we connect to our passion, that in itself will be regenerative; we won't have to wait for the energy, it will be there.

But how do we connect to that passion? One of my favorite phrases, which a friend taught me, is that we need to pay "exquisite attention" to our responses to things—noticing what makes our flame glow brighter. If we pay attention to those things, we'll be able to catch the flame and feed it.

Nina Simons
Quoted in *Utne Reader*, March-April 1996

Oh, the wild joys of living! the leaping from rock up to rock,
The strong rending of boughs from the fir-tree, the cool silver shock
Of the plunge in the pool's living water, the hunt of the bear,
And the sultriness showing the lion is couched in his lair.
And the meal, the rich dates yellowed over the gold dust divine,

And the locust-flesh steeped in the pitcher, the full draft of wine,
And the sleep in the dried river-channel where bulrushes tell
That the water was wont to go warbling so softly and well.
How good is man's life, the mere living! how fit to employ
All the heart and the soul and the senses forever in joy!

Robert Browning
Saul

I have never been happier, more exhilarated, at peace, rested, inspired, and aware
of the grandeur of the universe and the greatness of God than when I find myself
in a natural setting not much changed from the way He made it.

Jimmy Carter
An Outdoor Journal: Adventures and Reflections

Touch the earth, love the earth, honor the earth, her plains, her valleys, her hills,
and her seas; rest your spirit in her solitary places.

Henry Beston
The Outermost House

Life has a loveliness to sell,
All beautiful and splendid things,
Blue waves whitened on a cliff,
Soaring fire that sways and sings,
And children's faces looking up,
Holding wonder like a cup.

Life has loveliness to sell,
Music like a curve of gold,
Scent of pine trees in the rain,
Eyes that love you, arms that hold,
And for your spirit's still delight,
Holy thoughts that star the night.

Spend all you have for loveliness,
Buy it and never count the cost;

For one white singing hour of peace
Count many a year of strife well lost,
And for a breath of ecstasy
Give all you have been, or could be.

Sara Teasdale
"Barter"

Human reality authentically lived takes shape on different existential levels according to the hazards which have to be confronted at each stage. St. Augustine, for example, was compelled by the death of a young friend to take the decisive leap which changed his life. The Buddha, as a young prince, in a single flash of spiritual insight realized the suffering of the world. He stood up, we are told, and went out into homelessness...When some grief, shock, pain, compels us to rise to a higher plane of personal life, we must admit that they were in the service of life and hope. If we never lived through such times of mental and physical crisis our life would stagnate...Human life only progresses, rises higher, if it is forced out of the stage it has reached and ventures to break out of its petty limits. It is in suffering and pain that man realizes that he is not simply himself, that he has to achieve his own identity, that he is a hope. In suffering we learn that our real self has not yet been found, that we are still on the way. In order really to be able to live, one must have despaired of life at some time or another.

Ladislaus Boros
Living in Hope: Future Perspectives in Christian Thought

For whatsoever things were written aforetime were written for our learning, that we through patience and comfort of the scriptures might have hope.

Romans 15:4

I do not believe that sheer suffering teaches. If suffering alone taught, all the world would be wise, since everyone suffers. To suffering must be added mourning, understanding, patience, love, openness, and the willingness to remain vulnerable.

Anne Morrow Lindbergh
Quoted in *Time*, February 1973

It sometimes happens in this country that a poor person brings a gift to one not poor. If it is done in love and kindness or gratitude, then it should be received. Let us seek not so much to be consoled as to console, but when it is our turn to be consoled, then let us receive such consolation with humility and thanks.

Alan Paton
Instrument of Thy Peace

Our lives to be fruitful must be full of Christ. To be able to bring his peace, joy and love we must have it ourselves for we cannot give what we have not got, like the blind leading the blind. The poor in the slums are without Jesus and we have the privilege of entering their homes. What they think of us does not matter but what we are to them does matter. To go to the poor and the sick merely for the sake of going will not be enough to draw them to Jesus. If we are preoccupied with ourselves and our own affairs, we will not be able to live up to this ideal.

Mother Teresa
Life in the Spirit

I have known sorrow and learned to aid the wretched.

Virgil
Eclogues

Love cures people, the ones who receive love and the ones who give it, too

Karl A. Menninger
Sparks

The consumer society fails to deliver on its promise of fulfillment through material comforts because human wants are insatiable, human needs are socially defined, and the real sources of personal happiness are elsewhere. Indeed, the strength of social relations and the quality of leisure—both crucial psychological determinants of happiness in life—appear as much diminished as entrenched in the consumer class. The consumer society, it seems, has impoverished people by raising their incomes.

Alan Thein Durning
"Are We Happy Yet?" published in
Ecopsychology: Restoring the Earth, Healing the Mind

Asleep in his blue bed Joseph looked the picture of pleasant childlike thimble-work. Nora serenely simpered as she lifted him. Washed and powdered he sat on her lap. Fondly she slipped the gensai over his blonde head. His head tilted boldly forward then suddenly it shot backwards. He faced his mother. He gazed his hurt gaze, lip protruding, eyes busy in conversation. He ordered her to look out the window at the sunshine. He looked hard at her ear ordering her to listen to the birds singing. Then jumping on her knees he again asked her to cock her ear and listen to the village children out at play in the school yard. Now he jeered himself. He showed her his arms, his legs, his useless body. Beckoning his tears he shook his head. Looking at his mother he blamed her, he mouthed his cantankerous why, why, why me? Distracted by his youthful harshness of realization she tried to dis-tract him. Lifting him in her arms she brought him outside into the farmyard. 'Come on till I show you the calves,' she coaxed. His lonely tears reached even faster. He knew why she tried to divert his boyish questioning. He childishly deter-mined not to look at the calves and shaking his head he gazed the other way. His mother tried again. 'Look over at the lambs,' she said, pointing at the sheep feed-ing at their trough in the field. He cried so loud he brought her to her senses. 'Alright,' she said, 'we'll go back inside and talk.' Placing him in his chair she then sat down and faced her erstwhile boy, yes, her golden-haired accuser. Meanwhile he cried continuously, conning himself that he had beaten her to silence. Looking through his tears he saw her as she bent low in order to look into his eyes. 'I never prayed for you to be born crippled,' she said. 'I wanted you to be full of life, able to run and jump and talk just like Yvonne. But you are you, you are Joseph not Yvonne. Listen here Joseph, you can see, you can hear, you can think, you can understand everything you hear, you like your food, you like nice clothes, you are loved by me and Dad. We love you just as you are'...

The decision arrived at that day was burnt forever in his mind. He was only three years in age but he was now fanning the only spark he saw, his being alive and more immediate, his being wanted just as he was.

Dread-filled fretting marked Joseph Meehan's scene that day, but the scene and that day looked out through his eyes for the rest of his life. Comfort came in child-like notions, his clumsy body was his, but molested by mother-love he looked lollying looks at his limbs and liked Joseph Meehan.

Christopher Nolan
Under the Eye of the Clock

Think about [it] for just a minute. You are valuable just because you exist. Not because of what you do or what you have done, but simply because you are. Remember that. Remember that the next time you are left bobbing in the wake of someone's steamboat ambition. Remember that the next time some trickster tries to hang a bargain basement price tag on your self-worth. The next time someone tries to pass you off as a cheap buy, just think about the way Jesus honors you...and smile.

Max Lucado
No Wonder They Call Him the Savior

The person who loses a job is the same the day after notice of termination as the day before. His/her value is neither eradicated nor minimized. Only the direction in which to channel that value has been changed. Recognize that only your employment status is different, you aren't. Infinitely more tragic than unemployment is letting the best parts of yourself slip away with the job...

Keep moving. Stagnancy runs down your battery. Hope is the fuel that drives you forward; despair is the sinkhole that traps you. Cultivate new hope by meeting people, renewing old contacts, and making new ones. Join a support group for constructive commiseration...

Losing a job does not a failure make. Allowing it to affect what could be the rest of your life does. Remove labels. "I am..." should be followed by several sentences rather than just two words. Take a long look at the total person. See the many facets that make up the whole.

Cathy Beyer, Loretta McGovern, and Doris Pike
Surviving Unemployment: A Family Handbook for Weathering Hard Times

Our real blessings often appear to us in the shapes of pains, losses and disappointments; but let us have patience, and we soon shall see them in their proper figures.

Joseph Addison

Pain pushes you, sometimes gently, sometimes forcefully, but always in the direction of healing and growth.

Amy Dean
Proud to Be

Fog surrounds us not only in nature, but through our experiences in life. It could be the result of all illness, the loss of a loved one, losing a job, the dilemma of moving on to a new position, overwork or an unsolved problem. The list is endless. Do you feel afraid at a time like this?

To find solutions, sometimes it becomes necessary to go through the fog and look inward. Instead of rebelling, we can use this quiet time to help us sort out and clarify our thinking. It's like going through a valley.

Then, as the fog begins to lift, our eyes shift from looking downward to being lifted toward the horizon. The fog has now turned into a cloak of love till we are ready to have the confidence to step out once again onto the stage of life.

Ardath Rodale
"Stepping Through the Fog," Prevention, May 1996

We are healed of a suffering only by experiencing it to the full.

Marcel Proust
Remembrance of Things Past: The Sweet Cheat Gone

Laugh, and the world laughs with you;
Weep, and you weep alone;
For the sad old earth must borrow its mirth,
But has trouble enough of its own.
Sing, and the hills will answer;
Sigh, it is lost on the air;
The echoes bound to a joyful sound,
But shrink from voicing care.

Rejoice, and men will seek you;
Grieve, and they turn and go;
They want full measure of all your pleasure,
But they do not need your woe.
Be glad, and your friends are many;
Be sad, and you lose them all—
There are none to decline your nectared wine,
But alone you must drink life's gall.

Feast, and your halls are crowded;
Fast, and the world goes by.
Succeed and give, and it helps you live,
But no man can help you die.
There is room in the falls of pleasure
For a large and lordly train,
But one by one we must all file on
Through the narrow aisles of pain.

Ella Wheeler Wilcox
"Solitude"

Make no mistake: Grief will gain your attention. "Nowhere to hide" is accurate. There is no way under it, over it, or around it. One can only go through grief. Sadly, many believe mourning to be pathological or, at least, a weakness to overcome. We need courageous grievers who will experience their grief without hint of apology and who will...Set the model that mourning is not an illness, is not a weakness, is not a self indulgence or a reprehensible bad habit, but rather, mourning is an essential psychological process which must be recognized and facilitated. Learn to trust your own feelings.

Patrick J. Farmer
"Bereavement Counseling," Journal of Pastoral Care, Fall/Winter 1980

Rightly conceived, time is the friend of all who are in any way in adversity, for its many roads wind in and out of the shadows sooner or later into sunshine, and when one is at its darkest point one can be certain that presently it will grow brighter.

Arthur Bryant
Illustrated London News

Recovery from an ended relationship doesn't happen overnight, or by quickly finding someone else to attach ourselves to. It happens slowly, stage by stage, with time and effort. We may have a lot of old hurt, anger, and sadness to work through, we may have "lost years" to let go of before we can begin moving forward. Whatever our own circumstances, we have to turn to a new way of looking at things. A relationship has ended, and that part of our lives will never again be the same. We are shaken out of our old viewpoint and it is up to us to choose our new one. It is entirely within our power to choose a more positive one.

Veronica Ray
Choosing Happiness

"Time will heal" is a common saying. Part of it is true, and part is myth. Time will aid in recovery from grief, but it is time that needs to be used well. Time spent frantically running from grief—traveling, perhaps, or visiting relatives, keeping ever busy with never a moment to think about one's loss—will not help. Eventually, you will run out of places to go or things to do, and at that point you will have to face the void created by the death of your loved one. On the other hand, if you use your time to *mourn* your loss, to adjust to a different kind of life, and to get acquainted with your now somewhat altered (maybe greatly altered) identity, healing will occur faster.

Helen Fitzgerald
The Mourning Handbook

The next two weeks I cried until there were no more tears. I screamed until my throat was raw. I sulked in silence. I began to relive all the memories of my friends, laughing about the good times, crying about their deaths, allowing my anger because I felt cheated out of saying good-bye to them. I wrote letters to each one, saying the things I wanted to say. I wrote a goodbye to each, and then burned them all. As the smoke rose into the sky, I let my pain rise with it and let it go. The third week I rested, exhausted.

James P. Bell
"AIDS and the Hidden Epidemic of Grief,"
The American Journal of Hospice Care, May/June 1988

I have reconciled the deaths of friends by being grateful for having had such friendships. I have come to understand that Death ends life but certainly doesn't rob it of meaning. We all need to remember that in our lives we affect and change the people closest to us. Those changes have a considerable value. For instance, I am not the same person that I would have been had I not met James, Ruth, John, or the many others who have made a lasting impression on me. Some people even think of these changes as some form of immortality. They suggest that people who have died, or who are dying, do live on, in changes they have caused in those who survive them. Having a library or office block named after you cannot make people remember you. But if you've altered the way people think, then some of the meaning of your life will go on after your death.

Robert Buckman
I Don't Know What to Say

When you look into the night sky
and wonder, Where have they gone?
Place your hands over your heart space
and know they are right there.

Lon Nungesser
Axioms for Survivors

My heart still cries out. And I remember my seventeen-year-old prayer on the train from Charleston to Jacksonville when my father was dying: "Please, God, do whatever is best for Father. Please do whatever is best for Father." And that, of course, underlies all our praying. Do what is best, even if at this moment I cannot know what that best may be.

Madeleine L'Engle
Two-Part Invention

One of the experiences of prayer is that it seems that nothing happens. But when you stay with it and look back over a long period of prayer, you suddenly realize that something has happened. What is most close, most intimate, most present, often cannot be experienced directly but only with a certain distance. When I think that I am only distracted, just wasting my time, something is happening too immediate for knowing, understanding, and experiencing. Only in retrospect do I realize that something very important has taken place. Isn't this true of all the really important events of life? When I am together with someone I love very much, we seldom talk about our relationship. The relationship, in fact, is too central to be a subject of talk. But later after we have separated and write letters, we realize how much it all meant to us, and we even write about it.

Henri J. Nouwen
The Genesse Diary

He delivereth the poor in his affliction, and openeth their ears in oppression.

Job 36:15

In the book of Exodus we are told that a certain group of persons were slaves in Egypt, and that they suffered grievously as a result of their slavery. They were used as builders to build the cities of Egypt and perhaps those strange structures which are still to be found in Egypt today—the Pyramids. They engaged in all this hard labour for no pay at all, and, as you can expect, they used to lament and cry as a result of all this suffering.

Now the first and most important point is that God heard their cry and He saw their affliction. He revealed that He was a God who cares, even though He is in His heaven of heavens. He is very close to His people. Remember that, my dear friends—He hears, He sees.

Reverend Desmond Mpilo Tutu
Quoted in *Hope and Sufferings: Sermons and Speeches*

Blessed be God, even the Father of our Lord Jesus Christ, the Father of mercies, and the God of all comfort; who comforteth us in all our tribulation, that we may be able to comfort them which are in any trouble, by the comfort wherewith we ourselves are comforted of God.

2 Corinthians 1:3-4

Care is a state in which something does matter, care is the opposite of apathy. Care is important because it is what is missing in our day. What young people have been fighting, in revolts on college campuses and in the sweep of protests about the world, is the seeping, creeping conviction that nothing matters; the prevailing feeling that we can't do anything. The threat is apathy, uninvolvement, the grasping for external stimulants as found in drugs. Care is a necessary antidote for this.

Rollo May
Love and Will

The very presence of friends is pleasant in bad fortune as well as in good, for grief is lightened when friends sorrow with us.

Aristotle
Ethics

I don't think of my Teddy Bears as stuffed animals, I think of them as friends. Once or twice I've had to explain to people, "Listen, if you think my Teddy Bears are lame, you're thinking wrong. I don't play with stuffed animals." My Teddy Bears are connected to stuffed animals because when you are little, a stuffed animal takes away the bogeyman, and my Teddy Bears take away the cancer and the pain. The difference is that little kids put their friends into their teddy bears. If a little kid knew Carrie and Pete, he might put Carrie's smiling and caring, and Pete's ability to hope and survive and Anna's cheerfulness together in his teddy bear. He'd become imaginary friends with it because it's a symbol of those friends. But the Teddy Bears I use now are my *real* friends and then I draw them as teddy bears. I pick up the memory of stuffed animals because you have to remember friendship in all the ways that you can. It makes a smile on your face when you have someone to protect you.

Corey Svien, fourteen years old
I Will Sing Life

Fear thou not; for I am with thee: be not dismayed; for I am thy God: I will strengthen thee; yea, I will help thee; yea, I will uphold thee with the right hand of my righteousness.

Isaiah 41:10

You find no difficulty in trusting the Lord with the management of the universe, and all the outward creation, and can your case be any more complex or difficult than these, that you need to be anxious or troubled about His management of you? Away with such unworthy doubtings! Take your stand on the power and trustworthiness of your God, and see how quickly all difficulties will vanish before a steadfast determination to believe. Trust in the dark, trust in the light, trust at night and trust in the morning, and you will find that the faith which may begin by mighty effort, will end sooner or later by becoming the easy and natural habit of the soul.

Hannah Whitall Smith
The Christian's Secret of a Happy Life

I am a now person. A now person is a person that thinks of something to do and does it. Most people are "maybe" persons, and some people are "someday" persons...do you follow me? Some people are "I'll think about it" persons, you know? I'm not that kind of person. I'm an accidentally instant person. If I think of something, I'm gonna do it now. And it works for me, because, if I didn't do that, I'd be sitting in my studio and thinking about the past or I would make myself thoroughly miserable. Don't you realize that? 'Cause you always think about the things you should have done and didn't do, and maybe you should have done this instead of that; you know, you think about these things when you're alone. And then you say, "If I hadn't done this particular thing, it would have been much better." And you're right, but you can't change your past—you can't, you know. You see, the past is something that has flowed by you like a river. It's gone, and you can't change it. Now is all we have.

Theresa Bernstein Meyerowitz
Quoted in *The Search for Meaning:*
Americans Talk About What They Believe and Why

The happiest heart that ever beat
Was in some quiet breast
That found the common daylight sweet,
And left to Heaven the rest.

John Vance Cheney
"The Happiest Heart"

Have you ever felt as though your mind is going in a thousand directions, worrying about so many things you can't even keep track of them all? You're worried about the past, things you wish you could undo but you can't. You're worried about the present, everything that's going on in your life right now, making it seem like a three-ring circus. You're worried about the future; you see clouds stacking up on the dark horizon, and you wonder what storms might come sweeping down on you and your family. You wake up in the morning with so many things to do and to decide that you feel like crawling right back under your blankets.

Peter says, "Take all of that and cast it on to the Lord." Why? Because He really cares for you. He really cares about everything that happens in your life. He loves you!

David's son Solomon must have learned of this approach to life at his dad's knee. After Solomon assumed his father's throne and became king of Israel, he wrote these words:

"Commit to the LORD whatever you do, and your plans will succeed" (Proverbs 16:3, NIV).

And how true it was for Solomon. As long as he trusted wholly in the God of his father, his plans *did* succeed—and what great plans they were! He became wise beyond measure, wealthy beyond counting, and esteemed and honored all over the world. But when he turned away from the Lord and began trusting his own wisdom and worshiping other gods, his plans didn't succeed at all. He led his whole nation into brokenness and despair.

The truth is, God longs for us to commit our way to Him. He longs for us to trust Him with all our heart.

Ron Mehl
The Cure for a Troubled Heart

And it came to pass, as we went to prayer, a certain damsel possessed with a spirit of divination met us, which brought her masters much gain by soothsaying: The same followed Paul and us, and cried, saying, These men are the servants of the most high God, which shew unto us the way of salvation. And this did she many days. But Paul, being grieved, turned and said to the spirit, I command thee in the name of Jesus Christ to come out of her. And he came out the same hour. And when her masters saw that the hope of their gains was gone, they caught Paul and Silas, and drew them into the marketplace unto the rulers, and brought them to the magistrates, saying, These men, being Jews, do exceedingly trouble our city, and teach customs, which are not lawful for us to receive, neither to observe, being Romans. And the multitude rose up together against them: and the magistrates rent off their clothes, and commanded to beat them. And when they had laid many stripes upon them, they cast them into prison, charging the jailor to keep them safely: Who, having received such a charge, thrust them into the inner prison, and made their feet fast in the stocks. And at midnight Paul and Silas prayed, and sang praises unto God: and the prisoners heard them.

Acts 16:16-25

Know then, whatever cheerful and serene
Supports the mind, supports the body too:
Hence, the most vital movement mortals feel
Is hope, the balm and lifeblood of the soul.

John Armstrong
"Art of Preserving Health"

All human wisdom is summed up in two words,—wait and hope.

Alexander Dumas the Elder
The Count of Monte Cristo

It's really a wonder that I haven't dropped all my ideals, because they seem so absurd and impossible to carry out. Yet I keep them, because in spite of everything I still believe that people are really good at heart. I simply can't build up my hopes on a foundation consisting of confusion, misery, and death. I see the world gradually being turned into a wilderness, I hear the ever approaching thunder, which will destroy us too. I can feel the sufferings of millions and yet, if I look up into the heavens, I think that it will all come right, that this cruelty too will end, and that peace and tranquillity will return again.

In the meantime, I must uphold my ideals, for perhaps the time will come when I shall be able to carry them out.

Anne Frank
The Diary of a Young Girl

For more than three years I was in a prisoner-of-war camp and I understand something of the language of prisoners, the loneliness and the dreams of the "unhappy"...

Hope came to life as the prisoner accepted his imprisonment, affirmed the barbed wire, and in this situation discovered the real human being in himself and others. It was not at his release but even while in prison that the "resurrection from the dead" happened for him.

Jürgen Moltman
The Experiment Hope

During this time of recovery, I learned many things about myself...mainly that I could cope. I found myself able to do things and handle affairs which I never dreamed possible, and do them in a businesslike manner. I also became aware of the outside world around me instead of being in a sheltered world of homemaker. George would have been really surprised if he could see me now—maybe a little proud too. No, maybe a lot.

Widow, age 52
Quoted in *Surviving Grief…and Learning to Live Again*

Human misery must somewhere have a stop: there is no wind that always blows a storm.

Euripides
Heracles

the sun will rise
in a few minutes

it's been doing it
—regularly—
for as long as I
can remember.

maybe I should
pin my hopes
on important,
but often
unnoticed,
certainties
like that.

Peter McWilliams
Quoted in *How to Survive the Loss of a Love*

Walk on a rainbow trail; walk on a trail of song, and all about will be beauty. There is a way out of every dark mist, over a rainbow trail.

Navajo song

A walk. The atmosphere incredibly pure—a warm, caressing gentleness in the sunshine—joy in one's whole being...Every way I was happy—as idler, as painter, as poet. Forgotten impressions of childhood and youth came back to me—all those indescribable effects wrought by colour, shadow, sunlight, green hedges, and songs of birds, upon the soul just opening to poetry. I became young again, wondering, and simple, as candor and ignorance are simple. I abandoned myself to life and to nature, and they cradled me with an infinite gentleness. To open one's heart in purity to this ever pure nature, to allow this immortal life of things to penetrate into one's soul, is at the same time to listen to the voice of God.

Henri Frédéric Amiel
On Ideals

I love the stillness of the wood:
I love the music of the rill:
I love to couch in pensive mood
Upon some silent hill.

Scarce heard, beneath yon arching trees,
The silver-crested ripples pass;
And, like a mimic brook, the breeze
Whispers among the grass.

Here from the world I win release,
Nor scorn of men, nor footstep rude,
Break in to mar the holy peace
Of this great solitude.

Here may the silent tears I weep
Lull the vexed spirit into rest,
As infants sob themselves to sleep
Upon a mother's breast.

But when the bitter hour is gone,
And the keen throbbing pangs are still,

Oh, sweetest then to couch alone
Upon some silent hill!

To live in joys that once have been,
To put the cold world out of sight,
And deck life's drear and barren scene
 With hues of rainbow-light.

For what to man the gift of breath,
If sorrow be his lot below;
If all the day that ends in death
Be dark with clouds of woe?

Shall the poor transport of an hour
Repay long years of sore distress—
The fragrance of a lonely flower
Make glad the wilderness?

Ye golden hours of Life's young spring,
Of innocence, of love and truth!
Bright, beyond all imagining,
Thou fairy-dream of youth!

I'd give all wealth that years have piled,
The slow result of Life's decay,
To be once more a little child
For one bright summer-day.

Lewis Carroll
"Solitude"

Heaviness in the heart of man maketh it stoop: but a good word maketh it glad.
Proverbs 12:25

Given: Living will guarantee you adversity. The only question is how to deal with
it. When you get embarrassed, you can withdraw, cry, hit, develop ulcers, or even

die. Or, on occasion, you can employ humor…More often than not, humor will carry you through life's embarrassing moments. It will also help you deal with grief, interpersonal strife, marital conflict, workplace stress, life threatening illness, baldness, excess adipose, and teenage children. It will not help you with end-stage depression, Ralph Nader, or the IRS…

You can best understand humor's value in your life if you see humor in relation to adversity. You may want to ignore adversity, but life will not allow you this posture. It is through adversity that we learn the value of humor. Not just a trivial ornament appended to the human psyche, humor is a vehicle that bears us through the pain of life, its disappointments, its losses, and its cruelty.

Christian Hagaseth, III
A Laughing Place

They say that if you get bored enough with calamity you can learn to laugh.

Lawrence Durrell
Balthazar

"Ha, ha!" laughed Scrooge's nephew. "Ha, ha, ha!"

If you should happen, by any unlikely chance, to know a man more blest in a laugh than Scrooge's nephew, all I can say is, I should like to know him, too. Introduce him to me, and I'll cultivate his acquaintance.

It is a fair, even-handed, noble adjustment of things, that while there is infection and disease and sorrow, there is nothing in the world so irresistibly contagious as laughter and good-humor.

Charles Dickens
A Christmas Carol

My soul is refreshed.

I am grateful, for my life had become absurdly flat and dimensionless. It lacked humor and grace. My feelings had dried out.

This coming of spring has brought memories flooding in. I am surprised and delighted that in this moment I feel no regret. Yes, I am grateful for everything that has happened to me, everybody whom I have known, all that I have done. These are my life.

The future greets me in swiftly passing moments, including this one. I am curious. Oh, may the power of love fill me with the sweet anguish of caring deeply about life.

Malcolm Boyd

The Lover

In the depth of winter I finally learned there was in me invincible summer.

Albert Camus

Summer

Now the God of hope fill you with all joy and peace in believing, that ye may abound in hope, through the power of the Holy Ghost.

Romans 15:13

Learning to

LOVE

CHAPTER FIVE

LEARNING
TO LOVE

—⟨∿⟩—

If one wished to be perfectly sincere, one would have to admit that there are two
kinds of love—well-fed and ill-fed. The rest is pure fiction.

> Sidonie-Gabrielle Colette
> *The Last of Cheri*

Among those whom I like, I can find no common denominator, but among those
whom I love, I can: all of them make me laugh.

> W. H. Auden
> *The Dyer's Hand*

Love is mutually feeding each other, not one living on another like a ghoul.

> Bessie Head
> *A Question of Power*

Love doesn't just sit there, like a stone, it has to be made, like bread; re-made all
the time, made new.

> Ursula K. Le Guin
> *The Lathe of Heaven*

Love is not primarily a relationship to a specific person; it is an *attitude*, an *orientation* of *character* which determines the relatedness of a person to the world as a
whole, not toward one "object" of love. If a person loves only one other person and

is indifferent to the rest of his fellow men, his love is not love but a symbiotic attachment, or an enlarged egotism. Yet, most people believe that love is constituted by
the object, not by the faculty. In fact, they even believe that it is a proof of the intensity of their love when they do not love anybody except the "loved" person. This is
the same fallacy which we have already mentioned above. Because one does not see
that love is an activity, a power of the soul, one believes that all that is necessary to
find is the right object—and that everything goes by itself afterward. This attitude
can be compared to that of a man who wants to paint but who, instead of learning
the art, claims that he has just to wait for the right object, and that he will paint
beautifully when he finds it. If I truly love one person I love all persons, I love the
world, I love life. If I can say to somebody else, "I love you," I must be able to say, "I
love in you everybody, I love through you the world, I love in you also myself."

Erich Fromm
The Art of Loving

I wonder why love is so often equated with joy when it is everything else as well.
Devastation, balm, obsession, granting and receiving excessive value, and losing
it again. It is recognition, often of what you are not but might be. It sears and it
heals. It is beyond pity and above law. It can seem like truth.

Florida Scott-Maxwell
The Measure of My Days

Dear friends, let us love one another, for love comes from God. Everyone who
loves has been born of God and knows God. Whoever does not love does not
know God, because God is love.

1 John 4:7-8 (NIV)

Loving, like prayer, is a power as well as a process. It's curative. It is creative.

Zona Gale
Birth

Love and the hope of it are not things one can learn; they are a part of life's her-
itage.

Maria Montessori
The Absorbent Mind

Love stretches your heart and makes you big inside.

Margaret Walker
Jubilee

There is no surprise more magical than the surprise of being loved. It is the finger of God on a man's shoulder.

Charles Morgan
Quoted in *Reader's Digest,* November 1949

To love means to communicate to the other that you are all for him, that you will never fail him or let him down when he needs you, but that you will always be standing by with all the necessary encouragements. It is something one can communicate to another only if one has it.

Ashley Montagu
The Cultured Man

We may, it seems to me, find differences in love according to the esteem which we bear to the object loved as compared with oneself: for when we esteem the object of love less than ourselves, we have only a simple affection for it; when we esteem it equally with ourselves, that is called friendship; and when we esteem it more, the passion which we have may be called devotion.

René Descartes
Passions of the Soul

Love is the supreme value around which all moral values can be integrated into one ethical system valid for the whole of humanity.

Pitirim A. Sorokin
The Ways and Power of Love

Bitterness imprisons life; love releases it. Bitterness paralyzes life; love empowers it. Bitterness sickens life; love heals it. Bitterness blinds life; love anoints its eyes.

Harry Emerson Fosdick
Riverside Sermons

Respect is love in plain clothes.

Frankie Byrne
Quoted in *Reader's Digest*, April 1972

I did not lose my heart in summer's even
When roses to the moonrise burst apart:
When plumes were under heel and lead was flying,
In blood and smoke and flame I lost my heart.

I lost it to a soldier and a foeman,
A chap that did not kill me, but he tried;
That took the sabre straight and took it striking,
And laughed and kissed his hand to me and died.

A. E. Housman
"Love"

Hatred paralyzes life; love releases it. Hatred confuses life; love harmonizes it. Hatred darkens life; love illumines it.

Martin Luther King, Jr.
Strength to Love

Love is an act of endless forgiveness, a tender look which becomes a habit.

Peter Ustinov
Quoted in the *Christian Science Monitor,* December 9, 1958

It is pleasant to be loved, for this…makes a man see himself as the possessor of goodness, a thing that every being that has a feeling for it desires to possess: to be loved means to be valued for one's own personal qualities.

Aristotle
Rhetoric

In the Greek language there are four words for love. The first is *eros*. This is a "getting" love. *Eros* is usually associated with the physical aspect of sexual love. It is the feeling we have when someone pleases, the feeling of desire or sexual passion which responds to lovability. The basic element is desire, a will to possess seeking satisfaction. It sees something desirable in another. It can easily become selfish or shallow because if the one loved acts or reacts in a manner not desirable, this love grows cold and closes doors of communication and concern.

A second word for love is *stergo*. This is a "caring" love. This is the natural love which we have for others. As human beings we love persons as part of humanity. It is the quiet and abiding feeling within us, which, resting on an object near us, recognizes that we are closely bound together. We are dependent upon each other and obligated to each other. It is the natural love of humans because we sense our oneness with a common humanity. We are concerned about what happens to others because of a common kinship in creation.

Philos is a third word for love. This is a "sharing" love. This word means affection. It is called out of the heart by the pleasure one takes in another. The one loving finds a reflection of his own nature in the person loved. It is based on common interests, common attractions, and close sharing of many things, a sharing which attains its consummation in the sharing of one another's bodies.

A final Greek word for love is *agape*, which is a love called out of one's heart by the preciousness of the one loved. This is a "giving" love. It is a love which impels one to sacrifice for the benefit of the person loved. This love seeks to give rather than to get. *Agape* love keeps on loving without asking for return.

John M. Drescher
Meditations for the Newly Married

Love, whether sexual, parental, or fraternal, is essentially sacrificial, and prompts a man to give his life for his friends.

George Santayana
The Life of Reason: Reason in Religion

The loving are the daring.

Bayard Taylor
The Song of the Camp

In one sense, the opposite of fear is courage, but in the dynamic sense the opposite of fear is love, whether this be love of man or love of justice.

Alan Paton
"The Challenge of Fear"

The loss of love is a terrible thing;
They lie who say that death is worse.

Countee Cullen
"Variations on a Theme (The Loss of Love)"

The first stage is to believe that there is only one kind of love. The middle stage is to believe that there are many kinds of love and that the Greeks had a different word for each of them.

The last stage is to believe that there is only one kind of love.

The unabashed eros of lovers, the sympathetic philia of friends, agape giving itself freely no less for the murderer than for his victim (the King James version translates it as charity)—these are all manifestations of a single reality. To lose yourself in another's arms, or in another's company, or in suffering for all men who suffer, including the ones who inflict suffering upon you—to lose yourself in such ways is to find yourself. Is what it's all about. Is what love is.

Frederick Buechner
Wishful Thinking

Love is that condition in which the happiness of another person is essential to your own.

Robert A. Heinlein
Stranger in a Strange Land

Love is union with somebody, or something, outside oneself, under the condition of retaining the separateness and integrity of one's own self.

Erich Fromm
The Sane Society

To love a thing means wanting it to live.

K'ung Fu-tzu Confucius
Analects

The well-spring of social unity and spiritual love in the mystical worship of the God of love should never be forgotten. Religious worship, alone of all the forces known to man, is able to perform that miracle of pity and of hope which enables him who has seen God to see not his fellow worshipers only, but all mankind, as a potential Community of Love. That miracle, I say, for the natural man lacks this vision, and the presence of traces of such a feeling toward the human race is almost universally regarded as a token of the presence and work of God in the life of man.

Edgar S. Brightman
Religious Values

If I speak in the tongues of men and of angels, but have not love, I am only a resounding gong or a clanging cymbal. If I have the gift of prophecy and can fathom all mysteries and all knowledge, and if I have a faith that can move mountains, but have not love, I am nothing. If I give all I possess to the poor and surrender my body to the flames, but have not love, I gain nothing.

Love is patient, love is kind. It does not envy, it does not boast, it is not proud. It is not rude, it is not self-seeking, it is not easily angered, it keeps no record of wrongs. Love does not delight in evil but rejoices with the truth. It always protects, always trusts, always hopes, always perseveres.

Love never fails. But where there are prophecies, they will cease; where there are tongues, they will be stilled; where there is knowledge, it will pass away. For we know in part and we prophesy in part, but when perfection comes, the imperfect disappears. When I was a child, I talked like a child, I thought like a child, I reasoned like a child. When I became a man, I put childish ways behind me. Now we see but a poor reflection as in a miror; then we shall see face to face. Now I know in part; then I shall know fully, even as I am fully known.

And now these three remain: faith, hope and love. But the greatest of these is love.

1 Corinthians 13:1-13 (NIV)

Love dies only when growth stops.

Pearl S. Buck
To My Daughters, With Love

Love must be learned again and again; there is no end to it. Hate needs no instruction, but waits only to be provoked.

Katherine Anne Porter
The Days Before

You can give without loving, but you cannot love without giving.

Amy Carmichael

Love is a flame to burn out human wills,
Love is a flame to set the will on fire,
Love is a flame to cheat men into mire.
One of the three, we make Love what we choose.

John Masefield
"The Widow in the Bye Street"

It is a beautiful necessity of our nature to love something.

Douglas Jerrold

Love is love's reward.

John Dryden
Palamon and Arcite

Respect is what we owe; love, what we give.

Philip James Bailey

If mountains can be moved by faith,
Is there less power in love?

Frederick William Faber
Sermons

Love, like a spring rain, is pretty hard to be in the middle of without getting some on you.

Frank A. Clark
The Country Parson

If we wish to adhere to the true law of love, our eyes must chiefly be directed, not to man, the prospect of whom would impress us with hatred more frequently than with love, but to God, who commands that our love to him be diffused among all mankind; so that this must always be a fundamental maxim with us, that whatever be the character of a man, yet we ought to love him because we love God.

John Calvin
Institutes of the Christian Religion

Love does not die easily. It is a living thing. It thrives in the face of all life's hazards, save one—neglect.

James D. Bryden
Presbyterian Life

Love isn't like a reservoir. You'll never drain it dry. It's much more like a natural spring. The longer and the farther it flows, the stronger and the deeper and the clearer it becomes.

Eddie Cantor
The Way I See It

Love is the fire of life; it either consumes or purifies.

anonymous

A man of kindness, to his beast is kind,
Brutal actions show a brutal mind.
Remember, He who made the brute,
Who gave thee speech and reason, formed him mute;
He can't complain; but God's omniscient eye
Beholds thy cruelty. He hears his cry.
He was destined thy servant and thy drudge,
But know this: his creator is thy judge.

Robert White, Jr.
Admonition posted in Shaker barns

Love is the doorway through which the human soul passes from selfishness to service and from solitude to kinship with all mankind.

anonymous

It is not love, but lack of love, which is blind.

Glenway Wescott
Quoted in the *New York Herald Tribune*, December 19, 1965

I think true love is never blind
But rather brings an added light,
An inner vision quick to find
The beauties hid from common sight.

Phoebe Cary
"True Love"

Love talked about can be easily turned aside, but love demonstrated is irresistible.
W. Stanley Mooneyham
Come Walk the World

In real love you want the other person's good. In romantic love you want the other person.

Margaret Anderson
The Fiery Fountains

If love does not know how to give and take without restrictions, it is not love, but a transaction that never fails to lay stress on a plus and a minus.

Emma Goldman
"The Tragedy of Women's Emancipation"

Let me not to the marriage of true minds
Admit impediments. Love is not love
Which alters when it alteration finds,
Or bends with the remover to remove.
O, no! it is an ever-fixed mark
That looks on tempests and is never shaken;
It is the star to every wandering bark,
Whose worth's unknown, although his height be taken.
Love's not Time's fool, though rosy lips and cheeks

Within his bending sickle's compass come;
Love alters not with his brief hours and weeks,
But bears it out even to the edge of doom.

William Shakespeare
"Sonnet 116"

It is love that asks, that seeks, that knocks, that finds, and that is faithful to what it finds.

Saint Augustine

Love has no awareness of merit or demerit; it has no scale by which its portion may be weighed or measured. It does not seek to balance giving and receiving. Love loves; this is its nature.

Howard Thurman
Meditations of the Heart

There is a wealth of unexpressed love in the world. It is one of the chief causes of sorrow evoked by death: what might have been said or might have been done that never can be said or done.

Arthur Hopkins
Quoted in *Reader's Digest*, October 1937

As selfishness and complaint pervert and cloud the mind, so love with its joy clears and sharpens the vision.

Helen Keller
My Religion

We love the things we love in spite of what they are.

Louis Untermeyer
Love

If you love a person you love him or her in their stark reality, and refuse to shut your eyes to their defects and errors.

John MacMurray
Reason and Emotion

The happy man is he who lives the life of love, not for the honors it may bring, but for the life itself.

R. J. Baughan
Undiscovered Country

Dull sublunary lovers' love
(Whose soul is sense) cannot admit
Absence, because it doth remove
Those things which elemented it.

But we, by a love so much refined,
That ourselves know not what it is,
Inter-assured of the mind,
Care less, eyes, lips, and hands to miss.

Our two souls therefore, which are one,
Though I must go, endure not yet
A breach, but an expansion,
Like gold to airy thinness beat.

If they be two, they are two so
As stiff twin compasses are two,
Thy soul the fixt foot, makes no show
To move, but doth, if the other do.

And though it in the centre sit,
Yet when the other far doth roam,
It leans, and hearkens after it,
And grows erect, as that comes home.

Love reckons hours for months, and days for years;
And every little absence is an age.

John Dryden
Amphitryon

Love does not cause suffering: what causes it is the sense of ownership, which is love's opposite.

Antoine de Saint-Exupéry
The Wisdom of the Sands

Of all powers, love is the most powerful and the most powerless. It is the most powerful because it alone can conquer that final and most impregnable stronghold which is the human heart. It is the most powerless because it can do nothing except by consent.

Frederick Buechner
Wishful Thinking

Love is not love until love's vulnerable.

Theodore Roethke
"The Dream"

But if in your fear you would seek only love's peace and love's pleasure,
Then it is better for you that you cover your nakedness and pass out of love's
    threshing-floor,
Into the seasonless world where you shall laugh, but not all of your laughter,
    and weep, but not all of your tears.
Love gives naught but itself and takes naught but from itself.
Love possesses not nor would it be possessed;
For love is sufficient unto love...
Love has no other desire but to fulfill itself.
But if you love and must needs have desires, let these be your desires:
To melt and be like a running brook that sings its melody to the night.
To know the pain of too much tenderness.
To be wounded by your own understanding of love;
And to bleed willingly and joyfully.
To wake at dawn with a winged heart and give thanks for another day of
    loving;
To rest at the noon hour and meditate love's ecstasy;
To return home at eventide with gratitude;

And then to sleep with a prayer for the beloved in your heart and a song of praise upon your lips.

Kahlil Gibran
The Prophet

Immature love says: "I love you because I need you." Mature love says: "I need you because I love you."

Erich Fromm
The Art of Loving

It is love in old age, no longer blind, that is true love. For love's highest intensity doesn't necessarily mean its highest quality. Glamour and jealousy are gone; and the ardent caress, no longer needed, is valueless compared to the reassuring touch of a trembling hand. Passers-by commonly see little beauty in the embrace of young lovers on a park bench, but the understanding smile of an old wife to her husband is one of the loveliest things in the world.

Booth Tarkington
Quoted in *Reader's Digest*, December 1939

To love without criticism is to be betrayed.

Djuna Barnes
Nightwood

Whoever lives true life will love true love.

Elizabeth Barrett Browning
Aurora Leigh

Love is a tender plant; when properly nourished, it becomes sturdy and enduring, but neglected it will soon wither and die.

Hugh B. Brown

We should love those who point out our faults, but we seldom do.

anonymous

True love is but a humble low-born thing,
And hath its food served up in earthen ware;
It is a thing to walk with, hand in hand,
Through the every-dayness of this work-day world.

James Russell Lowell
"Love"

The greatest love is a mother's; then comes a dog's; then comes a sweetheart's.

Polish proverb

Money will buy a fine dog, but only love will make him wag his tail.

Ulster (Northern Ireland) *Post*

Kindness or humanity has a larger field than bare justice to exercise itself in; law and justice we cannot, in the nature of things, employ on others than men; but we may extend our goodness and charity even to irrational creatures; and such acts flow from a gentle nature, as water from an abundant spring. It is doubtless the part of a kind-natured man to keep even worn-out horses and dogs, and not only take care of them when they are foals and whelps, but also when they are grown old.

Plutarch
Marcus Cato

A joyous chattering broke out among the Animals, but stilled when the Man quietly rose and approached the tarpaulin. Very deliberately he loosed its fastenings and flung it clear. In the deep silence that followed it was almost possible to hear the sound of a hundred little breaths caught and released in a sigh of awe.

The Mole grasped Willie Fieldmouse's elbow. "Willie, what is it?" he whispered. "What is it? *Willie, be eyes for me.*"

Willie's voice was hushed and breathless—"Oh, Mole," he said. "Oh, Mole, it's so beautiful. It's Him, Mole, it's *Him* the Good Saint!"

"Him—of Assisi?" asked the Mole.

"Yes, Mole, *our* Saint. The good St. Francis of Assisi—him that's loved us and protected us Little Animals time out of mind—and, Oh, Mole, it's so beautiful! He's all out of stone, Mole, and his face is so kind and so sad. He's got a long robe on, old and poor like, you can see the patches on it.

"And all around his feet are the Little Animals. They're *us*, Mole, all out of stone. There's you and me and there's all the Birds and there's Little Georgie and Porkey and the Fox—even old Lumpy the Hop Toad. And His hands are held out in front of him sort of kind—like blessing things. And from his hands there's water dropping, Mole, clear, cool water. It drops into a pool there in front of him."

"I can hear it splashing," the Mole whispered, "and I can smell the good clear pool and feel its coolness. Go on, Willie, be eyes for me."

"It's a fine pool for drinking of, Mole, and at each end it's shallow like, so the Birds can bathe there. And, oh, Mole, all around the pool is broad flat stones, a sort of rim, like a shelf or something, and it's all set out with things to eat, like a banquet feast. And there's letters, there's words onto it, Mole, cut in the stones."

"What does it say, Willie, the printing?"

Willie spelled it out slowly, carefully. "It says—'There—is—enough—for—all—' There's enough for all, Mole. And there *is*.

"There's grain—corn and wheat and rye for us—and there's a big cake of salt for the Red Buck and there's vegetables, all kind of vegetables out of the garden, all fresh and washed clean, no dirt on *them* and there's clover and there's blue-grass and buckwheat. There's even nuts for the squirrels and chipmunks—and they're all starting in to eat them now, Mole, and if you don't mind—if you'll excuse me—I think I'll sort of join in."...

There was a steady sound of chewing and munching and champing. The Folks sat silent, the glow of the Man's pipe rising and falling with slow regularity, the Lady gently rubbing Mr. Muldoon's jowls. The Red Buck licked salt till his lips were thick with foam, took a long drink from the pool and then, tossing his head, snorted loudly. The eating stopped and Willie eased his belt a hole or two—his softly furred little stomach seemed to have suddenly swollen alarmingly...

The Red Buck snorted again and all gave attention as he spoke.

"We have eaten their food," his voice rang out impressively. "We have tasted their salt, we have drunk their water, and all are good." He tossed his proud head in the direction of the garden. "From now on this is forbidden ground." His chisel-sharp hoof rapped the earth. "Does anyone dispute me?"

None did and there was silence, broken at last by the voice of Uncle Anal-das. "Haow 'bout them dingblasted Cutworms?" he called. "They don't know no laws or decent regulations."

The Mole, who had been a little slower than the rest, leaned his elbows on the earth as he reared up from his just completed tunnel and turned his blind face toward the sound. "We'll patrol," he said smiling, "me and my brothers, night and day, turn and turn about. Good hunting too; got six on that trip."...

Each evening throughout the summer the kindly Saint's ledge was spread with a banquet, each morning it was clean and neatly swept. Each night the Red Buck, Phewie and the Gray Fox patrolled the premises against wandering marauders, the Mole and his stout brothers made their faithful rounds.

All summer, Mother and the other womenfolk preserved, packed and put away winter stores. Once again there were parties and merrymaking, laughter and dancing. Good days had come back to the Hill.

Tim McGrath surveyed the flourishing garden and lifted his voice in wonderment. "Louie," he said, "I just can't understand it. Here's these new folks with their garden and not a sign of a fence around it, no traps, no poison, no nothing; and not a thing touched, not a thing. Not a footprint onto it, not even a cutworm. Now me, I've got all them things, fences, traps, poisons; even sat up some nights with a shotgun—and what happens? All my carrots gone and half my beets, cabbages et into, tomatoes tromp down, lawn all tore up with moles. Fat-Man-down-to-the-Crossroads he keeps his dogs even and he ain't got a stalk of corn left standing, all his lettuce gone, most of his turnips. I can't understand it. Must just be Beginner's Luck."

"Must be," agreed Louie. "Must be that—or something."

Robert Lawson
Rabbit Hill

A man is ethical only when life, as such, is sacred to him, that of plants and animals as well as that of his fellowman, and when he devotes himself helpfully to all life that is in need of help.

Albert Schweitzer
Out of My Life and Thoughts

Many who have spent a lifetime in it can tell us less of love than the child that lost a dog yesterday.

Thornton Wilder
Quoted in *The American Scholar Reader*

'Tis much to gain universal admiration; more, universal love.

Baltasar Gracián
The Art of Wordly Wisdom

Love is not loved, my daughters! Love is not loved! And how can we remain cold, indifferent and almost without heart at this thought?...If we do not burn with love, we do not deserve the title which ennobles us, elevates us, makes us great, and even a portent to the angels in heaven.

Frances Xavier Cabrini
Quoted in *Too Small a World*

How strange it is to observe that in times like ours, when war has achieved a destructiveness without parallel...future plans for unity are made, which means not only that love exists, but that its power is fundamental.

Maria Montessori
The Absorbent Mind

But one of the attributes of love, like art, is to bring harmony and order out of chaos, to introduce meaning and affect where before there was none, to give rhythmic variations, highs and lows to a landscape that was previously flat.

Molly Haskell
From Reverence to Rape

Time flies,
Suns rise
And shadows fall.
Let time go by.
Love is forever over all.

from an English sun dial

Love is the most durable power in the world. This creative force is the most potent instrument available in mankind's quest for peace and security.

Martin Luther King, Jr.
Strength to Love

Shall I compare thee to a summer's day?
Thou art more lovely and more temperate:
Rough winds do shake the darling buds of May,
And summer's lease hath all too short a date:
Sometime too hot the eye of heaven shines,
And often is his gold complexion dimm'd;
And every fair from fair sometime declines,
By chance, or nature's changing course untrimm'd;
But thy eternal summer shall not fade,
Nor lose possession of that fair thou ow'st,
Nor shall death brag thou wander'st in his shade,
When in eternal lines to time thou grow'st,
So long as men can breathe, or eyes can see,
So long lives this, and this gives life to thee.

William Shakespeare
"Sonnet 18"

If we love a child, and the child senses that we love him, he will get a concept of love that all subsequent hatred in the world will never be able to destroy.

Howard Thurman
Disciplines of Spirit

Love conquers all; and we must yield to Love.

Virgil
Eclogues

Love is the strongest force the world possesses, and yet it is the humblest imaginable.

Mohandas K. Gandhi
Selections

One cannot be strong without love. For love is not an irrelevant emotion; it is the blood of life, the power of reunion of the separated.

Paul Tillich
The Eternal Now

It has been wisely said that we cannot really love anybody at whom we never laugh.

Agnes Repplier
Quoted in *Reader's Digest*, August 1962

Love knows hidden paths.

German proverb

With malice toward none; with charity for all; with firmness in the right as God gives us to see the right, let us strive on to finish the work we are in; to bind up the nation's wounds; to care for him who shall have borne the battle, and for his widow, and his orphan—to do all which may achieve and cherish a just and a lasting peace, among ourselves and with all nations.

Abraham Lincoln
Second Inaugural Address

Love is all we have, the only way that each can help the other.

Euripides
Orestes

Live and love,
Doing both nobly, because lowly;
Live and work strongly, because patiently.
That it be well done, unrepented of,
And not to loss.

Elizabeth Barrett Browning
"Live and Love"

With love one can live even without happiness.

Fyodor Dostoevsky
Notes from Underground

He who finds not love finds nothing.

Spanish proverb

Better a meal of vegetables where there is love than a fattened calf with hatred.

Proverbs 15:17 (NIV)

Someone has written that love makes people believe in immortality, because there seems not to be room enough in life for so great a tenderness, and it is inconceivable that the most masterful of our emotions should have no more than the spare moments of a few years.

Robert Louis Stevenson
Quoted in *Reader's Digest*, April 1960

How do I love thee? Let me count the ways.
I love thee to the depth and breadth and height
My soul can reach, when feeling out of sight
For the ends of Being and Ideal Grace.
I love thee to the level of every day's
Most quiet need, by sun and candle-light.
I love thee freely, as men strive for right;
I love thee purely, as they turn from praise.
I love thee with the passion put to use
In my old griefs; and with my childhood's faith.
I love thee with a love I seemed to lose
With my lost saints. I love thee with the breath,
Smiles, tears, of all my life!—and, if God choose,
I shall but love thee better after death.

Elizabeth Barrett Browning
Sonnets from the Portuguese

O love, resistless in thy might, thou triumphest even over gold!

Sophocles
Antigone

Life has taught us that love does not consist in gazing at each other but in looking outward together in the same direction.

Antoine de Saint-Exupéry
Wind, Sand, and Stars

We all have so many possible occasions for loving and yet there is so little demonstrated love in the world. People are dying alone, crying alone. Children are being abused and elderly people are spending their final days without tenderness and love. In a world where there is such an obvious need for demonstrated love, it is well to realize the enormous power we do have to help and to heal people in our lives with nothing more complicated than an outstretched hand or a warm hug. Teresa of Avila entreated us to "accustom yourself to make many acts of love, for they enkindle and melt the soul."

Day's end is a good time to reflect on what we have done to make the world a better, more caring and loving place. If nothing springs to mind night after night, this can also be an excellent time for us to consider how we can change the world for the better. We need not perform monumental acts, but act on the simple things which are readily accomplished: that phone call we have not made, that note we have put off writing, that kindness we have failed to acknowledge. When it comes to giving love, the opportunities are unlimited and we are all gifted.

Leo Buscaglia, Ph.D.
Born for Love

Religion that God our Father accepts as pure and faultless is this: to look after orphans and widows in their distress and to keep oneself from being polluted by the world.

James 1:27 (NIV)

I've decided to stick with love. Hate is too great a burden to bear.

Martin Luther King, Jr.

A pennyweight o' love is worth a pound o' law.

Scottish proverb

We are shaped and fashioned by what we love.

Johann Wolfgang von Goethe

Where love is, there's no lack.

Richard Brome
A Jovial Crew

How many times do I love thee, dear?
Tell me how many thoughts there be
In the atmosphere
Of a new-fall'n year,
Whose white and sable hours appear
The latest flake of Eternity:—
So many times do I love thee, dear.

How many times do I love again?
Tell me how many beads there are
In a silver chain
Of evening rain,
Unravelled from the tumbling main,
And threading the eye of a yellow star:—
So many times do I love again.

> Thomas Lovell Beddoes
> "Song"

Man has bought brains, but all the millions in the world have failed to buy love.
Man has subdued bodies, but all the power on earth has been unable to subdue
love. Man has conquered whole nations, but all his armies could not conquer
love. Man has chained and fettered the spirit, but he has been utterly helpless
before love. High on a throne, with all the splendor and pomp his gold can
command, man is yet poor and desolate, if loves passes him by. And if it stays,
the poorest hovel is radiant with warmth, with life and color. Thus love has the
magic power to make of a beggar a king. Yes, love is free; it can dwell in no
other atmosphere. In freedom it gives itself unreservedly, abundantly, completely.

> Emma Goldman
> "Marriage and Love"

Love makes the world go round.

> English proverb

One hour of downright love is worth an hour of dully living on.

Aphra Behn
The Rover

The divine miracle par excellence consists surely in the apotheosis of grief, the transfiguration of evil by good. The work of creation finds its consummation, and the eternal will of the Infinite Mercy finds its fulfillment only in the restoration of the free creature to God and of an evil world to goodness, through love.

Henri Frédéric Amiel
Journal Intime

It is only the souls that do not love that go empty in this world.

Robert Hugh Benson
The History of Richard Raynal Solitary

To love anyone is nothing else than to wish that person good.

Saint Thomas Aquinas

More and more clearly every day out of biology, anthropology, sociology, history, economic analysis, psychological insight, plain human decency, and common sense, the necessary mandate of survival that we shall love our neighbors as we do ourselves, is being confirmed and reaffirmed.

Ordway Tead
Illinois Medical Journal

Without love, life is pointless and dangerous. Man is on his way to Venus, but he still hasn't learned to live with his wife. Man has succeeded in increasing his life span, yet he exterminates his brothers six million at a whack. Man now has the power to destroy himself and his planet; depend upon it, he will—should he cease to love.

Harper Lee
"Love—In Other Words"

What we love we shall grow to resemble.

Saint Bernard of Clairvaux

Love will find a way.

English proverb

To love and be loved is to feel the sun from both sides.

David Viscott
How to Live with Another Person

Love should be a tree whose roots are deep in the earth, but whose branches extend into heaven.

Bertrand Russell
Marriage and Morals

The love we have in our youth is superficial compared to the love that an old man has for his old wife.

Will Durant
Quoted in the *New York Times*

When two people love each other, they don't look at each other, they look in the same direction.

Ginger Rogers
Quoted in *Parade*, March 8, 1987

The face of a lover is an unknown, precisely because it is invested with so much of oneself. It is a mystery, containing, like all mysteries, the possibility of torment.

James Baldwin
Another Country

There is nothing ridiculous in love.

Olive Schreiner
"The Buddhist Priest's Wife"

The fountains mingle with the river
And the rivers with the Ocean,
The winds of Heaven mix for ever
With a sweet emotion;

Nothing in the world is single;
All things by a law divine
In one spirit meet and mingle,
Why not I with thine?—

See the mountains kiss high Heaven
And the waves clasp one another;
No sister-flower would be forgiven
If it disdained its brother;
And the sunlight clasps the earth
And the moonbeams kiss the sea:
What is all this sweet work worth
If thou kiss not me?

Percy Bysshe Shelley
"Love's Philosophy"

Soon or late love is his own avenger.

George Gordon, Lord Byron
Don Juan

Until I truly loved, I was alone.

Caroline Sheridan Norton
The Lady of LaGaraye

The entire sum of existence is the magic of being needed by just one person.
Vi Putnam
Hard Hearts Are for Cabbage

Place me like a seal over your heart, like a seal on your arm; for love is as strong
as death, its jealousy unyielding as the grave. It burns like blazing fire, like a
mighty flame. Many waters cannot quench love; rivers cannot wash it away. If
one were to give all the wealth of his house for love, it would be utterly scorned.
Song of Solomon 8:6-7 (NIV)

A very small degree of hope is sufficient to cause the birth of love.

Stendhal
On Love

Love and hatred are natural exaggerators.

Hebrew proverb

There is no disguise which can hide love for long where it exists, or simulate it where it does not.

François de La Rochefoucauld
Maximes

I hold it true, whate'er befall;
I feel it, when I sorrow most;
'Tis better to have loved and lost
Than never to have loved at all.

Alfred, Lord Tennyson
"In Memoriam"

We must resemble each other a little in order to understand each other, but we must be a little different to love each other.

Paul Géraldy
L'Homme et l'amour

Love, the itch, and a cough cannot be hid.

Thomas Fuller
Gnomologia

It is with true love as with ghosts. Everyone talks of it, but few have ever seen it.

François de La Rochefoucauld
Maximes

Beauty without the beloved is like a sword through the heart.

anonymous

'Tis sweet to know there is an eye will mark
Our coming, and look brighter when we come.

George Gordon, Lord Byron
Don Juan

Loving can cost a lot but not loving always costs more, and those who fear to love often find that want of love is an emptiness that robs the joy from life.

Merle Shain
Some Men Are More Perfect Than Others

Love cures people, the ones who receive love and the ones who give it, too.

Karl A. Menninger
Sparks

In Love, if Love be Love, if Love be ours,
Faith and unfaith can ne'er be equal powers:
Unfaith in aught is want of faith in all.

It is the little rift within the lute,
That by and by will make the music mute,
And ever widening slowly silence all.

The little rift within the lover's lute,
Or little pitted speck in garnered fruit,
That rotting inward slowly moulders all.

It is not worth the keeping: let it go:
But shall it? answer, darling, answer, no.
And trust me not at all or all in all.

Alfred, Lord Tennyson
"Idylls of the King"

Don't miss love. It's an incredible gift. I love to think that the day you're born, you're given the world as your birthday present. It frightens me that so few people even bother to open up the ribbon! *Rip it open! Tear off the top!* It's just *full* of love and magic and life and joy and wonder and pain and tears. All of the things that are your gift for being human. Not only the really happy things—"I want to be happy all the time"—no, there's a lot of pain in there, a lot of tears. A lot of magic, a lot of wonder, a lot of confusion. But that's what it means. That's what life *is*. And all *so exciting.* Get into that box and you'll never be bored.

I see people who are always saying, "I'm a lover, I'm a lover. I really believe in love. I act the part." And then they shout at the waitress, *"Where's the water?!"* I will believe your love when you show it to me in action. When you can understand that everybody is teaching everybody to love at every moment. And when you ask yourself, "Am I the best teacher," and if your answer is "Yes"—great. Go around—listen to how many times a day you say, "I love," instead of, "I hate."

Leo Buscaglia, Ph.D.
Living, Loving & Learning

Love means exposing yourself to the pains of being hurt, deeply hurt by someone you trust.

Renita Weems
Quoted in *Essence,* October 1988

To love is to make of one's heart a swinging door.

Howard Thurman
Disciplines of Spirit

There can be no peace on earth until we have learned to respect the dignity of man and are willing to build on the foundation of human love the kind of world that the great teachers of mankind have portrayed to us from the time of the Ten Commandments and the Sermon on the Mount. These are the true lessons of mortal life.

David Lawrence
"Wisdom in a Troubled World"

Is it not by love alone that we succeed in penetrating to the very essence of a being?

Igor Stravinsky
An Autobiography

For one human being to love another: that is perhaps the most difficult of all our tasks, the ultimate, the last test and proof, the work for which all other work is but preparation.

Rainer Maria Rilke
Letters to a Young Poet

The entire law is summed up in a single command: "Love your neighbor as yourself."

Galatians 5:14 (NIV)

Glory be to those who maintain their balance in spite of how we see them, who speak from the best in themselves even when we don't see it, those solid ones who know what they are and what they are doing, or are finding out. They don't give themselves up for a word, for a look, for anything. Our job is to help them stay like that, and to give the same kind of freedom to others whenever we can.

There's a big reward for *seeing* people. They *become* real, to us and to themselves. Look beneath the surface and invite the real man to speak—and invite again, and again. He'll come out. This is liking people, seeing them instead of their shells.

To condemn them, to be disappointed and withdraw, to think we know them too well, to be afraid of them, to give up our own good view for their poor one, to react to something other than the best in them, to hold on to past poor views of them—these are bad habits. They hurt us, cut us down, separate us, and help nobody. It means we're not getting *at* people, *to* them, *with* them—*not seeing* them. Then how can we *like* them?

Robert A. Jackson
How to Like People

If you'd be loved, be worthy to be loved.

Ovid
The Art of Love

We don't love qualities, we love persons; sometimes by reason of their defects as well as of their qualities.

Jacques Maritain
Reflections on America

The love we give away is the only love we keep.

Elbert Hubbard
The Note Book

Love sought is good, but given unsought is better.

William Shakespeare
Twelfth Night

Love of one's enemies may be understood in three ways. First, as though we were to love our enemies as enemies; this is perverse, and contrary to charity, since it implies love of that which is evil in another.

Secondly love of one's enemies may mean that we love them as to their nature, but in a universal way, and in this sense charity requires that we should love our enemies, namely, that in loving God and our neighbor, we should not exclude our enemies from the love given to our neighbour in general.

Thirdly love of one's enemies may be considered as specially directed to them, namely, that we should have a special movement of love towards our enemies. Charity does not require this absolutely, because it does not require that we should have a special movement of love to every individual man, since this would be impossible. Nevertheless charity does require this, in respect of our being prepared in mind, namely that we should be ready to love our enemies individually, if the necessity were to occur.

That man should actually do so, and love his enemy for God's sake, without it being necessary for him to do so, belongs to the perfection of charity.

Saint Thomas Aquinas
Summa Theologica

My heart is open wide tonight
For stranger, kith or kin.
I would not bar a single door
Where love might enter in.

Kate Douglas Wiggin
"The Romance of a Christmas Card"

There is more pleasure in loving, than in being beloved.

Thomas Fuller
Gnomologia

Love is the irresistible desire to be desired irresistibly.

Louis Ginsberg
Reading at St. Mark's in the Bowery, April 1, 1968

If you would be loved, love and be lovable.

Benjamin Franklin
Poor Richard's Almanac

One Friday afternoon I was on my way to set up for a book fair in San Francisco. Waiting at a stoplight in front of the convention center, I noticed a handicapped woman on the street corner. She was sitting against a fence, a walker by her side, surrounded by what was probably all of her belongings. As I watched, another woman, perfectly coiffed, in high heels and a power suit, came up to her with a bag. Without a word, the businesswoman proceeded to lay out prepared food, which she had obviously bought "to go," around the street person so that she could easily reach the food from a sitting position. The homeless woman looked on in grateful amazement, as if her guardian angel had appeared out of nowhere just in time. In fact, she had. Three days later, when I was leaving the convention center, I passed the same woman leaning against the same fence. This time, a man in a van was at the stoplight, honking and holding money out to the woman. She was trying to move, but couldn't get up. Quickly, I ran to the van, grabbed the money, and brought it to her. I felt so happy to see people taking care of this woman, and pleased that my weekend was bracketed by tokens of generosity.

Random Acts of Kindness

But though natural likings should normally be encouraged, it would be quite wrong to think that the way to become charitable is to sit trying to manufacture affectionate feelings. Some people are "cold" by temperament; that may be a misfortune for them, but it is no more a sin than having a bad digestion is a sin; and it does not cut them out from the chance, or excuse them from the duty, of learning charity. The rule for all of us is perfectly simple. Do not waste time bothering whether you "love" your neighbour; act as if you did. As soon as we do this we find one of the great secrets. When you are behaving as if you loved someone, you will presently come to love him. If you injure someone you dislike, you will find yourself disliking him more. If you do him a good turn, you will find yourself disliking him less. There is, indeed, one exception. If you do him a good turn, not to please God and obey the law of charity, but to show him what a fine forgiving chap you are, and to put him in your debt, and then sit down to wait for his "gratitude," you will probably be disappointed. (People are not fools: they have a very quick eye for anything like showing off, or patronage.) But whenever we do good to another self, just because it is a self, made (like us) by God, and desiring its own happiness as we desire ours, we shall have learned to love it a little more or, at least, to dislike it less.

C. S. Lewis
Mere Christianity

No show of bolts and bars
Can keep the foeman out,
Or 'scape his secret mine
Who enter'd with the doubt
That drew the line.
No warder at the gate
Can let the friendly in;
But, like the sun, o'er all
He will the castle win,
And shine along the wall.

Implacable is Love—
Foes may be bought or teased
From their hostile intent,
But he goes unappeased
Who is on kindness bent.

Henry David Thoreau
"Love"

Love your enemies.

Matthew 5:44 (NIV)

Ask any decent person what he thinks matters most in human conduct: five to one his answer will be "kindness."

Lord Kenneth Clark
Quoted in *Reader's Digest*, June 1971

To be loved, love.

Decimus Magnus Ausonius
Epigrams

CHAPTER SIX

Enjoying a

GOOD MARRIAGE

ENJOYING A GOOD MARRIAGE

—◈◈◈—

Therefore shall a man leave his father and his mother, and shall cleave unto his wife: and they shall be one flesh.

Genesis 2:24

There is no more lovely, friendly and charming relationship, communion or company than a good marriage.

Martin Luther
Table Talk

Perhaps the answer is in that deceptively simple remark made by the greatest psychologist of all time, Jesus, when asked about the great commandments. We must do two things, he said: love God and love our neighbor as ourself. By obeying the first, we acquire a balanced perspective on the self. When one is at worship it is impossible to engage in either arrogance or self-contempt. The paradox of the second command is that we discover ourselves best while loving another.

Alan Loy McGinnis
The Romance Factor

If you'd be loved, be worthy to be loved.

Ovid
The Art of Love

After a youth and manhood passed half in unutterable misery and half in dreary solitude, I have for the first time found what I can truly love—I have found *you*. You are my sympathy—my better self—my good angel—I am bound to you with a strong attachment. I think you good, gifted, lovely: a fervent, a solemn passion is conceived in my heart; it leans to you, draws you to my centre and spring of life, wraps my existence about you—and, kindling in pure, powerful flame, fuses you and me in one.

It was because I felt and knew this, that I resolved to marry you.

Charlotte Brontë
Jane Eyre

The best friend is likely to acquire the best wife, because a good marriage is based on the talent for friendship.

Friedrich Nietzsche
Human, All Too Human

For a good wife contains so many persons in herself. What was H. not to me? She was my daughter and my mother, my pupil and my teacher, my subject and my sovereign; and always, holding all these in solution, my trusty comrade, friend, shipmate, fellow-soldier.

C. S. Lewis
A Grief Observed

Remember, that if thou marry for beauty, thou bindest thyself all thy life for that which perchance will neither last nor please thee one year; and when thou hast it, it will be to thee of no price at all; for the desire dieth when it is attained, and the affection perisheth when it is satisfied.

Sir Walter Raleigh
Instructions to His Son

Who can find a virtuous woman? for her price is far above rubies. The heart of her husband doth safely trust in her, so that he shall have no need of spoil...Strength and honour are her clothing; and she shall rejoice in time to come. She openeth her mouth with wisdom: and in her tongue is the law of kindness.

Proverbs 31:10-11, 25-26

Marriage, to woman as to men, must be a luxury, not a necessity; an incident of life, not all of it.

Susan B. Anthony
Speech, 1875

Dear Larry,

Here it is, four in the morning, and you're about to receive a letter from your brother-in-law because your sister, or my wife, however you want to refer to her, is out of town. I never sleep well when Lily is away.

Your sister has made many impressions on me over the years and affected me in ways I'm still discovering. But the best thing she did was remind me of what's truly important. Falling more and more in love with Lily has made me realize that nothing is as important as being with her.

You're probably thinking, "Yeah, I've heard this before." But it wasn't until the night we lost the campaign, as I drove home way after midnight, that I saw, when all was said and done, that it was Lily who mattered—not my work, the campaign, or the "cause." It was Lily who would always be there for me, no matter what.

This realization liberated me. It uncluttered my mind. So I offer some observations on marriage, since you'll be getting married very shortly.

Talk to each other. I always wonder about couples who come into a restaurant, order their meals, wait, eat in silence, pay the check, and leave without engaging in a discussion. Read a book and talk about it. Listen to the news and argue about what's going on. Discuss a purchase or renovation or what flowers to plant.

If one of you is a planner, make plans and agree to the ground rules. Some people go with the flow, others need goals and plans to accomplish them. We've had to remember that plans should be about dreams, not about limits. And settle the issue of children early on. Do you want them, how many, and when? Don't wait so long that you begin to feel pressure about advancing age.

Have some rituals to look forward to each week, such as watching a TV show or doing Saturday errands together or fixing her breakfast on Sunday mornings. Remember that surprises count, too. Unexpected flowers, gifts, or a night on the town keep us from getting into ruts.

Join your wife in one of her activities. It's easy to go off in another room and read or work while she's involved elsewhere in the house. Pick yourself up and become part of her life. Learn how to do what she's doing and do it with her. There's a difference between two people living with each other under the same roof and two people sharing a life together.

The sharing aspect is hardest for me. It's easier to help Lily than it is to ask for her help or disclose what's on my mind. But, believe me, if you don't make yourself vulnerable and your wife does, pretty soon she'll resent the one-sidedness of the relationship. Sharing goes both ways.

Finally, marriage isn't about reforming your partner. She brings to the table a whole lifetime of experiences that make her who she is. Every time you get upset and try to change her, you'll diminish her. I always catch myself, either right before or, usually, right after I say, "Why can't you change?" She can't, and I shouldn't ask. Instead of trying to reform her, the most important thing I can do is respect and love her.

When getting married opens up whole new possibilities and opportunities, when tolerating differences becomes the norm rather than the exception, and when the same face looks better and better as the years pass, you can be sure you have a special kind of love. Living together isn't easy. But knowing Lily is there for me beats everything. Which is why I don't get much sleep when she isn't around.

See you at your wedding.

Billy
Quoted in *From the Heart*
by Dale Atkins and Meris Powell

Give your hearts, but not into each other's keeping.
For only the hand of Life can contain your hearts.
And stand together yet not too near together:
For the pillars of the temple stand apart,
And the oak tree and the cypress grow not in each other's shadow.

Kahlil Gibran
The Prophet

The more personal harmony we feel the more we will be able to give in a loving relationship. All the elements necessary for a genuine, loving relationship with someone else are the same ingredients we need in order to fully love ourselves. Respect, confidence, good values, tolerance, open-mindedness, sincerity, benevolence—we share this inner contentment and self-love with someone. First, it has to be inside us.

Alexandra Stoddard
Living Beautifully Together

An essential part of becoming marriageable is to be a maker, a person who cultivates a life of beauty, rich texture, and creative work. If we understand marriage only as the commitment of two individuals to each other, then we overlook its soul, but if we see that it also has to do with family, neighborhood, and the greater community, and with our own work and personal cultivation, then we begin to glimpse the *mystery* that is marriage.

Thomas Moore
Soul Mates

And Laban said unto Jacob, Because thou art my brother, shouldest thou therefore serve me for nought? tell me, what shall thy wages be? And Laban had two daughters: the name of the elder was Leah, and the name of the younger was Rachel. Leah was tender eyed; but Rachel was beautiful and well favoured. And Jacob loved Rachel; and said, I will serve thee seven years for Rachel thy younger daughter. And Laban said, It is better that I give her to thee, than that I should give her to another man: abide with me. And Jacob served seven years for Rachel; and they seemed unto him but a few days, for the love he had to her.

Genesis 29:15-20

When a man and woman first meet and there seems to be...a bond between them, they explore each other in a cautious, perhaps uncertain way. Maybe the relationship develops into intimacy, families become involved, and a marriage proposal is accepted and consummated. This sounds like a happy ending to a delightful story, but it's just the introduction to a marriage.

What makes a marriage? Is a personal union built or strengthened mainly by dramatic events? I would say no. It's the year-by-year, dozen-times-a-day demonstration of the little things that can destroy a marriage or make it successful. The ability to communicate is most important…Times arise when the husband and wife look on the same event with different perspectives. If they can talk about their views with honesty and mutual respect—a big if—many problems can be avoided.

We have to be willing to forgive, because mistakes are going to be made. There is going to be anger and even, at times, deliberately hurtful words, so understanding and flexibility are required. And it is crucial during times of crisis to maintain an overriding sense of permanence…

If we outline the basic elements of a marriage, we see that the same things apply in our relationship with Christ: love, forgiveness, loyalty, flexibility, the admission of mistakes; looking inward; the ability to ask, What is there about my own life that is not acceptable to Christ, and am I willing to change, to repent?

Jimmy Carter
Living Faith

Two pure souls fused into one by an impassioned love—friends, counselors—a mutual support and inspiration to each other amid life's struggles, must know the highest human happiness;—this is marriage; and this is the only corner-stone of an enduring home.

Elizabeth Cady Stanton
History of Woman Suffrage

That I may come near to her, draw me nearer to thee than to her; that I may know her, make me to know thee more than her; that I may love her with the perfect love of a perfectly whole heart, cause me to love thee more than her and most of all. Amen. Amen.

That nothing may be between me and her, be thou between us, every moment. That we may be constantly together, draw us into separate loneliness with thyself. And when we meet breast to breast, my God, let it be on thine own. Amen. Amen.

Temple Gairdner

The minutes and hours we have shared together, the thoughtfulness and tender-ness we have shown to each other, or simply the willingness to be ourselves—for the sake of the other—assures us that we are already intimate, and making love can only be the culmination of all this. As I see it, lovemaking is a total act embracing every minute of one's day. And I think Fromm was right when he said people think they want intimacy; but actually they avoid it all the time, because in order to confront another person with intimacy, you have to be willing to show yourself and be yourself, to shed that image you like to protect. It requires a certain readiness to see oneself as one is and to see another person. It requires even a certain sense of humanity to let a person be and to let oneself be—without being indignant or over-tolerant.

> Sister Joan (now Fran Eder)
> Letter to Robert Eder (then a parish priest)
> Quoted in *Married Priests & Married Nuns*

You are so beautiful to me, your physical beauty, your mind, yes, your soul, even your arrogance (!), your optimism, your smile. Would you allow me to share your life? I do so much want to take you for my wife and make you happy. I want to live for you, and through you, for the whole world.

> Robert Eder (then a parish priest)
> Letter to Sister Joan (now Fran Eder)
> Quoted in *Married Priests & Married Nuns*

I like not only to be loved, but also to be told that I am loved.

> George Eliot

Romance is about the little things. It's much more about the small gestures—the little ways of making daily life with your lover a bit more special—than it is about extravagant, expensive gestures.

> Gregory J. P. Godek
> *1001 Ways to Be Romantic*

There is nothing more soothing and loving than a gentle caress, a hug, a pat on the fanny or the back. This tenderness, these affectionate caresses, are love in action.

> Alexandra Stoddard
> *Living Beautifully Together*

The first thing I see, as I open my eyes, is the morning making a pink glow on the trunks of the three birch trees outside our window. Between two of the trunks hangs the moon, just past full and sinking in the west, the same pale, chalky-pink color as the papery bark of the birches. Both trees and moon appear almost translucent, as if lit from behind.

But the whole morning is translucent. The air holds light like a goblet. Even the mountain, that most opaque of God's creations, glows with an inner light...

This is the scene I wake up to every morning, here where I live, to the accompaniment of one of those frothing, silver-blue, rushing mountain rivers whose sound fills my ears the way the dawn light fills my eyes. And yet even that is not all. There is something else. Something more breathtaking than any of these other stupendous and beautiful things, and even more radiant with light.

There is a woman in bed beside me. Right this moment I could reach out my hand and touch her, as easily as I touch myself, and as I think about this, it is more staggering than any mountain or moon. It is even more staggering, I think, than if this woman happened instead to be an angel (which, come to think of it, she might well be). There are only two factors which prevent this situation from being so overpoweringly awesome that my heart would explode just trying to take it in: one is that I have woken up just like this, with the same woman beside me, hundreds of times before; and the other is that millions of other men and women are waking up beside each other, just like this, each and every day all around the world, and have been for thousands of years.

Mike Mason
The Mystery of Marriage

The husband should fulfil his marital duty to his wife, and likewise the wife to her husband. The wife's body does not belong to her alone but also to her husband. In the same way, the husband's body does not belong to him alone but also to his wife.

1 Corinthians 7:3-4 (NIV)

Communicate. That's the advice many experts give for a successful marriage. Exchange ideas, ask questions, keep no secrets. It's worthwhile advice, but I've found that certain questions *don't* enhance a marriage; they threaten it.

For instance, I called my wife from work a while back. No particular reason. I needed a break and simply wanted to say "Hi."

I said, "Hi."

She said, "Hi."

"I just thought I'd call," I said.

"Good," she said.

"I'll probably be home on time tonight."

"Wonderful."

"What's for dinner?" I asked.

Click. Dial tone.

That made me suspect something was wrong. So when I got home, I communicated. "What's wrong?" I asked.

"Nothing."

In a marriage, when you know something is wrong and you ask what it is, the response "nothing" is a euphemism for just about everything.

"Was it my call earlier?" I asked.

It was.

She said, "Why did you ask what we were having for dinner?"

"I don't know. I suppose I just wanted to know what we were having for dinner."

"No, 'How was your day?' No, 'I love you?' Just 'What's for dinner?' "

This is where communication helps. I listened and learned. A few weeks later, I called again from work. "I just called because I missed you," I said. "And to tell you I love you."

"Why don't we meet at home for lunch," she suggested.

"Why would I do that?" I asked.

"Oh, we'll think of something to do," she said.

"You know, I might," I said. "What are you having for lunch?"

Click. Dial tone.

Gene Perret
"Please, Don't Ask Me That!" *Good Housekeeping*, January 1997

To be concentrated in relation to others means primarily to be able to listen. Most people listen to others, or even give advice, without really listening. They do not take the other person's talk seriously, they do not take their own answers seriously either. As a result, the talk makes them tired. They are under the illusion that they would be even more tired if they listened with concentration. But the opposite is true.

Erich Fromm
The Art of Loving

Communication is both talking and silence; it is touching and a quiet look.

Communication is the process of sharing yourself both verbally and nonverbally in such a way that the other person can understand and accept what you are sharing. Of course, it means you also have to attend with your ears and eyes so that the other person can communicate with you.

Communication is accomplished only when the other person receives the message you send, whether verbal or nonverbal. Communication can be effective, positive and constructive, or it can be ineffective, negative and destructive. While one spouse may intend the message to be positive, the other spouse may receive it as a negative...

When a couple marries, two distinct cultures and languages come together. In fact, you are actually marrying a foreigner. Surprised? You may be! But each of you speaks a different language with different meanings to the same words. If each of you does not define your words, then assumptions and misunderstandings will occur...

Hearing is basically to gain content or information for your own purposes. Listening is caring for and being empathic toward the person who is talking. Hearing means that you are concerned about what is going on inside *you* during the conversation. Listening means you are trying to understand the feelings of *the other person* and are listening for his sake...

You can learn to listen, for it is a skill to be learned. Your mind and ears can be taught to hear more clearly. Your eyes can be taught to see more clearly. But the reverse is also true. You can learn to *hear* with your *eyes* and *see* with your *ears*.

H. Norman Wright
So You're Getting Married:
The Keys to Building a Strong, Lasting Relationship

Marriage involves big compromises all the time. International-level compromises. You're the U.S.A., he's the USSR, and you're talking nuclear warheads.

Bette Midler
Quoted in *Parade Magazine*, February 5, 1989

To repress a harsh answer, to confess a fault, and to stop (right or wrong) in the midst of self-defence, in gentle submission, sometimes requires a struggle like life and death; but these *three* efforts are the golden threads with which domestic happiness is woven; once begin the fabric with this woof, and trials shall not break or sorrow tarnish it.

Caroline Gilman
Recollections of a Southern Matron

Criticism should not be querulous and wasting, all knife and root-puller, but guiding, instructive, inspiring, a south wind, not an east wind.

Ralph Waldo Emerson
Journals

Recently I asked myself whether it was necessary to tell Mark his habit of leaving the cap off the toothpaste makes me nuts. I decided it wasn't. Why? Because if I called him on every one of his habits that irked me, or vice versa, we'd be at each other constantly.

Deirdre Martin
"Why Fighting Is Good for Your Marriage," *McCall's*, January 1997

In a successful marriage, there is no such thing as one's way. There is only the path of both, the bumpy, difficult but always mutual path.

Phyllis McGinley
The Province of the Heart

When wronged by those we love, we seem to devalue years of relationship—a relationship that may have brought us many joys and which required much intellectual and emotional energy to have lasted so long. Still, with a single harsh statement, a thoughtless act, an unfeeling criticism, we are capable of destroying even the closest of our relationships. We quickly forget the good and set out to rationalize scenarios of hate. We do this rather than take up the challenge of honest evaluation and confrontation. We ignore the possibility that in the act of forgiving and showing compassion we are very likely to discover new depths in ourselves and new possibilities for relating in the future...We fail to realize that when we refuse to engage in forgiving behaviors, it is we who assume the useless weight of hate, pain and vengeance which is neverending, and, instead, weighs upon us rather than the wrongdoer...

True forgiveness will become easier when we learn to empathize and apologize; when we admit we are human too, capable of wrongdoing; when we make allowances for circumstances we may not understand;...when we are willing to start again with compassion and without grudges.

Leo Buscaglia, Ph.D.
Loving Each Other

I am not much concerned about a moderate amount of disagreement or even bickering, for it is not unnatural that a certain amount of conflict should exist between human beings living in close proximity. I have never been impressed by the statement often made that a husband and wife have lived together for, let us say, forty years, and never had a cross word. Ignoring the question of whether the assertion is true, it still remains that it would be a rather dull existence for two people to live together on such an insipid plane that there never would be any argument. A good, robust difference of opinion strenuously engaged in is not bad for human beings provided they never let the sun go down on their wrath...Battle the issues out if you must but get them settled and forgive any sharpness before you go to sleep for the night...

Think appreciation rather than criticism...set up a family conference and get everything out on the table but don't snip and snarl and condemn and look askance. Do not develop the habit of seeing the things that are wrong. Condition your attention to the things that are right and appreciate them, *and say so,* and say so *often.*

Norman Vincent Peale
A Guide to Confident Living

Marriage is three parts love and seven parts forgiveness of sins.

Langdon Mitchell
The New York Idea

You can bear your own faults, and why not a fault in your wife?

Benjamin Franklin
Poor Richard's Almanac

We seem to have realized that the thing which cannot *possibly* be revealed to the other *can* be revealed, the problem which you *must keep* to yourself can be shared. While many times we have temporarily lost this learning, it has always returned in periods of crisis…

There have been periods of greater remoteness from each other, and periods of great closeness. There have been periods of real stress, squabbles, annoyance, and suffering—though we are not the kind who fight—and periods of enormous love and supportiveness. And we have always continued to share. Neither has become so involved in his own life and activity that he has had no time for sharing with the other.

Carl R. Rogers, Ph.D.
Becoming Partners

The essence of chastity is not the suppression of lust, but the total orientation of one's life towards a goal.

Dietrich Bonhoeffer
Letters and Papers from Prison

One man should love and honor one:
A bride-bed
Theirs alone till life's done.

Euripides
Andromache

When people get married because they think it's a long-time love affair, they'll be divorced very soon, because all love affairs end in disappointment. But marriage is recognition of a spiritual identity. If we live a proper life, if our minds are on the right qualities in regarding the person of the opposite sex, we will find our proper male or female counterpart. But if we are distracted by certain sensuous interests, we'll marry the wrong person. By marrying the right person, we reconstruct the image of the incarnate God, and that's what marriage is.

Joseph Campbell
The Power of Myth

A Prince and a Princess were still celebrating their honeymoon. They were extremely happy; only one thought disturbed them, and that was how to retain their present happiness. For that reason they wished to own a talisman with which to protect themselves against any unhappiness in their marriage.

Now, they had often been told about a man who lived out in the forest, acclaimed by everybody for his wisdom and known for his good advice in every need and difficulty. So the Prince and Princess called upon him and told him about their heart's desire. After the wise man had listened to them he said, "Travel through every country in the world, and wherever you meet a completely happily married couple, ask them for a small piece of the linen they wear close to the body, and when you receive this, you must always carry it with you. That is a sure remedy!"

The Prince and the Princess rode forth, and on their way they soon heard of a knight and his wife who were said to be living the most happily married life. They went to the knight's castle and asked him and his wife if their marriage was truly as happy as was rumored.

"Yes, of course," was the answer, "with the one exception that we have no children!"

Here then the talisman was not to be found, and the Prince and Princess continued their journey in search of the completely happily married couple.

As they traveled on, they came to a country where they heard of an honest citizen who lived in perfect unity and happiness with his wife. So to him they went, and asked if he really was as happily married as people said.

"Yes, I am," answered the man. "My wife and I live in perfect harmony; if only we didn't have so many children, for they give us a lot of worries and sorrows!"

So neither with him was the talisman to be found, and the Prince and the Princess continued their journey through the country, always inquiring about happily married couples; but none presented themselves.

One day, as they rode along fields and meadows, they noticed a shepherd close by the road, cheerfully playing his flute. Just then a woman carrying a child in her arm, and holding a little boy by the hand, walked towards him. As soon as the shepherd saw her, he greeted her and took the little child, whom he kissed and caressed. The shepherd's dog ran to the boy, licked his little hand, and barked and jumped with joy. In the meantime, the woman arranged a meal she had brought along, and then said, "Father, come and eat now!" The man sat down and took of the food, but the first bite he gave to the little boy, and the second he divided between the boy and the dog. All this was observed by the Prince and the Princess, who walked closer, and spoke to them, saying, "You must be a truly happily married couple."

"Yes, that we are," said the man. "God be praised; no prince or princess could be happier than we are!"

"Now listen then," said the Prince. "Do us a favor, and you shall never regret it. Give us a small piece of the linen garment you wear close to your body!"

As he spoke, the shepherd and his wife looked strangely at each other, and finally he said, "God knows we would be only too happy to give you not only a small piece, but the whole shirt, or undergarment, if we only had them, but we own not as much as a rag!"

So the Prince and the Princess journeyed on, their mission unaccomplished. Finally, their unsuccessful roaming discouraged them, and they decided to return home. As they passed the wise man's hut, they stopped by, related all their travel experiences, and reproached him for giving them such poor advice.

At that the wise man smiled and said, "Has your trip really been all in vain? Are you not returning richer in knowledge?"

"Yes," answered the Prince, "I have gained *this* knowledge, that contentment is a rare gift on this earth."

"And I have learned," said the Princess, "that to be contented, one needs nothing more than simply—to be contented!"

Whereupon the Prince took the Princess' hand; they looked at each other with an expression of deepest love. And the wise man blessed them and said, "In your own hearts you have found the true talisman! Guard it carefully, and the evil spirit of discontentment shall never in all eternity have any power over you!"

Hans Christian Andersen

"The Talisman"

To keep the marriage brimming
With love in the loving cup
When you're wrong, admit it
When you're right, shut up.

Ogden Nash

We have lived and loved together
Through many changing years;
We have shared each other's gladness
And wept each other's tears;
I have known ne'er a sorrow
That was long unsoothed by thee;
For thy smiles can make a summer
Where darkness else would be.

Like the leaves that fall around us
In autumn's fading hours,
Are the traitor's smiles, that darken
When the cloud of sorrow lowers;
And though many such we've known, love,
Too prone, alas, to range,
We bothe can speak of one love
Which time can never change.

We have lived and loved together
Through many changing years;
We have shared each other's gladness
And wept each other's tears,
And let us hope the future
As the past has been will be:
I will share with thee my sorrows,
And thou thy joys with me.

Charles Jeffreys
"We Have Lived and Loved Together"

Wedlock—the deep, deep peace of the double bed after the hurly-burly of the chaise-longue.

Mrs. Patrick Campbell
Quoted in *Jennie*

Whenever I see my mother and father together, I know they're residing in a state where I want to live with Camille, a state of such blessed mellowness that they make the Dalai Lama seem like a Type A personality.

I will never forget my first awareness that my mother and father had ascended to a matrimonial plane where only God knew what they were doing—perhaps. We were driving to Philadelphia from Atlantic City, with my father at the wheel, my mother beside him, and me in the back.

"Oh, there's a car from Pittsburgh," said my mother, looking at a license plate in the next lane.

"How do you know it's from Pittsburgh?" said my father.

"Because I couldn't think of Pennsylvania," she replied.

And I waited for my father to respond to this Einsteinian leap into another dimension, but he didn't speak. He simply continued to drive, a supremely contented man.

Because he had understood.

He had understood that my mother's Pittsburgh was a mythical place, located where the Monongahela entered the twilight zone. My mother also had not been able to think of Afghanistan, but she didn't say that the car was from Kabul. However, *had* she said that the car was from Kabul, my father would have understood it bore Afghans moving to Allentown.

For the next twenty minutes, I thought about fifty-three years of marriage and how they had bonded my parents in this remarkable Zen rapport; but then I was suddenly aware that my father had just driven past the exit for Philadelphia. Not the exit for Pennsylvania or for North America, but for Philadelphia, the literal city.

"Mom," I said, "didn't Dad just pass the exit we want?"

"Yes, he did," she replied.

"Well, why don't you *say* something?"

"Your father knows what he's doing."

Had *I* driven past the proper exit, my wife would have said, *Please pull over* and let me out. I'd like to finish this trip by hitching a ride on a chicken truck.

But if Camille and I can just stay together another twenty-five years, then we also will have reached the Twilight Zone, where one of us will do something idiotic and the other one not only will understand it but admire it as well.

You turned out the light when I'm reading, I will tell her. *Thank you for the surprise trip to the planetarium.*

You left your shoes in the bathtub, she will tell me. *Thank you for giving me two more boats.*

One morning a few days after that memorably roundabout trip to Philadelphia, I got another glimpse of the lotus land where my parents dwelled. My father came into the house, took off his hat, put it on a chair, gave some money to my children, and then went back and sat on his hat.

"You just sat on your hat," my mother told him.

"Of course I did," he replied, and then neither one of them said another word about hat reduction. When the time came to leave, my father picked up the crushed hat and put it on his head, where it sat like a piece of Pop Art. My mother glanced at it, as if to make sure that it would not fall off, and then she took his arm and they walked out the door, ready to be the sweethearts of the Mummers parade.

However, if I ever sat on my hat, Camille would say, *Can't you feel that you're sitting on your hat?*

And I would reply, *It's a tradition in my family for a man to sit on his hat. It's one of the little things that my father did for my mother.*

Yes, twenty-five years, happy as they have been, are still not enough to have given Camille and me that Ringling Brothers rhythm my mother and father enjoy. But we can hear the circus calling to us.

Bill Cosby
Love and Marriage

A man reserves his true and deepest love not for the species of woman in whose company he finds himself electrified and enkindled, but for that one in whose company he may feel tenderly drowsy.

George Jean Nathan
The Theatre Book of the Year

Same old slippers,
Same old rice,
Same old glimpse of
Paradise.

William James Lampton
"Slippers and Rice"

Our love has been anything but perfect and anything but static. Inevitably there have been times when one of us has outrun the other and has had to wait patiently for the other to catch up. There have been times when we have misunderstood each other, demanded too much of each other, been insensitive to the other's needs. I do not believe there is any marriage where this does not happen. The growth of love is not a straight line, but a series of hills and valleys. I suspect in every good marriage there are times when love seems to be over. Sometimes these desert lines are simply the only way to the next oasis, which is far more lush and beautiful after the desert crossing than it could possibly have been without it.

Madeleine L'Engle
Two-Part Invention

Ideals are like stars in the sky for a ship navigator. They are always there, they never vary, and they guide one through the voyage he is taking. If two marriage partners have the same ideal, they will continue to draw closer together, no matter what their temporary goals may be. But they have to know what an ideal is, and they must be convinced that it is worthwhile.

William McGarey, M.D. and Gladys McGarey, M.D.
There Will Your Heart Be Also

We should measure affection, not like youngsters by the ardor of its passion, but by its strength and constancy.

Marcus Tullius Cicero
De Officiis

"Haven't you read," he replied, "that at the beginning the Creator 'made them male and female,' and said, 'For this reason a man will leave his father and mother and be united to his wife, and the two will become one flesh'? So they are no longer two, but one. Therefore what God has joined together, let man not separate."

Matthew 19:4-6 (NIV)

In a constructive marriage...partners must regularly, routinely and predictably, attend to each other and their relationship no matter how they feel...Couples sooner or later always fall out of love, and it is at the moment when the mating instinct has run its course that the opportunity for genuine love begins. It is when the spouses no longer feel like being in each other's company always, when they would rather be elsewhere some of the time, that their love begins to be tested and will be found to be present or absent.

M. Scott Peck, M.D.
The Road Less Traveled

A good marriage is one where love is not destroyed. Love changes, of course, in its manifestation as time goes on and as individuals achieve higher levels of maturity, but change does not mean destruction. It can and should mean growth. A good marriage is one which allows for change and growth in the individuals and in the way they express their love.

Pearl S. Buck
To My Daughters, With Love

There are two sorts of constancy in love; the one comes from the constant discovery in our beloved of new grounds for love, and the other comes from making it a point of honour to be constant.

François de La Rochefoucauld
Maximes

Chains do not hold a marriage together. It is threads, hundreds of tiny threads which sew people together through the years. That is what makes a marriage last—more than passion or even sex!

Simone Signoret
Quoted in the Daily Mail, July 4, 1978

There is a courtesy of the heart. It is akin to love. Out of it arises the purest courtesy in the outward behavior.

Johann Wolfgang von Goethe
Elective Affinities

When you're with [your wife] watching a Bo Derek movie, say, "Come on sweetheart, let's get out of here. I don't know what they see in her."

Instead of reading the newspaper at the kitchen table, try talking to your wife. You might learn a few things, like your kids have grown up and moved out.

Remember those important dates: her birthday, Valentine's Day, your anniversary, your first date together, your first trip together, and above all what happened the day you forgot one of those days you were supposed to remember.

Praise her in public. Let her hear you telling others how much you depend on her judgment and value her intelligence. What you say behind her back is up to you.

George Burns
Dr. Burns' Prescription for Happiness

If you cannot inspire a woman with love of you, fill her above the brim with love of herself—all that runs over will be yours.

Charles Caleb Colton
Lacon

Homes that are gay with laughter and good cheer bear the burdens of life more easily, and blows of difficulty and adversity do not destroy them. Fun and laughter lighten burdens of fatigue and care, and at the same time promote harmony and give life a good taste. Recreation is well named when it recreates, and every home ought to build into its experience plenty of good times planned and carried out together.

Reverend Leland Foster Wood, Ph.D.
Harmony in Marriage

Nurturing a relationship is an act as familiar as kissing hello, as flamboyant as a surprise birthday party, as unique to your relationship as a love note written with your pet names, or as universal as regularly voicing your appreciation for your partner. Nurturing your relationship means keeping it current, warm, juicy, sparkling with gratitude, burnished with respect. Nurturing your love means you give it the same attention you do your career, your children, or your commitment to your community. *It is the act of creating an environment in which the relationship, and each person, can flourish.*

To nurture another human being is to accept that person for who he or she is. To nurture is to honor your lover as the magnificent human being she or he is inside. It is to support your partner's growth toward wholeness. It means you honestly care about your partner's thoughts, feelings, wants, and especially needs. It is *always* a reciprocal process. One partner does not do all the nurturing: that is excessive caretaking, and that eventually leads to resentment, burnout, and finally bitterness and alienation.

Jennifer Louden
The Couple's Comfort Book

One must not be mean with affections; what is spent of the funds is renewed in the spending itself. Left untouched for too long, they diminish imperceptibly or the lock gets rusty; they are there all right but one cannot make use of them.

Sigmund Freud
Letter to Martha Bernays

Some people think that the only way to get romance back in their marriage is to get into a different marriage. But many people who opt out of a romanceless marriage find themselves, two or three years later, in another romanceless marriage. They thought they needed a new partner, but what they really needed was a new pattern of relating and expressing love. They thought they needed a new marriage, but what they really needed was a new motivation for rekindling their old one…

If you want to rekindle romance, you should commit yourself to meaningful conversation, court creatively, learn one another's language of love, and now, start to have some fun again…

Even the best marriages take a tremendous amount of work. If there is no fun to balance out the work, even the most earnest spouses begin to lose motivation and energy. And the more challenging a marriage is, the more important fun is. We have learned that mutually enjoyable, fun experiences can help heal tender wounds and become a bridge across frustrating differences.

Bill and Lynne Hybels
Fit to Be Tied

Trusty, dusky, vivid, true,
With eyes of gold and bramble-dew,
Steel true and blade-straight,
The great artificer
Made my mate.

Honour, anger, valour, fire;
A love that life could never tire,
Death quench or evil stir,
The mighty master
Gave to her.

Teacher, tender, comrade, wife,
A fellow-farer true through life,
Heart-whole and soul-free,
The august father
Gave to me.

Robert Louis Stevenson
"A Husband to a Wife"

Billy [Graham] recalls that when he and Ruth were about to celebrate their thirty-fifth wedding anniversary, a friend wanted to know if the evangelist had ever seriously considered divorce. "No," Graham replied truthfully. "It never even entered my mind."

The next question asked was, "What's your secret?"

Billy said that God had given us certain guidelines for marriage, and when they are neglected, the likelihood of marital difficulty is greatly increased. For years he and Ruth have followed what may be called *The Grahams' Ten Commandments for a Happy Marriage.*

1. *Put God in your marriage.* I mention this first because I am convinced that

this is the most important key for a solid marital union. It must have a solid rock upon which to build—it cannot be half and half. If you want certain discord in your home, have deep-seated religious differences. There must be a spiritual understanding.

2. *Learn the act of mutual acceptance.* Respecting each other without constantly wishing things were different is crucial. That doesn't mean a husband or wife simply relaxes and casually decides it is unimportant to change. If the couple honestly wants to improve their marriage, they will seek to overcome irritants. Frustration, disappointment and sorrow are an inevitable part of life. Happiness is hoped for but not promised. It must be merited.

3. *Accept your individual responsibilities.* Not only should the mates accept each other, but they should accept the responsibilities each has as husband and wife. Obvious? It is surprising how many letters I get groaning about these failures—each blaming the other. Self-righteousness is a menace to marriage.

4. *Communicate.* This is essential. One of the saddest things I have heard married people say is, "We don't really have anything to talk about anymore." I know of couples who remain silent with each other the entire day. In the restaurant, just look at a table next to you shared by a husband and wife. Often, nothing is said during the entire meal. A wonderful way to rekindle conversation is by discussing the Bible.

5. *Take time with each other.* For two people to get married only to go their separate ways is illogical and against God's plan for marriage. Modern life may appear to require perpetual running—I urge you to slow down.

6. *Give attention to the little things.* What do I mean by "little things"? It may be removing the curlers from your hair before your husband comes home. It may mean taking out the trash without protesting. *Simple things,* but oh so important.

7. *Beware of pitfalls and learn to forgive.* Each marriage is unique, and each faces its own peculiar problems. Recognize them and try to avoid them. But if they do occur—forgive. To have a successful marriage you need two forgivers.

8. *Recognize the greatest enemy of your marriage—selfishness.* Have you ever asked yourself what the opposite of love is? Many of us would say, "hate." But this is an incomplete answer. The real opposite of love is selfishness. Being aware of this fact is an important step in the right direction. A happy marital partnership has to be dominated by love—two people seeking out ways to do what is best for the other.

9. *Learn to grow—together.* Too often one mate has matured remarkably but the other one is left far behind. Ruth and I have learned to listen carefully and respectfully to the other's point of view. We find it healing to kneel together at least once a day. I pray for her and she in turn prays for me. Let not the sun go down upon your wrath.

10. *See your marriage as opportunity to serve.* God has not given us marriage just to be selfishly enjoyed. He wants us to use our marriage to benefit others. You will feel enriched when you do.

Jhan Robbins
Marriage Made in Heaven:
The Story of Billy & Ruth Graham

Two such as you with such a master speed
Cannot be parted nor be swept away
From one another once you are agreed
That life is only life forevermore
Together wing to wing and oar to oar.

Robert Frost
"The Master Speed"
(inscribed on the gravestone of Frost and his wife, Elinor)

Love seems the swiftest, but it is the slowest of all growths. No man or woman really knows what perfect love is until they have been married a quarter of a century.

Mark Twain
Notebook

Dear Jane,

This weekend Bill and I celebrated our twentieth anniversary, and it was probably the most important one of all. I've always loved our anniversaries. It's become a date to remember the major events of the year (wonderful and sad), close doors on mistakes, and put our relationship in perspective.

It's so easy to get preoccupied with our needs and wants during daily living. I get annoyed by his irritating little habits, he feels hurt when I promise to do something and forget, and we both get resentful about hard things like compromising ("giving in," when I have to do it; "being reasonable," when I want it to come from him). Every year we talk, and it always comes back to the same issue. We feel stressed and misunderstood when we don't have enough time. Time together, time by ourselves, just time. This year we decided to do something about it. For our anniversary we stayed home. Friday night and all day Saturday and Sunday.

We didn't answer the phone (this is hard). We didn't turn on the TV (easier than expected). We didn't look at the mail (what a relief!). We didn't do any chores, yard work, or fixing. We went to the grocery store Thursday night and stocked up on lots of salad stuff and frozen things and fun food for easy eating. So during the weekend we didn't do any of the ordinary daily living things that are always there to distract us and that fill up so much time. Friday night was great. We felt reprieved from all of our responsibilities, with a touch of giddiness and a hint of guilt, like we were getting away with something. We agreed not to talk about work, the house, relatives, or money. We had a long, leisurely picnic dinner on the floor of the living room, listening to music. Listening—the music wasn't just background noise for our talking. Amazing.

It wasn't easy. We kept catching ourselves, or each other, bringing up some bit of chronically unfinished business (next week we have to call the insurance company, plumber, etc.) or recycled personal news (I talked to Bob, Sarah, Ted, your mother today and she or he said...). It became clear that our conversations had taken on a pattern of reacting to other people and outside events. Weren't we once more innovative—and interesting? That's when we got into our discussion about time.

Our time is filled with careers, home keeping, social obligations (both the required and fun kinds), television, computers, and a continuous barrage of temptations from movies, malls, and new and improved things to try.

We've forgotten—or never learned—how to just be. We never have the time to linger in a garden, park, or art gallery. We have many old friends who live within a day's drive whom we never see—none of us has the time, but we keep promising one another that "some weekend this fall..." We live by the clock, everywhere. Our creativity has gone into our work (which we both love), but it's all outside of us. We have no balance. Even our relaxation and fun are scheduled and pressured by time.

We spent most of Saturday sitting in our backyard, which is lovely. We usually just look at it in passing or glance at it over the newspaper. We ate brunch there, and lunch, and even napped for a while. We could hear the messages piling up on our machine, and this kept us a little on edge. So we cheated a little—we listened to messages twice a day.

We talked about our personal yearnings. I can't even draw a tree, but I've always wanted to paint. And I've wanted to make quilts but don't have the slightest idea how to begin, and haven't had time to find out. Bill has spent years waiting for time to take guitar lessons and rekindle his love for photography. Each of us had assumed that somehow time would automatically open up, or that maybe when we retired…We attacked our assumptions with great vigor. Who was going to step in and give us this time we craved? How would we feel if we got to retirement and didn't have the health or opportunity to ever dabble in some creative adventures? What about the next twenty-plus years before retirement?

Saturday evening we left the house and drove to a secluded lookout to watch the sunset. We lingered there, holding hands on a park bench. It was magical.

By Sunday we realized we have to do something about our lives. We love each other deeply, we're best friends, and in a crisis we're always there for each other. But somehow we've lost our vitality, our spontaneity, our personal creativity. Our lives aren't in balance, either for ourselves or for each other. When we're stressed with our own frustrations, we often take it out on each other. We don't want to live this way anymore.

Our goal is to really examine our work lives, and within six months we'll take Fridays off to be together, whether it's going and doing or just hanging out. We need to know we'll have sustained, unhurried time with each other on a regular, predictable basis. We know we won't have the time, so we must make the time. It'll never happen without major surgery to our busy lives.

We've been living but we haven't been growing, so we're each going to do some personal expanding. This is exciting stuff. And so my first project will be to make a quilt for you, because you're my best friend and you'll be celebrating your tenth anniversary in a year (which is about how long this will take—if it's small) and because you'll love it even if it isn't perfect.

This was the best weekend of my life.

Pru
Quoted in *From the Heart: Men and Women Write
Their Private Thoughts About Their Married Lives*
by Dale Atkins and Meris Powell

Dawn love is silver,
Wait for the west:
Old love is gold love—
Old love is best.

Katharine Lee Bates
"For a Golden Wedding"

Love is not simply a feeling of romantic excitement; it is more than a desire to marry a potential partner; it goes beyond intense sexual attraction; it exceeds the thrill at having "captured" a highly desirable social prize. These are emotions that are unleashed at first sight, but they *do not constitute love.* I wish the whole world knew that fact. These temporary feelings differ from love in that they place the spotlight on the one experiencing them. "What is happening to *me?!* This is the most fantastic thing *I've* ever been through! *I* think *I* am in love!" You see, these emotions are selfish in the sense that they are motivated by our gratification. They have little to do with the new lover. Such a person has not fallen in love with another person; *he has fallen in love with love!* And there is an enormous difference between the two...

Real love, in contrast to popular notions, is an expression of the deepest appreciation for another human being; it is an intense awareness of his or her needs and longings—past, present, and future. It is unselfish and giving and caring. And believe me, friends, these are not attitudes one "falls" into at first sight, as though we were tumbling into a ditch. I have developed a lifelong love for my wife, but it was not something I fell into. I *grew* into it, and that process took time.

Dr. James C. Dobson
What Wives Wish Their Husbands Knew about Women

One dollar and eighty-seven cents. That was all. And sixty cents of it was in pennies. Pennies saved one and two at a time by bulldozing the grocer and the vegetable man and the butcher until one's cheeks burned with the silent imputation of parsimony that such close dealing implied. Three times Della counted it. One dollar and eighty-seven cents. And the next day would be Christmas.

There was clearly nothing to do but flop down on the shabby little couch and howl. So Della did it. Which instigates the moral reflection that life is made up of sobs, sniffles, and smiles, with sniffles predominating.

While the mistress of the home is gradually subsiding from the first stage to the second, take a look at the home. A furnished flat at $8 per week. It did not exactly beggar description, but it certainly had that word on the lookout for the mendicancy squad.

In the vestibule below was a letter-box into which no letter would go, and an electric button from which no mortal finger could coax a ring. Also appertaining thereunto was a card bearing the name "Mr. James Dillingham Young."

The "Dillingham" had been flung to the breeze during a former period of prosperity when its possessor was being paid $30 per week. Now, when the income was shrunk to $20, the letters of "Dillingham" looked blurred, as though they were thinking seriously of contracting to a modest and unassuming D. But whenever Mr. James Dillingham Young came home and reached his flat above he was called "Jim" and greatly hugged by Mrs. James Dillingham Young, already introduced to you as Della. Which is all very good.

Della finished her cry and attended to her cheeks with the powder rag. She stood by the window and looked out dully at a gray cat walking a gray fence in a gray backyard. Tomorrow would be Christmas Day and she had only $1.87 with which to buy Jim a present. She had been saving every penny she could for months, with this result. Twenty dollars a week doesn't go far. Expenses had been greater than she had calculated. They always are. Only $1.87 to buy a present for Jim. Her Jim. Many a happy hour she had spent planning for something nice for him. Something fine and rare and sterling—something just a little bit near to being worthy of the honor of being owned by Jim.

There was a pier-glass between the windows of the room. Perhaps you have seen a pier-glass in an $8 flat. A very thin and very agile person may, by observing his reflection in a rapid sequence of longitudinal strips, obtain a fairly accurate conception of his looks. Della, being slender, had mastered the art.

Suddenly she whirled from the window and stood before the glass. Her eyes were shining brilliantly, but her face had lost its color within twenty seconds. Rapidly she pulled down her hair and let it fall to its full length.

Now, there were two possessions of the James Dillingham Youngs in which they both took a mighty pride. One was Jim's gold watch that had been his father's and his grandfather's. The other was Della's hair. Had the queen of Sheba lived in the flat across the airshaft, Della would have let her hair hang out the window some day to dry just to depreciate Her Majesty's jewels and gifts. Had

King Solomon been the janitor, with all his treasures piled up in the basement, Jim would have pulled out his watch every time he passed, just to see him pluck at his beard from envy.

So now Della's beautiful hair fell about her rippling and shining like a cascade of brown waters. It reached below her knee and made itself almost a garment for her. And then she did it up again nervously and quickly. Once she faltered for a minute and stood still while a tear or two splashed on the worn red carpet.

On went her old brown jacket; on went her old brown hat. With a whirl of skirts and with the brilliant sparkle still in her eyes, she fluttered out the door and down the stairs to the street.

Where she stopped the sign read: "Mme. Sofronie. Hair Goods of All Kinds." One flight up Della ran, and collected herself, panting. Madame, large, too white, chilly, hardly looked the "Sofronie."

"Will you buy my hair?" asked Della.

"I buy hair," said Madame. "Take yer hat off and let's have a sight at the looks of it."

Down rippled the brown cascade.

"Twenty dollars," said Madame, lifting the mass with a practised hand.

"Give it to me quick," said Della.

Oh, and the next two hours tripped by on rosy wings. Forget the hashed metaphor. She was ransacking the stores for Jim's present.

She found it at last. It surely had been made for Jim and no one else. There was no other like it in any of the stores, and she had turned all of them inside out. It was a platinum fob chain simple and chaste in design, properly proclaiming its value by substance alone and not by meretricious ornamentation—as all good things should do. It was even worthy of The Watch. As soon as she saw it she knew that it must be Jim's. It was like him. Quietness and value—the description applied to both. Twenty-one dollars they took from her for it, and she hurried home with the 87 cents. With that chain on his watch Jim might be properly anxious about the time in any company. Grand as the watch was, he sometimes looked at it on the sly on account of the old leather strap that he used in place of a chain.

When Della reached home her intoxication gave way a little to prudence and reason. She got out her curling irons and lighted the gas and went to work repairing the ravages made by generosity added to love. Which is always a tremendous task, dear friends—a mammoth task.

Within forty minutes her head was covered with tiny, close-lying curls that made her look wonderfully like a truant schoolboy. She looked at her reflection in the mirror long, carefully, and critically.

"If Jim doesn't kill me," she said to herself, "before he takes a second look at me, he'll say I look like a Coney Island chorus girl. But what could I do—oh! what could I do with a dollar and eighty-seven cents?"

At 7 o'clock the coffee was made and the frying-pan was on the back of the stove hot and ready to cook the chops.

Jim was never late. Della doubled the fob chain in her hand and sat on the corner of the table near the door that he always entered. Then she heard his step on the stair away down on the first flight, and she turned white for just a moment. She had a habit of saying little silent prayers about the simplest everyday things, and now she whispered: "Please God, make him think I am still pretty."

The door opened and Jim stepped in and closed it. He looked thin and very serious. Poor fellow, he was only twenty-two—and to be burdened with a family! He needed a new overcoat and he was without gloves.

Jim stepped inside the door, as immovable as a setter at the scent of quail. His eyes were fixed upon Della, and there was an expression in them that she could not read, and it terrified her. It was not anger, nor surprise, nor disapproval, nor horror, nor any of the sentiments that she had been prepared for. He simply stared at her fixedly with that peculiar expression on his face.

Della wriggled off the table and went for him.

"Jim, darling," she cried, "don't look at me that way. I had my hair cut off and sold it because I couldn't have lived through Christmas without giving you a present. It'll grow out again—you won't mind, will you? I just had to do it. My hair grows awfully fast. Say 'Merry Christmas!' Jim, and let's be happy. You don't know what a nice—what a beautiful, nice gift I've got for you."

"You've cut off your hair?" asked Jim, laboriously, as if he had not arrived at that patent fact yet even after the hardest mental labor.

"Cut it off and sold it," said Della. "Don't you like me just as well, anyhow? I'm me without my hair, ain't I?"

Jim looked about the room curiously.

"You say your hair is gone?" he said, with an air almost of idiocy.

"You needn't look for it," said Della. "It's sold, I tell you—sold and gone, too. It's Christmas Eve, boy. Be good to me, for it went for you. Maybe the hairs on my head were numbered," she went on with sudden serious sweetness, "but nobody could ever count my love for you. Shall I put the chops on, Jim?"

Out of his trance Jim seemed quickly to wake. He enfolded his Della. For ten seconds let us regard with discreet scrutiny some inconsequential object in the other direction. Eight dollars a week or a million a year—what is the difference? A mathematician or a wit would give you the wrong answer. The magi brought valuable gifts, but that was not among them. This dark assertion will be illuminated later on.

Jim drew a package from his overcoat pocket and threw it upon the table.

"Don't make any mistake, Dell," he said, "about me. I don't think there's anything in the way of a haircut or a shave or a shampoo that could make me like my girl any less. But if you'll unwrap that package you may see why you had me going a while at first."

White fingers and nimble tore at the string and paper. And then an ecstatic scream of joy; and then, alas! a quick feminine change to hysterical tears and wails, necessitating the immediate employment of all the comforting powers of the lord of the flat.

For there lay The Combs—the set of combs, side and back, that Della had worshipped for long in a Broadway window. Beautiful combs, pure tortoise shell, with jewelled rims—just the shade to wear in the beautiful vanished hair. They were expensive combs, she knew, and her heart had simply craved and yearned over them without the least hope of possession. And now, they were hers, but the tresses that should have adorned the coveted adornments were gone.

But she hugged them to her bosom, and at length she was able to look up with dim eyes and a smile and say: "My hair grows so fast, Jim!"

And then Della leaped up like a little singed cat and cried, "Oh, oh!"

Jim had not yet seen his beautiful present. She held it out to him eagerly upon her open palm. The dull precious metal seemed to flash with a reflection of her bright and ardent spirit.

"Isn't it a dandy, Jim? I hunted all over town to find it. You'll have to look at the time a hundred times a day now. Give me your watch. I want to see how it looks on it."

Instead of obeying, Jim tumbled down on the couch and put his hands under the back of his head and smiled.

"Dell," said he, "let's put our Christmas presents away and keep 'em a while.

They're too nice to use just at present. I sold the watch to get the money to buy your combs. And now suppose you put the chops on."

The magi, as you know, were wise men—wonderfully wise men—who brought gifts to the Babe in the manger. They invented the art of giving Christmas presents. Being wise, their gifts were no doubt wise ones, possibly bearing the privilege of exchange in case of duplication. And here I have lamely related to you the uneventful chronicle of two foolish children in a flat who most unwisely sacrificed for each other the greatest treasures of their house. But in a last word to the wise of these days let it be said that of all who give gifts these two were the wisest. Of all who give and receive gifts, such as they are wisest. Everywhere they are wisest. They are the magi.

O. Henry
The Gift of the Magi

When you love you wish to do things for. You wish to sacrifice for. You wish to serve.

Ernest Hemingway
A Farewell to Arms

Love is that condition in which the happiness of another person is essential to your own.

Robert A. Heinlein
Stranger in a Strange Land

Far too many young people approach marriage with a romantic and egocentric attitude, full of daydreams which are concerned with *getting,* never with *giving.* They have not progressed emotionally beyond the "gimme" stage. Such an attitude is not only wishful thinking, it is turning the church aisle into a warpath. Here the desire for a happy home is only a desire for the benefits of a happy home, not a readiness to accept the responsibility and the work of producing the necessary conditions to create a happy home. This is expecting too much. Of course it leads to bitter disillusionment. Daydreaming of the end result, with no regard for means, is only silly sentimentalism.

Richard M. Magoun
Love and Marriage

Real marriage is sacrificing your ego, not for the other person, but for the relationship.

Oprah Winfrey
Quoted in *Ladies Home Journal*, May 1990

There will be less disillusion and heartache in marriage when we begin to understand that from the illusions of romance a deep and abiding love may emerge. *Love is the passionate and abiding desire on the part of two or more people to produce together conditions under which each can be, and spontaneously express, his real self; to produce together an intellectual soil and an emotional climate in which each can flourish, far superior to what either could achieve alone.* In a true marriage, man and woman think more *of the partnership* than they do of themselves. It is an interweaving of interests and a facing of sacrifice together for the sake of both. Its feeling of security and contentment comes from mutual efforts. In marriage, as in dancing, the happiness does not stem from the way the individual moves, but in the togetherness of the behavior…

We may think we are in love because of the way another person makes us feel, but love is not delight in ME, love is self-realization together in us.

F. Alexander Magoun
Love and Marriage

So ought men to love their wives as their own bodies. He that loveth his wife loveth himself.

Ephesians 5:28

Passionate love is a fragile flower; it wilts in time. Companionate love is a sturdy evergreen; it thrives with contact.

Elaine Walster and G. William Walster
A New Look at Love

I define a healthy marriage as: Two people who have committed themselves to take individual responsibility to work together for the fulfillment of each other…

The healthy relationship is the collaborative marriage relationship. Here two people have individually committed themselves to the marriage relationship and have stepped inside the marriage circle. They remain within the marriage boundaries because they continue to choose to do so. They maintain their own individuality, yet work together as a team. They are not overly dependent upon each other, nor are they trying to escape from each other. The optimal marital commitment is demonstrated by the collaborative relationship in which both people are cooperatively committed to each other and to Jesus Christ.

In summary, healthy marriages are not made up of people who live under the illusion of having a perfect marriage, nor do they need to be married to the perfect partner. Instead, healthy marriages consist of people who are committed to the process of growing and living together. They are dedicated to understanding and adjusting to each other. They accept the complex task of mutual adjustment.

David Field
Marriage Personalities

There is nothing nobler or more admirable than when two people who see eye to eye keep house as man and wife, confounding their enemies and delighting their friends.

Homer
Odyssey

Life has taught us that love does not consist in gazing at each other but in looking outward together in the same direction.

Antoine de Saint-Exupéry
Wind, Sand, and Stars

It was a momentous day for us when, nine years after we met and seven years after we were married, Ralph finally had both graduate school and the Navy behind him, and was able to open his office. There had been plenty of sacrifice on both our parts, and we had looked forward to this day for a long, long time.

Several weeks after Ralph was officially open for business, I picked him up after work and we decided to stop at our favorite ice-cream parlor on the way home.

"Hi, Ralph. Hi, Louise," said our waitress. "Don't tell me—one hot-fudge sundae with vanilla, one dish of butter pecan, and bring the hot fudge on the side so you can split it, right?"

(It's almost frightening when people know you that well.)

"No," said Ralph, "we are entering a new era in our lives. We will have two hot-fudge sundaes."

Then we went across the street to the nearest department store and bought Ralph his first full-price, nonirregular shirt.

"Maybe this is premature," I said anxiously to Ralph, who was counting out $12.00 in nickels, dimes, and quarters for the sales clerk. (Business wasn't exactly booming yet.)

Then we went home for a steak dinner, a bottle of wine, and an acute depressive reaction.

"This is going to sound absurd," said Ralph, "but what is there to live for when you can buy two hot-fudge sundaes outright?"

"You know," I said, "that's exactly what I was thinking."

We were silent for a moment, reminiscing.

"Remember when you graduated from school," I said, "and we traded in Aunt Mara's Cross pen for a top sheet?"

Ralph brightened immediately. "Remember how we used to get my shirts at that outlet store on the Lower East Side that sold irregulars? The ones where the buttonholes never matched up to the button and you had to make sure they had two sleeves?"

"Yes, but they were great bargains," I recalled. "Remember how we'd go to Chinatown afterward and get pork fried rice and drink tea out of hospital glasses at that really cheap place where you got food poisoning?"

"Those were the days," said Ralph wistfully. "You know, I wish I hadn't bought that shirt. I thought it was going to make me so happy."

"We could always return it," I said tentatively. "Real stores let you return things."

"All these years I've been working toward this day, to be out of school, to be through with the Navy, to open up my own office. The Big Reward."

"Well, I guess this is the Big Reward," I said. "Feel any different?"

"No," said Ralph. "You?"

"No," I said.

We were silent for a while.

"I guess I never really realized it before," said Ralph finally.

"Realized what?" I said.

Ralph smiled wryly. "That the Big Reward was all along."

Louise DeGrave
From This Day Forward

The early excited years together had settled into a passionate affection so unexpected to both of us that we were as shy and careful with each other as courting children. Without words, we knew that we had survived for the best of all reasons, the pleasure of each other.

Lillian Hellman
Pentimento

Being a

GOOD PARENT

BEING A GOOD PARENT

—⦿⦿—

There's no vocabulary
For love within a family, love that's lived in
But not looked at, love within the light of which
All else is seen, the love within which
All other love finds speech.
This love is silent.

T. S. Eliot
The Elder Statesman

Govern a family as you would cook a small fish—very gently.

Chinese proverb

To make a happy fire-side clim
To weans and wife,
That's the true pathos and sublime
Of human life.

Robert Burns
"To Dr. Blacklock"

How can love, hate, cherishing, rejection, pity, and broken promises all coexist without canceling each other out? Such mysteries are the heart of family bonds; they transcend analysis.

Elizabeth Peer
Quoted in *Newsweek*, July 24, 1978

There is little less trouble in governing a private family than a whole kingdom.

Michel Eyquem de Montaigne
Essays

Bringing up a family should be an adventure, not an anxious discipline in which everybody is constantly graded for performance.

Milton R. Sapirstein
Paradoxes of Everyday Life

Here all mankind is equal: rich and poor alike, they love their children.

Euripides
Heracles

The character and history of each child may be a new and poetic experience to the parent, if he will let it.

Margaret Fuller
Summer on the Lakes

You may give them [your children] your love but not your thoughts,
For they have their own thoughts.
You may house their bodies but not their souls.
For their souls dwell in the house of tomorrow, which you cannot visit, not
even in your dreams.

Kahlil Gibran
The Prophet

We never know the love of our parents for us till we have become parents.

Henry Ward Beecher
Proverbs from Plymouth Pulpit

Parents lend children their experience and a vicarious memory; children endow their parents with a vicarious immortality.

George Santayana
The Life of Reason: Reason in Society

Children know the grace of God
Better than most of us. They see the world
The way the morning brings it back to them.
New and born and fresh and wonderful.

Archibald MacLeish
JB

That energy which makes a child hard to manage is the energy which afterward makes him a manager of life.

Henry Ward Beecher
Proverbs from Plymouth Pulpit

Children are God's apostles, day by day
Sent forth to preach of love, and hope, and peace.

James Russell Lowell
"On the Death of a Friend's Child"

Marriage partners are to…raise their children honorably, lovingly, and with detachment. A child is a guest in the house, to be loved and respected—never possessed, since he belongs to God. How wonderful, how sane, how beautifully difficult, and therefore true. The joy of responsibility for the first time in my life.

J. D. Salinger
Raise High the Roof Beam, Carpenters

Cleaning your house while your kids are still growing is like shoveling the walk before it stops snowing.

Phyllis Diller
Quoted in *Women's Day*, May 13, 1997

Blessed be childhood, which brings down something of heaven into the midst of our rough earthliness.

Henri Frédéric Amiel
Journal

If you will stop and think a minute—if you will go back 50 to 100 years to your early married life and recontemplate your first baby—you will remember that he amounted to a good deal, and even something over. You soldiers all know that when that little fellow arrived at family headquarters you had to hand in your resignation. He took entire command. You became his lackey—his mere body-servant, and you had to stand around, too. He was not a commander who made allowances for time, distance, weather, or anything else. You had to execute his order whether it was possible or not. And there was only one form of marching in his manual of tactics, and that was the double-quick. He treated you with every sort of insolence and disrespect, and the bravest of you didn't dare to say a word. You could face the death storm of Donelson and Vicksburg, and give back blow for blow, but when he clawed your whiskers, and pulled your hair, and twisted your nose, you had to take it. When the thunders of war were sounding in your ears you set your faces toward the batteries, and advanced with steady tread, but, when he turned on the terrors of his war-whoop, you advanced in the other direction, and mighty glad of the chance too.

Mark Twain
"The Babies"
Speech to a reunion of the Armies of the Tennessee,
printed in the *Chicago Tribune*, November 14, 1879

'I have no name:
I am but two days old.'
What shall I call thee?
'I happy am.
Joy is my name.'
Sweet joy befall thee!
Pretty Joy!
Sweet Joy, but two days old,
Sweet Joy, I call thee:

Thou dost smile,
I sing the while,
Sweet joy befall thee!

William Blake
"Infant Joy," *Songs of Innocence*

The right moment to begin the requisite moral training is the moment of birth, because then it can be begun without disappointing expectations.

Bertrand Russell
On Education, especially in Early Childhood

...The finches sing my thoughts away. I feel so happy, so green and so full of shoots. Over my head sits a little bird with beautifully shiny feathers, soulful eyes and vibrancy in his voice.

"Take spring when it comes, and rejoice...Take happiness when it comes, and rejoice...Take love when it comes, and rejoice..."

The sun shines, the anemones nod in the wind. The trees are budding while the worms burrow and the earth is full of eggs and seeds.

I bow to the law of God...Here where everything is birth and spring I pray for the child which is being born to me.

He shall grow up among the people of the earth as the anemones here—with his feet in the soil and his face lifted high toward the brilliant sun. He shall grow strong and straight...May he be a gentleman of life. May his curiosity be fathomless, like his courage, his passion, his love and his anger...

May he find God Eternal...

This I promise: I shall cast no shadow over his youth, nor break his spirit, nor make my old clothes over to fit him. I shall acknowledge him when he appears in the oddest garb and with the strangest speech.

I shall grant him his dreams...

Carl Ewald
"My Little Boy/My Big Girl"

The best learning occurs in the context of a shared experience. When an adult leaves the parental perch to come alongside the child, something special happens.

At that moment, the parent asks to be invited into the child's world. Your aim as a parent should be to find some creative ways to capitalize on the child's mental and emotional eagerness.

...there is more to helping your child shine than showing up with the proper equipment. Activities with your child should tap enthusiasm for learning and supply healthy doses of confidence and self-worth in the process.

Kenny Luck
52 Ways to Nurture Your Child's Natural Abilities

None of us is perfect, and there is room in this world for every individual into whom an eternal soul has been breathed. My advice is to take the child God sends to you and "go with the flow." You and he will be much more contented for it!

Dr. James C. Dobson
Parenting Isn't for Cowards

During a prayer time, as I cried out to the Lord for help with my temper, especially with my son, an idea formed I believe was heaven-sent because it made a difference.

I was to pray with Marty before I administered any form of discipline. Sometimes those prayers sounded strange and strained as I almost shouted, "Dear Lord, help this miserable little boy and help his miserable mommy who wants so desperately to raise him in a way that would honor You."

By the time I said "amen," I was almost a reasonable person. I was able to see past my emotions and do what was in Marty's best interest.

Sometimes he needed a firm hand, but he was dealt with in love instead of anger, and the moment drew us together instead of tearing us apart. Many times all he needed was time and a mother's tender touch.

But one day that boy really ticked me off! I remember heading across the room for him like a high-speed locomotive, steam coming out all sides. I had one goal and intent—get the kid, get the kid, get the kid!

Just as I loomed over him, his eyes the size of saucers, he held up one hand and yelled, "Let's pray!"

Marty had learned a valuable lesson in life: "When Mommy talks to Jesus, we're all a lot better off."

Patsy Clairmont
God Uses Cracked Pots

Through your honesty children learn that it's okay to be less than perfect. Having faults, worries, and failures does not make a person weird or inferior. On the contrary, it is the strong person who can admit his weaknesses.

Dr. Kevin Leman
Making Children Mind Without Losing Yours

The real menace in dealing with a five-year-old is that in no time at all you begin to sound like a five-year-old.

Jean Kerr
Please Don't Eat the Daisies

I call that parent rash and wild
Who'd reason with a six-year child,
Believing little twigs are bent
By calm considered argument.

Phyllis McGinley
"The Velvet Hand"

The rod and reproof give wisdom, but a child left to himself bringeth his mother shame.

Proverbs 29:15

It is alleged by a friend of my family that I used to suffer from insomnia at the age of four; and that when she asked me how I managed to occupy my time at night I answered: 'I lie awake and think about the past.'

Ronald Knox
Literary Distractions

It goes without saying that you should never have more children than you have car windows.

Erma Bombeck
Quoted in *Women's Day*, May 5, 1997

Thou pretty opening rose!
(Go to your mother, child, and wipe your nose!)
Balmy and breathing music like the South,
(He really brings my heart into my mouth!)
Fresh as the morn, and brilliant as its star,—
(I wish that window had an iron bar!)
Bold as the hawk, yet gentle as the dove,—
(I'll tell you what, my love,
I cannot write, unless he's sent above!)

Thomas Hood
"A Parental Ode to my Son, Aged Three Years and Five Months"

Seventeen—certainly the age when sons react most strongly against their parents.
Stephen Spender
World Within World

Some parents may argue with me, but I still believe that Mother and Dad always remain the key role models for their children. I realize the power of the peer group is great. And I realize that as children get older they often are deeply impressed by a certain teacher, coach, or even a movie star or professional athlete. But the ones they live with day in and day out are their parents. Your children do learn by watching you and, believe me, they watch much more carefully than you would ever imagine.

Dr. Kevin Leman
Making Children Mind Without Losing Yours

Last year, when Jeffrey turned fourteen and Matilda twelve, they had begun to change; to grow rude, coarse, selfish, insolent, nasty, brutish and tall. It was as if she were keeping a boarding house in a bad dream, and the children she loved were turning into awful lodgers—lodgers who paid no rent, whose leases could not be terminated. They were awful at home and abroad; in company and alone; in the morning, the afternoon and the evening.

Alison Lurie
The War Between the Tates

At sixteen, the adolescent knows about suffering because he himself has suffered, but he barely knows that other beings also suffer; seeing without feeling is not knowledge.

Jean Jacques Rousseau
Emile

Neither must we think, that the life of Man begins when he can feed himself or walk alone, when he can fight, or beget his like; for so he is contemporary with a camel, or a cow; but he is first a man when he comes to a certain, steady use of reason, according to his proportion, and when that is, all the world of men cannot tell precisely. Some are called *at age*, at fourteen, some at one and twenty, some never; but all men, late enough; for the life of a man comes upon him slowly and insensibly.

Jeremy Taylor
The Rule and Exercises of Holy Dying, 1650

I hid myself within myself, I only considered myself and quietly wrote down all my joys, sorrows and contempt in my diary...I used to be furious with Mummy, and still am sometimes. It's true that she doesn't understand me, but I don't understand her either.

Anne Frank
The Diary of a Young Girl

There is nothing wrong with being human, but there is a great deal wrong with being hypocritical. I believe that when I freely admit my humanness to my children, I am taking advantage of an ideal opportunity to teach them dependence upon the grace of God. As I admit to my children that I don't always have all the answers and as I pray with them and share with them, they see me depending upon the strength of the Holy Spirit and my walk with Jesus Christ as I deal with the everyday hassles of life.

Dr. Kevin Leman
Making Children Mind Without Losing Yours

If you can keep your head when all about you
Are losing theirs and blaming it on you;

If you can trust yourself when all men doubt you,
But make allowance for their doubting too;
If you can wait and not be tired by waiting,
Or being lied about, don't deal in lies,
Or being hated don't give way to hating,
And yet don't look too good, nor talk too wise:

If you can dream—and not make dreams your master;
If you can think—and not make thoughts your aim;
If you can meet with Triumph and Disaster
And treat those two impostors just the same;
If you can bear to hear the truth you've spoken
Twisted by knaves to make a trap for fools,
Or watch the things you gave your life to, broken,
And stop and build 'em up with worn-out tools:

If you can make one heap of all your winnings
And risk it on one turn of pitch-and-toss,
And lose, and start again at your beginnings
And never breathe a word about your loss;
If you can force your heart and nerve and sinew
To serve your turn long after they are gone,
And so hold on when there is nothing in you
Except the Will which says to them: "Hold on!"

If you can walk with crowds and keep your virtue,
Or walk with Kings—nor lose the common touch,
If neither foes nor loving friends can hurt you,
If all men count with you, but none too much;
If you can fill the unforgiving minute
With sixty seconds' worth of distance run,
Yours is the earth and everything that's in it,
And—which is more—you'll be a Man, my son.

Rudyard Kipling
"If"

If you are only half convinced of your beliefs, [your children] will quickly discern that fact. Any ethical weak spot—any indecision on your part—will be incorporated and then magnified in your sons and daughters. Like it or not, we are on the hook. Their faith or faithlessness will be a reflection of our own...our children will eventually make their own choices and set the course of their lives, but those decisions will be influenced by the foundations we have laid. Someone said, "The footsteps a boy follows are the ones his father thought he covered up." It is true.

Dr. James C. Dobson
Parenting Isn't for Cowards

Children are the anchors that hold a mother to life.

Sophocles
Phaedra

The mother-child relationship is paradoxical and, in a sense, tragic. It requires the most intense love on the mother's side, yet this very love must help the child grow away from the mother, and to become fully independent.

Erich Fromm
The Sane Society

I opine..."Judicious mothers will always keep in mind, that they are the first book read, and the last put aside, in every child's library."

C. Lenox Remond
*The Mind of the Negro As Reflected in Letters
Written During the Crisis, 1800-1860*

The ideal mother, like the ideal marriage, is a fiction.

Milton R. Sapirstein
Paradoxes of Everyday Life

Some are kissing mothers and some are scolding mothers, but it is love just the same, and most mothers kiss and scold together.

Pearl S. Buck
To My Daughters, With Love

...You had a dam that loved you well,
That did what could be done for young,
And nursed you up till you were strong,
And 'fore she once would let you fly,
She showed you joy and misery;
Taught what was good, and what was ill,
What would save life, and what would kill.
Thus gone, amongst you I may live,
And dead, yet speak, and counsel give:
Farewell, my birds; farewell, adieu,
I happy am, if well with you.

Anne Dudley Bradstreet
"In Reference to Her Children"

I remember one summer, living in a friend's house in Vermont. My husband was working abroad for several weeks, and my three sons—nine, seven, and five years old—and I dwelt for most of that time by ourselves. Without a male adult in the house, without any reason for schedules, naps, regular mealtimes, or early bedtimes so the two parents could talk, we fell into what I felt to be a delicious and sinful rhythm. It was a spell of unusually hot, clear weather, and we ate nearly all our meals outdoors, hand-to-mouth; we lived half-naked, stayed up to watch bats and stars and fireflies, read and told stories, slept late...I remember thinking: This is what living with children could be—without school hours, fixed routines, naps, the conflict of being both mother and wife with no room for being, simply, myself. Driving home once after midnight from a late drive-in movie, through the foxfire and stillness of a winding Vermont road, with three sleeping children in the back of the car, I felt wide awake, elated; we had broken together all the rules of bedtime, the night rules, rules I myself thought I had to observe in the city or become a "bad mother." We were conspirators, outlaws from the institution of motherhood; I felt enormously in charge of my life.

Adrienne Rich
"Of Woman Born"

Her children rise up, and call her blessed; her husband also, and he praiseth her.
Proverbs 31:28

A father is a banker provided by nature.

French proverb

There never was a child so lovely but his mother was glad to get him asleep.

Ralph Waldo Emerson
Journals, 1836

Once, when ransacking the barn with my brothers for eggs, I somehow slipped under a mass of hay, and was so oppressed by it, and so scared, that I could scarcely make a sound. Robert heard my faint cries, but could not find me, and he ran to call my father, who, with some friends who happened to be with him, soon extricated me. From their caresses and conversation I inferred that my danger of suffocation had been imminent…How brightly are some points in our childhood's path illuminated, while all along, before and behind, the track is dim or lost in utter darkness! We can not always recall the feeling that fixed these bright passages in our memory. They are the shrines for our hearts' saints, and there the light never goes out.

Catherine Maria Segwick
From Recollections of Childhood

This is what a father ought to be about: helping his son to form the habit of doing right on his own initiative, rather than because he's afraid of some serious consequence.

Terence
The Brothers

…I ran up the steps and into the house. Aunt Alexandra had gone to bed, and Atticus's room was dark. I would see if Jem might be reviving. Atticus was in Jem's room, sitting by his bed. He was reading a book.

"Is Jem awake yet?"

"Sleeping peacefully. He won't be awake until morning."

"Oh. Are you sittin' up with him?"

"Just for an hour or so. Go to bed, Scout. You've had a long day."

"Well, I think I'll stay with you for a while."

"Suit yourself," said Atticus. It must have been after midnight, and I was puzzled by his amiable acquiescence. He was shrewder than I, however; the moment I sat down I began to feel sleepy.

"Whatcha readin'?" I asked.

Atticus turned the book over. "Something of Jem's. Called *The Gray Ghost...*"

"Read it out loud, please, Atticus. It's real scary."...

I moved over and leaned my head against his knee...

I willed myself to stay awake, but the rain was so soft and the room was so warm and his voice was so deep and his knee was so snug that I slept.

Seconds later, it seemed, his shoe was gently nudging my ribs. He lifted me to my feet and walked me to my room...

His hands were under my chin, pulling up the cover, tucking it around me.

He turned out the light and went into Jem's room. He would be there all night, and he would be there when Jem waked up in the morning.

Harper Lee
To Kill a Mockingbird

There must always be a struggle between a father and son, while one aims at power and the other at independence.

Samuel Johnson
Quoted in *The Life of Samuel Johnson*

When my grown children confess what they did behind my back when they were kids, it doesn't occur to them that I was also doing a few things behind their backs. In the spirit of fairness to my wife and children, I confess:

I used the wok once to change the oil in the car.

And I used the sewing scissors to cut canvas.

I used the kitchen-sink sponge to clean my shoes...

Yes, it was me who ate the baking chocolate.

The hamsters didn't die from old age.

I deliberately left price tags on presents sometimes.

Even raised them.

I always took a private cut of the money Grandmother sent for Christmas.

I lied when I said you looked beautiful when you were a teenager...

I know who sent you anonymous cards for Valentine's Day.

I know who took money out of my wallet.

But I know you know who took money out of the piggy banks.

At times I said I missed you when, in fact, I was glad to be alone for a
   while.
I always said I was proud of you—even when I knew you could do better.
I let you lie to me sometimes because the truth was too hard for all of us.
Sometimes I said "I love you" when I didn't love anyone, not even me.
Your mother and I both played Santa Claus on Christmas Eve.
But I was always the Easter Bunny.

Robert Fulghum
Maybe (Maybe Not)

To an old father, nothing is more sweet than a daughter. Boys are more spirited,
but their ways are not so tender.

Euripides
The Suppliant Women

My dear Mellyn,
If you will:
   Receive and believe what God says,
   Treasure with high value His commandments,
   Listen attentively to His wisdom,
   Draw your heart to understanding Him,
   Cry out for discernment,
   Raise your voice for understanding,
   Seek Him more than silver or hidden treasures,
   Then, you, my daughter, will understand how to
      honor God.
God will give you knowledge and wisdom. From Him you will receive under-
standing, for God has been storing up wisdom for you because you have sought
Him above all else.
"He will be your shield, your bodyguard, and He will preserve your way"
(Proverbs 2:1-8).
I love you.
You are a woman of honor!

Marilyn Willett Heavilin
Mother to Daughter: Becoming a Woman of Honor

The Mother weeps
At that white funeral of the single life,
Her maiden daughter's marriage; and her tears
Are half of pleasure, half of pain.

Alfred, Lord Tennyson
"To H.R.H. Princess Beatrice"

Crowded lives produce fatigue—and fatigue produces irritability—and irritability produces indifference—and indifference can be interpreted by a child as a lack of genuine affection and personal esteem.

Dr. James C. Dobson
Dr. Dobson Answers Your Questions

At some distant point a daughter may be able to look at her mother with appreciation. It may take all of her adolescent years, but she eventually will realize that mothers have rights and feelings.

Girls do not want to lose their mothers' affection, although they seem to spurn it. As they get older and lose their egocentricity, they will probably tolerate their mothers' ideas. The stress that a girl feels in school and with her friends is masking her affection for her family, but if a mother can be patient, her daughter's true self will emerge again.

A twenty-five-year-old woman laughed as she recalled her adolescent fights with her mother. Their arguments were so intense, she said, that her mother was sure her daughter hated her. At one point she yelled at her mother, "How could I hate you so much if I didn't love you?" This comment really stopped her mother "in her tracks," and they both burst out laughing.

Ann F. Caron, Ed.D.
Don't Stop Loving Me

He who has daughters is always a shepherd.

Spanish proverb

Everyone calls his son his son, whether he has talents or has not talents.

K'ung Fu-tzu Confucius
Analects

Bright clasp of her whole hand around my finger,
My daughter, as we walk together now,
All my life I'll feel a ring invisibly
Circle this bone with shining: when she is grown
Far from today as her eyes are far already.

Stephen Spender
"To My Daughter"

A wise son maketh a glad father: but a foolish son is the heaviness of his mother.

Proverbs 10:1

How easily a father's tenderness is recalled, and how quickly a son's offenses vanish at the slightest words of repentance!

Molière
Don Juan

Today is Father's Day. A day of cologne. A day of hugs, new neckties, long-distance telephone calls, and Hallmark cards.

Today is my first Father's Day without a father. For thirty-one years I had one. I had one of the best. But now he's gone; he's buried under an oak tree in a west Texas cemetery. Even though he's gone, his presence is very near—especially today.

It seems strange that he isn't here. I guess that's because he was never gone. He was always close by. Always available. Always present. His words were nothing novel. His achievements, though admirable, were nothing extraordinary.

But his presence was.

Like a warm fireplace in a large house, he was a source of comfort. Like a sturdy porch swing or a big-branched elm in the backyard, he could always be found...and leaned upon.

During the turbulent years of my adolescence, Dad was one part of my life that was predictable. Girlfriends came and girlfriends went, but Dad was there. Football season turned into baseball season and turned into football season again and Dad was always there. Summer vacation, Homecoming dates, algebra, first car, driveway basketball—they all had one thing in common: his presence.

And because he was there life went smoothly. The car always ran, the bills got paid, and the lawn stayed mowed. Because he was there the laughter was fresh and the future was secure. Because he was there my growing up was what God intended growing up to be: a storybook scamper through the magic and mystery of the world.

Because he was there we kids never worried about things like income tax, saving accounts, monthly bills or mortgages. Those were the things on Daddy's desk.

We have lots of family pictures without him. Not because he wasn't there, but because he was always behind the camera.

He made the decisions, broke up the fights, chuckled at Archie Bunker, read the paper every evening, and fixed breakfast on Sundays. He didn't do anything unusual. He only did what dads are supposed to do—be there. He taught me how to shave and how to pray. He helped me memorize verses for Sunday school and taught me that wrong should be punished and that rightness has its own reward. He modeled the importance of getting up early and of staying out of debt. His life expressed the elusive balance between ambition and self-acceptance.

He comes to mind often. When I smell "Old Spice" after-shave, I think of him. When I see a bass boat I see his face. And occasionally, not too often, but occasionally when I hear a good joke, (the kind Red Skelton would tell), I hear him chuckle. He had a copyright chuckle that always came with a wide grin and arched eyebrows.

Daddy never said a word to me about sex nor told his life story. But I knew that if I ever wanted to know, he would tell me. All I had to do was ask. And I knew if I ever needed him he'd be there.

Like a warm fireplace.

Maybe that's why this Father's Day is a bit chilly. The fire has gone out. The winds of age swallowed the last splendid flame, leaving only golden embers. But there is a strange thing about those embers. Stir them a bit and a flame will dance. It will dance only briefly, but it will dance. And it will knock just enough chill out of the air to remind me that he is still…in a special way, very present.

Max Lucado
God Came Near

Jesus continued: "There was a man who had two sons. The younger one said to his father, 'Father, give me my share of the estate.' So he divided his property between them.

"Not long after that, the younger son got together all he had, set off for a distant country and there squandered his wealth in wild living. After he had spent everything, there was a severe famine in that whole country, and he began to be in need. So he went and hired himself out to a citizen of that country, who sent him to his fields to feed pigs. He longed to fill his stomach with the pods that the pigs were eating, but no one gave him anything.

"When he came to his senses, he said, 'How many of my father's hired men have food to spare, and he to spare, and here I am starving to death! I will set out and go back to my father and say to him: Father, I have sinned against heaven and against you. I am no longer worthy to be called your son; make me like one of your hired men.' So he got up and went to his father. But while he was still a long way off, his father saw him and was filled with compassion for him; he ran to his son, threw his arms around him and kissed him.

"The son said to him, 'Father, I have sinned against heaven and against you. I am no longer worthy to be called your son.'

"But the father said to his servants, 'Quick! Bring the best robe and put it on him. Put a ring on his finger and sandals on his feet. Bring the fattened calf and kill it. Let's have a feast and celebrate. For this son of mine was dead and is alive again; he was lost and is found.' So they began to celebrate.

"Meanwhile, the older son was in the field. When he came near the house, he heard music and dancing. So he called one of the servants and asked him what was going on. 'Your brother has come,' he replied, 'and your father has killed the fattened calf because he has him back safe and sound.'

"The older brother became angry and refused to go in. So his father went out and pleaded with him. But he answered his father, 'Look! All these years I've been slaving for you and never disobeyed your orders. Yet you never gave me even a young goat so I could celebrate with my friends. But when this son of yours who has squandered your property with prostitutes comes home, you kill the fattened calf for him!'

"'My son,' the father said, 'you are always with me, and everything I have is yours. But we had to celebrate and be glad, because this brother of yours was dead and is alive again; he was lost and is found.'"

Luke 15:11-32 (NIV)

Sons have always a rebellious wish to be disillusioned by that which charmed their fathers.

Aldous Huxley
Music at Night

You don't raise heroes, you raise sons. And if you treat them like sons, they'll turn out to be heroes, even if it's just in your own eyes.

Walter Schirra, Sr.
This Week, February 3, 1963

And, ye fathers, provoke not your children to wrath, but bring them up in the nurture and admonition of the Lord.

Ephesians 6:4

When you encourage your teen in the context of a biblical relationship, you are offering a powerful motivator for right behavior. Outside that context, however, encouraging words can sound hypocritical. The comments of a father who does not take the time to establish a trusting relationship with his son or daughter are meaningless. Hearing an encouraging word is not the same as having an encouraging parent.

Unfortunately, this is an area in which many parents fail, particularly during the teen years. During this time, parents are so preoccupied with getting things under control by continually correcting, they generally forget to encourage. And as we all know from personal experience, the absence of encouragement is the same thing as discouragement.

There are a number of ways to encourage teens…Verbal praise, physical touch, simple gifts, spending time together, acts of service—each expression of love sends the message that we notice what our kids do and we care about them. But encouragement doesn't just happen. No matter which form of it we use, we must take the time to really notice behavior and then single out the positive aspects of it in regard to the individual doing it. Encouragement requires parents to go an extra mile because it forces them to be proactive. Here are some specific ways you can encourage your teen.

With Words

In healthy relationships, verbal affirmation is never redundant. Each of us enjoys receiving a pat on the back or hearing "well done" from someone we respect. We appreciate hearing how our actions pleased or helped another. Teens are no different. Like the rest of us, they are powerfully encouraged when justifiable praise comes their way.

If you are not verbalizing your encouragement, what message are you sending? Verbally encourage your teens in the little things and the big. It's easier to catch their big efforts, but many times it's the daily stuff that makes or breaks relationships. Sometimes a simple "thank you" can go a long way.

Another way to verbally encourage a child is to say, "I need your help," instead of "I want it," or just "Do this." Humbly asking for help elevates the person whose help is being sought.

If you are just getting started on the encouragement side of your relationship, be careful not to qualify your encouragement. Don't say, "Thanks for doing the dishes tonight. Miracles never cease," or "You prepared a great meal; too bad it's burnt." Such qualified encouragement is not encouragement at all.

With Touch

The touch of a gentle hand, a tender hug, or a pat on the back can convey a message of encouragement. Physical encouragement communicates support, whether in victory or defeat. It fills in when words fail or aren't enough.

To hold or be held communicates vulnerability and a closeness that is reserved for trusting members of a family. Those with a struggling relationship with their teens may need to start slowly by simply placing a hand on a son's or daughter's shoulder and saying, "Great game," "Great job," or "Thank you." At other times, a high-five or a hug may be best. Whatever the case, don't underestimate the powerful influence of physical encouragement on your teenage son or daughter.

Anne Marie has always been great at combining words of encouragement and simple but meaningful expressions of physical touch. Sometimes she would just stop the kids, put her hands on their shoulders, and with great sincerity say, "I just want you to know how much I appreciate the way you…" Verbal affirmation combined with physical touch are an unbeatable combination.

There is a tendency to use the encouragement of touch only when we're happy. But believe me, if we'd had a bad day, our teens would notice when we put a gentle hand on their shoulders to say so. Consciously or unconsciously, they'd register the added emotional effort that the gesture cost.

Gift-Giving

Teens relish being appreciated. One way to show this is through gift-giving. Giving a gift in response to a child's act of loving service is a great way to remind the child that you have not forgotten what he or she did.

We have tried to practice spontaneous gift-giving in our home. There were occasions when my wife and I rushed out the door to a meeting, leaving the kitchen in disarray. Coming home to a spotless kitchen without having prompted the girls to clean up created in us a desire to express our appreciation with more than a simple "thank you." The next day Anne Marie would pick up a couple of thank you cards and write the girls a note of thanks on behalf of the two of us. Sometimes she would slip an inexpensive pair of earrings in with each card.

This cost very little time or money, yet it communicated our deep appreciation for our daughters' kindness and our desire to celebrate our love for them. It also added quality the next time we said, "Thank you."

Whether you are working at reclaiming a relationship with your teen or just working to improve it, consider saying "I appreciate you" with a simple gift. However, try to avoid some common pitfalls. Don't attach any strings or conditions to your gift. Don't do it just because the idea is in this book. Make it a genuine gift from your heart. Don't give with expectations. If you find yourself saying, "How could you do that after I gave you...?" realize you're giving with expectations. And don't use it as a defense during later conflicts.

With Service

Closely associated with gift-giving is saying thank you through acts of service. In the kitchen-cleaning incident, we could also have expressed our thanks by doing something for the kids that we knew they would appreciate—something over and above what we would normally do.

The teen years were hectic in our home, and there were times when the girls' rooms showed it. Although the girls often kept them neat, there were seasons of clutter. Sometimes during these busy times, Anne Marie would clean their rooms. She wanted to say, "I love and appreciate you" in a tangible way. That act of service communicated the value we placed on what our children were giving to our lives. We appreciated it, and they knew it.

Quality Time

A fifth way to show encouragement to our teens is by giving them our time. As parents, we all struggle to balance competing demands. Work quotas, family responsibilities, friendships, ministry opportunities, personal interests—all these and more cry out for our attention.

Your teen is probably well aware of the battle you wage—after all, he or she lives with you. Better than anyone else, your family knows how little time you have to spare. With that in mind, what could be more encouraging than to show up to cheer at your child's drama production, band concert, or soccer game? Or you could take your teen to lunch one day to demonstrate your appreciation for a special act such as helping a younger brother with his homework, making peace with a friend, or fixing dinner the night Mom was sick.

These are just some of the many ways we can encourage our kids. But don't let the suggestions we've outlined limit you. Remember, any action that you do as a parent that instills in your teen the courage to do right is encouragement.

We asked one hundred teens between ninth and twelfth grade to list for us what their parents do or say that encourages them most. Here are the top five responses in order of their ranking.

1. Teens feel motivated to do right when they have a sense that their parents trust them.

2. Teens feel motivated to do right when they feel respected by their parents. That is, encouragement works better than put-downs.

3. Teens feel motivated to do right when their parents live the standard they are being asked to live.

4. Teens feel motivated to do right when they are given the moral reasons why.

5. Teens feel motivated to do right when parents are willing to acknowledge their own mistakes, instead of making up excuses.

Gary and Anne Marie Ezzo
Reaching the Heart of Your Teen

Endeavouring to make children prematurely wise is useless labour. Suppose they have more knowledge at five or six years old than other children, what use can be made of it? It will be lost before it is wanted, and the waste of so much time and labour of the teacher can never be repaid. Too much is expected from precocity, and too little performed.

Samuel Johnson
Quoted in *The Life of Samuel Johnson*

A rich child often sits in a poor mother's lap.

Danish proverb

I call drugs and alcohol the great tricksters because they hide their true faces from our view. They begin by enhancing the ordinary, but end in their own darkness.

This sounds dramatic and full of false alarm. But it's a sad truth that too many learn too late. In fact, when you first feel that rush of clarity from a drug or first find yourself filled with loving warmth from a few drinks, it is inconceivable that there can be trouble waiting. Your first response is, "There's nothing to fear here. This can be good if I use it correctly. It's excess that causes the problems, and I don't need excess."

But drugs and alcohol are great seducers and deceivers. They offer you the world in a new way, but from that first moment they are at work on your chemistry. And your chemistry has a logic of its own.

Soon, in subtle ways, they begin to own you and demand that you serve their will. And it is only a matter of time until they cause you to harm yourself or other people.

And you never see it coming.

Consider alcohol. A few drinks and the lights become brighter, the colors richer. Your tongue begins to speak from your heart. The world becomes graceful and suffused with a warm glow. You are at peace.

What can be wrong with something that produces such truth and such honesty?

You will never know until the day when it tricks you. And it will. There will come a moment when the alcohol will tell you what to do, and you will follow.

Maybe you'll be lucky. Maybe it will only cause you to utter a hurtful word, or perform some foolish and embarrassing action.

Maybe you'll be unlucky and great harm will be done. Maybe you'll get a girl pregnant because your love seemed so strong and real. Maybe you'll take the life of a friend, because the warmth that surrounded you made you feel that you could drive faster or longer or with less care...

You will never know which of these awaits you. But one of them does. Drinking is a devil's bargain. You get something extra in the present, but you pay for it in the future. And you never know the real price until it is due.

Drugs are even more seductive. They make you think you have control, then deceive you by taking control themselves, and making you the pawn in a great chemical game that the human system is powerless to resist.

They are even more treacherous than alcohol, because at first they seem to offer so much more…

In my youth, when I did a lot of drugs, I always said that they moved my life from black and white to technicolor…All was new and full of joy.

Then slowly, I saw it all turn. Words would escape me. My memory would fail and my mental quickness was gone. I felt vague pains in my body and vague fears overtook my mind. Free time became dead time; I wanted to fill it with drugs, because reality without drugs seemed boring and drab.

I saw my friends who did not do drugs as fearful, their lives as lacking. I could not imagine that they were having the fun I had because they were not seeing the world as I saw it. I found myself hanging out with people with whom I had nothing more in common than the drugs we shared.

Soon a friend died. Other friends began coughing up blood. One lost his mind, and it had been a beautiful mind. He returned to his parents' home where he lives even today lost in wild and terrifying delusions…

I don't know how to explain this in a way that will touch your heart. The world is full of slick slogans, like "Just say No"—slogans meant to simplify and scare and sell abstinence. Everyone who has seen the down side will tell you horror stories calculated to stop you out of fear. But the true issue is much more complicated.

Drugs and alcohol…carry the seeds of dark and abysmal horrors, and they plant them in your mind, your heart, your very chemical makeup. No matter how benign they seem, no matter how elevated the experience they create, they are giving you something at the expense of something else. They are a devil's bargain—a promise of power in exchange for a service yet unnamed—and it is up to you if you wish to make that bargain.

I am afraid of that bargain for you, because I do not know what service will be demanded…

The world contains enough to fill us a thousand times. I would not trade five minutes of being with you for all the…drugs I ever took. I would not trade a moment of your mother's love for every…second spent in the thrall of alcohol…

It takes courage to step across the line into drugs, but it is a courage based on weakness. The hunger for new experience, the desire to reach new heights and depths, is really an admission that the world is not enough. And that admission is ignorant and false.

To see a solar eclipse when the earth goes dark and the birds tuck their heads under their wings to sleep, to see a child born into the world from the body of a woman you love, to hear the silence of eternity as you stand on a windswept mountain pass—these are enough. And the drugs and the alcohol do not increase them; they merely move them further from life and closer to dream. They give them to you in the moment but they take them from you in your memory. They cannot take root and enlarge your spirit.

Do not be seduced by the tricksters. Do not be deceived by their promises. Health has been given to you. Fineness of mind and fitness of body are ours. If you choose to play with drugs and alcohol, you reach behind a door where darkness has no name.

Better men than you or I have been destroyed by the hand that will not let go.

Kent Nerburn
Letters to My Son: Reflections on Becoming a Man

I have found the best way to give advice to your children is to find out what they want and then advise them to do it.

Harry S. Truman
Television interview, May 27, 1955

"You don't love me!" How many times have your kids laid that one on you? Someday when my children are old enough to understand the logic motivating a mother, I'll tell them:

I loved you enough to bug you about where you were going and what time you would get home.

I loved you enough to let you discover your friend was a creep.

I loved you enough to stand over you for two hours while you cleaned your bedroom, a job that would have taken me 15 minutes.

I loved you enough to ignore what every other mother did or said.

I loved you enough to let you stumble, fall, hurt and fail.

I loved you enough to accept you for what you are, not what I wanted you to be.

Most of all, I loved you enough to say no when you hated me for it.

...I see children as kites. You spend a lifetime trying to get them off the ground. You run with them until you're both breathless...they crash...you add a longer tail. You patch and comfort, adjust and teach—and assure them that someday they will fly.

Finally they are airborne, but they need more string, and you keep letting it out...You know it won't be long before that beautiful creature will snap the life-line that bound you together and soar—free and alone. Only then do you know you did your job.

Erma Bombeck
Forever Erma

To a hoarding father succeeds an extravagant son.

Spanish proverb

Children need models rather than critics.

Joseph Joubert
Pensées

And these words, which I command thee this day, shall be in thine heart; And thou shalt teach them diligently unto thy children, and shalt talk of them when thou sittest in thine house, and when thou walkest by the way, and when thou liest down, and when thou risest up.

Deuteronomy 6:6-7

If you must give your child lessons, send him to driving school. He is far more likely to end up owning a Datsun than he is a Stradivarius.

Fran Lebowitz
Social Studies

Our children do not want models of perfection, neither do they want us to be buddies, friends, or confidants who never rise above their own levels of maturity and experience. We need to walk that middle ground between perfection and peerage, between intense meddling and apathy—the middle ground where our values, standards, and expectations can be shared with our children. The very act of bringing a child into the world has bestowed a responsibility and obligation on us which our children do not share or totally understand yet. By the very fact that we are parents, we owe them the wisdom of our years.

I often visit families mourning the death of a parent or grandparent who was dearly loved. I've noticed over the years that people do not dwell on what their parents or grandparents did for a living, what kind of car they drove, or how much they paid for their house. They talk of menschlichkeit. Particularly in close families where the lives of family members were intertwined, people tell me of the small everyday gestures of love and kindness that made a lasting impression. "Grandpa took me to the zoo on Sunday." "Mom always waited for me at the bus stop so that she could ask about my day."…"One cold night I was late from a date and Dad met me at the subway with his overcoat over his pajamas." These are the memories that last.

Neil Kurshan
*Raising Your Child to Be a Mensch**
**Decent, responsible, caring person*

A torn jacket is soon mended; but hard words bruise the heart of a child.
Henry Wadsworth Longfellow
Driftwood

Parents must make a careful distinction between goals and desires for their children. Although it is my desire that my daughter maintain at least a B average in school, keep her room neat, and pick up after herself, these things should never be my goals as a parent. If they are, I will be frustrated and angry if my daughter (who has total control of making these things happen) blocks them by not performing well.

Instead, I should express these things as desires, both to Christi and to God, and make it my goal to lovingly control my responses toward Christi when she fails to meet them. My goal should be to respond to her in a way that communicates unconditional involvement no matter how she responds to my requests. But I also want to be uncompromisingly responsive if she decides to ignore them (e.g., withdrawing privileges until my requests are honored).

To achieve such goals I need only control myself, not her, thus relieving the frustration I would experience if I tried to control her. At the same time, she will learn that she is the one responsible for controlling her impulses, not me. By making it my goal to consistently provide painful consequences for my daughter's disobedient or destructive choices, I provide the best environment for teaching her the necessity of self control…

Wise parents understand that negative emotions can tell them something very important about themselves. If a plan of theirs for finding fulfillment is being thwarted by their adolescent, they recognize their foolishness in trying to control what they can never control. *They allow their emotions to alert them to their need for some fundamental changes in what they are pursuing.*

Even pursuits that seem to parents to be in their adolescent's best interest can be based on foolish goals. For example, although it should be every parent's desire to see his child become a godly person, it must never become part of a parent's strategy for finding life. If it does, it shifts his center of dependence away from Christ and onto his child or on his abilities to raise his child a certain way. *A parent can maintain a deep desire to see his kid turn out well without making his own life and fulfillment dependent on whether it happens or not.* Wise parents make it their goal to stay in the ministry model no matter what kind of person their adolescent becomes. They understand that *life does not depend on the results of their parenting, but in whom they trust as they parent.*

Kevin Huggins
Parenting Adolescents

Parents who have failed to train their children properly often identify a patsy to blame for negatively influencing them. Teachers, other children, TV, and even the church often receive this blame. However, God holds only the parent accountable for training children. Therefore, it is the parents' responsibility to control what influences their children.

Children may be taught things at school that oppose the teaching of their parents, but it is the parents' responsibility to determine where the children go to school and what they are taught. Children can be influenced by their peers, but it is the parents' responsibility to control with whom their children associate. Children are definitely influenced by what they see on television…but it is still the parent who is ultimately responsible for choosing to what his child is to be exposed. Children can ignore what is taught in church, but it is the parent whom God holds accountable for a child's instruction in the Word.

Another technique of parents in attempting to avoid their responsibility is to pass the buck to God. This is done by telling a child who will not obey that God will punish him for his disobedience...Parents cannot pass the responsibility back to God. God's Word tells parents that they are not only to tell their children what to do, but also to enforce obedience to their instructions. This is the parents' job, not God's. A child learns obedience to parents as a preparation for his obeying God.

J. Richard Fugate
What the Bible Says About...Child Training

Children have never been very good at listening to their elders, but they have never failed to imitate them.

James Baldwin
Nobody Knows My Name

Parents can only give good advice or put them on the right paths, but the final forming of a person's character lies in their own hands...

Anne Frank
The Diary of a Young Girl

Correct thy son, and he shall give thee rest; yea, he shall give delight unto your soul.

Proverbs 29:17

If a well-intentioned person says to you, "Now it's none of my business, but if that were my child, I would...," please, for the sake of our Lord, stifle your impulse to choke them.

Before our first child was born, my wife and I read several books about parenting. When Spencer arrived, we discovered just how useful those books can be, particularly for chewing on.

When our second son, Sam, was born, my mother came to help. She's a smart woman who reads quite a bit. She had just read a book about parenting and was eager to share her knowledge. Spencer, then two years old, threw a tantrum while Mom was with us. I hadn't slept for two days, and after an hour of crying—mine, not his—I gave Spencer what he wanted.

"Boy, that was a mistake," Mom warned. And she proceeded to tell me that if Spencer gets what he wants by throwing a fit, there's no telling where he'll end up.

"Probably in Congress," I told her.

Mom even had advice about sleeping. She advised us to have baby Sam lie on his back to prevent crib death. But someone else said they should lie on their stomachs for the same reason. So to be safe, I built a rotisserie crib.

Be sure to pray that your child escapes the usual infant ailments, because giving up vacation time to watch your kid is a real drag. But also because advice givers come out of the woodwork when they catch a whiff of sickness. Surprisingly, many people spoke about the curative power of whiskey in small doses. So I tried it, but it only made me lightheaded and woozy.

The worst advice we received was from a man who told us that holding our baby would spoil him. Obviously, he didn't understand how babies require the intimacy that cuddling provides. Besides, cuddling babies is fun and almost makes up for what our children do to us as teenagers.

The best advice we received was from the lady who told us about babysitters.

The Bible offers parenting advice. It speaks of sparing the rod and spoiling the child. Some folks think this means spanking your child, but the psalmist speaks of a rod which gives comfort. "Thy rod and they staff they comfort me." So it really has more to do with gentle guidance.

I believe I've got this advice thing figured out. It isn't that we think we know more than the parents. It's mostly about lending a hand with something as neat as raising a child. It's the same principle behind planting a tree. Twenty years later, we come upon it and delight that we had a part in its growing.

So when folks start telling you how to raise your child, don't think of them as busybodies, but as tree planters. That way, if your little sapling goes bad, you'll have someone else to blame.

Philip Gulley
Front Porch Tales

Train up a child in the way he should go and, when he is old, he will not depart from it.

Proverbs 22:6

1. You are not to blame for the temperament with which your child was born...

2. He *is* in greater danger because of his inclination to test the limits and scale the walls...

3. If you fail to understand his lust for power and independence, you can exhaust your resources and bog down in guilt...

4. Hold tight to the reins of authority in the early days, and build an attitude of respect during your brief window of opportunity...

5. Don't panic, even during the storms of adolescence. Better times are ahead...

6. Stay on your child's team, even when it appears to be a *losing* team...

7. Give him time to find himself, even if he appears not to be searching.

8. Most importantly, I urge you to hold your children before the Lord in fervent prayer throughout their years at home. I am convinced there is no other source of confidence and wisdom in parenting...We must bathe them in prayer every day of their lives. The God who made your children *will* hear your petitions. He has promised to do so. After all, He loves them more than you do.

Dr. James C. Dobson
Parenting Isn't for Cowards

Being a

GOOD FRIEND

CHAPTER EIGHT

BEING A
GOOD FRIEND

———

To be capable of steady friendship or lasting love, are the two greatest proofs, not only of goodness of heart, but of strength of mind.

William Hazlitt

All kinds of things rejoiced my soul in their [my friends'] company—to talk and laugh and do each other kindnesses; read pleasant books together, pass from lightest jesting to talk of the deepest things and back again; differ without rancour, as a man might differ with himself, and when most rarely dissension arose find our normal agreement all the sweeter for it; teach each other or learn from each other; be impatient for the return of the absent, and welcome them with joy on their home-coming; these and such like things, proceeding from our hearts as we gave affection and received it back, and shown by face, by voice, by the eyes, and a thousand other pleasing ways, kindled a flame which fused our very souls and of many made us one. This is what men value in friends.

Saint Augustine
Confessions

A man cannot be said to succeed in this life who does not satisfy one friend.

Henry David Thoreau
Winter: Journal, February 19, 1857

Friendship is unnecessary, like philosophy, like art...It has no survival value; rather it is one of those things that give value to survival.

C. S. Lewis
The Four Loves, Friendship

Nothing shall I, while sane, compare with a dear friend.

Quintus Horatius Flaccus

My fellow, my companion, held most dear,
My soul, my other self, my inward friend.

Mary Sidney Herbert
The Psalmes of David

That perfect tranquillity of life, which is nowhere to be found but in retreat, a faithful friend, and a good library...

Aphra Behn
The Lucky Mistake

There's a kind of emotional exploration you plumb with a friend that you don't really do with your family.

Bette Midler
Quoted in *Parade Magazine*, February 5, 1989

Though Love be deeper, Friendship is more wide...

Corinne Roosevelt Robinson
"Friendship"

A true friend is a pearl. He reads
Your deepest needs
And so spares you the shame
Of giving your heart's hidden desires a name.

Jean de La Fontaine
"The Two Friends"

The balm of life, a kind and faithful friend.

> Mercy Otis Warren
> *Miscellaneous Poems*

Animals are such agreeable friends—they ask no questions, they pass no criticisms.

> George Eliot
> *Scenes of Clerical Life*

I have always detested the belief that sex is the chief bond between man and women. Friendship is far more human.

> Agnes Smedley
> *Battle Hymn of China*

The more people are reached by mass communication, the less they communicate with each other. The proliferation of one-way messages, whether in print or on air, seems to have increased rather than lessened the alienation of the individual. Friendly, gregarious America is full of intensely lonely people for whom radio and television provide the illusory solace of company.

> Marya Mannes
> *But Will It Sell?*

Good friends are good for your health.

> Dr. Irwin Sarason
> Quoted in the *New York Times*, August 27, 1985

A faithful friend is the medicine of life.

> Apocrypha: Ecclesiasticus 6:16

One of the ways social interest can be trained is though friendship. We learn in friendship to look with the eyes of another person, to listen with his ears and to feel with his heart. If a child is frustrated, if he is always watched and guarded, if he grows up isolated, without comrades and friends, he does not develop this ability to identify himself with another person. He always thinks himself the most important being in the world and is always anxious to secure his own welfare. Training in friendship is preparation for marriage.

Alfred Adler
What Life Should Mean to You

"Madame, people very seldom die because they lost someone. I believe they die more often because they haven't had someone."

Sidonie-Gabrielle Colette
"The Photographer's Missus"

The loneliest woman in the world is a woman without a close woman friend.

Toni Morrison
Speech, Sarah Lawrence College, 1978

Few comforts are more alluring for a woman than the rich intimate territory of women's talk...A woman friend will say, "You are not alone. I have felt that way, too. This is what happened to me." Home, in other words.

Elsa Walsh
Quoted in *In the Company of Women*

Those friends thou hast, and their adoption tried,
Grapple them to thy soul with hoops of steel.

William Shakespeare
Hamlet

Books and friends should be few but good.

proverb

Character is so largely affected by associations that we cannot afford to be indifferent as to who and what our friends are. They write their names in our albums, but they do more, they help make us what we are. Be therefore careful in selecting them and when wisely selected, never sacrifice them.

M. Hulburd

One friend in a lifetime is much; two are many; three are hardly possible.

Henry Adams
The Education of Henry Adams

Be slow in choosing a friend, slower in changing.

Benjamin Franklin
Poor Richard's Almanac

Be courteous to all, but intimate with few, and let those few be well tried before you give them your confidence. True friendship is a plant of slow growth, and must undergo and withstand the shocks of adversity before it is entitled to the appellation.

George Washington
Letter, Newburgh, New York,
January 15, 1783

Fate chooses your relations, you choose your friends.

Jacques Delille
Malheur et pitie

As adults, there's no one like a sister to remind you of who you once were, what your foibles are, what history you hail from, and most of all, what mistakes and sins you've committed...

Underlying our history from the womb on, a belief in each other surfaces despite the conflicts. There's little more powerful than that belief. She knows who I am. She's been there since my beginning. She'll always be there. We share a language only families understand: a heart kind of Braille. Touching, knowing, supporting.

I've come to understand that in my sister's shadow there is shade for me. In her, I've found a lifetime companion.

Sherry Von Ohlsen
Quoted in *In the Company of Women*

I prefer to strive in bravery with the bravest, rather than in wealth with the wealthiest, or in greed with the greediest.

Plutarch
Lives

Oh the comfort, the inexpressible comfort of feeling safe with a person: having neither to weigh thoughts nor measure words, but to pour them out. Just as they are—chaff and grain together, knowing that a faithful hand will take and sift them, keep what is worth keeping, and then with the breath of kindness, blow the rest away.

George Eliot

"Yes'm, old friends is always best, 'less you can catch a new one that's fit to make an old one out of."

Sarah Orne Jewett
The Country of the Pointed Furs and Other Stories

Trust, honesty, respect, commitment, safety, support, generosity, loyalty, mutuality, constancy, understanding, acceptance. These are the most widely heralded qualities of friendship, the minimum requirements, if you will, to be counted as a friend.

Lillian B. Rubin
Just Friends

No man is the whole of himself. His friends are the rest of him.

Good Life Almanac
Solway Community Press

Tell me what company thou keepest, and I'll tell thee what thou art.

Miguel de Cervantes
Don Quixote

Associate yourself with men of good quality if you esteem your own reputation; for 'tis better to be alone than in bad company.

George Washington
Rules of Civility

Always, Sir, set a high value on spontaneous kindness. He whose inclination prompts him to cultivate your friendship of his own accord, will love you more than one whom you have been at pains to attach to.

Samuel Johnson
Quoted in *The Life of Samuel Johnson*

Their belief in one another seeks no results.

David Michaelis
The Best of Friends

A friend is a present you give yourself.

Robert Louis Stevenson

A friend's only gift is himself…To praise the utility of friendship, as the ancients so often did, and to regard it as a political institution justified, like victory or government, by its material results, is to lose one's moral bearings…We are not to look now for what makes friendships useful, but for whatever may be found in friendship that may lend utility to life.

George Santayana
The Life of Reason

The only gift is a portion of thyself.

Ralph Waldo Emerson

Between two friends neither one should rule.

Marie de Ventadorn

Friends—and I mean real friends—reserve nothing:
The property of one belongs to the other.

Euripides
Andromache

You've probably heard the powerful story coming out of World War I of the deep friendship of two soldiers in the trenches. Two buddies were serving together in the mud and misery of that wretched European stalemate (one version even identifies them as actual brothers). Month after month they lived out their lives in the trenches, in the cold and the mud, under fire and under orders.

From time to time one side or the other would rise up out of the trenches, fling their bodies against the opposing line and slink back to lick their wounds, bury their dead, and wait to do it all over again. In the process, friendships were forged in the misery. Two soldiers became particularly close. Day after day, night after night, terror after terror, they talked of life, of families, of hopes, of what they would do when (and if) they returned home from this horror.

On one more fruitless charge, "Jim" fell, severely wounded. His friend, "Bill," made it back to the relative safety of the trenches. Meanwhile Jim lay suffering beneath the night flares. Between the trenches. Alone.

The shelling continued. The danger was at its peak. Between the trenches was no place to be. Still, Bill wished to reach his friend, to comfort him, to offer what encouragement only friends can offer. The officer in charge refused to let Bill leave the trench. It was simply too dangerous. As he turned his back, however, Bill went over the top. Ignoring the smell of cordite in the air, the concussion of incoming rounds, and the pounding in his chest, Bill made it to Jim.

Sometime later he managed to get Jim back to the safety of the trenches. Too late. His friend was gone. The somewhat self-righteous officer, seeing Jim's body, cynically asked Bill if it had been "worth the risk." Bill's response was without hesitation.

"Yes, sir, it was," he said. "My friend's last words made it more than worth it. He looked up at me and said, 'I knew you'd come.'"

Stu Weber
Locking Arms

The doer of the favour is the firmer friend of the two, in order by continued kindness to keep the recipient in his debt; while the debtor feels less keenly from the very consciousness that the return he makes will be a payment, not a free gift.

Thucydides
Peloponnesian War

The man who treasures his friends is usually solid gold himself.

Marjorie Holmes
Love and Laughter

If a man does not make new acquaintance as he advances through life, he will soon find himself left alone. A man, Sir, should keep his friendship *in constant repair.*

Samuel Johnson
Quoted in *The Life of Samuel Johnson*

Little acts of kindness which we render to each other in everyday life, are like flowers by the way-side to the traveler: they serve to gladden the heart and relieve the tedium of life's journey.

Eunice Bathrick
Quoted in *Simple Wisdom: Shaker Sayings, Poems, and Songs*

We care when our friends are fine and we worry and are concerned when they aren't. There are so many wonderful ways to share and express our warm feelings toward others. Do it as a natural part of your life, of your day. When you do things for yourself, include others in them. The next time you roast walnuts, roast some extra ones and wrap them to give to a friend you're meeting for lunch tomorrow. When you discover a wine you particularly enjoy, buy an extra bottle, tie it with a ribbon and bring it to a friend. Drop a few museum postcards off at a friend's apartment house on your way home from work with a note, "Thinking of you." After you've been to a special museum exhibit, take the catalogue to an elderly friend who is confined to her home.

Sharing doubles joy and diminishes sorrow...In the give-and-take of a healthy relationship both people grow by the exchange. In the happiness of loving another, we feel better about ourselves, too.

Alexandra Stoddard
Living a Beautiful Life

To live in prayer together is to walk in love together.

Margaret Moore Jacobs

We should not let the grass grow on the path of friendship.

Marie Thérèse Rodet Geoffrin
Quoted in *Biography of Distinguished Women*

Friendship is in loving rather than in being lov'd.

Robert Bridges
The Testament of Beauty

A slender acquaintance with the world must convince every man, that actions, not words, are the true criterion of the attachment of friends; and that the most liberal professions of good-will are very far from being the surest marks of it.

George Washington
Social Maxims: Friendship

There isn't much that I can do, but I can share my bread with you, and sometimes share a sorrow, too—as on our way we go.

There isn't much that I can do, but I can sit an hour with you, and I can share a joke with you, and sometimes share reverses, too—as on our way we go.

There isn't much that I can do, but I can share my flowers with you, and I can share my books with you and sometimes share your burdens, too—as on our way we go.

There isn't much that I can do, but I can share my songs with you, and I can share my mirth with you, and sometimes come and laugh with you—as on our way we go.

There isn't much that I can do, but I can share my hopes with you, and I can share my fears with you, and sometimes shed some tears with you—as on our way we go.

There isn't much that I can do, but I can share my friends with you, and I can share my life with you, and oftentimes share a prayer with you—as on our way we go.

anonymous

Rebbe Uri, the celebrated Seraphin of Strelisk, needed money to marry off an old maid, orphan to boot. Where could he go? To people who had money. The problem was, he didn't know any; he knew only people who needed money—for themselves or for others. One of them was his friend Reb Moshe-Leib of Sassov, who also was running around the country collecting funds for beggars. He went to see him. At first, the two remained quiet for several hours, reflecting. Then Reb Moshe-Leib turned to his friend and said, "Uri, my friend, I wish I could help you with money but I have none. Still, there is something I can do for you: I shall dance for you." And he danced for his friend all night. Next morning, after prayers, he told his friend: "I must go. Wait for me." He left and returned two days later, with a considerable sum of money. "Let me tell you what happened," he said. "Years ago, I came into a strange city and was lucky enough to find a young boy who consented to be my guide. In return I promised him that I would come and dance at his wedding. Passing through Zlotchov after I left you, I heard music and singing. There was a wedding going on. Though I was not invited, I went closer—and recognized the bridegroom. I remembered my promise and kept it: I danced for the young couple and did my best to give them joy. When they heard my story—your story, Uri—they felt sorry for the poor old maid and they and their guests opened their hearts and their pockets. Here is the money, Uri, go and tell the girl that now it is her turn to rejoice."

Concluded Reb Moshe-Leib, "When somebody asks something impossible of me, I know what I must do: I must dance."

From the encounter of the two Rebbes we thus learn that there is always *something* one can do for one's friends. What is Hasidism if not the belief that man must have faith in God *and* in people? You suffer? Pray to God but speak to your friend.

Elie Wiesel
Somewhere a Master

The only way to have a friend is to be one.

Ralph Waldo Emerson
Essays, First Series: Friendship

"Harville," he said to me as he slumped into the chair, "I feel really terrible. I just don't have any friends."

I was sympathetic with him. "You must be very sad. It's lonely not having any friends."

"Yeah. I can't seem to…I don't know. There are no friends in my life. I keep looking and looking, and I can't seem to find any."

Walter was locked into a view of the world that went something like this: wandering around the world were people on whose forehead were stamped the words "Friends of Walter," and his job was merely to search until he found them.

"Walter," I said with a sigh, "do you understand why you don't have any friends?"

He perked up. "No. Tell me!"

"The reason you don't have any friends is that there aren't any friends out there."

His shoulders slumped.

I was relentless. "That's right," I told him. "There are no friends out there. What you want does not exist." I let him stew in this sad state of affairs for a few seconds. Then I leaned forward in my chair and said, "Walter—listen to me! All people in the world are strangers. If you want a friend, you're going to have to go out and make one!"

Harville Hendrix
Getting the Love You Want

To cement a new friendship, especially between foreigners or persons of a different social world, a spark with which both were secretly charged must fly from person to person, and cut across the accidents of place and time.

George Santayana
Persons and Places: The Middle Span

We cannot tell the precise moment when friendship is formed. As in filling a vessel drop by drop, there is at last a drop which makes it run over; so in a series of kindnesses there is at last one which makes the heart run over.

James Boswell
The Life of Samuel Johnson

Geometry forgotten, they sat in Lester's room for hours, reciting to each other the lines that helped to harness the chaos and confusions in their fourteen-year-old worlds. Bloody noses had made them friends, but giving sound to the bruised places in their hearts made them brothers.

Gloria Naylor
Linden Hills

Friendship of a kind that cannot easily be reversed tomorrow must have its roots in common interests and shared beliefs, and even between nations, in some personal feeling.

> Barbara Tuchman
> Quoted in *Harper's*, December 1972

Two may walk together under the same roof for many years, yet never really meet; and two others at first speech are old friends.

> Mary Catherwood
> *Mackinac and Lake Stories*

Poets and friends are born to what they are.

> Katherine Fowler Philips
> "Friendship"

A Father's a Treasure; a Brother's a Comfort; a Friend is both.

> Benjamin Franklin
> *Poor Richard's Almanac*

Friendship needs no words—it is a loneliness relieved of the anguish of loneliness.

> Dag Hammarskjöld
> *Markings*

A rail-thin nine-year-old named Toussaint LaRue looked on during these beatings and only hit me once. I therefore assumed that he occupied some lower social niche than mine. Like a snail's.

He took no pleasure in the China Boy rituals. He instead talked to me. I suspected that he had devised a new method of pain infliction.

"Toussaint," he said, offering his hand. "Ya'lls supposed ta shake it." He grinned when I put my hand out with the same enthusiasm with which I would pet Mr. Carter's bulldog...

Toussaint would become my guide to American boyhood.

My primary bond to him was for the things he did not do. He did not pound or trap me. He never cut me down. Or laughed with knives in his eyes. Then he opened his heart by explaining things to me, giving me his learning, and taking me into his home...

He made his closest buddies tolerate me. His mother took me to the church of Reverend Jones on Sundays...The simple presence of his company, and that of his pals, saved me from innumerable trashings and gave me time to breathe.

I had never had a friend before, and I cared for him as few lads have for another. My heart fills now when I think of him. That will never change.

Gus Lee
China Boy

Friendships, like geraniums, bloom in kitchens. Love runs up and down a flight of stairs and enters one flat and another in the housing projects.

Blanche H. Gelfant
Women Writing in America: Voices in Collage

When a friend speaks to me, whatever he says is interesting.

Jean Renoir
Quoted in the New York Times, September 28, 1969

Only solitary men know the full joys of friendship. Others have their family; but to a solitary and an exile his friends are everything.

Willa S. Cather
Shadows on the Rock

A Friend may well be reckoned the masterpiece of Nature.

Ralph Waldo Emerson
Essays

You meet your friend, your face brightens—you have struck gold.

Kassia

Friendship is the greatest enrichment that I have found.

Adlai E. Stevenson
(at the funeral of Lloyd Lewis, Libertyville, Illinois, 1949)

Gentle ladies, you will remember till old age what we did together in our brilliant youth!

Sappho

Without friends no one would choose to live, though he had all other goods; even rich men and those in possession of office and of dominating power are thought to need friends most of all; for what is the use of such prosperity without the opportunity of beneficence, which is exercised chiefly and in its most laudable form towards friends? Or how can prosperity be guarded and preserved without friends? The greater it is, the more exposed is it to risk. And in poverty and in other misfortunes men think friends are the only refuge. It helps the young, too, to keep from error; it aids older people by ministering to their needs and supplementing the activities that are failing from weakness; those in the prime of life it stimulates to noble actions...for with friends men are more able both to think and to act...

Perfect friendship is the friendship of men who are good, and alike in virtue; for these wish well alike to each other *qua* good, and they are good in themselves. Now those who wish well to their friends for their sake are most truly friends; for they do this by reason of their own nature and not incidentally; therefore their friendship lasts as long as they are good—and goodness is an enduring thing...

But it is natural that such friendships should be infrequent; for such men are rare. Further, such friendship requires time and familiarity; as the proverb says, men cannot know each other till they have 'eaten salt together'; nor can they admit each other to friendship or be friends till each has been found lovable and been trusted by each. Those who quickly show the marks of friendship to each other wish to be friends, but are not friends unless they both are lovable and know the fact; for a wish for friendship may arise quickly, but friendship does not.

Aristotle
Ethics

I find friendship to be like wine, raw when new, ripened with age, the true old man's milk and restorative cordial.

Thomas Jefferson
Writings

Forsake not an old friend; for the new is not comparable to him: a new friend is as new wine; when it is old, thou shalt drink it with pleasure.

Apocrypha: Ecclesiasticus 9:10

Surely we ought to prize those friends on whose principles and opinions we may constantly rely—of whom we may say in all emergencies, "I know what they would think."

Hannah Farnham Lee
The Log Cabin; or, The World Before You

It is not so much our friends' help that helps us as the confident knowledge that they will help us.

Epicurus

After David had finished talking with Saul, Jonathan became one in spirit with David, and he loved him as himself. And Jonathan made a covenant with David because he loved him as himself. Jonathan took off the robe he was wearing and gave it to David, along with his tunic, and even his sword, his bow and his belt.

Saul told his son Jonathan and all the attendants to kill David. But Jonathan was very fond of David and warned him, "My father Saul is looking for a chance to kill you. Be on your guard tomorrow morning; go into hiding and stay there. I will go out and stand with my father in the field where you are. I'll speak to him about you and will tell you what I find out."

Jonathan spoke well of David to Saul his father and said to him, "Let not the king do wrong to his servant David; he has not wronged you, and what he has done has benefited you greatly…Why then would you do wrong to an innocent man like David by killing him for no reason?"

Saul listened to Jonathan and took this oath: "As surely as the LORD lives, David will not be put to death."

But an evil spirit from the LORD came upon Saul as he was sitting in his house with his spear in his hand. While David was playing the harp, Saul tried to pin him to the wall with his spear, but David eluded him as Saul drove the spear into the wall. That night David made good his escape.

Then David…went to Jonathan and asked, "What have I done? What is my crime? How have I wronged your father, that he is trying to take my life?"

"Never!" Jonathan replied. "Your are not going to die! Look, my father doesn't do anything, great or small, without confiding in me. Why would he hide this from me? It's not so!"

But David took an oath and said, "Your father knows very well that I have found favor in your eyes, and he has said to himself, 'Jonathan must not know this or he will be grieved.' Yet as surely as the LORD lives and as you live, there is only a step between me and death."

Jonathan said to David, "Whatever you want me to do, I'll do for you."

1 Samuel 18:1, 3-4; 19:1-6, 9-10; 20:1-4 (NIV)

A friend in need is a friend indeed.

proverb

And I will gladly share with you your pain,
If it turn out I can no comfort bring;
For 'tis a friend's right, please let me explain,
To share in woeful as in joyful things.

Geoffrey Chaucer
Troilus and Cressida

Real friendship is shown in times of trouble; prosperity is full of friends.

Euripides
Hecuba

A friend loves at all times, and a brother is born for adversity.

Proverbs 17:17 (NIV)

Two men were traveling together, when a bear suddenly met them on their path. One of them climbed up quickly into a tree, and concealed himself in the branches. The other, seeing that he must be attacked, fell flat on the ground, and when the Bear came up and felt him with his snout, and smelt him all over, he held his breath, and feigned the appearance of death as much as he could. The Bear soon left him, for it is said he will not touch a dead body. When he was quite gone, the other traveler descended from the tree, and accosting his friend, jocularly inquired, "what it was the Bear had whispered in his ear?" He replied, "He gave me this advice: Never travel with a friend who deserts you at the approach of danger."

Misfortune tests the sincerity of friends.

Æsop
Fables

Best friend, my well-spring in the wilderness!

George Eliot
"The Spanish Gypsy"

But every road is tough to me
that has no friend to cheer it.

Elizabeth Shane
"Sheskinbeg"

Two are better than one; because they have a good reward for their labour. For if they fall, the one will lift up his fellow: but woe to him that is alone when he falleth; for he hath not another to help him up. Again, if two lie together, then they have heat: but how can one be warm alone? And if one prevail against him, two shall withstand him; and a threefold cord is not quickly broken.

Ecclesiastes 4:9-12

So closely interwoven have been our lives, our purposes, and experiences that, separated, we have a feeling of incompleteness—united, such strength of self-assertion that no ordinary obstacles, differences, or dangers ever appear to us insurmountable.

Elizabeth Cady Stanton
Eighty Years and More

A friend hears the song in my heart and sings it to me when my memory fails.

Pioneer Girls Leaders' Handbook

Our friends are among our life's greatest treasures. They help us negotiate the difficult hurdles of life. What would we have done without friends in adolescence to help us navigate the travails of puberty and deal with our "unreasonable" parents? And what about our twentysomething romances? Whom do we go to for emotional rescue when in the dating years the man of our dreams becomes the stuff of nightmares? We go to our friends. Later, they coach us through first-time motherhood. Years later as we help our kids pack for college, they witness our tears. Our friends walk with us through menopause as, once again, we are caught up in the hormonal crazies, and they listen as we fantasize about fleeing to the Caribbean or a convent.

In their presence, we laugh about what drove us crazy hours before; with them we cry without shame, knowing we will be understood.

Brenda Hunter, Ph.D.
In the Company of Women

When two go together, one of them at least looks forward to see what is best; a man by himself, though he be careful, still has less mind in him than two, and his wits have less weight.

Homer
Iliad

Love is like the wild rose-briar;
Friendship like the holly-tree.
The holly is dark when the rose-briar blooms,
But which will bloom most constantly?

Emily Brontë
"Love and Friendship"

"Pooh, *promise* you won't forget about me, ever. Not even when I'm a hundred."

Pooh thought for a little.

"How old shall I be then?"

"Ninety-nine."

Pooh nodded.

"I promise," he said.

Still with his eyes on the world Christopher Robin put out a hand and felt for Pooh's paw.

"Pooh," said Christopher Robin earnestly, "if I—if I'm not quite—" he stopped and tried again—"Pooh, *whatever happens*, you *will* understand, won't you?"

"Understand what?"

"Oh, nothing." He laughed and jumped to his feet. "Come on!"

"Where?" said Pooh.

"Anywhere," said Christopher Robin.

So they went off together. But wherever they go, and whatever happens to them on the way, in that enchanted place on top of the Forest, a little boy and his Bear will always be playing.

A. A. Milne
The House at Pooh Corner

A true friend unbosoms freely, advises justly, assists readily, adventures boldly, takes all patiently, defends courageously, and continues a friend unchangeably.

William Penn
Fruits of Solitude

Deft thieves can break your locks and carry off
your savings, fire consume your home,
debtors default on principal and interest, failed crops
return not even the seed you'd sown,
cheating women run up your charge accounts,
storm overwhelm ships freighted with all your goods—
fortune can't take way what you give friends:
that wealth stays yours forever.

Lucius Valerius Martialis
Epigrams

A man of many companions may come to ruin, but there is a friend who sticks closer than a brother.

Proverbs 18:24 (NIV)

I shall ask into my shell only those friends with whom I can be completely honest. I find I am shedding hypocrisy in human relationships. What rest that will be! The most exhausting thing in life, I have discovered, is being insincere. That is why so much of social life is exhausting; one is wearing a mask. I have shed my mask.

Anne Morrow Lindberg
A Gift from the Sea

When friends stop being frank and useful to each other, the whole world loses some of its radiance.

Anatole Broyard
Quoted in the *New York Times*, September 1, 1985

Friends should not be chosen to flatter. The quality we should prize is that rectitude which will shrink from no truth. Intimacies which increase vanity destroy friendship.

William Ellery Channing
Note-Book: Friendship

What is a Friend? I will tell you. It is a person with whom you dare to be yourself.

Frank Crane
A Definition of Friendship

We love those who know the worst of us and don't turn their faces away.

Walker Percy

Your friend is the man who knows all about you, and still likes you.

Elbert Hubbard
The Roycroft Dictionary and Book of Epigrams

It is more shameful to distrust one's friends than to be deceived by them.

François de La Rochefoucauld
Maximes

There is nothing in all the world so precious as a friend who is at once wise and true.

Herodotus
History

Better be a nettle in the side of your friend than his echo.

Ralph Waldo Emerson
Essays, First Series: Friendship

We need very strong ears to hear ourselves judged frankly; and because there are few who can endure frank criticism without being stung by it, those who venture to criticize us perform a remarkable act of friendship; for to undertake to wound and offend a man for his own good is to have a healthy love for him.

Michel Eyquem de Montaigne
Essays

There can be no Friendship where there is no *Freedom*. Friendship loves a *Free Air*, and will not be fenced up in straight and narrow Enclosures.

William Penn
Fruits of Solitude

The more we love our friends, the less we flatter them; it is by excusing nothing that pure love shows itself.

Molière
Le Misanthrope

Without friendship and the openness and trust that go with it, skills are barren and knowledge may become an unguided missile.

Frank H. T. Rhodes
Commencement address, Cornell University, May 29, 1983

Do not remove a fly from your friend's forehead with a hatchet.

Chinese proverb

Fine as friendship is, there is nothing irrevocable about it. The bonds of friend-ship are not iron bonds, proof against the strongest of strains and the heaviest of assaults. A man by becoming your friend has not committed himself to all the demands which you may be pleased to make upon him. Foolish people like to test the bonds of their friendships, pulling upon them to see how much strain they will stand. When they snap, it is as if friendship itself had been proved unworthy.

But the truth is that good friendships are fragile things and require as much care in handling as any other fragile and precious things. For friendship is an adventure and a romance, and in adventures it is the unexpected that happens. It is the zest of peril that makes the excitement of friendship. All that is unpleasant and unfavorable is foreign to its atmosphere; there is no place in friendship for harsh criticism or fault-finding. We will "take less" from a friend than we will from one who is indifferent to us.

Randolph S. Bourne
"Youth and Life"

One may be my very good friend, and yet not of my opinion.

Margaret Cavendish
Sociable Letters

Friendship is almost always the union of a part of one mind with a part of another: People are friends in spots.

George Santayana

There is no man so imperfect that we cannot have for him a very perfect friendship, when we are loved by him, and when we have a truly noble and generous soul.

René Descartes
Passions of the Soul

Yes, friendship is a kaleidoscopic and complicated thing; it affords many possible grounds for suspicion and offense, but a truly wise man always finds it possible to avoid them or smooth them over or put up with them. One thing however must be shunned, and that is hypersensitivity, if we are to preserve the mutual confidence and practical value of friendship. For it often happens that friends must be admonished and even reprimanded, and this we must take in good part when it is offered in a spirit of charity...

...In this whole matter, then, we must be reasonable and cautious. We may admonish, but we must not scold; we may reprimand, but we must not humiliate...

It is an essential part of true friendship, then, to offer and to receive admonition; but it must be offered courteously, not peremptorily, and received with forbearance, not with resentment. By the same sign, we must maintain that there is no danger more deadly to friendship than servility, sycophancy, flattery—put as many names as you like upon it, but let it be branded as the vicious practice of disloyal, untruthful men, who measure everything they say by what people want to hear, and never anything by the truth.

Now in all matters, hypocrisy is vicious (for it distorts and destroys our judgment), but it is particularly inimical to friendship, for it makes honesty impossible, and without honesty the word "friendship" has no meaning. For the essence of friendship consists in the fact that many souls, so to speak, become one, and how can that take place if even in the one individual the soul is not single and forever the same, but various, changeable, kaleidoscopic?…

…For in friendship unless, as we say, you see the naked heart and let your own be seen, there is nothing that you can deem trustworthy or reliable, not even the mere fact of loving and being loved, since you cannot know how genuine the sentiment is…

I tell you,…it is virtue, yes virtue, that initiates and preserves friendship. For it is virtue that is the source of the rational, the stable, the consistent element in life. When virtue raises herself up and displays her light, and sees and recognizes the same light in another, she moves toward it and shares reciprocally in that which the other possesses; from this a flame bursts forth, whether of love or of friendship. Both terms after all are derived from the verb "to love"…, and "to love" means nothing but to cherish the person for whom one feels affection, without any special need and without any thought of advantage—although advantage in fact does grow out of friendship, even if one does not seek it…

But since human life is a fragile and unstable thing, we have no choice but to be ever on the search for people whom we may love, and by whom we may be loved in turn, for if charity and goodwill are removed from life, all the joy is gone out of it.

Marcus Tullius Cicero
On Friendship

A friend will be sure to act the part of an advocate before he will assume that of a judge.

Robert South
Sermons

I was sitting, torn by grief. Someone came and talked to me of God's dealings, of why it happened, of hope beyond the grave. He talked constantly, he said things I knew were true. I was unmoved except to wish he'd go away. He finally did.

Another came and sat beside me. He just sat beside me for an hour and more, listened when I said something, answered briefly, prayed simply, left. I was moved. I was comforted. I hated to see him go.

Joseph Bayly
(written after he laid three of his sons in the grave)
Quoted in *Acts of Love*

Friends should consider themselves as the sacred guardians of each other's virtue; and the noblest testimony they can give of their affection is the correction of the faults of those they love.

Anna Letitia Barbauld
"On Friendship"

I am speaking now of the highest duty we owe our friends, the noblest, the most sacred—that of keeping their own nobleness, goodness, pure and incorrupt...If we *let* our friend become cold and selfish and exacting without a remonstrance, we are no true lover, no true friend.

Harriet Beecher Stowe
Little Foxes

When our friends fall into sin, we ought not to deny them the benefits of friendship so long as there is hope of their mending their ways, and we ought to help them more readily to regain virtue than to recover money, had they lost it, since virtue is more akin than money to friendship. When, however, they fall into very great wickedness, and become incurable, we ought no longer to show them friendliness.

Saint Thomas Aquinas
Summa Theologica

Happy is he to whom, in the maturer season of life, there remains one tried and constant friend.

Anna Letitia Barbauld
"On Friendship"

Lord, make me an instrument of Thy peace.
Where there is hatred, let us sow love;
where there is despair, hope;
where there is sadness, joy;
where there is darkness, light.
O Divine Master,
grant that we may not so much seek to be consoled, as to console;
not so much to be loved, as to love.
For it is in giving that we receive,
it is in pardoning that we are pardoned,
it is in dying that we are born again to eternal life.

Saint Francis of Assisi

To act the part of a true friend requires more conscientious feeling than to fill with credit and complacency any other station or capacity in social life.

Sarah Ellis
Pictures of Private Life

Thank you for the birthday card. Old Dad Time trades little that men want. He has traded me wrinkles for teeth, stiff legs for limber ones. But cards like yours tell me he has left me my friends. For that great kindness I forgive him.

Good friends make the roughest trail easy.

Charles M. Russell
Letter to Josephine Trigg,
March 27, 1924

Should auld acquaintance be forgot,
And never brought to min'?

Robert Burns
Auld Lang Syne

And great and numerous as are the blessings of friendship, this certainly is the sovereign one, that it gives us bright hopes for the future and forbids weakness and despair. In the face of a true friend a man sees as it were a second self. So that where his friend is he is; if his friend be rich, he is not poor; though he be weak, his friend's strength is his; and in his friend's life he enjoys a second life after his own is finished. This last is perhaps the most difficult to conceive. But such is the effect of the respect, the loving remembrance, and the regret of friends which follow us to the grave. While they take the sting out of death, they add a glory to the life of the survivors.

Marcus Tullius Cicero
On Friendship

I met Tim in the second grade. We sat together in Mrs. Worrel's class. We became friends when we discovered no other group would have us. We weren't athletic enough to be jocks. The girls didn't like us because we looked funny. Even the Scouts, who had taken a solemn oath to be kind and charitable, steered clear of us.

Tim lived on a farm. I lived in town. When we hit fourth grade, our parents let us ride our bikes back and forth to each other's houses. Our social life increased exponentially. On Fridays, Tim would ride in to my house to spend the night. We'd go to the movies up at the Royal Rathole. The jocks would sit near the back and neck with the girls, and we'd sit behind them and make kissing noises.

On Saturdays, I'd ride my Schwinn Varsity out to Tim's. We'd stay up late to watch *Planet of the Apes*. His mom was a night-shift nurse at the county hospital. She'd bring us a tray of Cokes and Pringles, give us both a good night kiss, and head into work. She was real nice. A lot of mothers don't like having extra kids around, but she never seemed to mind. I always felt welcome. I'm going to try and remember that when my boys start bringing their friends home.

When we were in the eighth grade, I invited a girl named Amy to the spring dance. Tim came along. We wore plaid leisure suits and drank a lot of punch. Amy spent most of her time in the bathroom.

Then we went to high school. We took all the same classes so we could be together. We were both girl crazy. Unfortunately, our feelings weren't recipro-cated. The prettiest girl in school was named Laura. She was a cheerleader, and Tim loved her. She was a friend of my brother's, who was a jock, so I asked her for her picture. She signed it "to someone I really admire." I think it's because she didn't remember my name. I sold it to Tim for two bucks. Friendship had its limits.

When we graduated from high school, we got jobs. I worked in an office for an electric utility. Tim was a mechanic at Logan's Mobil. I'd stop by every morning on my way to work for a dollar's worth of gas and conversation. Then at night we'd get in his car and drive to McDonald's in the next town over.

Flush with money from our jobs, we decided to buy motorcycles. Tim bought one that had a custom paint job. It didn't run well, but it looked good. We'd ride every Sunday afternoon and most nights. A lot of times we'd end up at the Dairy Queen, where we'd sit on our bikes and talk about stuff that doesn't seem too important now, but was incredibly so then.

One night, about two o'clock, I got a phone call from the sheriff's chaplain, Joe Stump. He told me my best friend since Mrs. Worrel's second grade class had been hit by a drunken driver and was dead. They were afraid I had been hit too, so they were calling to check on me.

Tim's funeral was three days later. I was a pallbearer and sat on the front row. His parents sat across from me. His mother was a knot of grief; his dad was bent and weighed. We buried him at the South Cemetery. All I remember now is the crying.

There are a lot of things about Tim I've forgotten. I do remember that he liked *The Dukes of Hazzard* and that he was taking a correspondence course on how to be a diesel mechanic. I remember his laugh. And I remember that in the fourteen years of our friendship, I never once heard him ridicule anyone.

When Tim died, a lot of people took it upon themselves to explain to me why it happened. I would listen and smile and nod my head, mostly so they'd go away and leave me alone.

There are some things about this life I'll never understand. One of them is why a drunken driver dies of old age when a never-hurt-a-flea young man barely sees twenty. Someday I'm going to see God face to face. And when I do, I'm going to ask Him why that is.

Philip Gulley
Front Porch Tales

Thinking of departed friends is to me something sweet and mellow. For when I had them with me it was with the feeling that I was going to lose them, and now that I have lost them I keep the feeling that I have them with me still.

Lucius Annaeus Seneca
Letters to Lucilius

This is the comfort of friends, that though they may be said to die, yet their friendship and society are, in the best sense, ever present, because immortal.

William Penn
Fruits of Solitude

Hand grasps at hand, eye lights eye in good friendship,
And great hearts expand
And grow one in the sense of this world's life.

Ralph Waldo Emerson

Greater love hath no man that this, that a man lay down his life for his friends.

John 15:13

Being a

GOOD CITIZEN

CHAPTER NINE

BEING A GOOD CITIZEN

———

Citizens are not born, but made.

Baruch Spinoza
Tractatus Politicus

Whatever makes men good Christians, makes them good citizens.

Daniel Webster
Speech, December 22, 1820

But I say unto you which hear, Love your enemies, do good to them which hate you. Bless them that curse you, and pray for them which despitefully use you. And unto him that smiteth thee on the one cheek offer also the other; and him that taketh away thy cloke forbid not to take thy coat also. Give to every man that asketh of thee; and of him that taketh away thy goods ask them not again. And as ye would that men should do to you, do ye also to them likewise. For if ye love them which love you, what thank have ye? for sinners also love those that love them. And if ye do good to them which do good to you, what thank have ye? for sinners also do even the same. And if ye lend to them of whom ye hope to receive, what thank have ye? for sinners also lend to sinners, to receive as much again. But love ye your enemies, and do good, and lend, hoping for nothing again; and your reward shall be great, and ye shall be the children of the

Highest: for he is kind unto the unthankful and to the evil. Be ye therefore merciful, as your Father also is merciful. Judge not, and ye shall not be judged: condemn not, and ye shall not be condemned: forgive, and ye shall be forgiven: Give, and it shall be given unto you; good measure, pressed down, and shaken together, and running over, shall men give into your bosom. For with the same measure that ye mete withal it shall be measured to you again.

Luke 6:27-38

If a man be gracious and courteous to strangers, it shows he is a citizen of the world, and that his heart is no island cut off from other lands, but a continent that joins to them.

Francis Bacon
Essays

You must give time to your fellow men—even if it's a little thing, do something for others—something for which you get no pay but the privilege of doing it.

Albert Schweitzer

Scrooge fell upon his knees, and clasped his hands before his face.

"Mercy!" he said. "Dreadful apparition, why do you trouble me?"

"Man of the worldly mind!" replied the Ghost, "do you believe in me or not?"

"I do," said Scrooge. "I must. But why do spirits walk the earth, and why do they come to me?"

"It is required of every man," the Ghost returned, "that the spirit within him should walk abroad among his fellow-men, and travel far and wide, and if that spirit goes not forth in life, it is condemned to do so after death. It is doomed to wander through the world—oh, woe is me!—and witness what it cannot share, but might have shared on earth, and turned to happiness!"…

"But you were always a good man of business, Jacob," faltered Scrooge, who now began to apply this to himself.

"Business!" cried the Ghost, wringing its hands again. "Mankind was my business; the common welfare was my business; charity, mercy, forbearance, and benevolence, were, all, my business. The dealings of my trade were but a drop of water in the comprehensive ocean of my business!"

It held up its chain at arm's length, as if that were the cause of all its unavailing grief, and flung it heavily upon the ground again.

"At this time of the rolling year," the spectre said, "I suffer most. Why did I walk though crowds of fellow-beings with my eyes turned down, and never raised them to that blessed Star which led the Wise Men to a poor abode! Were there no poor homes to which its light would have conducted me!"

Charles Dickens
A Christmas Carol

The primary idea in all of my work was to help the farmer and fill the poor man's empty dinner pail...My idea is to help the "man farthest down." This is why I have made every process just as simple as I could to put it within his reach.

George Washington Carver
Quoted in *George Washington Carver in His Own Words*

I got the finest letter tonight. It was from a blind girl, and she sent me one of my Sunday articles and it was all written out in Braille.

I don't know how long that system of writing has been out. It may have been before the Nobel Prize was given out for outstanding achievement. But Braille, or whoever he was, should have had that prize...

Think of helping the world like that.

Will Rogers
Quoted in *Will Rogers Speaks*

If I can stop one heart from breaking,
I shall not live in vain;
If I can ease one life the aching,
Or cool one pain,
Or help one fainting robin
Unto his nest again,
I shall not live in vain.

Emily Dickinson
"If I Can Stop One Heart From Breaking"

A man of humanity is one who, in seeking to establish himself, finds a foot-hold for others and who, desiring attainment for himself, helps others to attain.

K'ung Fu-tzu Confucius
Analects

Some men succeed by what they know; some by what they do; and a few by what they are.

Elbert Hubbard
The Note Book

I want to see you game, boys. I want to see you brave and manly, and I also want to see you gentle and tender.

Be practical as well as generous in your ideals. Keep your eyes on the stars and your feet on the ground.

Courage, hard work, self-mastery and intelligent effort are all essential to a successful life.

Character in the long run is the decisive factor in the life of an individual and of nations alike.

Theodore Roosevelt
"Youth"

There is no end to the sufficiency of character. It can afford to wait; it can do without what is called success; it cannot but succeed. To a well-principled man existence is victory. He defends himself against failure in his main design by making every inch of the road to it pleasant. There is no trifle, and no obscurity to him: he feels the immensity of the chain whose last link he holds in his hand, and is led by it. Having nothing, this spirit hath all. It asks, with Marcus Aure-lius, "What matter by whom the good is done?" It extols humility,—by every self-abasement lifted higher in the scale of being. It makes no stipulations for earthly felicity,—does not ask, in the absoluteness of its trust, even for the assurance of continued life.

Ralph Waldo Emerson
"Character"

Man is made by his belief. As he believes, so he is.

Bhagavad-Gita

He does not believe that does not live according to his belief.

Thomas Fuller
Gnomologia

I believe that we can live on earth according to the teachings of Jesus, and that the greatest happiness will come to the world when man obeys His command-ment "Love ye one another."

I believe that every question between man and man is a religious question, and that every social wrong is a moral wrong.

I believe that we can live on earth according to the fulfilment of God's will, and that when the will of God is done on earth as it is done in heaven, every man will love his fellow men, and act towards them as he desires they should act towards him. I believe that the welfare of each is bound up in the welfare of all.

Helen Keller
Midstream

And, behold, a certain lawyer stood up, and tempted him, saying, Master, what shall I do to inherit eternal life? He said unto him, What is written in the law? how readest thou? And he answering said, Thou shalt love the Lord thy God with all thy heart, and with all thy soul, and with all thy strength, and with all thy mind; and thy neighbour as thyself. And he said unto him, Thou hast answered right; this do, and thou shalt live. But he, willing to justify himself, said unto Jesus, And who is my neighbour?

And Jesus answering said, A certain man went down from Jerusalem to Jeri-cho, and fell among thieves, which stripped him of his raiment, and wounded him, and departed, leaving him half dead. And by chance there came down a certain priest that way: and when he saw him, he passed by on the other side. And likewise a Levite, when he was at the place, came and looked on him, and passed by on the other side. But a certain Samaritan, as he journeyed, came where he was: and when he saw him, he had compassion on him. And went to him, and bound up his wounds, pouring in oil and wine, and set him on his own beast, and brought him to an inn, and took care of him. And on the morrow when he departed, he took out two pence, and gave them to the host, and said unto him, Take care of him; and whatsoever thou spendest more, when I come again, I will repay thee.

Which now of these three, thinkest thou, was neighbour unto him that fell among the thieves? And he said, He that shewed mercy on him. Then said Jesus unto him, Go, and do thou likewise.

Luke 10:25-37

Who is my neighbor?

I was taught as a child that it is the person who lives next door. But then I had to ask, did that person cease to be my neighbor by the simple act of moving away? I began wondering if someone living as far away as the next block could be my neighbor. Could someone in the next town, or a city five thousand or even fifty thousand miles away, be my neighbor?

Growing up, I learned that my neighbor is both highly specific and legion. He lives next door or halfway around the world. He shares my values or utterly opposes them. He resembles me or looks completely different.

But if my neighbor, whoever or wherever he may be, is persecuted for his beliefs, am I not persecuted, too? If my neighbor's humanity is called into question, is not my humanity called into question, too?

Malcolm Boyd
The Lover

The world has narrowed to a neighborhood before it has broadened to brotherhood.

Lyndon Baines Johnson
Quoted in Public Papers of the Presidents of the United States,
Lyndon B. Johnson: 1963-64

Every experience proves that the real problem of our existence lies in the fact that we ought to love one another, but do not.

Reinhold Niebuhr
Christian Realism and Political Problems

Our true nationality is mankind.

> H. G. Wells
> *The Outline of History*

To see the earth as we now see it, small and beautiful in that eternal silence where it floats, is to see ourselves as riders on the earth together, brothers on that bright loveliness in the unending night—brothers who see now they are truly brothers.

> Archibald MacLeish
> "Riders on Earth Together, Brothers in Eternal Cold,"
> *New York Times*, December 25, 1968

Oh, East is East, and West is West, and never the twain shall meet,
Till Earth and Sky stand presently at God's great Judgement Seat;
But there is neither East nor West, Border, nor Breed, nor Birth,
When two strong men stand face to face, though they come from the ends
    of the earth.

> Rudyard Kipling
> "The Ballad of East and West"

Wherever there is a human being, I see God-given rights inherent in that being whatever may be the sex or complexion.

> William Lloyd Garrison
> *Life*

Let us discard all this quibbling about this man or the other man, this race or that race and the other race being inferior and therefore they must be placed in an inferior position—discarding our standard that we have left us! Let us discard all these things and unite as one people throughout this land until we shall once more stand up declaring that all men are created equal.

> Abraham Lincoln
> Speech, July 10, 1858

I am the inferior of any man whose rights I trample under foot.

> Robert G. Ingersoll
> *Prose-Poems and Selections*

All, too, will bear in mind this sacred principle, that though the will of the majority is in all cases to prevail, that will, to be rightful, must be reasonable; that the minority possess their equal rights, which equal laws must protect, and to violate which would be oppression. Let us, then, fellow citizens, unite with one heart and one mind. Let us restore to social intercourse that harmony and affection without which liberty and even life itself are but dreary things. And let us reflect that having banished from our land that religious intolerance under which mankind so long bled and suffered, we have yet gained little if we countenance a political intolerance as despotic, as wicked, and capable of as bitter and bloody persecutions.

Thomas Jefferson
Democracy

I say to you today even though we face the difficulties of today and tomorrow, I still have a dream. It is a dream that is deeply rooted in the American dream. I have a dream that one day this nation will rise up, live out the true meaning of its creed. We hold these truths to be self-evident, that all men are created equal. I have a dream that one day on the red hills of Georgia the sons of former slaves and the sons of former slave-owners will be able to sit down together at the table of brotherhood…I have a dream that one day every valley shall be exalted, every hill and mountain shall be made low. The rough places will be made plain and the crooked places will be made straight.

Martin Luther King, Jr.
Speech at the Civil Rights March on
Washington, D.C., August 28, 1963

Prejudice is the child of ignorance.

William Hazlitt
Sketches and Essays

A Fox who had never yet seen a Lion, when he fell in with him by a certain chance for the first time in the forest, was so frightened that he was near dying with fear. On his meeting with him for the second time, he was still much alarmed, but not to the same extent as at first. On seeing him the third time, he

so increased in boldness that he went up to him, and commenced a familiar conversation with him.

   Acquaintance softens prejudices.

Æsop
Fables

Race prejudice is not only a shadow over the colored—it is a shadow over all of
us, and the shadow is darkest over those who feel it least and allow its evil effects
to go on.

Pearl S. Buck
What America Means to Me

There are cases where not to speak is a strong form of assertion—not to condemn
is to approve—When a great moral question is made a test question before the
public mind—or a great evil is threatening to spread in a community—and any
body of men professing eminently to be the representative men of Christianity,
decline publicly & clearly to express any opinion about it this want of assertion
is immediately received by the powers of evil as the strongest affirmation.

Harriet Beecher Stowe
"The Church and the Slave Trade"

Forty years ago, a young man awoke, and he found himself an orphan in an
orphaned world. What have I learned in the last forty years? Small things. I
learned the perils of language and those of silence. I learned that in extreme situations when human lives and dignity are at stake, neutrality is a sin. It helps the
killers, not the victims…

   April 19, 1943, the Warsaw Ghetto rose in arms against the onslaught of the
Nazis. They were so few and so young and so helpless. And nobody came to their
help…They managed to fight and resist and push back those Nazis and their
accomplices for six weeks. And yet the leaders of the free world…knew everything and did so little, or nothing, or at least nothing specifically to save Jewish
children from death…One million Jewish children perished. If I spent my entire
life reciting their names, I would die before finishing the task…

   I have learned the danger of indifference, the crime of indifference. For the opposite of love, I have learned, is not hate, but indifference. Jews were killed by the enemy but betrayed by their so-called allies, who found political reasons to justify their indifference or passivity.

Elie Wiesel
The Kingdom of Memory

Dearest Mother:

...We have had the greatest heroine of the age here, Harriet Tubman, a black woman, and a fugitive slave, who has been back eight times secretly and brought out in all sixty slaves with her, including all her own family, besides aiding many more in other ways to escape. Her tales of adventure are beyond anything in fiction and her ingenuity and generalship are extraordinary. I have known her for some time and mentioned her in speeches once or twice—the slaves call her Moses. She has had a reward of twelve thousand dollars offered for her in Maryland and will probably be burned alive whenever she is caught, which she probably will be, first or last, as she is going again...She is jet black and cannot read or write, only talk, besides acting.

Colonel Thomas Wentworth Higginson
Quoted in *Harriet Tubman*

During my lifetime I have dedicated myself to this struggle of the African people. I have fought against White domination, and I have fought against Black domination. I have cherished the ideal of a democratic and free society in which all persons live together in harmony and with equal opportunities. It is an ideal which I hope to live for and to achieve. But if needs be, it is an ideal for which I am prepared to die.

Nelson Mandela
No Easy Walk to Freedom

To accomplish great things, we must not only act but also dream, not only plan but also believe.

Anatole France

And Haman said unto king Ahasuerus, There is a certain people scattered abroad and dispersed among the people in all the provinces of thy kingdom; and their laws are diverse from all people; neither keep they the king's laws: therefore it is not for the king's profit to suffer them. If it please the king, let it be written that they may be destroyed: and I will pay ten thousand talents of silver to the hands of those that have the charge of the business, to bring it into the king's treasuries. And the king took his ring from his hand, and gave it unto Haman the son of Hammedatha the Agagite, the Jews' enemy. And the king said unto Haman, The silver is given to thee, the people also, to do with them as it seemeth good to thee. Then were the king's scribes called on the thirteenth day of the first month, and there was written according to all that Haman had commanded unto the king's lieutenants, and to the governors that were over every province, and to the rulers of every people of every province according to the writing thereof, and to every people after their language; in the name of king Ahasuerus was it written, and sealed with the king's ring. And the letters were sent by posts into all the king's provinces, to destroy, to kill, and to cause to perish, all Jews, both young and old, little children and women, in one day, even upon the thirteenth day of the twelfth month, which is the month Adar, and to take the spoil of them for a prey. The copy of the writing for a commandment to be given in every province was published unto all people, that they should be ready against that day. The posts went out, being hastened by the king's commandment, and the decree was given in Shushan the palace. And the king and Haman sat down to drink; but the city Shushan was perplexed.

When Mordecai perceived all that was done, Mordecai rent his clothes, and put on sackcloth with ashes, and went out into the midst of the city, and cried with a loud and a bitter cry; And came even before the king's gate: for none might enter into the king's gate clothed with sackcloth. And in every province, whithersoever the king's commandment and his decree came, there was great mourning among the Jews, and fasting, and weeping, and wailing; and many lay in sackcloth and ashes.

So Esther's maids and her chamberlains came and told it to her. Then was the queen exceedingly grieved; and she sent raiment to clothe Mordecai, and to take away his sackcloth from him: but he received it not. Then called Esther for Hatach, one of the king's chamberlains, whom he had appointed to attend upon her, and gave him a commandment to Mordecai, to know what it was, and why it was. So Hatach went forth to Mordecai unto the street of the city, which was before the king's gate. And Mordecai told him of all that had happened unto him, and of the sum of the money that Haman had promised to pay to the king's treasuries for the Jews, to destroy them. Also he gave him the copy of the writing of the decree that was given at Shushan to destroy them, to shew it unto Esther, and to declare it unto her, and to charge her that she should go in unto the king, to make supplication unto him, and to make request before him for her people. And Hatach came and told Esther the words of Mordecai. Again Esther spake unto Hatach, and gave him commandment unto Mordecai; All the king's servants, and the people of the king's provinces, do know, that whosoever, whether man or woman, shall come unto the king into the inner court, who is not called, there is one law of his to put him to death, except such to whom the king shall hold out the golden sceptre, that he may live: but I have not been called to come in to the king these thirty days. And they told to Mordecai Esther's words. Then Mordecai commanded to answer Esther, Think not thyself that thou shalt escape in the king's house, more than all the Jews. For if thou altogether holdest thy peace at this time, then shall there enlargement and deliverance arise to the Jews from another place; but thou and thy father's house shall be destroyed: and who knoweth whether thou art come to the kingdom for such a time as this?

Then Esther bade them return Mordecai this answer, Go gather together all the Jews that are present in Shushan, and fast ye for me, and neither eat nor drink three days, night or day: I also and my maidens will fast likewise; and so will I go in unto the king, which is not according to the law: and if I perish, I perish. So Mordecai went his way, and did according to all that Esther had commanded him.

Now it came to pass on the third day, that Esther put on her royal apparel, and stood in the inner court of the king's house, over against the king's house: and the king sat upon his royal throne in the royal house, over against the gate of the house. And it was so, when the king saw Esther the queen standing in the court, that she obtained favour in his sight; and the king held out to Esther the golden sceptre that was in his hand. So Esther drew near, and touched the top of the sceptre. Then said the king unto her, What wilt thou, queen Esther? and what is thy request? it shall be even given thee to the half of the kingdom. And Esther answered, If it seem good unto the king, let the king and Haman come this day unto the banquet that I have prepared for him. Then the king said, Cause Haman to make haste, that he may do as Esther hath said. So the king and

Haman came to the banquet that Esther had prepared.

And the king said unto Esther at the banquet of wine, What is thy petition? and it shall be granted thee: and what is they request? even to the half of the kingdom it shall be performed…

Then Esther the queen answered and said, If I have found favour in thy sight, O king, and if it please the king, let my life be given me at my petition, and my people at my request: For we are sold, I and my people, to be destroyed, to be slain, and to perish. But if we had been sold for bondmen and bondwomen, I had held my tongue, although the enemy could not countervail the king's damage.

Then the king Ahasuerus answered and said unto Esther the queen, Who is he, and where is he, that durst presume in his heart to do so? And Esther said, The adversary and enemy is this wicked Haman. Then Haman was afraid before the king and the queen.

And the king arising from the banquet of wine in his wrath went into the palace garden: and Haman stood up to make request for his life to Esther the queen; for he saw that there was evil determined against him by the king. Then the king returned out of the palace garden into the place of the banquet of wine; and Haman was fallen upon the bed whereon Esther was. Then said the king, Will he force the queen also before me in the house? As the word went out of the king's mouth, they covered Haman's face…So they hanged Haman on the gallows…

And Esther spake yet again before the king, and fell down at his feet, and besought him with tears to put away the mischief of Haman the Agagite, and his device that he had devised against the Jews. Then the king held out the golden scepter toward Esther. So Esther arose, and stood before the king, and said, If it please the king, and if I have found favour in his sight, and the thing seem right before the king, and I be pleasing in his eyes, let it be written to reverse the letters devised by Haman the son of Hammedatha the Agagite, which he wrote to destroy the Jews which are in all the king's provinces: For how can I endure to see the evil that shall come unto my people? or how can I endure to see the destruction of my kindred? Then the king Ahasuerus said unto Esther the queen and to Mordecai the Jew, Behold, I have given Esther the house of Haman, and him they have hanged upon the gallows, because he laid his hand upon the Jews…

Therefore the Jews of the villages, that dwelt in the unwalled towns, made the fourteenth day of the month Adar a day of gladness and feasting, and a good day, and of sending portions one to another.

Esther 3:8–5:6; 7:3-8,10; 8:3-7; 9:19

If we are markt to die, we are enow
To do our country loss; and if to live,
The fewer men, the greater share of honour.
God's will! I pray thee, wish not one man more.
By Jove, I am not covetous for gold;
Nor care I who doth feed upon my cost;
It yearns me not if men my garments wear;
Such outward things dwell not in my desires:
But if it be a sin to covet honour,
I am the most offending soul alive.
No, faith, my coz, wish not a man from England:
God's peace! I would not lose so great an honour,
As one man more, methinks, would share from me,
For the best hope I have. O, do not wish one more!
Rather proclaim it, Westmoreland, through my host,
That he which hath no stomach to this fight,
Let him depart; his passport shall be made,
And crowns for convoy put into his purse:
We would not die in that man's company
That fears his fellowship to die with us.
This day is call'd the feast of Crispian:
He that outlives this day, and comes safe home,
Will stand a tip-toe when the day is named,
And rouse him at the name of Crispian.
He that shall live this day, and see old age,
Will yearly on the vigil feast his neighbours,
And say, 'To-morrow is Saint Crispian:'
Then will he strip his sleeve and show his scars,
And say, 'These wounds I had on Crispin's day.'
Old men forget; yet all shall be forgot,
But he'll remember with advantages

What feats he did that day: then shall our names,
Familiar in their mouths as household words,—
Harry the king, Bedford and Exeter,
Warwick and Talbot, Salisbury and Gloster,—
Be in their flowing cups freshly remember'd.
This story shall the good man teach his son;
And Crispin Crispian shall ne'er go by,
From this day to the ending of the world,
But we in it shall be remembered,—
We few, we happy few, we band of brothers;
For he to-day that sheds his blood with me
Shall be my brother; be he ne'er so vile,
This day shall gentle his condition:
And gentlemen in England now a-bed
Shall think themselves accurst they were not here;
And hold their manhoods cheap whiles any speaks
That fought with us upon Saint Crispin's day.

William Shakespeare
Henry V

There is something better, if possible, that a man can give than his life. That is his living spirit to a service that is not easy, to resist counsels that are hard to resist, to stand against purposes that are difficult to stand against.

Woodrow Wilson
Speech, May 30, 1919

I cannot and will not recant anything, for to go against conscience is neither right nor safe. Here I stand, I can do no other, so help me God. Amen.

Martin Luther
Speech, April 18, 1521

Let us be true: this is the highest maxim of art and of life, the secret of eloquence and of virtue, and of all moral authority.

Henri Frédéric Amiel
Journal

I want to declare to the world that, whatever may be said to the contrary, and although I might have forfeited the regard and even the trust of many in the West—and I bow my head low—but even for their friendship or their love, I must not suppress that voice within, call it conscience, call it the prompting of my inner basic nature. There is something within me impelling me to cry out my agony. I have known exactly what it is. That something in me which never deceives me tells me now: 'You have to stand against the whole world although you may have to stand alone. You have to stare at the world in the face although the world may look at you with blood-shot eyes. Do not fear. Trust that little thing in you which resides in the heart and says: Forsake friends, wife, all; but testify to that for which you have lived and for which you have to die.'

Mohandas K. Gandhi
All Men Are Brothers

Fortitude is the capacity to say "no" when the world wants to hear "yes."

Erich Fromm
The Revolution of Hope

He has honor if he holds himself to an ideal of conduct though it is inconvenient, unprofitable, or dangerous to do so.

Walter Lippmann
A Preface to Morals

Nebuchadnezzar the king made an image of gold, whose height was threescore cubits, and the breadth thereof six cubits: he set it up in the plain of Dura, in the province of Babylon. Then Nebuchadnezzar the king sent to gather together the princes, the governors, and the captains, the judges, the treasurers, the counsellors, the sheriffs, and all the rulers of the provinces, to come to the dedication of the image which Nebuchadnezzar the king had set up. Then the princes, the governors, and captains, the judges, the treasurers, the counsellors, the sheriffs, and all the rulers of the provinces, were gathered together unto the dedication of the image that Nebuchadnezzar the king had set up; and they stood before the image that Nebuchadnezzar had set up. Then an herald cried aloud, To you it is commanded, O people, nations, and languages, That at what time ye hear the sound of the cornet, flute, harp, sackbut, psaltery, dulcimer, and all kinds of musick, ye fall down and worship the golden image that Nebuchadnezzar the king hath set up: And whoso falleth not down and worshippeth shall the same hour be cast into the midst of a burning fiery furnace. Therefore at that time, when all the people heard the sound of the cornet, flute, harp, sackbut, psaltery, and all kinds of musick, all the people, the nations, and the languages, fell down and worshipped the golden image that Nebuchadnezzar the king had set up.

Wherefore at that time certain Chaldeans came near, and accused the Jews. They spake and said to the king Nebuchadnezzar, O king, live for ever. Thou, O king, hast made a decree, that every man that shall hear the sound of the cornet, flute, harp, sackbut, psaltery, and dulcimer, and all kinds of musick, shall fall down and worship the golden image: And whoso falleth not down and worshippeth, that he should be cast into the midst of a burning fiery furnace. There are certain Jews whom thou hast set over the affairs of the province of Babylon, Shadrach, Meshach, and Abednego; these men, O king, have not regarded thee: they serve not thy gods, nor worship the golden image which thou hast set up.

Then Nebuchadnezzar in his rage and fury commanded to bring Shadrach, Meshach, and Abednego. Then they brought these men before the king. Nebuchadnezzar spake and said unto them, Is it true, O Shadrach, Meshach, and Abednego, do not ye serve my gods, nor worship the golden image which I have set up? Now if ye be ready that at what time ye hear the sound of the cornet, flute, harp, sackbut, psaltery, and dulcimer, and all kinds of musick, ye fall down and worship the image which I have made; well: but if ye worship not, ye shall be cast the same hour into the midst of a burning fiery furnace; and who is that God that shall deliver you out of my hands?

Shadrach, Meshach, and Abednego, answered and said to the king, O Nebuchadnezzar, we are not careful to answer thee in this matter. If it be so, our God whom we serve is able to deliver us from the burning fiery furnace, and he will deliver us out of thine hand, O king. But if not, be it known unto thee, O king, that we will not serve thy gods, nor worship the golden image which thou hast set up.

Then was Nebuchadnezzar full of fury, and the form of his visage was changed against Shadrach, Meshach, and Abednego: therefore he spake, and commanded that they should heat the furnace seven times more than it was wont to be heated. And he commanded the most mighty men that were in his army to bind Shadrach, Meshach, and Abednego, and to cast them into the burning fiery furnace. Then these men were bound in their coats, their hosen, and their hats, and their other garments, and were cast into the midst of the burning fiery furnace. Therefore because the king's commandment was urgent, and the furnace exceeding hot, the flame of the fire slew those men that took up Shadrach, Meshach, and Abednego. And these three men, Shadrach, Meshach, and Abednego, fell down bound into the midst of the burning fiery furnace.

Then Nebuchadnezzar the king was astonished, and rose up in haste, and spake, and said unto his counsellors, Did not we cast three men bound into the midst of the fire? They answered and said unto the king, True, O king. He answered and said, Lo, I see four men loose, walking in the midst of the fire, and they have no hurt; and the form of the fourth is like the Son of God. Then Nebuchadnezzar came near to the mouth of the burning fiery furnace, and spake, and said, Shadrach, Meshach, and Abednego, ye servants of the most high God, come forth, and come hither. Then Shadrach, Meshach, and Abednego, came forth of the midst of the fire. And the princes, governors, and captains, and the king's counsellors, being gathered together saw these men, upon whose bodies the fire had no power, nor was an hair of their head singed, neither were their coats changed, nor the smell of fire had passed on them.

Then Nebuchadnezzar spake, and said, Blessed be the God of Shadrach, Meshach, and Abednego, who hath sent his angel, and delivered his servants that trusted in him, and have changed the king's word, and yielded their bodies, that they might not serve nor worship any god, except their own God. Therefore I make a decree, That every people, nation, and language, which speak any thing amiss against the God of Shadrach, Meshach, and Abednego, shall be cut in pieces, and their houses shall be made a dunghill: because there is no other God that can deliver after this sort. Then the king promoted Shadrach, Meshach, and Abednego, in the province of Babylon.

Daniel 3

Character is much easier kept than recovered.

Thomas Paine
The American Crisis

The honor of a gentleman demands the inviolability of his word, and the incorruptibility of his principles. He is the descendant of the knight, the crusader; he is the defender of the defenseless and the champion of justice—or he is not a gentleman.

Emily Post
Etiquette

The place to improve the world is first in one's own heart and head and hands, and then work outward from there.

Robert M. Pirsig
Zen and the Art of Motorcycle Maintenance

You cannot hope to build a better world without improving the individuals. To that end each of us must work for his own improvement, and at the same time share a general responsibility for all humanity, our particular duty being to aid those to whom we think we can be most useful.

Marie Curie
Pierre Curie

The stream of life through millions of years, the stream of human lives through countless centuries. Evil, death and dearth, sacrifice and love—what does "I" mean in such a perspective? Reason tells me that I am bound to seek my own good, seek to gratify my desires, win power for myself and admiration from others. And yet I "know"—know without knowing—that, in such a perspective, nothing could be less important.

Dag Hammarskjöld
Markings

I am told that the world is selfish, that men seek only outward aggrandizement and temporal prosperity. I assuredly see much of this, but society would cease to exist if liberality and enlarged principles of action did not more prevail. I discover that negligence and folly, vice and crime, sweep widely and fearfully; but I cannot be blind to the fact that there must be a greater amount of care and reflection, of purity and integrity, else the fabric of social life would fall in ruins, and the intellectual become subservient to animal life.

Dorothea L. Dix
Poverty, U.S.A.

"You love to feed the hungry, don't you, Elizabeth?"

"Yes, I do!" she said, with emphasis.

"Then you know what the delight of Heaven is, to wit, 'the doing good to others.' It is all the delight God has, and therefore it is a principle of Heaven that man never owns any good until he gives it away—then he treasures it up. Not only does God's happiness consist in doing good to the neighbor, but it makes the joy and growth of all his angels. It is the only genuine joy of earth and Heaven. Indeed, it must become our joy here, or it can never be there. The good we do others, we do to ourselves."

Reverend Jermain Wesley Loguen
*The Rev. J. W. Loguen, as a Slave and
as a Freeman. A Narrative of Real Life.*

Men and nations sink or soar, survive or perish, as they choose to be dominated by sin or righteousness.

A. P. Gouthey

We have not all been born with the same gifts.

A gift is anything that we have that we did not work for. People born to wealth have more advantages than those born in poverty. People with a high intelligence will probably fare better than those born with low intelligence. It is known that people who are blond, tall, and good-looking will be more likely to succeed than those who are not...

Those of us who were raised in good families have a gift. Not everyone was raised with love, security, positive feedback, and values...The "work ethic" is also a gift. Some parents taught it to their kids and some parents did not...

The bottom line is to understand that what we have and who we are has a lot to do with factors we received in a package deal when we came into the world. If that realization doesn't make you thankful, nothing will...

Clearly some people are short of gifts and some have gifts and do not use them well. For both groups their security and quality of life runs a deficit....

But what of the rest of us whose gifts (and usually some effort) have yielded a surplus? It is easy to find people who have surpluses...most of us do. And most of us squander huge amounts of surplus money or time on personal gratification and give very little or nothing in return.

The attitude of "I worked hard and I deserve…" does not consider the very large degree that our gifts contributed to what we have…

By donating some of our surplus time, energy, and money we express thankfulness for the abundance of gifts with which we were born.

Amy Dacyczyn
The Tightwad Gazette

Charity never humiliated him who profited from it, nor ever bound him by the chains of gratitude, since it was not to him but to God that the gift was made.

Antoine de Saint-Exupéry
Flight to Arras

The sage does not hoard.
Having bestowed all he has on others, he has yet more;
Having given all he has to others, he is richer still.

Lao-Tzu
Tao-te-ching

It is not uncommon in a society where there is great disparity of wealth for the "haves" to argue amongst themselves as to whether the "have-nots" are grateful or ungrateful. Some "haves" are obsessed with a belief in the ingratitude of the "have-nots," to the extent that they are embittered by it. "I gave him this and I gave him that, and look what he did to me!" That there are cases of ingratitude one cannot doubt, but apart from those it is my experience that those who complain of ingratitude never give themselves with their gifts. It is the gift, the thing, the money, that they expect to evoke the response, and very often it does not. But when we give ourselves, not seeking gratitude, we are often overwhelmed by the response in some other person who at that moment gives himself to us. It is in that moment that we receive; it is in that moment that God is; it is in that place that God is. That, above all, is what we receive, and it is an experience of joy.

Alan Paton
Instrument of Thy Peace

Isn't it better to have men being ungrateful than to miss a chance to do good?
Denis Diderot
Discours Sur la Poésie Dramatique

To give and then not feel that one has given is the very best of all ways of giving.
Max Beerbohm
And Even Now

The giving is the hardest part; what does it cost to add a smile?
Jean de la Bruyère
Characters

Compassion is not quantitative. Certainly it is true that behind every human being who cries out for help there may be a million or more equally entitled to attention. But this is the poorest of all reasons for not helping the person whose cries you hear. Where, then, does one begin or stop? How to choose? How to determine which one of a million sounds surrounding you is more deserving than the rest? Do not concern yourself in such speculations. You will never know; you will never need to know. Reach out and take hold of the one who happens to be nearest. If you are never able to help or save another, at least you will have saved one. To help put meaning into a single life may not produce universal regeneration, but it happens to represent the basic form of energy in a society. It also is the test of individual responsibility.

Norman Cousins
Human Options

Let him that desires to see others happy, make haste to give while his gift can be enjoyed, and remember that every moment of delay takes away something from the value of his benefaction.

Samuel Johnson
The Idler

In the time of swords and periwigs and full-skirted coats with flowered lappets—when gentlemen wore ruffles, and gold-laced waistcoats of paduasoy and taffeta—there lived a tailor in Gloucester.

He sat in the window of a little shop in Westgate Street, cross-legged on a table, from morning till dark.

All day long while the light lasted he sewed and snippeted, piecing out his satin and pompadour, and lute-string; stuffs had strange names, and were very expensive in the days of the Tailor of Gloucester.

But although he sewed fine silk for his neighbours, he himself was very, very poor—a little old man in spectacles, with a pinched face, old crooked fingers, and a suit of thread-bare clothes…

One bitter cold day near Christmas-time the tailor began to make a coat— a coat of cherry-coloured corded silk embroidered with pansies and roses, and a cream-coloured satin waistcoat—trimmed with gauze and green worsted chenille—for the Mayor of Gloucester…

There were twelve pieces for the coat and four pieces for the waistcoat; and there were pocket flaps and cuffs, and buttons all in order. For the lining of the coat there was fine yellow taffeta; and for the button-holes of the waistcoat, there was cherry-coloured twist. And everything was ready to sew together in the morning, all measured and sufficient—except that there was wanting just one single skein of cherry-coloured twisted silk.

The tailor came out of his shop at dark, for he did not sleep there at nights; he fastened the window and locked the door, and took away the key. No one lived there at night but little brown mice, and they run in and out without any keys…

But the tailor came out of his shop, and shuffled home through the snow. He lived quite near by in College Court, next the doorway to College Green; and although it was not a big house, the tailor was so poor he only rented the kitchen.

He lived alone with his cat; it was called Simpkin…

"Miaw?" said the cat when the tailor opened the door. "Miaw?"

The tailor replied—"Simpkin, we shall make our fortune, but I am worn to a ravelling. Take this groat (which is our last fourpence) and Simpkin, take a china pipkin; buy a penn'orth of bread, a penn'orth of milk and a penn'orth of sausages. And oh, Simpkin, with the last penny of our fourpence buy me one penn'orth of cherry-coloured silk. But do not lose the last penny of the fourpence, Simpkin, or I am undone and worn to a thread-paper, for I have NO MORE TWIST."

Then Simpkin again said, "Miaw?" and took the groat and the pipkin, and went out into the dark.

The tailor was very tired and beginning to be ill. He sat down by the hearth and talked to himself about that wonderful coat...

Then the tailor started; for suddenly, interrupting him, from the dresser at the other side of the kitchen came a number of little noises—

Tip tap, tip tap, tip tap tip!

"Now what can that be?" said the Tailor of Gloucester, jumping up from his chair. The dresser was covered with crockery and pipkins, willow pattern plates, and tea-cups and mugs.

The tailor crossed the kitchen, and stood quite still beside the dresser, listening, and peering through his spectacles. Again from under a tea-cup, came those funny little noises—

Tip tap, tip tap, tip tap tip!

"This is very peculiar," said the Tailor of Gloucester; and he lifted up the tea-cup which was upside down. Out stepped a little live lady mouse, and made a curtsey to the tailor! Then she hopped away down off the dresser, and under the wainscot.

The tailor sat down again by the fire, warming his poor cold hands, and mumbling to himself...

But all at once, from the dresser, there came other little noises:

Tip tap, tip tap, tip tap tip!

"This is passing extraordinary!" said the Tailor of Gloucester, and turned over another tea-cup, which was upside down. Out stepped a little gentleman mouse, and made a bow to the tailor!

And then from all over the dresser came a chorus of little tappings, all sounding together, and answering one another, like watch-beetles in an old worm-eaten window-shutter—

Tip tap, tip tap, tip tap tip!

And out from under tea-cups and from under bowls and basins, stepped other and more little mice who hopped away down off the dresser and under the wainscot.

The tailor sat down, close over the fire, lamenting—"One-and-twenty button-holes of cherry-coloured silk! To be finished by noon of Saturday: and this is Tuesday evening. Was it right to let loose those mice, undoubtedly the property of Simpkin? Alack, I am undone, for I have no more twist!"

The little mice came out again, and listened to the tailor; they took notice of the pattern of that wonderful coat. They whispered to one another about the taffeta lining, and about little mouse tippets.

And then all at once they all ran away together down the passage behind the wainscot, squeaking and calling to one another, as they ran from house to house; and not one mouse was left in the tailor's kitchen when Simpkin came back with the pipkin of milk…

The poor old tailor was very ill with a fever, tossing and turning in his four-post bed; and still in his dreams he mumbled—"No more twist! No more twist!"

All that day he was ill, and the next day, and the next; and what should become of the cherry-coloured coat? In the tailor's shop in Westgate Street the embroidered silk and satin lay cut out upon the table—one-and-twenty button-holes—and who should come to sew them, when the window was barred, and the door was fast locked?

But that does not hinder the little brown mice; they run in and out without any keys through all the old houses in Gloucester…

When the tailor awoke in the morning, the first thing which he saw upon the patchwork quilt, was a skein of cherry-coloured twisted silk…

"Alack, I am worn to a ravelling," said the Tailor of Gloucester, "but I have my twist!"

The sun was shining on the snow when the tailor got up and dressed, and came out into the street with Simpkin running before him…

"Alack," said the tailor, "I have my twist; but no more strength—nor time—than will serve to make me one single button-hole; for this is Christmas Day in the Morning! The Mayor of Gloucester shall be married by noon—and where is his cherry-coloured coat?"

He unlocked the door of the little shop in Westgate Street…

But upon the table—oh joy! the tailor gave a shout—there, where he had left plain cuttings of silk—there lay the most beautifullest coat and embroidered satin waistcoat that ever were worn by a Mayor of Gloucester.

There were roses and pansies upon the facings of the coat; and the waistcoat was worked with poppies and corn-flowers.

Everything was finished except just one single cherry-coloured button-hole, and where that button-hole was wanting there was pinned a scrap of paper with these words—in little teeny weeny writing—

NO MORE TWIST

And from then began the luck of the Tailor of Gloucester; he grew quite stout, and he grew quite rich.

He made the most wonderful waistcoats for all the rich merchants of Gloucester, and for all the fine gentlemen of the country around.

Never were seen such ruffles, or such embroidered cuffs and lappets! But his button-holes were the greatest triumph of it all.

The stitches of those button-holes were so neat—*so neat*—I wonder how they could be stitched by an old man in spectacles, with crooked fingers, and a tailor's thimble.

The stitches of those button-holes were so small—*so small*—they looked as if they had been made by little mice!

Beatrix Potter
"The Tailor of Gloucester"

There are some things we do simply because the doing is a success.

Nikki Giovanni
Racism 101

When the candle is burning, who looks at the wick? When the candle is out, who needs it? But the world without light is wasteland and chaos, and a life without sacrifice is abomination.

Annie Dillard
Holy the Firm

We ourselves feel that what we are doing is just a drop in the ocean. But if that drop was not in the ocean, I think the ocean would be less because of that missing drop.

Mother Teresa
A Gift for God

"Let me light my lamp,"
says the star,
"And never debate
if it will help to remove the darkness."

Rabindranath Tagore
Fireflies

I am only one,
But still I am one.
I cannot do everything,
But still I can do something;
And because I cannot do everything
I will not refuse to do the something that I can do.

Edward E. Hale
"Lend a Hand"

When you're growing up, your ambitions are to have a reasonable amount of money and a lot of fun. But this unbelievable experience changed my values, my attitude, my whole life. I had not been politically active or even aware before the war, but I became so afterwards. And whenever I feel that one person cannot do much, or that what I'm doing is not important or not having any effect, I remember the Germans saying, "No, we are not responsible," and our answer, "Yes, you are. You allowed it to happen."

Kay Bonner Nee
Quoted in *Witnesses to the Holocaust:*
An Oral History

The ratification of the Treaty of Geneva was an enormous triumph for Clara Barton. She lobbied against a bureaucracy that was convinced any agreement with a foreign nation was not only unnecessary but meant compromising America's autonomy. That she persevered to erode this antiquated opinion was a test of her own determination and tenacity, more so because she worked alone; though she could never believe that "someone would not rise up for its help," no one ever did. She labored in an exclusively male world, among politicians and diplomats who had no reason to even consider receiving a disenfranchised female. Yet Barton was received, and listened to, and her treaty was considered— a testament to both the respect she had inspired with her Civil War work and to her self-possession and formidable powers of persuasion. Her success is to be measured not only against the goals of humanitarians—where it stands as a stunning achievement—but also with the work of diplomats, for with the passage of the Treaty of Geneva the United States shed its young timidity and began to define the ideals it held in common with the other nations of the world. The American

Red Cross stands, one hundred years later, a monument to Clara Barton's fore-
sight, courage, and perseverance.

Elizabeth Brown Pryor
Clara Barton: Professional Angel

Like the star
Shining afar
Slowly now
And without rest,
Let each man turn, with steady sway,
Round the task that rules the day
And do his best.

Johann Wolfgang von Goethe
"Example"

There is nothing in the universe that I fear but that I shall not know all my duty,
or shall fail to do it.

Mary Lyon
Quoted in *Eminent Missionary Women*

I believe that every right implies a responsibility; every opportunity, an obligation;
every possession, a duty.

I believe that the law was made for man and not man for the law; that government is the servant of the people and not their master.

I believe in the dignity of labor, whether with head or hand; that the world
owes no man a living but that it owes every man an opportunity to make a living.

I believe that thrift is essential to well-ordered living and that economy is a
prime requisite of a sound financial structure, whether in government, business,
or personal affairs.

I believe that truth and justice are fundamental to an enduring social order.

I believe in the sacredness of a promise, that a man's word should be as good
as his bond, that character—not wealth or power or position—is of supreme
worth.

I believe that the rendering of useful service is the common duty of mankind and that only in the purifying fire of sacrifice is the dross of selfishness consumed and the greatness of the human soul set free.

I believe in an all-wise and all-loving God, …and that the individual's highest fulfillment, greatest happiness, and widest usefulness are to be found in living in harmony with his will.

I believe that love is the greatest thing in the world; that it alone can overcome hate; that right can and will triumph over might.

John D. Rockefeller, Jr.
"I Believe"

It is not the function of our Government to keep the citizen from falling into error; it is the function of the citizen to keep the Government from falling into error.

Robert H. Jackson
American Communications Association v. Douds

We live in a contaminated moral environment. We have fallen morally ill because we became used to saying one thing and thinking another. We have learned not to believe in anything, to ignore each other, to care only about ourselves. Notions such as love, friendship, compassion, humility, or forgiveness have lost their depth and dimensions; for many of us, they represent nothing more than the psychological idiosyncrasies, or appear to be some kind of relic from times past, rather comical in the era of computers and spaceships…

It is up to all of us, and only us, to do something about it. We cannot blame the previous rulers for everything—not only because it would be untrue but also because it could weaken our sense of duty, our obligation to act independently, freely, sensibly, and quickly. Let us not be mistaken: even the best government in the world, the best parliament, and the best president cannot do much on their own. And in any case, it would be wrong to expect a cure-all from them alone. Freedom and democracy, after all, require everyone to participate and thus to share responsibility.

Václav Havel
Open Letters

Rights! There are no rights whatever without corresponding duties.

Samuel Taylor Coleridge
Table-Talk

The long fight to save wild beauty represents democracy at its best. It requires citizens to practice the hardest of virtues—self-restraint.

Edwin Way Teale
Circle of the Seasons

The basic value of a sustainable society, the ecological equivalent of the Golden Rule, is simple: each generation should meet its needs without jeopardizing the prospects of future generations to meet their own needs. We can curtail our use of those things that are ecologically destructive, such as fossil fuels, minerals, and paper. And we can cultivate the deeper, nonmaterial sources of fulfillment that are the main psychological determinants of happiness: family and social relationships, meaningful work, and leisure. Or we can abrogate our responsibilities and let our life-style ruin the Earth.

Alan Thein Durning
"Are We Happy Yet?" published in
Ecopsychology: Restoring the Earth, Healing the Mind

There is a lovely road that runs from Ixopo into the hills. These hills are grass-covered and rolling, and they are lovely beyond any singing of it. The road climbs seven miles into them, to Carisbrooke; and from there, if there is no mist, you look down on one of the fairest valleys of Africa. About you there is grass and bracken and you may hear the forlorn crying of the titihoya, one of the birds of the veld. Below you is the valley of the Umzimkulu, on its journey from the Drakensberg to the sea; and beyond and behind the river, great hill after great hill; and beyond and behind them, the mountains of Ingeli and East Griqualand.

The grass is rich and matted, you cannot see the soil. It holds the rain and the mist, and they seep into the ground, feeding the streams in every kloof. It is well-tended, and not too many cattle feed upon it; not too many fires burn it, laying bare the soil. Stand unshod upon it, for the ground is holy, being even as it came from the Creator. Keep it, guard it, care for it, for it keeps men, guards men, cares for men. Destroy it and man is destroyed.

Where you stand the grass is rich and matted, you cannot see the soil. But the rich green hills break down. They fall to the valley below, and falling, change their nature. For they grow red and bare; they cannot hold the rain and mist, and the streams are dry in the kloofs. Too many cattle feed upon the grass, and too many fires have burned it. Stand shod upon it, for it is coarse and sharp, and the stones cut under the feet. It is not kept, or guarded, or cared for, it no longer keeps men, guards men, cares for men. The titihoya does not cry here any more.

The great red hills stand desolate, and the earth has torn away like flesh. The lightning flashes over them, the clouds pour down upon them, the dead streams come to life, full of the red blood of the earth. Down in the valleys women scratch the soil that is left, and the maize hardly reaches the height of a man. They are valleys of old men and old women, of mothers and children. The men are away, the young men and the girls are away. The soil cannot keep them any more.

Alan Paton
Cry, the Beloved Country

That which is not good for the bee-hive cannot be good for the bees.

Marcus Aurelius
Meditations

Years ago I had a dear friend who married a man who was addicted to gardening. They were a perfect match. Joe had charm; Delia had money. She loved flowers, and he was a gardener. He moved into her beautiful house, and within a week he had the bulldozers and the Vermeer tree movers in to rearrange the topography as the first step in his gardening plan.

Joe was a brilliant gardener, and soon he had altered Delia's acreage, which had been pleasant enough in its neglected state, almost beyond recognition. Where there had been a few ancient camellias straggling down a ragged sloping lawn, now there were terraces with rock walls and herbaceous borders. The over-grown pecan orchard was pushed up, and in its place was a field of Japanese flowering almonds and drifts of daffodils. At the bottom of the garden, where there had been a bog and a thicket, there was now a sylvan glade with the graceful fronds of maidenhair fern dropping into a still, dark pool. There was the sound of water, gouts of sunlight in the shade, and beyond that, a bright meadow of wildflowers surrounded by a carefully ordered and calculated wilderness.

Joe felt that he had gotten a late start with this garden, so he pushed his plantings for maximum growth with tons of fertilizer. His relentless pest management program involved a complicated sprinkling system that would automatically apply pesticides and fungicides in the proper proportions exactly twenty-four hours before the first swarm of aphids hit the budding trees, or the first black spot appeared on a rose leaf.

After just five years of this vigorous encouragement, the garden achieved its mature beauty. The hybrid tea roses with their glossy, flawless foliage stood as tall and dense as a phalanx of soldiers and bloomed until midwinter. The river birch trees spread their silvery shade over the slate walkways. The great coral pink and sunny yellow lotus blossoms swayed on their tall stems above the pool. Plants that weren't even supposed to grow in south Georgia thrived under Joe's care, and horticulturists came from miles around to visit the garden and talk to Joe about his methods.

Then one spring Delia developed allergies. She broke out in great welts and rashes, she itched all over, she couldn't sleep. She thought she was allergic to her cosmetics, so she threw out all her creams and lotions and powders. Her wide, bald-looking eyes stared hopefully out of her pale face, but still she itched and couldn't sleep. Joe decided she was allergic to synthetic fibers, and he bought her all new, expensive clothes made out of Sea Island cotton, linen, and silk. But still she itched and coughed and sneezed. Her eyes watered and her throat hurt.

Then Joe started taking her to special clinics, and she began having all her extra organs removed, just in case. Finally, after the hysterectomy, there was nothing left to take out, and she settled down to a life of torment. Joe was sweet to her. He did everything he could to make her comfortable, and he surrounded her with beautiful things. Every day he brought armloads of flowers in to her, and the bright rooms of the house were filled with bowls of peonies, roses with three-foot stems, blue flag irises, and lilies.

After nearly a year the doctors finally found something. It was cancer. Before three months passed, Delia was on her deathbed. I went to see her, but she didn't recognize me and just kept tossing her head feebly and mumbling the names of flowers. On her last night, Joe said, she sat up in bed with staring eyes, clutched the covers to her neck, and cried out, "Roses!" Then she died.

Joe organized a beautiful private ceremony, and Delia was buried in his rose garden.

Sometimes I go and visit my old friend's grave. Joe doesn't like us to bring flowers from outside, because of the threat of introducing some deadly spore, so I stand empty-handed and admire the sweep and the colors and the forms of the garden. On spring days when the roses are in full bloom, the air is saturated with their color. But, I notice, from the trees and hedges and borders not one bird sings, and from the sylvan glade not one spring peeper can be heard, and from those roses, so tall and dense, just the faintest whiff of malathion rises on the breeze.

Bailey White
Sleeping at the Starlite Motel and
Other Adventures on the Way Back Home

I am I plus my surroundings and if I do not preserve the latter, I do not preserve myself.

José Ortega y Gasset
Meditations on Quixote

It is good to realize that, if love and peace can prevail on earth, and if we can teach our children to honor nature's gifts, the joys and beauties of the outdoors will be here forever.

Jimmy Carter
An Outdoor Journal: Adventures and Reflections

We are not going to be able to operate our spaceship earth successfully nor much longer unless we see it as a whole spaceship and our fate as common. It has to be everybody or nobody.

Buckminster Fuller
Operating Manual for Spaceship Earth

Emperors, kings, artisans, peasants, big people, little people—at the bottom we are all alike and all the same; all just alike on the inside, and when our clothes are off, nobody can tell which of us is which.

Mark Twain
"Does the Race of Man Love a Lord,"
North American Review, April 1902

So once I shut down my privilege of disliking anyone I chose and holding myself aloof if I could manage it, greater understanding, growing compassion came to me.

Catherine Marshall

Christy

An hour before sunset, on an October evening in 1815, a man travelling afoot entered the village of D——. A few people saw him walk into the town and looked at him with suspicion. His sun-tanned face was half hidden by a leather cap, and was dripping with sweat. His shaggy breast could be seen through a coarse yellow shirt; his tie was twisted like a rope; his worn blue trousers were shabby, with holes in the knees; and he wore a ragged grey blouse, roughly patched with green cloth sewed with twine. On his back was a strongly buckled knapsack, well-filled and quite new; in his hand was a heavy knotted stick; his stockingless feet were in hobnailed shoes; his hair was cropped close, and his beard was long.

The sweat, the heat, and the dust from his long journey added greatly to the wretchedness of his appearance.

The same evening, after a stroll through the town, the Bishop of D—— stayed quite late in his room, working on his great treatise on Duty. At eight o'clock, knowing that the table was laid for supper, and that his sister, Mlle. Baptistine, was waiting, he left his work and went into the dining room.

The housekeeper, Mme. Magloire, was setting the plates for the brother and sister, when there was a loud knocking at the door.

"Come in!" said the bishop.

The door opened, and the traveller entered, knapsack on his back, stick in his hand, and a weary but hard and fierce look in his eyes. Mme. Magloire stood trembling, her mouth open as though she would scream with fright. Mlle. Baptistine started up, at first alarmed; then, slowly turning, she looked at her brother and her face resumed its usual calm.

The bishop looked at the man with a tranquil eye, and started to speak, to ask the stranger what he wanted; but the man, without waiting for the bishop to begin, said in a loud voice:

"My name is Jean Valjean. I am a convict; I have spent nineteen years in the galleys. Four days ago I was set free, and in those four days I have walked from

Toulon. Today I walked twelve leagues. When I reached this town tonight, I went to an inn, and they would not take me in because of my yellow passport, which I had to show at the mayor's office. I went to another inn; no one would have me. I went to the prison, and the jailer would not let me in. I crept into a kennel, and the dog bit me and drove me away; you would have said he knew who I was. I went into a field to sleep beneath the stars, but there were no stars, and I thought it would rain, so I came back to the town to find shelter in some doorway. There in the square I lay down upon the stone; a good woman showed me your house and said, 'Knock there.' I have knocked. What is this place? Are you an inn? I have money: one hundred and nine francs and fifteen sous, my savings from what I earned in the galleys those nineteen years. Can I stay?"

"Mme. Magloire," said the bishop, "put on another plate."

The man came near the table.

"Stop, " he exclaimed, "didn't you understand me? I am a galley-slave—a convict—I have just left the galleys." He drew from his pocket a large sheet of yellow paper. "See, here is what they have put in the passport: 'Jean Valjean, a liberated convict, native of ——, nineteen years in the galleys. This man is very dangerous.' "

"Mme. Magloire," said the bishop, "put some sheets on the bed in the alcove."

Mme. Magloire went out to fulfill her orders, and the bishop turned to the man:

"Monsieur, sit down and warm yourself; we are going to take supper presently, and your bed will be made ready while you sup."

Now the man understood; his face, which had been gloomy and hard, expressed stupefaction and joy, and he began to stutter like a madman.

"Is it true? You will keep me, a convict? You call me 'Monsieur' and don't say 'Get out, dog!' like every one else! I shall have a supper! a bed like other people, with a mattress and sheets! Why, it is nineteen years since I slept in a bed. You are really willing for me to stay? You are good people! And I have money; I will pay well. I beg your pardon, Monsieur Innkeeper, but what is your name?"

"I am a priest who lives here," said the bishop.

"A priest!" said the man. "Oh, noble priest! Then you do not ask any money?"

"No," said the bishop, "keep your money."

Mme. Magloire brought in a plate and put it on the table.

"Mme. Magloire," said the bishop, "put this man's place near the fire." Then, turning to his guest, he added: "The night wind is raw in the Alps, Monsieur; you must be cold."

"Mme. Magloire," said the bishop, "this lamp gives a very poor light."

Mme. Magloire understood, and taking the two silver candlesticks from the mantle, she lighted the candles and placed them on the table.

"Monsieur le Curé," said the man, "you are very good. You take me into your house and light your candles for me. I haven't hid from you what I am, and yet you do not despise me."

The bishop touched his hand and said: "This is not my house, it is the house of Christ. It does not ask any comer what he is, but whether he has an affliction. You are suffering; you are cold and hungry; be welcome. And do not thank me or tell me that I have taken you into my house; for this is the home of no man, except him who needs a refuge. You, who are a traveller, are more at home here than I; whatever is here is yours."

"Stop, monsieur le Curé," exclaimed the man. "I was cold and hungry when I came in, but you are so kind that now I don't know what I am. All that is gone."

The bishop looked at him again and said, "You have seen much suffering?"

"Yes," said the man. "The ball and chain, the plank to sleep on, the heat, the cold, the lash, the double chain for nothing, the dungeon for a word,—even when sick, the chain. The dogs are happier! Nineteen years, and I am forty-six and have a yellow passport and that is all."

"Yes," said the bishop, "you have left a place of great suffering. But listen, there will be more joy in heaven over the tears of one repentant sinner than over the salvation of a hundred good men. If you leave that place with hate and anger against men, you are worthy of compassion; if you leave it with good will and gentleness, you are better than any of us."

Mme. Magloire had served up supper, which consisted of soup, a scrap of pork, a bit of mutton, figs, cheese, and a loaf of bread; and she had added without asking a bottle of fine old wine. "To supper," the bishop said briskly, and he seated the man at his right, while Mlle. Baptistine took her place at his left. The bishop said the blessing, and served the soup himself; the stranger ate greedily, like a starving man, and paid attention to no one.

After supper, the bishop said goodnight to his sister, took one of the silver candlesticks from the table, handed the other to his guest, and said to him, "Monsieur, I will show you to your room."

The alcove where the man was to sleep could be reached only by passing through the bishop's bed chamber, and just as they were passing through this room, Mme. Magloire was putting away the silver in the cupboard at the head of the bed, as was her nightly custom. The bishop left his guest in the alcove, where there was a clean white bed.

"A good night's rest to you," said the bishop, "and tomorrow morning before you go, you shall have a cup of warm milk from our cows."

As the cathedral clock struck two, Jean Valjean awoke. What awakened him was that it was too good a bed. For nineteen years he had not slept in a bed, and his sleep was unquiet.

Many thoughts came to him as he lay there, but one repeated itself and drove away all others. For he remembered the six silver plates and the large silver ladle that he had seen Mme. Magloire putting away in the cupboard, and the thought of them took possession of him. There they were, a few steps away. They were solid, and old silver; they would bring at least two hundred francs, double what he had earned in those long years of imprisonment.

His mind struggled with this thought for an hour, when the clock struck three. He opened his eyes, thrust out his legs, placed his feet on the ground, and sat on the edge of the bed, lost in thought. He might have remained there until daybreak, if the clock had not struck the quarter-hour. It seemed to say to him, "Come along!"

He rose to his feet, hesitated for a moment, and listened. All was still. He walked cautiously toward the window; it had no bars, opened into the garden, and was unfastened. The garden was enclosed with a low white wall, that he could easily scale.

He turned quickly, like a man with mind made up, went to the alcove, where he took his haversack, put his shoes into a pocket, swung his bundle upon his shoulders, put on his cap and pulled it down over his eyes. Holding his breath, he moved toward the door of the bishop's room with stealthy steps. There was not a sound.

Jean Valjean pushed open the door.

A deep calm filled the chamber. At the further end of the room he could hear the quiet breathing of the sleeping bishop. A ray of moonlight, coming through the high window, suddenly lighted up the bishop's pale face. He slept tranquilly. His head had fallen on the pillow in an attitude of untroubled slumber; over the side of the bed hung his hand, ornamented with the pastoral ring. His counte-nance was lit with an expression of hope and happiness.

For a moment Jean Valjean did not remove his eyes from the face of the old man. Then he walked quickly along the bed straight to the cupboard at its head; the key was in it; he opened it and took the basket of silver, crossed the room with hasty stride, stepped out the window, put the silver in his knapsack, threw away the basket, ran across the garden, leaped over the wall like a tiger, and fled.

The next day at sunrise, the bishop was walking in the garden, when Mme. Magloire came running out of the house quite beside herself.

"Monseigneur, monseigneur," she cried. "Does your excellency know where the basket of silver is?"

"Yes," said the bishop.

"God be praised," she said. "I did not know what had become of it."

The bishop had just found the basket in a flower-bed. He handed it to Mme. Magloire and said, "Here it is."

"But...there is nothing in it!" she exclaimed. "Where is the silver?"

"Ah!" said the bishop, "it is the silver then that troubles you. I do not know where that is."

"Good heavens! It is stolen! That man who came last night must have taken it!"

The bishop was silent for a moment, then raising his serious eyes, he said qui-etly to Mme. Magloire:

"Now, first, did this silver belong to us?"

Mme. Magloire did not answer, and the bishop continued:

"Mme. Magloire, for a long time I have wrongfully withheld this silver; it belonged to the poor. Who was that man? A poor man, evidently."

In a few minutes he was breakfasting with his sister at the same table where Jean Valjean had sat the night before.

Just as the bishop and Mlle. Baptistine were rising from the table, there was a knock at the door.

"Come in," said the bishop.

The door opened. A strange, unruly group appeared on the threshold; three gendarmes were holding Jean Valjean by the collar. A brigadier of gendarmes appeared to head the group, and advanced toward the bishop, giving a military salute.

"Monseigneur," he said…

At this, Jean Valjean raised his head with a stupefied air.

"Monseigneur!" he murmured. "Then it is not the curé!"

"Silence!" and the brigadier. "It is monseigneur, the bishop."

The bishop had risen and walked toward the group.

"Ah, there you are!" he said, looking toward Jean Valjean. "I am glad to see you. But…I gave you the candlesticks also, which are silver like the rest, and would bring another two hundred francs. Why did you not take them along with your plates?"

Jean Valjean looked at the bishop amazedly.

"Monseigneur," said the brigadier, "then what this man said was true? He was hurrying away like a man who was running away, and we arrested him in order to see. In his knapsack he had this silver."

"And he told you," said the bishop, with a smile, "that it had been given him by a good priest with whom he had passed the night. I see it all. And you brought him back here? That was a mistake."

"If that is so," said the brigadier, "we can let him go."

"Certainly," replied the bishop.

The gendarmes released Jean Valjean, who shrank away from them.

"Is it true that they have let me go?" he asked, in a voice almost inaudible.

"Yes, you can go," said a gendarme. "Don't you understand?"

"My friend," said the bishop, "before you leave, here are your candlesticks. Take them."

He went to the mantelpiece, took the two candlesticks, and handed them to Jean Valjean. The two women beheld the action without a word or gesture that might disturb the bishop.

Jean Valjean was trembling. He took the two candlesticks mechanically.

"Now," said the bishop, "go in peace. And, friend, when you come again, you need not come through the garden; you can always come in and go out by the front door, for it is closed only with a latch, day or night."

Then, turning to the gendarmes, he said:

"Messieurs, you may retire."

The men withdrew.

Jean Valjean looked like a man about to faint. The bishop approached him, and said in a low voice:

"Forget not, never forget that you have promised me to use this silver to become an honest man."

Jean Valjean, who had no recollection of such a promise, stood confused. The bishop had laid much stress upon these words as he uttered them, and he continued solemnly:

"Jean Valjean, my brother; you belong no longer to evil, but to good. It is your soul that I am buying for you. I withdraw it from dark thoughts and from the spirit of perdition, and I give it to God!"

Adapted from Victor Hugo's
Les Misérables in *Treasures of Love and Inspiration*

Man and his deed are two distinct things. Whereas a good deed should call forth approbation and a wicked deed disapprobation, the doer of the deed, whether good or wicked, always deserves respect or pity as the case may be. 'Hate the sin and not the sinner' is a precept which, though easy enough to understand is rarely practised, and that is why the poison of hatred spreads in the world.

Mohandas K. Gandhi
All Men Are Brothers

To Jesus, each human being is of infinite worth to God and before God; there is one God, and to that One God every human being in the world is related. A man's significance is precisely in that fact. Therefore, in dealings with other human beings I must act from within that presupposition. How terrible that is! It means that social classifications, within which my life and your life exist, have no validity. A Republican and a Democrat, a Socialist and a Communist, a Methodist and a Baptist, a Buddhist and a Hindu, a poor man and a rich man, a male human being and a female human being, an ignorant person and a learned person, a sick person and a well person—none of these classifications has meaning before God. Each one is a human being, not because of his social standing, not because of his relation to another human being, not according to his context, or to the character of his life—No! Every human being as a human being relates to God. That is the point!

Howard Thurman
The Growing Edge

Thirty-seven years old. Thin, almost frail. Balding and bespectacled. An electronics buff. Law-abiding and timid. Certainly not a description you would give a vigilante. Certainly not the person who you would cast to play Robin Hood or the Lone Ranger.

But that didn't bother the American public. When Bernhard Hugo Goetz blasted four would-be muggers in a New York subway, he instantly became a hero.

It's not hard to see why.

Bernhard Goetz was an American fantasy come true. He did what every citizen wants to do. He fought back. He "kicked the bully in the shins." He "punched the villain in the nose." He "clobbered evil over the head." This unassuming hero embodied a nationwide, even world-wide anger: a passion for revenge...

We're tired. We're tired of being bullied, harassed, and intimidated. We're weary of the serial murders, rapists, and hired assassins.

We're angry at someone, but we don't know who...

Anger. It's a peculiar yet predictable emotion. It begins as a drop of water. An irritant. A frustration. Nothing big, just an aggravation. Someone gets your parking place. Someone pulls in front of you on the freeway. A waitress is slow and you are in a hurry. The toast burns. Drops of water. Drip. Drip. Drip. Drip.

Yet, enough of these seemingly innocent drops of anger and before long you've got a bucket full of rage. Walking revenge. Blind bitterness. Unharnessed hatred. We trust no one and bare our teeth at anyone who gets near. We become walking time bombs that, given just the right tension and fear, could explode like Mr. Goetz.

Now, is that any way to live? What good has hatred ever brought? What hope has anger ever created? What problems have ever been resolved by revenge?

No one can blame the American public for applauding the man who fought back. Yet, as the glamour fades on such acts, reality makes us ask the questions: What good was done? Is that really the way to reduce the crime rate? Are subways forever safer? Are the streets now free of fear? No. Anger doesn't do that. Anger only feeds a primitive lust for revenge that feeds our anger that feeds our revenge that feeds our anger—you get the picture. Vigilantes are not the answer...

My point is this: Uncontrolled anger won't better our world, but sympathetic understanding will. Once we see the world and ourselves for what we are, we can help. Once we understand ourselves we begin to operate not from a posture of anger but of compassion and concern. We look at the world not with bitter frowns but with extended hands. We realize that the lights are out and a lot of people are stumbling in the darkness. So we light candles.

Max Lucado
No Wonder They Call Him the Savior

I find a little paragraph in my notebook, "Michael Martin, porter, idle for five years, brought in $2."

It was a thanksgiving offering, he explained, and he wanted to give it to some of our children in honor of his daughter in Ireland.

And I remembered how I spoke down in Palm Beach last month before the Four Arts Club, on the invitation of a convert. They told me, when I had finished, "Miss Day, I hope you can convey to your readers and listeners that we would give our very souls to help the poor, if we saw any constructive way of doing it"…

But as I thought of our breakfast line, our crowded house with people sleeping on the floor, when I thought of cold tenement apartments around us, and the lean gaunt faces of the men who come to us for help, desperation in their eyes, it was impossible not to hate, with a hearty hatred and with a strong anger, the injustices of this world.

St. Thomas says that anger is not a sin, provided there is no undue desire for revenge. We want no revolution; we want the brotherhood of men. We want men to love one another. We want all men to have sufficient for their needs.

Dorothy Day
By Little and By Little:
The Selected Writings of Dorothy Day

We must be willing to learn the lesson that cooperation may imply compromise, but if it brings a world advance it is a gain for each individual nation.

Eleanor Roosevelt
"My Day," newspaper column, January 21, 1946

In heaven,
Some little blades of grass
Stood before God.
"What did you do?"
Then all save one of the little blades
Began eagerly to relate
The merits of their lives.
This one stayed a small way behind,
Ashamed.
Presently, God said,
"And what did you do?"
The little blade answered, "O my lord,
Memory is bitter to me,
For, if I did good deeds,
I know not of them."
Then God, in all His splendour,
Arose from His throne.
"O best little blade of grass!" He said.

Stephen Crane
"In Heaven"

Then came Peter to him, and said, Lord, how oft shall my brother sin against me, and I forgive him? till seven times? Jesus saith unto him, I say not unto thee, Until seven times: but, Until seventy times seven.

Therefore is the kingdom of heaven likened unto a certain king, which would take account of his servants. And when he had begun to reckon, one was brought unto him, which owed him ten thousand talents. But forasmuch as he had not to pay, his lord commanded him to be sold, and his wife, and children, and all that he had, and payment to be made. The servant therefore fell down, and worshipped him, saying, Lord, have patience with me, and I will pay thee all. Then the lord of that servant was moved with compassion, and loosed him, and forgave him the debt. But the same servant went out, and found one of his fellowservants, which owed him an hundred pence: and he laid hands on him, and took him by the throat, saying, Pay me that thou owest. And his fellowservant fell down at his feet, and besought him, saying, Have patience with me, and I will pay thee all. And he would not: but went and cast him into prison, till he should pay the debt. So when his fellowservants saw what was done, they were very sorry, and came and told unto their lord all that was done. Then his lord, after that he had called him, said unto him, O thou wicked servant, I forgave thee all that debt, because thou desiredst me: Shouldest not thou also have had compassion on thy fellowservant, even as I had pity on thee? And his lord was wroth, and delivered him to the tormentors, till he should pay all that was due unto him.

So likewise shall my heavenly Father do also unto you, if ye from your hearts forgive not every one his brother their trespasses.

Matthew 18:21-35

Saying and Doing the

RIGHT THING

CHAPTER TEN

SAYING AND DOING THE RIGHT THING

—⟳—

During my eighty-seven years I have witnessed a whole succession of technolog-
ical revolutions. But none of them has done away with the need for character in
the individual or the ability to think.

Bernard M. Baruch
Baruch: My Own Story

Live among men as if God beheld you; speak to God as if men were listening.

Lucius Annaeus Seneca
Epistles

The best index to a person's character is (a) how he treats people who can't do
him any good, and (b) how he treats people who can't fight back.

Abigail Van Buren
"Dear Abby," May 16, 1974

The thing that must survive you is not just the record of your practice, but the
principles that are the basis of your practice.

Bernice Johnson Reagon
Home Girls

It is the motive, and not the result, that constitutes the crime.

Marguerite Blessington
The Victims of Society

What good will it be for a man if he gains the whole world, yet forfeits his soul?

Matthew 16:26 (NIV)

I know what I have done, and Your Honor knows what I have done…Somewhere between my ambition and my ideals, I lost my ethical compass.

Jeb Stuart Magruder
Quoted in *Time*, June 3, 1974

There are two classes of moralists: those who seek to improve the quality of other people's lives, and those who are content to improve their own.

Paul Gruchow
Our Sustainable Table

It is awfully important to know what is and what is not your business.

Gertrude Stein
"What Is English Literature"

One should examine oneself for a very long time before thinking of condemning others.

Molière

Explore thyself. Herein are demanded the eye and the nerve.

Henry David Thoreau
Walden

We never remark any passion or principle in others, of which, in some degree or other, we may not find a parallel in ourselves.

David Hume
A Treatise of Human Nature

The unexamined life is not worth living.

Socrates
Quoted in *Apology*

Integrity without knowledge is weak and useless, and knowledge without integrity is dangerous and dreadful.

Samuel Johnson
Rasselas

There, my blessings with thee!
And these few precepts in thy memory
Look thou character. Give thy thoughts no tongue,
Nor any unproportioned thought his act.
Be thou familiar, but by no means vulgar;
The friends thou hast, and their adoption tried,
Grapple them to thy soul with hoops of steel;
But do not dull thy palm with entertainment
Of each new-hatched, unfledged comrade. Beware
Of entrance to a quarrel, but, being in,
Bear't that the opposèd may beware of thee.
Give every man thine ear, but few thy voice;
Take each man's censure, but reserve thy judgement.
Costly thy habit as thy purse can buy,
But not expressed in fancy, rich, not gaudy;
For the apparel oft proclaims the man,
And they in France of the best rank and station
Are most select and generous, chief in that.
Neither a borrower, nor a lender be;
For loan oft loses both itself and friend,
And borrowing dulls the edge of husbandry.
This above all: to thine own self be true,
And it must follow, as the night the day,
Thou canst not then be false to any man.

William Shakespeare
Hamlet

[Conscience] is the voice of our ideal self, our complete self, our real self, laying its call upon the will.

Rufus Jones
The Nature and Authority of Conscience

It is necessary to the happiness of man that he be mentally faithful to himself. Infidelity does not consist in believing, or in disbelieving, it consists in professing to believe what one does not believe.

Thomas Paine
The Age of Reason

'I'm a self-made man, you know,' explained a certain magnate of modern business to Dr. Joseph Parker, who immediately replied, 'Sir, you have lifted a great load of responsibility from the Almighty.'

John Baillie
Invitation to Pilgrimage

When you know you're right, you don't care what others think. You know sooner or later it will come out in the wash.

Barbara McClintock
Quoted in *Time*, October 24, 1983

Morality is not an imposition removed from life and reason; it is a compendium of the minimum of sacrifices necessary for man to live in company with other men, without suffering too much or causing others to suffer.

Gina Lombroso
The Tragedies of Progress

How far you go in life depends on your being tender with the young, compassionate with the aged, sympathetic with the striving, and tolerant of the weak and the strong—because someday you will have been all of these.

George Washington Carver
Quoted in *Reader's Digest*, January 1997

If you think you are standing firm, be careful that you don't fall.

1 Corinthians 10:12 (NIV)

An ideal cannot wait for its realization to prove its validity.

George Santayana
The Life of Reason

Whoever exalts himself will be humbled, and whoever humbles himself will be exalted.

Matthew 23:12 (NIV)

I don't claim anything of the work. It is his work. I am like a little pencil in his hand. That is all. He does the thinking. He does the writing. The pencil has nothing to do with it. The pencil has only to be allowed to be used.

Mother Teresa
Speech, Awakening Conference, June 15, 1986

What comes from the heart, goes to the heart.

Samuel Taylor Coleridge
Table-Talk

Humility does not mean thinking less of yourself than of other people, nor does it mean having a low opinion of your own gifts. It means freedom from thinking about yourself one way or the other at all…The humility which consists in being a great deal occupied about yourself, and saying you are of little worth, is not Christian humility. It is one form of self-occupation and a very poor and futile one at that.

William Temple
Christ in his Church

Whatever perfections you may have, be assured people will find them out; but whether they do or not, nobody will take them on your own word.

A Juvenile Guide, or Manual of Good Manners

In many things we shall do well to follow Galileo's recommendation to his readers 'to pronounce that wise, ingenious and modest sentence, "I do not know" '.

C. A. Coulson
Science and Christian Belief

You must believe in yourself, my son, or no one else will believe in you. Be self-confident, self-reliant, and even if you don't make it, you will know you have done your best. Now, go to it.

Mary Hardy MacArthur
Quoted in *Reminiscences*

It is never right to compromise with dishonesty.

Henry Cabot Lodge, Jr.
Quoted in *Thomas E. Dewey and His Times*

Honesty is the best policy.

proverb

If I'm elected, at the end of four years or eight years I hope people will say, "You know, Jimmy Carter made a lot of mistakes, but he never told me a lie."

Jimmy Carter
Interview, Bill Moyers, May 6, 1976

It is impossible that a man who is false to his friends and neighbours should be true to the public.

Bishop Berkeley
Maxims Concerning Patriotism

To make your children *capable of honesty* is the beginning of education.

John Ruskin
Time and Tide

An honest man's word is as good as his bond.

proverb

We are meant to speak the truth in love…

> Ephesians 4:15 (The New Testament in Modern English)

Speak clearly, if you speak at all;
Carve every word before you let it fall.

> Oliver Wendell Holmes
> *A Rhymed Lesson*

Eloquence is the power to translate a truth into language perfectly intelligible to the person to whom you speak.

> Ralph Waldo Emerson
> *Letters and Social Aims: Eloquence*

When you've got a thing to say,
Say it! Don't take half a day.
When your tale's got little in it,
Crowd the whole thing in a minute!

> Joel Chandler Harris
> *Advice to Writers for the Daily Press*

It is with narrow-souled people as with narrow-necked bottles: the less they have in them, the more noise they make in pouring it out.

> Alexander Pope
> *Thoughts on Various Subjects*

In general those who nothing have to say
Contrive to spend the longest time in doing it,
They turn and vary it in every way,
Hashing it, stewing it, mincing it, *ragouting* it.

> James Russell Lowell
> *An Oriental Apologue*

He who guards his mouth and his tongue keeps himself from calamity.

> Proverbs 21:23 (NIV)

Precision of communication is important, more important than ever, in our era of hair-trigger balances, when a false, or misunderstood word may create as much disaster as a sudden thoughtless act.

James Thurber
*Lanterns and Lances: Friends,
Romans, Countrymen, Lend Me Your Muffs*

Words can destroy. What we call each other ultimately becomes what we think of each other, and it matters.

Jeane Kirkpatrick
Speech, AntiDefamation League, February 11, 1982

There is no inspiration in evil and…no man ever made a great speech on a mean subject.

Eugene V. Debs
Efficient Expression

A tart temper never mellows with age, and a sharp tongue is the only edged tool that grows keener with constant use.

Washington Irving
The Sketch Book

Be humble and gentle in your conversation; and of few words, I charge you; but always pertinent when you speak.

William Penn
Letters to His Wife and Children

The music that can deepest reach,
And cure all ill, is cordial speech.

Ralph Waldo Emerson
Conduct of Life: Considerations by the Way

Never throw mud. You may miss your mark; but you *must* have dirty hands.

Joseph Parker

They sing. They hurt. They teach. They sanctify. They were man's first, immeasurable feat of magic. They liberated us from ignorance and our barbarous past.

Leo Rosten
The Many Worlds of L*E*O*R*O*S*T*E*N:
The Power of Words

Praise no man too liberally before his face, nor censure any man severely behind his back.

Shaker proverb

Keep clear of personalities in conversation. Talk of things, objects, thoughts. The smallest minds occupy themselves with persons. Do not needlessly report ill of others. As far as possible, dwell on the good side of human beings. There are family boards where a constant process of depreciating, assigning motives, and cutting up character, goes forward. They are not pleasant places. One who is healthy does not wish to dine at a dissecting table. There is evil enough in man, God knows. But it is not the mission of every young man and woman to detail and report it all. Keep the atmosphere as pure as possible, and fragrant with gentleness and charity.

John Hall

Without discipline, there's no life at all.

Katharine Hepburn
Interview, *Dick Cavett Show,* April 4, 1975

Speak as little as may be of thy neighbour or of anything that concerns him, unless an opportunity offers to say something good of him.

Lorenzo Scupoli
The Spiritual Combat

Words are what hold society together.

Stuart Chase and Marion T. Chase
Power of Words

A Slip of the Foot you may soon recover,
But a Slip of the Tongue you may never get over.

Benjamin Franklin
Poor Richard's Almanac

Everybody gets so much information all day long that they lose their common sense.

Gertrude Stein
"Reflection on the Atomic Bomb"

A single conversation across the table with a wise man is better than ten years' study of books.

Henry Wadsworth Longfellow
Hyperion

A good conversationalist is not one who remembers what was said, but says what someone wants to remember.

Rosellen Brown
Quoted in *Esquire*, April 1960

Language—even literacy—alone does not lead automatically to reflective, abstract thought. In order for reflection to occur, the oral and written forms of language must pass back and forth between persons who both speak and listen or read and write—sharing, expanding, and reflecting on each other's experiences. Such interchanges lead to ways of knowing that enable individuals to enter into the social and intellectual life of their community. Without them, individuals remain isolated from others; and without tools for representing their experiences, people also remain isolated from the self.

Mary Field Belenky
The Ways of Knowing

It is easy to relate what is of no importance.

Sidonie-Gabrielle Colette
"The Photographer's Missus"

I find it fascinating to think about what the world is going to be like when people won't talk anymore. There are probably brilliant people, geniuses, alive today who don't even know how to say, "Hello, how do you do?" because their minds are absorbed with electronic images.

Beth Henley
Quoted in *Interview With Contemporary Women Playwrights*

We have to face the fact that either all of us are going to die together or we are going to learn to live together and if we are to live together we have to talk.

Eleanor Roosevelt
Quoted in the *New York Times*, October 15, 1960

Since language and speech are the cement of human society whoever falsifies them should be punished for counterfeit or for poisoning the public water well.

Marie de Jars
"Advis"

Speak gently to the young, for they
Will have enough to bear;
Pass through this life as best they may,
'Tis full of anxious care.

Shaker poem
"Speak Gently"

May I softly walk and wisely speak,
Lest I harm the strong or wound the weak;
For all those wounds I yet must feel,
And bathe in love until they heal.
Why should I carelessly offend,
Since many of life's joys depend
On gentle words and peaceful ways;
Which spread such brightness o'er our days.

Shaker poem
New Lebanon, New York, 1869

Conversation is the vent of character as well as of thought.

Ralph Waldo Emerson
Society and Solitude: Clubs

A compliment is a gift, not to be thrown away carelessly unless you want to hurt the giver.

Eleanor Hamilton
Partners in Love

Never promise more than you can perform.

Shaker proverb

So much to say. And so much not to say; some things are better left unsaid. But so many unsaid things can become a burden.

Virginia Mae Axline
Dibs: In Search of Self

A wise old owl sat on an oak,
The more he saw the less he spoke;
The less he spoke the more he heard;
Why aren't we like that wise old bird?

Edward Hersey Richards
A Wise Old Owl

There is a grace of kind listening, as well as a grace of kind speaking.

Frederick William Faber
Spiritual Conferences

When I was in the fourth grade, I was offered a job as a paper boy. It didn't pay much money, but I knew having a job would build my character so I took it, good character being important to fourth-graders. My lessons started the first day on the job. A customer paying his bill asked me if I wanted a tip, and I said, "Sure." He said, "Stay away from wild women."

One of my customers was a lady named Mrs. Stanley. She was a widow and not prone to wild living, so I took to lingering on her front porch during my rounds. She'd watch for me to come down her street, and by the time I'd pedaled up to her house, there'd be a slushy bottle of Coke waiting for me. I'd sit and drink while she talked. That was our understanding—I drank, she talked.

The widow Stanley talked mostly about her dead husband, Roger. "Roger and I went grocery shopping this morning over to the IGA," she'd say. The first time she said that, the Coke went up my nose. That was back in the days when Coke going up your nose wasn't a crime, just a mite uncomfortable.

Went home and told my father about Mrs. Stanley and how she talked as if Mr. Stanley were still alive. Dad said she was probably lonely, and that maybe I just ought to sit and listen and nod my head and smile, and maybe she'd work it out of her system. So that's what I did. I figured this was where the character-building came into play. Turned out Dad was right. After a few summers, she seemed content to leave her husband over at the South Cemetery.

Nowadays, we'd send Mrs. Stanley to a psychiatrist. But all she had back then was a front porch rocker and her paper boy's ear, which turned out to be enough.

I quit my paper route after her healing. Moved on to the lucrative business of lawn mowing. Didn't see the widow Stanley for several years. Then we crossed paths up at the Christian Church's annual fund-raiser dinner. She was standing behind the steam table spooning out mashed potatoes and looking radiant. Four years before she'd had to bribe her paper boy with a Coke to have someone to talk with; now she had friends brimming over. Her husband was gone, but life went on. She had her community and was luminous with love.

Community is a beautiful thing; sometimes it even heals us and makes us better than we would otherwise be.

I live in the city now. My front porch is a concrete slab. And my paper boy is a lady named Edna with three kids and a twelve-year-old Honda. Every day she asks me how I'm doing. When I don't say "fine," she sticks around long enough to find out why. She's such a nice lady that sometimes I act as if I have a problem, just so she'll tarry. She's lived in the city all her life, but she knows about community, too.

Community isn't so much a locale as it is a state of mind. You find it when-ever folks ask how you're doing because they care, and not because they're get-ting paid to inquire.

Two thousand years ago, a church elder named Peter wrote the recipe for community. "Above all else," he wrote, "hold unfailing your love for one another, since love covers a multitude of sins" (1 Peter 4:8). That means when you love a person, you occasionally have to turn a blind eye toward their shortcomings.

Kind of like what my dad told me about the widow Stanley. Sometimes it's better to nod your head and smile.

Psychiatrists call that "enabling denial," but back when I delivered papers, we called it "compassion."

Philip Gulley
Front Porch Tales

You ain't learnin' nothing when you're talking.

anonymous

There is no such thing as a worthless conversation, providing you know what to listen for. And questions are the breath of life for a conversation.

James Nathan Miller
Quoted in *Reader's Digest*, September 1965

It is better to ask some of the questions than to know all the answers.

James Thurber
"The Scotty Who Knew Too Much"

It was hard to communicate with you. You were always communicating with yourself. The line was busy.

Jean Kerr
Mary, Mary

Years ago, I tried to top everybody, but I don't anymore. I realized it was killing conversation. When you're always trying for a topper you aren't really listening. It ruins communication.

Groucho Marx
The Groucho Phile

Even a fool is thought wise if he keeps silent, and discerning if he holds his tongue.

Proverbs 17:28 (NIV)

For the most part we are much too busy living and thinking to have leisure to be silent and see.

Aurobindo

What shall I say to you? What can I say better than silence is?

Henry Wadsworth Longfellow
"Morituri Salutamus"

When I was first diagnosed with leukemia, people would say the strangest things to me. They would make offhand speculations about possible sins in my life, or remark about my lack of faith, or take me aside to share some bizarre cure they had heard from a great aunt in Delaware. Already struggling with worry, I wasn't helped or comforted at all by their "counsel." It would have been better had they just said they would pray for me—or said nothing at all.

Ron Mehl
The Cure for a Troubled Heart

Lord, the Scripture says: 'There is a time for silence and a time for speech'. Saviour, teach me the silence of humility, the silence of wisdom, the silence of love, the silence of perfection, the silence that speaks without words, the silence of faith.

Lord, teach me to silence my own heart that I may listen to the gentle movement of the Holy Spirit within me and sense the depths which are of God.

Frankfurt prayer

He speaketh not; and yet there lies
A conversation in his eyes.

Henry Wadsworth Longfellow
The Hanging of the Crane

That silence is one of the great arts of conversation is allowed by Cicero himself, who says, there is not only an art, but even an eloquence in it.

Hannah More
"Thoughts on Conversation"

Talking is like playing on the harp; there is as much in laying the hands on the string to stop their vibration as in twanging them to bring out the music.

Oliver Wendell Holmes
The Autocrat of the Breakfast-Table

Not knowing what else to do, I stood motionless behind the grown son who held the hand of his dying father. It was my first church, my first month. I had never walked the road of cancer with a parishioner before. I was almost surprised at how deeply I cared for the man in the hospital bed. I didn't understand yet that God planned for me to love that bedridden man like Christ loved him. I didn't know yet that when God ordains a pastor, He provides the pastor's heart. So I just stood silently, surprised by the depth of my love, but disappointed by my feelings of pastoral ineptness.

Lester winced with pain. His medication at the time wasn't strong enough to mask his physical anguish. So his body constricted because of the pain emanating from his bones. He drew in a short breath and then exhaled slowly. As he breathed outward, Lester rhythmically stretched out a moan. "O-h-h-h me." It was a pain-filled, mournful moan. But, at the same time, it possessed a compelling beauty. It was not just a cry of distress. It was a sigh of the soul. The more I listened, the more it sounded like a song rather than a moan. "O-h-h-h me. O-h-h-h me."

The tender son leaned forward. I had been to seminary. I had been trained. But I watched this son carefully. His confident demeanor proved he knew how to care for his beloved father better than I. With a clasped hand and a hint of a smile, the son brought his face down close to his dad's.

Lester moaned again, "O-h-h-h me."

Then, what I could have never imagined to happen occurred. The song echoed back, "O-h-h-h me."

The white-haired patient moaned louder, "O-h-h-h me."

Again, the unfathomable echo came back from the son, "O-h-h-h me."

What was I beholding? Was such insensitivity possible? Could a son actually mock his dying father's moan?

I considered interrupting the son's echo of anguish. I contemplated pulling the man away from the bed to save his father from the humiliation. But, oddly,

Lester seemed comforted, not agitated by his son's peculiar imitation. So, I stood silently and waited.

I was about to learn a holy lesson in compassion that I would never forget.

After watching this amazing father-son duet of moans for some time, I stepped out of the hospital room with the son. He explained.

When I first met this saintly, aging man, he was at home, not in the hospital. Though Lester's health was declining rapidly and his pain was increasing at the same rate, there was no place of healing like home. Lester was thankful for a fine hospital, but the hospital had no home-cooked meals, no view of Rose of Sharon Road, and no Wesley.

Wesley was Lester's two-year-old grandson. I knew this toddler to be a blond-haired barrel of fun who was bound to bring sunshine to the darkest of days. I had seen Lester's smile broaden when Wesley was around. I knew that Wesley's presence helped alleviate Lester's anguish. I knew how much he loved the little boy. But what Lester's son told me outside the hospital room that day touched my heart forever.

At home, as Lester's health worsened, he rarely walked. When he did, Lester supported himself with a walker. Each grueling step brought shooting pain. His walk was more of a shuffle, each slide of the foot an accomplishment. And with each foot forward, each lift of the walker, Lester would exhale his usual moan. "O-h-h-h me." Step. "O-h-h-h me." Step.

One day, unprompted, little Wesley came alongside his shuffling, moaning grandfather. He placed his two-year-old hand at the base of Lester's walker, and with each painful step, Wesley "helped." With all his two-year-old strength, Wesley helped lift the walker upward and forward.

And following each of Lester's mournful moans, a two-year-old voice echoed back. "O-h-h me. O-h-h me."

Although I would like to have beheld the scene firsthand, I am more nourished by the picture I carry of it in my imagination. How different the man and the boy. There were more than seventy years between them. One had lived a lifetime; the other had hardly lived. One had bones brittle enough to make every trip down the hall risky, the other had bones supple enough to bounce on beds and fall off couches unharmed.

And yet, as Wesley echoed his grandfather's moan, how similar they were.

Though the toddler was quicker, the size of their stride was about the same. Though Lester was a friendly talker, when in pain, his vocabulary was not much larger than little Wesley's. The old man and the little boy had a unique, beautiful connection as they walked and moaned together.

My seminary professors and pastoral mentors had taught me consistently, but never so powerfully or eloquently as that two-year-old boy, the most important pastoral lesson of all. When people are hurting their worst, our words need to be fewest. Aching saints do not need long-winded preachers or glib cheerleaders. They need someone who will come alongside them and, step by grueling step, acknowledge their pain. Hurting people need someone who, in the apostle Paul's words, will "mourn with those who mourn."

Alan D. Wright
A Chance at Childhood Again

Love silence, even in the mind; for thoughts are to that as words are to the body, troublesome: much speaking, as much thinking, spends. True silence is the rest of the mind; and it is to the spirit what sleep is to the body, nourishment and refreshment.

William Penn
Advice to His Children

Persons in public positions—including me—miss too many chances to keep their mouths shut. I'm not passing up my chance tonight.

Dwight D. Eisenhower
June 7, 1964

We often repent of what we have said, but never, never, of that which we have not.

Thomas Jefferson
Writings

Better to remain silent and be thought a fool than to speak out and remove all doubt.

Abraham Lincoln

When words are many, sin is not absent, but he who holds his tongue is wise.

Proverbs 10:19 (NIV)

To forbear replying to an unjust reproach, and overlook it with a generous, or, if possible, with an entire neglect of it, is one of the most heroic acts of a great mind.

Joseph Addison
The Tatler

Sometimes when you get in a fight with a skunk, you can't tell who started it.

Lloyd Doggett
Quoted in *Time*, November 5, 1984

Without wood a fire goes out; without gossip a quarrel dies down.

Proverbs 26:20 (NIV)

If you argue your case with a neighbor, do not betray another man's confidence.

Proverbs 25:9 (NIV)

The world is a fine place and worth fighting for.

Ernest Hemingway
For Whom the Bell Tolls

You cannot choose your battlefield,
The gods do that for you,
But you can plant a standard
Where a standard never flew.

Nathalia Crane
"The Colors"

If a man hasn't discovered something that he will die for, he isn't fit to live.

Martin Luther King, Jr.
Speech, Detroit, Michigan, June 23, 1963

All truths must not be told at all times.

Henry C. Blinn

You have much more power when you are working for the right thing than when you are working against the wrong thing.

Peace Pilgrim
Peace Pilgrim: Her Life and Work
in Her Own Words

"No one ever wins a fight"—thoughtfully, and with eyes searching the depths of me, my grandmother repeated the words. I was something to behold. One eye was swollen, my jacket was ripped with all the buttons torn from their places, and there was a large tear in the right knee of my trousers. It was a hard and bitter fight. I had stood all I could, until at last I threw discretion to the winds and the fight was on. The fact that he was larger and older and had brothers did not matter. For four blocks we had fought and there was none to separate us. At last I began to gain in power; with one tremendous effort I got him to the ground and, as the saying went, "made him eat dirt." Then I had to come home to face my grandmother. "No one ever wins a fight," were her only words as she looked at me. "But I beat him," I said. "Yes, but look at you. You beat him, but you will learn someday that nobody ever wins a fight." Many years have come and gone since that afternoon in early summer. I have seen many fights, big and little. I have lived through two world wars. The wisdom of these telling words becomes clearer as the days unfold. There is something seductive about the quickening sense of power that comes when the fight is on. There is a bewitching something men call honor, in behalf of which they often do and become the dishonorable thing. It is all very strange. How often honor is sacrificed in defense of honor. Honor is often a strange mixture of many things—pride, fear, hate, shame, courage, truth, cowardice—many things. The mind takes many curious twistings and turnings as it runs the interference for one's survival. And yet the term survival alone is not quite what is meant. Men want to survive, yes, but on their own terms. And this is most often what is meant by honor. "No one ever wins a fight." This suggests that there is always some other way; or does it mean that man can always choose the weapons he shall use? Not to fight at all is to choose a weapon by which one fights. Perhaps the authentic moral stature of a man is determined by his choice of weapons which he uses in his fight against the adversary. Of all weapons, love is the most deadly and devastating, and few there be who dare trust their fate in its hands.

Howard Thurman
Deep Is the Hunger

It is easier to fight for one's principles than to live up to them.

Alfred Adler
Quoted in *Alfred Adler*

The greatest mistake you can make in life is to be continually fearing that you will make one.

Elbert Hubbard
The Note Book

Perhaps it is better to be irresponsible and right than to be responsible and wrong.

Winston S. Churchill
Party political broadcast, London, August 26, 1950

If in my high moments, I have done some good, offered some service, shed some light, healed some wounds, rekindled some hope, or stirred someone from apathy and indifference, or in any way along the way helped somebody, then this campaign has not been in vain...If in my low moments, in word, deed or attitude, through some error of temper, taste or tone, I have caused anyone discomfort, created pain or revived someone's fears, that was not my truest self...I am not a perfect servant. I am a public servant doing my best against the odds. As I develop and serve, be patient. God is not finished with me yet.

Jesse Jackson
Speech, Democratic National Convention,
July 16, 1984

There is nothing final about a mistake, except its being taken as final.

Phyllis Bottome
Strange Fruit

Every great mistake has a halfway moment, a split second when it can be recalled and perhaps remedied.

Pearl S. Buck
What America Means to Me

In the movie *Rob Roy*, the character of Rob Roy is asked by his son, "Father, what is honor?" Rob Roy tells him, "Honor is something no man can give to you and no man can take away. Honor is a man's gift to himself."

In this case, honor and integrity are used synonymously. Integrity, like honor, cannot be bestowed upon you. It can only come from yourself. And when you give it to yourself, everyone knows. It's obvious. You have a relaxed confidence and an unshakable security because you have an integrity that comes from a devout belief in yourself, in your God-given abilities, and even more importantly, in the trustworthiness of your God who both supersedes and empowers all of your assets.

A life of personal integrity is in large measure a matter of holding true to your assets. It is understanding your values and refusing to compromise them.

It's not always so easy to be a woman or man of integrity. You have daily temptations to compromise, temptations in the form of money, power, and fame. Sometimes it's just a whole lot easier to compromise. But remember the eternal truth: Easy things give immediate joy but generally offer longer-term pain, while hard things bring immediate pain with longer-term satisfaction and joy.

Charlie Hedges
Getting the Right Things Right

It may be necessary temporarily to accept a lesser evil, but one must never label a necessary evil as good.

Margaret Mead
Quoted in *Redbook*, November 1978

In his own way each man must struggle, lest the moral law become a far-off abstraction utterly separated from his active life.

Jane Addams
Twenty Years at Hull House

True gratitude, like true love, must find expression in acts, not words.

R. Mildred Barker

Live truth instead of professing it.

Elbert Hubbard
The Roycroft Dictionary and Book of Epigrams

Truth is given, not to be contemplated, but to be done. Life is an action, not a thought.

F. W. Robertson
Sermons

Morality, including political morality, has to do with the definition of right *conduct,* and this not simply by way of the ends of action. *How* we do what we do is as important as our goals.

Paul Ramsey
War and the Christian Conscience

Of course, fortune has its part in human affairs, but conduct is really much more important.

Jeanne Detourbey
Quoted in *Forty Years of Partisan Society*

Blessed is he who has regard for the weak; the LORD delivers him in times of trouble.

Psalm 41:1 (NIV)

No man or woman of the humblest sort can really be strong, gentle, pure, and good, without the world being the better for it, without somebody being helped and comforted by the very existence of that goodness.

Phillips Brooks

Then the King will say to those on his right, "Come, you who are blessed by my Father; take your inheritance, the kingdom prepared for you since the creation of the world. For I was hungry and you gave me something to eat, I was thirsty and you gave me something to drink, I was a stranger and you invited me in, I needed clothes, and you clothed me, I was sick and you looked after me, I was in prison and you came to visit me."

Matthew 25:34-36 (NIV)

The greatest pleasure I know, is to do a good action by stealth, and to have it found out by accident.

Charles Lamb
The Athenaeum

He who would do good to another must do it in Minute Particulars. General Good is the plea of the scoundrel, hypocrite, and flatterer.

William Blake
Jerusalem

I expect to pass through this world but once; any good thing therefore that I can do, or any kindness that I can show to any fellow-creature, let me do it now; let me not defer or neglect it, for I shall not pass this way again.

Stephen Grellet

How far that little candle throws his beams!
So shines a good deed in a naughty world.

William Shakespeare
The Merchant of Venice

Be good, sweet maid, and let who can be clever;
Do lovely things, not dream them, all day long;
And so make Life, and Death, and that For Ever,
One grand sweet song.

Charles Kingsley
"A Farewell to C. E. G."

One must think like a hero to behave like a merely decent human being.

May Sarton
Journal of a Solitude

We do not live to extenuate the miseries of the past nor to accept as uncurable those of the present.

Fairfield Osborn
The Limits of the Earth

Neither do men light a candle, and put it under a bushel, but on a candlestick; and it giveth light unto all that are in the house. Let your light so shine before men, that they may see your good works, and glorify your Father which is in heaven.

Matthew 5:15-16

Always do right—this will gratify some and astonish the rest.

Mark Twain
Message to Young People's Society,
Greenpoint Presbyterian Church, Brooklyn, New York,
February 16, 1901

If you open it, close it.
If you turn it on, turn it off.
If you unlock it, lock it up.
If you break it, admit it.
If you can't fix it, call in someone who can.
If you borrow it, return it.
If you value it, take care of it.
If you make a mess, clean it up.
If you move it, put it back.
If it belongs to someone else and you want to use it, get permission.
If you don't know how to operate it, leave it alone.
If it's none of your business, don't ask questions.
If it ain't broke, don't fix it.
If it will brighten someone's day, say it.
If it will tarnish someone's reputation, keep it to yourself.

anonymous
"Golden Rules for Living"

Character isn't inherited. One builds it daily by the way one thinks and acts, thought by thought, action by action. If one lets fear or hate or anger take possession of the mind, they become self-forged chains.

Helen Gahagan Douglas
Speech, Marlboro College, 1975

Enter through the narrow gate. For wide is the gate and broad is the road that leads to destruction, and many enter through it. But small is the gate and narrow the road that leads to life, and only a few find it.

Matthew 7:13-14 (NIV)

Do all the good you can,
By all the means you can,
In all the ways you can,
In all the places you can,
At all the times you can,
To all the people you can,
As long as ever you can.

John Wesley
John Wesley's Rule

The society which scorns excellence in plumbing because plumbing is a humble activity and tolerates shoddiness in philosophy because it is an exalted activity will have neither good plumbing nor good philosophy. Neither its pipes nor its theories will hold water.

John W. Gardner
Excellence: Can We Be Equal and Excellent Too?

And what does the LORD require of you? To act justly and to love mercy and to walk humbly with your God.

Micah 6:8 (NIV)

Excellence costs a great deal.

May Sarton
The Small Room

From everyone who has been given much, much will be damanded; and from the one who has been entrusted with much, much more will be asked.

Luke 12:48 (NIV)

Man transcends death by finding meaning in his life…It is the burning desire for the creature to count…What man really fears is not so much extinction, but extinction with *insignificance.*

Ernest Becker
Quoted in *In Search of Excellence*

There are events without which one's life becomes unimportant, a worthless toy; and there are times when one is commanded to do something, even at the price of one's life.

Hannah Senesh
Hannah Senesh: Her Life and Diary

And God spoke all these words:

"I am the LORD your God…You shall have no other gods before me. You shall not make for yourself an idol in the form of anything in heaven above or on the earth beneath or in the waters below. You shall not bow down to them or worship them; for I, the LORD your God, am a jealous God, punishing the children for the sin of the fathers to the third and fourth generation of those who hate me, but showing love to a thousand generations of those who love me and keep my commandments.

"You shall not misuse the name of the LORD your God, for the LORD will not hold anyone guiltless who misuses his name.

"Remember the Sabbath day by keeping it holy. Six days you shall labor and do all your work, but the seventh day is a Sabbath to the LORD your God. On it you shall not do any work, neither you, nor your son or daughter, nor your manservant or maidservant, nor your animals, nor the alien within your gates. For in six days the LORD made the heavens and the earth, the sea, and all that is in them, but he rested on the seventh day. Therefore the LORD blessed the Sabbath day and made it holy.

"Honor your father and your mother, so that you may live long in the land the LORD your God is giving you.

"You shall not murder.

"You shall not commit adultery.

"You shall not steal.

"You shall not give false testimony against your neighbor.

"You shall not covet your neighbor's house. You shall not covet your neighbor's wife, or his manservant or maidservant, his ox or donkey, or anything that belongs to your neighbor."

Exodus 20:1-17 (NIV)

Morality, if it is not fixed by custom and authority, becomes a mere matter of taste determined by the idiosyncrasies of the moralist.

Walter Lippmann
A Preface to Morals

The world has achieved brilliance without wisdom, power without conscience. Ours is a world of nuclear giants and ethical infants.

Omar Bradley
Speech, Boston, Massachusetts, November 10, 1948

A word to the wise ain't necessary—it's the stupid ones who need the advice.

Bill Cosby
Fat Albert's Survival Kit

A good scare is worth more to a man than good advice.

Edgar Watson Howe
Country Town Sayings

Knowledge alone is not enough. It must be leavened with magnanimity before it becomes wisdom.

Adlai E. Stevenson
Call to Greatness

Nine-tenths of wisdom consists in being wise in time.

Theodore Roosevelt
Speech, Lincoln, Nebraska, June 14, 1917

O God, help us not to despise or oppose what we do not understand.

William Penn

Granma's name was Bonnie Bee. I knew that when I heard him late at night say, "I kin ye, Bonnie Bee," he was saying, "I love ye," for the feeling was in the words.

And when they would be talking and Granma would say, "Do you kin me, Wales?" and he would answer, "I kin ye," it meant, "I understand ye." To them, love and understanding was the same thing. Granma said you couldn't love something you didn't understand; nor could you love people, nor God, if you didn't understand the people and God.

Granpa and Granma had an understanding, and so they had a love. Granma said the understanding run deeper as the years went by, and she reckined it would get beyond anything mortal folks could think upon or explain. And so they called it "kin."

Granpa said back before his time "kinfolks" meant any folks that you understood and had an understanding with, so it meant "loved folks." But people got selfish, and brought it down to mean just blood relatives; but that actually it was never meant to mean that.

Granpa said when he was a little boy his Pa had a friend who ofttimes hung around their cabin. He said he was an old Cherokee named 'Coon Jack, and he was continually distempered and cantankerous. He couldn't figure out what his Pa saw in old 'Coon Jack.

He said they went irregular to a little church house down in a hollow. One Sunday it was testifying time, when folks would stand up, as they felt the Lord called on them, and testify as to their sins and how much they loved the Lord.

Granpa said at this testifying time, " 'Coon Jack stood up and said, 'I hear tell they's some in here been talking about me behind my back. I want ye to know that I'm awares. I know what's the matter with ye; ye're jealous because the Deacon Board put me in charge of the key to the songbook box. Well, let me tell ye; any of ye don't like it, I got the difference right here in my pocket.' "

Granpa said, shore enough, 'Coon Jack lifted his deer shirt and showed a pistol handle. He was stomping mad.

Granpa said that church house was full of some hard men, including his Pa, who would soon as not shoot you if the weather changed, but nobody raised an eyebrow. He said his Pa stood up and said, " 'Coon Jack, every man here admires the way ye have handled the key to the songbook box. Best handling ever been done. If words has been mistook to cause ye discomfort, I here and now state the sorrow of every man present."

'Coon Jack set down, total mollified and contented, as was everybody else.

On the way home, Granpa asked his Pa why 'Coon Jack could get away with such talk, and Granpa said he got to laughing about 'Coon Jack acting so important over the key to the songbook box. He said his Pa told him, "Son, don't laugh at 'Coon Jack. Ye see, when the Cherokee was forced to give up his home and go to the Nations, 'Coon Jack was young, and he hid out in these mountains, and he fought to hold on. When the War 'tween the States come, he saw maybe he could fight that same guvmint and get back the land and homes. He fought hard. Both times he lost. When the War ended, the politicians set in, trying to git what was left of what we had. 'Coon Jack fought, and run, and hid, and fought some more. Ye see, 'Coon Jack come up in the time of fighting. All he's got now is the key to the songbook box. And if 'Coon Jack seems cantankerous...well, there ain't nothing left for 'Coon Jack to fight. He never knowed nothing else."

Granpa said, he come might near crying fer 'Coon Jack. He said after that, it didn't matter what 'Coon Jack said, or did...he loved him, because he understood him.

Granpa said that such was "kin," and most of people's mortal trouble come about by not practicing it...

I could see that right off, and might near cried about 'Coon Jack myself.

Forrest Carter
The Education of Little Tree

The root of the matter is a very simple and old-fashioned thing, a thing so simple that I am almost ashamed to mention it for fear of the derisive smile with which wise cynics will greet my words. The thing I mean—please forgive me for mentioning it—is love, Christian love, or compassion.

Bertrand Russell
Impact of Science on Society

The eternal *not ourselves* that makes for righteousness.

Matthew Arnold
Literature and Dogma

The code of morality is to do unto others as you would have them do unto you. If you make that the central theme of your morality code, it will serve you well as a moral individual.

Barbara Jordan
Quoted in *Parade*, February 16, 1986

One night at 11:30, an older African-American woman was standing on the side of an Alabama highway trying to endure a lashing rain storm. Her car had broken down and she desperately needed a ride. Soaking wet, she decided to flag down the next car. A young white man stopped to help her—generally unheard of in the deep South during those conflict-filled 1960s. The man took her to safety, helped her get assistance and put her into a taxi cab. She seemed to be in a big hurry! She wrote down his address, thanked him and rode away.

Seven days went by and a knock came on the man's door. To his surprise, a giant combination console color TV and stereo record player were delivered to his home. A special note was attached. The note read:

Dear Mr. James:

Thank you so much for assisting me on the highway the other night. The rain drenched not only my clothes but my spirits. Then you came along. Because of you, I was able to make it to my dying husband's bed-side just before he passed away. God bless you for helping me and unselfishly serving others.

Sincerely,

Mrs. Nat King Cole

Dan Clark
Just in Time

Decency—generosity—cooperation—assistance in trouble—devotion to duty; these are the things that are of greater value than surface appearances and customs.

Dwight D. Eisenhower
Letter to Mamie Doud Eisenhower,
June 11, 1943

If a man be gracious and courteous to strangers, it shews he is a citizen of the world, and that his heart is no island cut off from other lands, but a continent that joins to them.

Francis Bacon
Of Goodness and Goodness of Nature

Have you had a kindness shown?
Pass it on;
'Twas not given for thee alone,
Pass it on;
Let it travel down the years,
Let it wipe another's tears,
'Till in Heaven the deed appears—
Pass it on.

Henry Burton
Pass It On

Do not forget to entertain strangers, for by so doing some people have entertained angels without knowing it.

Hebrews 13:2 (NIV)

That best portion of a good man's life, His little, nameless, unremembered acts of kindness and of love.

William Wordsworth
Lines above Tintern Abbey

Don't be selfish; don't live to make a good impression on others. Be humble, thinking of others as better than yourself. Don't just think about your own affairs, but be interested in others, too...Your attitude should be the kind that was shown us by Jesus Christ, who, though he was God, did not demand and cling to his rights as God, but laid aside his mighty power and glory, taking the disguise of a slave and becoming like men.

Philippians 2:3–7 (TLB)

Only a life lived for others is the life worth while.

Albert Einstein
Quoted in the *New York Times*, June 20, 1932

A Lion having laid down to take his repose under the spreading boughs of a shady tree, a company of Mice scampered over his back and waked him. Upon which, starting up, he clapped his paw upon one of them, and was just going to put it to death, when the little suppliant implored his mercy, begging him not to stain his noble character with the blood of so small and insignificant a creature. The Lion, touched with compassion, instantly released his little trembling captive. Not longer after, traversing the forest in search of his prey, he chanced to run into the toils of the hunters, and not being able to disengage himself, he set up a loud roar. The Mouse hearing the voice, and knowing it to be the Lion's, immediately repaired to the place, and bade him fear nothing, for that he was his friend. Instantly he fell to work and with his little sharp teeth gnawed asunder the knots and fastenings of the toils, and set the royal brute at liberty.

APPLICATION

They who generously shower benefits on their fellow-creatures, seldom fail of inspiring the great bulk of them with a benevolent regard for their benefactors, and often receive returns of kindness which they never expected. Mercy is of all other virtues the most likely to kindle gratitude in those to whom it is extended, and it is difficult to find an instance of a conqueror who ever had occasion to repent of his humanity and clemency. The Fable gives us to understand, that there is no person in the world so little, but even the greatest may, at some time or other, stand in need of his assistance; and consequently, it is good to shew favour, when there is room for it, towards those who fall into our power. As the lowest people in life may, upon occasion, be able either to serve or hurt us, it is as much our interest as our duty to behave with good nature and lenity towards all with whom we have any intercourse. A great soul is never so much delighted as when an opportunity offers of making a return for favours received; and a sensible man, however exalted his station, will never consider himself secure from the necessity of accepting a service from the poorest.

Æsop
Fables

The quality of mercy is not strain'd,
It droppeth as the gentle rain from heaven.

William Shakespeare
The Merchant of Venice

To be able to practise five things everywhere under heaven constitutes perfect virtue…gravity, generosity of soul, sincerity, earnestness, and kindness.

K'ung Fu-tzu Confucius
Analects

Be kind and compassionate to one another, forgiving each other, just as in Christ God forgave you.

Ephesians 4:32 (NIV)

Teach us delight in simple things,
And mirth that has no bitter springs;
Forgiveness free of evil done,
And love to all men 'neath the sun!

Rudyard Kipling
The Children's Song

Abashed the devil stood,
And felt how awful goodness is.

John Milton
Paradise Lost

Mr. President, it constantly amazes me that you seem always to know what is the right thing to do.

"Oh, I don't think knowing what's the right thing to do ever gives anybody too much trouble. It's *doing* the right thing that seems to give a lot of people trouble."

You said the other day that Justice Holmes attributed his long and successful life to the fact that he discovered at an early age that he wasn't God. To what, sir, do you attribute your long and remarkable life?

"Well, I never thought I was God; that's one thing for sure. I grew up wanting to be as good a man as my father was and as my mother wanted me to be. I never had the notion that I was anything special at all; even when I got that job in the White House, I didn't. And I never had the notion that there weren't a lot of people who couldn't do whatever it was better than I could.

"But that never worried me. All that ever concerned me was that I wanted to do it as best I could. So I guess I'd have to say to that, to your question, that I always tried to be satisfied with what I was and what I was doing. My father used to say that a man ought to leave the world a little better than it was when he came into it, and if that can be said about me, I guess you'll have to say I lived a successful life."

Did it bother you, leaving the pomp and circumstance of Washington? Of the White House?

"Never gave me any trouble at all. I always kept in mind something old Ben Franklin said at that meeting in Philadelphia we were talking about. They had a big discussion about what should be done about ex-Presidents, and Alexander Hamilton I think it was said that it would be a terrible thing to degrade them by putting them back among the common people after they'd had all that power. But old Ben Franklin didn't agree. It's here someplace…I've got it, what he said…Here, read it."

Franklin said, "In free governments the rulers are the servants and the people their superiors and sovereigns. For the former therefore to return among the latter is not to degrade them but to promote them."

Mr. Truman smiled, and he said, "I kept that in mind when I was in the White House, and I've had it in mind ever since I got my…promotion."

Merle Miller
Plain Speaking: An Oral Biography of Harry S. Truman

Finally, brethren, whatsoever things are true, whatsoever things are honest, whatsoever things are just, whatsoever things are pure, whatsoever things are lovely, whatsoever things are of good report; if there be any virtue, and if there be any praise, think on these things.

Philippians 4:8

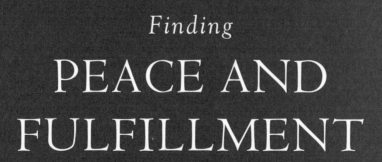

Finding

PEACE AND
FULFILLMENT

CHAPTER ELEVEN

FINDING PEACE AND FULFILLMENT

————

The mind is its own place, and in itself
Can make a Heaven of Hell, a Hell of Heaven.

John Milton
Paradise Lost

People often ask me, "Joni, how does the devil get to you? What kind of fiery darts really get under your skin?"

I'm not sure if folks expect a laundry list of vices and temptations, but what I tell them most often is this: Satan digs at me hardest when things break down.

My comfort and independence rest heavily on bits and pieces of adaptive equipment. When that equipment fails—a buckle on a corset snap or a clamp on a leg bag or a tire on a wheelchair—well, it really gets to me.

I was explaining that to a friend not long ago.

We wrapped up our conversation as I wheeled into my van. I cranked the engine and was just about to push the control to close the electric-powered door, when my friend reached over, grabbed the handle, and slammed the door shut.

A friendly gesture. One that anybody might do as you're saying goodbye. My car door, however, is loaded with fragile chains and springs and switches. With one good yank from my "helpful" friend—and before I could cry "Stop!"—the door chain snapped.

He was thoroughly embarrassed and I was almost irritated. But we both laughed over our reactions.

You probably feel the same way when your washing machine gets rusty joints, when the printer on your computer freezes up, or your car's air conditioner takes a vacation. Take heart! If God can make axheads float as He did in 2 Kings 6, or if He can cause the wheels to fall off Egyptian chariots as He did in Exodus 15, then God must be in control of the springs and hinges and widgets and all the rest of those little mechanical doodads that seem to break down at the wrong time.

The Bible makes it clear God's control extends beyond the "big things" of life, like our dreams and destiny. We all know the Lord has His hand in those monumental decisions of our lives. But Scripture also tells us the Lord gets down into the nuts and bolts of little things.

I'm trying hard to remember that whenever my wheelchair batteries konk out on me, leaving me stranded where I don't want to be. I'm trying to remember to have a good attitude about those kinds of things, to remember that God is still in control.

The next time you have to call a plumber or have a mechanic look under your hood, remember that the King's sovereignty extends to such lowly, utilitarian objects like refrigerators, toasters, transistors, and oil filters. Even in these, He is Lord.

So hang in there. Be patient. Call a handyman. Pay the bill.

But trust God.

Joni Eareckson Tada
Glorious Intruder

To live with serenity does not necessarily mean that outward conditions have changed. *Serenity is an inner peace that is present even in difficult surroundings.*

William V. Pietsch
The Serenity Prayer Book

If you observe a really happy man you will find him building a boat, writing a symphony, educating his son, growing double dahlias in his garden, or looking for dinosaur eggs in the Gobi desert. He will not be searching for happiness as if it were a collar button that has rolled under the radiator. He will not be striving for it as if it were a goal in itself, nor will he be seeking for it among the nebulous wastes of metaphysics.

To find happiness we must seek for it in a focus outside ourselves.

W. Beran Wolfe
How To Be Happy Though Human

In my life, I have found there are two things about which I should never worry. First, I shouldn't worry about the things I can't change. If I can't change them, worry is certainly most foolish and useless. Second, I shouldn't worry about the things I can change. If I can change them, then taking action will accomplish far more than wasting my energies in worry. Besides, it is my belief that, 9 times out of 10, worrying about something does more danger than the thing itself. Give worry its rightful place—out of your life.

anonymous
"Two Things Not to Worry About"

Do not be anxious about anything, but in everything, by prayer and petition, with thanksgiving, present your requests to God. And the peace of God, which transcends all understanding, will guard your hearts and your minds in Christ Jesus.

Philippians 4:6-7 (NIV)

Peace I leave with you; my peace I give you. I do not give to you as the world gives. Do not let your hearts be troubled and do not be afraid.

John 14:27 (NIV)

Therefore I tell you, do not worry about your life, what you will eat or drink; or about your body, what you will wear. Is not life more important than food, and the body more important than clothes? Look at the birds of the air; they do not sow or reap or store away in barns, and yet your heavenly Father feeds them. Are you not much more valuable than they? Who of you by worrying can add a single hour to his life?

And why do you worry about clothes? See how the lilies of the field grow. They do not labor or spin. Yet I tell you that not even Solomon in all his splendor was dressed like one of these. If that is how God clothes the grass of the field, which is here today and tomorrow is thrown into the fire, will he not much more clothe you, O you of little faith? So do not worry, saying, "What shall we eat?" or "What shall we drink?" or "What shall we wear?" For the pagans run after all these things, and your heavenly Father knows that you need them. But seek first his kingdom and his righteousness, and all these things will be given to you as well. Therefore do not worry about tomorrow, for tomorrow will worry about itself. Each day has enough trouble of its own.

Matthew 6:25-34 (NIV)

And remember, there are two things which are more utterly incompatible than even oil and water, and these two are trust and worry. Would you call it trust if you should give something into the hands of a friend to attend to for you, and then should spend your nights and days in anxious thought and worry as to whether it would be rightly and successfully done? And can you call it trust, when you have given the saving and keeping of your soul into the hands of the Lord, if day after day, and night after night you are spending hours of anxious thought and questionings about the matter? When a believer really trusts anything, he ceases to worry about that thing which he has trusted. And when he worries, it is plain proof that he does not trust.

Hannah Whitall Smith
The Christian's Secret of a Happy Life

Drop thy still dew of quietness,
Till all our striving cease;
Take from our souls the strain and stress,
And let our ordered lives confess
The beauty of thy peace.

John Greenleaf Whittier
Prayer

God, give us grace
to accept with serenity the things that cannot be changed,
courage to change the things which should be changed
and the wisdom to distinguish the one from the other.

Reinhold Niebuhr
Part of a sermon

I would like to beg of you, dear friend, as well as I can, to have patience with everything that remains unsolved in your heart. Try to love the *questions them-selves*, like locked rooms and like books written in a foreign language. Do not now look for the answers. They cannot now be given to you because you could not live them. It is a question of experiencing everything. At present you need to live the question. Perhaps you will gradually, without even noticing it, find yourself experiencing the answer, some distant day.

Rainer Maria Rilke
Letters to a Young Poet

Nowhere in the Bible does it say that God is going to give you a plan for your entire life. He never said that He would lay out His plan for your life in cine-mascope so you can view it in its entirety. What He does promise is to lead you as you go; to direct you day by day; to show you His will hour by hour.

Tony Campolo
You Can Make a Difference

It once occurred to a certain king, that if he always knew the right time to begin everything; if he knew who were the right people to listen to, and whom to avoid; and, above all, if he always knew what was the most important thing to do, he would never fail in anything he might undertake.

And this thought having occurred to him, he had it proclaimed throughout his kingdom that he would give a great reward to any one who would teach him what was the right time for every action, and who were the most necessary people, and how he might know what was the most important thing to do.

And learned men came to the King, but they all answered his questions dif-ferently.

In reply to the first question, some said that to know the right time for every action, one must draw up in advance, a table of days, months and years, and must live strictly according to it. Only thus, said they, could everything be done at its proper time. Others declared that it was impossible to decide beforehand the right time for every action; but that, not letting oneself be absorbed in idle pas-times, one should always attend to all that was going on, and then do what was most needful. Others, again, said that however attentive the King might be to what was going on, it was impossible for one man to decide correctly the right time for every action, but that he should have a Council of wise men, who would help him to fix the proper time for everything.

But then again others said there were some things which could not wait to be laid before a Council, but about which one had at once to decide whether to undertake them or not. But in order to decide that, one must know beforehand what was going to happen. It is only magicians who know that; and, therefore, in order to know the right time for every action, one must consult magicians.

Equally various were the answers to the second question. Some said, the people the King most needed were his councilors; others, the priests; others, the doctors; while some said the warriors were the most necessary.

To the third question, as to what was the most important occupation: some replied that the most important thing in the world was science. Others said it was skill in warfare; and others, again, that it was religious worship.

All the answers being different, the King agreed with none of them, and gave the reward to none. But still wishing to find the right answers to his questions, he decided to consult a hermit, widely renowned for his wisdom.

The hermit lived in a wood which he never quitted, and he received none but common folk. So the King put on simple clothes, and before reaching the hermit's cell dismounted from his horse, and, leaving his bodyguard behind, went on alone.

When the King approached, the hermit was digging the ground in front of his hut. Seeing the King, he greeted him and went on digging. The hermit was frail and weak, and each time he stuck his spade into the ground and turned a little earth, he breathed heavily.

The King went up to him and said: "I have come to you, wise hermit, to ask you to answer three questions: How can I learn to do the right thing at the right time? Who are the people I most need, and to whom should I, therefore, pay more attention than to the rest? And, what affairs are the most important, and need my first attention?"

The hermit listened to the King, but answered nothing. He just spat on his hand and recommenced digging.

"You are tired," said the King, "let me take the spade and work awhile for you."

"Thanks!" said the hermit, and, giving the spade to the King, he sat down on the ground.

When he had dug two beds, the King stopped and repeated his questions.

The hermit again gave no answer, but rose, stretched out his hand for the spade, and said:

"Now rest awhile—and let me work a bit."

But the King did not give him the spade, and continued to dig. One hour passed, and another. The sun began to sink behind the trees, and the King at last stuck the spade into the ground, and said:

"I came to you, wise man, for an answer to my questions. If you can give me none, tell me so, and I will return home."

"Here comes some one running," said the hermit, "let us see who it is."

The King turned round, and saw a bearded man come running out of the wood. The man held his hands pressed against his stomach, and blood was flowing from under them. When he reached the King, he fell fainting on the ground moaning feebly. The King and the hermit unfastened the man's clothing. There was a large wound in his stomach. The King washed it as best he could, and bandaged it with his handkerchief and with a towel the hermit had. But the blood would not stop flowing, and the King again and again removed the bandage soaked with warm blood, and washed and rebandaged the wound. When at last the blood ceased flowing, the man revived and asked for something to drink. The King brought fresh water and gave it to him. Meanwhile the sun had set, and it had become cool. So the King, with the hermit's help, carried the wounded man into the hut and laid him on the bed. Lying on the bed the man closed his eyes and was quiet; but the King was so tired with his walk and with the work he had done, that he crouched down on the threshold, and also fell asleep—so soundly that he slept all through the short summer night. When he awoke in the morning, it was long before he could remember where he was, or who was the strange bearded man lying on the bed and gazing intently at him with shining eyes.

"Forgive me!" said the bearded man in a weak voice, when he saw that the King was awake and was looking at him.

"I do not know you, and have nothing to forgive you for," said the King.

"You do not know me, but I know you. I am that enemy of yours who swore to revenge himself on you, because you executed his brother and seized his property. I knew you had gone alone to see the hermit, and I resolved to kill you on your way back. But the day passed and you did not return. So I came out from my ambush to find you, and I came upon your bodyguard, and they recognized me, and wounded me. I escaped from them, but should have bled to death had you not dressed my wound. I wished to kill you, and you have saved my life. Now, if I live, and if you wish it, I will serve you as your most faithful slave, and will bid my sons do the same. Forgive me!"

The King was very glad to have made peace with his enemy so easily, and to have gained him for a friend, and he not only forgave him, but said he would send his servants and his own physician to attend him, and promised to restore his property.

Having taken leave of the wounded man, the King went out into the porch and looked around for the hermit. Before going away he wished once more to beg an answer to the questions he had put. The hermit was outside, on his knees, sowing seeds in the beds that had been dug the day before.

The King approached him, and said:

"For the last time, I pray you to answer my questions, wise man."

"You have already been answered!" said the hermit, still crouching on his thin legs, and looking up at the King, who stood before him.

"How answered? What do you mean?" asked the King.

"Do you not see," replied the hermit. "If you had not pitied my weakness yesterday, and had not dug those beds for me, but had gone your way, that man would have attacked you, and you would have repented of not having stayed with me. So the most important time was when you were digging the beds; and I was the most important man; and to do me good was your most important business. Afterwards when that man ran to us, the most important time was when you were attending to him, for if you had not bound up his wounds he would have died without having made peace with you. So he was the most important man, and what you did for him was your most important business. Remember then: there is only one time that is important—Now! It is the most important time because it is the only time when we have any power. The most necessary man is he with whom you are, for no man knows whether he will ever have dealings with any one else: and the most important affair is, to do him good, because for that purpose alone was man sent into this life!"

Leo Tolstoy
"Three Questions"

Peace *with* God brings the peace *of* God. It is a peace that settles our nerves, fills our mind, floods our spirit, and in the midst of the uproar around us, gives us the assurance that everything is all right.

Bob Mumford

Throw out the ballast and the balloon will rise.

James Barr

Two roads diverged in a yellow wood,
And sorry I could not travel both
And be one traveler, long I stood
And looked down one as far as I could
To where it bent in the undergrowth;

Then took the other, as just as fair,
And having perhaps the better claim,
Because it was grassy and wanted wear;
Though as for that, the passing there
Had worn them really about the same,

And both that morning equally lay
In leaves no step had trodden black.
Oh, I kept the first for another day!
Yet knowing how way leads on to way,
I doubted if I should ever come back.

I shall be telling this with a sigh
Somewhere ages and ages hence:
Two roads diverged in a wood, and I—
I took the one less traveled by,
And that has made all the difference.

Robert Frost
"The Road Not Taken"

We can live any way we want. People take vows of poverty, chastity, and obedi-ence—even of silence—by choice. The thing is to stalk your calling in a certain skilled and supple way, to locate the most tender and live spot and plug into that pulse. This is yielding, not fighting. A weasel doesn't "attack" anything; a weasel lives as he's meant to, yielding at every moment to the perfect freedom of single necessity.

I think it would be well, and proper, and obedient, and pure, to grasp your one necessity and not let it go, to dangle from it limp wherever it takes you.

Annie Dillard
Teaching a Stone to Talk

1. You will receive a body.

You may like it or hate it, but it will be yours for the entire period of this time around.

2. You will learn lessons.

You are enrolled in a full-time informal school called Life. Each day in this school you will have the opportunity to learn lessons. You may like the lessons or think them irrelevant and stupid.

3. There are no mistakes, only lessons.

Growth is a process of trial and error: Experimentation. The "failed" experi-ments are as much a part of the process as the experiment that ultimately "works."

4. A lesson is repeated until learned.

A lesson will be presented to you in various forms until you have learned it. When you have learned it, you can then go on to the next lesson.

5. Learning lessons does not end.

There is no part of life that does not contain its lessons. If you are alive, there are lessons to be learned.

6. "There" is no better than "here."

When your "there" has become a "here," you will simply obtain another "there" that will again look better than "here."

7. Others are merely mirrors of you.

You cannot love or hate something about another person unless it reflects something you love or hate about yourself.

8. What you make of your life is up to you.

You have all the tools and resources you need. What you do with them is up to you. The choice is yours.

9. Your answers lie inside you.

The answers to Life's questions lie inside you. All you need to do is look, listen and trust.

10. You will forget all this.

Chérie Carter-Scott
"The Rules for Being Human"

I am me.

In all the world, there is no one else exactly like me. There are people who have some parts like me but no one adds up exactly like me. Therefore, everything that comes out of me is authentically mine because I alone choose it.

I own everything about me—my body, including everything it does; my mind, including all my thoughts and ideas; my eyes, including the images of all they behold; my feelings, whatever they might be—anger, joy, frustration, love, disappointment, excitement; my mouth and all the words that come out of it—polite, sweet or rough, correct or incorrect; my voice, loud or soft; and all my actions, whether they be to others or myself.

I own my own fantasies, my dreams, my hopes, my fears.

I own all my triumphs and successes, all my failures and mistakes.

Because I own all of me, I can become intimately acquainted with me. By so doing, I can love me and be friendly with me in all my parts. I can then make it possible for all of me to work in my best interests.

I know there are aspects about myself that puzzle me, and other aspects that I do not know. But as long as I am friendly and loving to myself, I can courageously and hopefully look for the solutions to the puzzles and for ways to find out more about me.

However I look and sound, whatever I say and do, and whatever I think and feel at a given moment in time is me. This is authentic and represents where I am at that moment in time.

When I review later how I looked and sounded, what I said and did, and how I thought and felt, some parts may turn out to be unfitting. I can discard that which is unfitting and keep that which proved fitting, and invent something new for that which I discarded.

I can see, hear, feel, think, say and do. I have the tools to survive, to be close to others, to be productive, to make sense and order out of the world of people and things outside of me.

I own me and therefore I can engineer me.

I am me and I am okay.

Virginia Satir
"My Declaration of Self-Esteem"

Christ Jesus…made himself nothing.

He made himself nothing, emptied himself—the great kenosis. He made himself no reputation, no image.

I can recall my father shaking his head and repeating over and over to himself, "If I only knew what this meant. There is something powerful here. If I only understood it." Maybe that is why this Scripture has glued itself to my mind and equally disturbs me. Reputation is so important to me. I want to be seen with the right people, remembered in the right light, advertised with my name spelled right, live in the right neighborhood, drive the right kind of car, wear the right kind of clothing. But Jesus made himself of no reputation!

Gayle D. Erwin
The Jesus Style

There was once a fisherman who lived with his wife in a pigsty not far from the sea, and every day the fisherman went fishing. And he fished and he fished.

One day he was sitting with his line, looking into the smooth water. And he sat and he sat.

His line sank to the bottom, deep deep down, and when he pulled it up there was a big flounder on it. And the flounder said: "Look here, fisherman. Why not let me live? I'm not a real flounder, I'm an enchanted prince. What good would it do you to kill me? I wouldn't be much good to eat. Put me back in the water and let me go." "Save your breath," said the fisherman. "Do you think I'd keep a talking flounder?" So he put him back in the smooth water, and the flounder swam down to the bottom, leaving a long trail of blood behind him. Whereupon the fisherman got up and went home to his wife in the pigsty.

"Husband," said the wife, "haven't you caught anything today?" "No," said the fisherman. "I caught a flounder who said he was an enchanted prince, so I let him go." "Didn't you make a wish?" the wife asked. "No," he said. "What should I wish for?" "That's easy," said the wife. "It's so dreadful having to live in this pigsty. It stinks, it's disgusting: you could have wished for a little cottage. Go back and tell him we want a little cottage. He's sure to give us one." "How can I go back again?" said the husband. "Didn't you catch him and let him go?" said the wife. "He's bound to do it. Go right this minute." The husband didn't really want to go, but neither did he want to cross his wife, so he went to the shore.

When he got there, the sea was all green and yellow and not nearly as smooth as before. He stood there and said:

> "Little man, whoever you be,
> Flounder, flounder in the sea,
> My wife, her name is Ilsebil,
> Has sent me here against my will."

The flounder came swimming and asked: "Well, what does she want?" "It's like this," said the fisherman. "I caught you, didn't I, and now my wife says I should have wished for something. She's sick of living in a pigsty. She wants a cottage." "Just go home," said the flounder. "She's already got it."

The fisherman went home and his wife wasn't sitting in their pigsty any more. She was sitting on a bench outside a little cottage. She took him by the hand and said: "Come on in; look, it's much nicer." They went in, and there was a little hallway and a lovely little parlor and a bedroom with a bed for each of them, and a kitchen and a pantry, all with the best of furnishings and utensils, tinware and brassware, and everything that was needed. And behind the cottage there was a small barnyard with chickens and ducks in it and a little garden full of vegetables and fruit. "See," said the wife. "Isn't it nice?" "Yes indeed," said the husband. "If only it lasts, we shall live happy and contented." "We'll see about that," said the wife. Then they had something to eat and went to bed.

All went well for a week or two. Then the wife said: "Listen to me, husband. This cottage is too cramped and the garden and barnyard are too small. The flounder could have given us a bigger house. I'd like to live in a big stone castle. Go to the flounder and tell him to give us a castle." "Wife, wife," said the husband, "this cottage is plenty good enough. Why would we want to live in a castle?" "Don't argue," said the wife. "Just get going. The flounder can do that for us." "No, wife," said the husband. "The flounder has just given us a cottage, I don't think I ought to go back so soon, he might not like it." "Get going," said the wife. "It's no trouble at all to him and he'll be glad to do it." The husband's heart was heavy; he didn't want to go. He said to himself: "It's not right." But he went.

When he got to the sea, the water wasn't green and yellow any more, it was purple and dark-blue and gray and murky, but still calm. He stood there and said:

>"Little man, whoever you be,
>Flounder, flounder in the sea,
>My wife, her name is Ilsebil,
>Has sent me here against my will."

"Well, what does she want?" said the flounder. "Dear me!" said the fisherman in distress. "Now she wants to live in a big stone castle." "Just go home," said the flounder. "She's standing at the gate."

So the man started off and thought he was going home, but when he got there he found a big stone castle, and his wife was standing at the top of the stair-case ready to go in. She took him by the hand and said: "Come on in." He went in with her and inside there was a great hall with a marble floor and lots of servants, who flung the big doors open, and the walls were all bright and covered with beautiful tapestries, and in the rooms all the tables and chairs were of gold. Crystal chandeliers hung from the ceiling, and all the halls and bedchambers had carpets, and the tables were so weighed down with victuals and the very best of wine that you'd have thought they'd collapse. And behind the house there was a big yard with barns and stables, and the very best of carriages, and there was also a wonderful big garden with the loveliest flowers and fruit trees, and a park that must have been half a mile long, with stags and deer and hares in it and everything you could possibly wish for. "Well," said the wife. "Isn't it nice?" "Yes, indeed," said the husband. "If only it lasts! We will live in this beautiful castle and be contented." "We'll see about that," said the wife. "We'll sleep on it." And with that they went to bed.

Next morning the wife woke up first. It was just daybreak, and from her bed she could see the beautiful countryside around her. Her husband was still stretching when she poked him in the side with her elbow and said: "Husband, get up and look out of the window. See here. Couldn't we be king over all that country? Go to the flounder and tell him we want to be king." "Wife, wife," said the husband. "What do we want to be king for? I don't want to be king." "Well," said the wife, "if you don't want to be king, then I'll be king. Go to the flounder. I want to be king." "But wife," said the fisherman, "why do you want to be king? I can't tell him that!" "Why not?" asked the wife. "Get going this minute. I must be king." Then the husband went, and he was very unhappy because of his wife wanting to be king. "It's not right, it's not right at all," he thought. And he didn't want to go, but he went.

When he got to the sea, it was all gray-black, and the water came churning up from the depths and it had a foul smell. And he stood there and said:

> "Little man, whoever you be,
> Flounder, flounder in the sea,
> My wife, her name is Ilsebil,
> Has sent me here against my will."

"Well, what does she want?" said the flounder. "Dear me," said the man. "She wants to be king." "Just go home," said the flounder, "she is already."

So the man went home, and when he got there the castle was much larger and had a big tower with marvelous ornaments. A sentry was standing at the gate, and there were lots of soldiers and drums and trumpets. And when the fisherman went inside, everything was made of pure marble and gold, with velvet covers and big golden tassels. The doors of the great hall opened, and there was the whole royal household, and his wife was sitting on a high throne of gold and diamonds, wearing a big golden crown and holding a scepter made of pure gold and precious stones, and on both sides of her ladies-in-waiting were standing in rows, each a head shorter than the last. He went and stood there and said: "My goodness, wife! So now you're king?" "That's right," said his wife. "Now I'm king." So he stood there and looked at her and after he'd looked awhile he said: "Now that you're king, suppose we let well enough alone. Let's stop wishing." "No, husband," she said, and she looked very upset. "Already the time is hanging heavy on my hands. I can't stand it any more. Go to the flounder. I'm king, but I've got to be emperor too." "Wife, wife," said the man, "why do you want to be emperor?" "Husband," she said, "go to the flounder. I want to be emperor." "Woman," said the fisherman, "he can't make you emperor. I can't tell the flounder that! There's only one emperor in the empire. The flounder can't make you emperor, he just can't." "Fiddlesticks," said the woman. "I'm the king and you're only my husband, so do as you're told. If he can make a king he can also make an emperor. I want to be emperor and that's that. Get going." So he had to go. But on the way he was frightened, and he thought to himself: "This won't end well. Emperor is too much of a good thing. The flounder must be getting sick of all this."

When he got to the sea, it was all black and murky, the water came churning up from the depths and throwing up bubbles, and the wind was so strong that
the sea frothed and foamed. The fisherman was filled with dread. And he stood
there and said:

> "Little man, whoever you may be,
> Flounder, flounder in the sea,
> My wife, her name is Ilsebil,
> Has sent me here against my will."

"Well, what does she want?" said the flounder. "Oh, flounder," he said, "my
wife wants to be emperor." "Just go home," said the flounder. "She is already."

So the fisherman went home, and when he got there, the whole palace was
made of polished marble with alabaster figures and golden ornaments. Soldiers
were marching and blowing trumpets and beating drums outside, and inside the
building barons and counts and dukes were going about the duties of servants.
They opened the doors for him and the doors were pure gold. When he went in,
his wife was sitting on a throne which was all one block of gold and at least two
miles high; and on her head she was wearing a big golden crown that was three
ells high and studded with diamonds and rubies. In one hand she was holding the
scepter and in the other the Imperial Orb, and on either side of her stood a row
of lifeguards, each shorter than the one before him, from the most enormous
giant, who was two miles high, to the tiniest dwarf, who was no bigger than my
little finger. And before her stood a crowd of princes and dukes. Her husband
went and stood among them and said: "Well, wife. It looks like you're emperor
now." "That's right," she said. "I'm emperor." He stood there and took a good
look at her, and when he'd been looking for a while, he said: "Well, wife, now that
you're emperor, suppose we let well enough alone." "Husband," she said, "what
are you standing there for? Yes, yes, I'm emperor, but now I want to be pope too,
so go to the flounder." "Woman, woman," said the husband, "what won't you be
asking next! You can't get to be pope, there's only one pope in all Christendom.
He can't make you pope." "Husband," she said, "I want to be pope, so do as you're
told. I insist on being pope before the day is out." "No, wife," said the husband,
"I can't tell him that, it's too much; the flounder can't make you pope." "Husband," said the woman. "That's poppycock. If he can make an emperor, he can
make a pope. Do as you're told. I'm the emperor and you're only my husband, so
you'd better get going." At that he was afraid and went, but he felt faint. He shiv-

ered and shook and he was wobbly at the knees. A strong wind was blowing, the clouds were flying fast, and toward evening the sky darkened. The leaves were blowing from the trees, the water roared and foamed as if it were boiling, and the waves pounded against the shore. In the distance he saw ships that were bobbing and bounding in the waves, and firing guns in distress. There was still a bit of blue in the middle of the sky, but there was red all around it as in a terrible storm. He stood there in fear and despair and said:

> "Little man, whoever you be,
> Flounder, flounder in the sea,
> My wife, her name is Ilsebil,
> Has sent me here against my will."

"Well, what does she want?" said the flounder. "Dear me!" said the fisherman. "She wants to be pope." "Just go home," said the flounder, "she is already."

So he went home, and when he got there, he found a big church with palaces all around it. He pushed through the crowd. Inside, the whole place was lighted with thousands and thousands of candles, and his wife, dressed in pure gold, was sitting on a throne that was even higher, much higher, and she was wearing three big golden crowns. All around her were church dignitaries, and on both sides of her there were rows of candles, from the biggest, which was as tall and thick as the biggest tower, down to the smallest kitchen candle. And all the emperors and kings were down on their knees to her, kissing her slipper. "Well, wife," said the fisherman, watching her closely, "so now you're pope?" "That's right," she said. "I'm pope." He stood there looking at her, and he felt as if he were looking into the bright sun. Then, after he'd been looking at her for a while, he said: "Well, wife, now that you're pope, suppose we let well enough alone!" But she sat there as stiff as a board, she didn't stir and she didn't move. "Wife," he said to her, "you'd better be satisfied now. You can't get to be anything better than pope." "I'll see about that," said the wife, and then they both went to bed. But she wasn't satisfied, her ambition wouldn't let her sleep, and she kept wondering what more she could get to be.

The fisherman slept soundly, for he had covered a lot of ground that day, but his wife couldn't get to sleep. All night she tossed and turned, wondering what more she could get to be, but she couldn't think of a single thing. Then the sun began to rise, and when she saw the red glow, she sat up in bed and looked out of the window. And when she saw the sun rising, she thought: "Ha! Why couldn't

I make the sun and the moon rise? Husband!" she cried, poking him in the ribs. "Wake up. Go and see the flounder. I want to be like God." The fisherman was still half-asleep, but her words gave him such a start that he fell out of bed. He thought he'd heard wrong and he rubbed his eyes. "Wife, wife!" he cried out, "what did you say?" "Husband," she said, "if I can't make the sun and moon rise it will be more than I can bear. If I can't make them rise I'll never have another moment's peace." She gave him a grisly look that sent the cold shivers down his spine and cried: "Get going now. I want to be like God." "Wife, wife!" he cried, falling down on his knees, "the flounder can't do that. He can make an emperor and a pope, but please, please, think it over and just go on being pope." At that she grew angry, her hair flew wildly around her head. She tore her nightgown to shreds, and gave him a kick. "I won't stand for it!" she cried. "I won't stand for it another minute. *Will* you get a move on?" Then he pulled on his trousers and ran out like a madman.

A storm was raging. The wind was blowing so hard he could hardly keep his feet. Trees and houses were falling, the mountains were trembling, great boulders were tumbling into the sea, the sky was as black as pitch, the thunder roared, the lightning flashed, the sea was rising up in great black waves as big as mountains and church towers, and each one had a crown of foam on top. He couldn't hear his own words, but he shouted:

> "Little man, whoever you be,
> Flounder, flounder in the sea,
> My wife, her name is Ilsebil,
> Has sent me here against my will."

"Well, what does she want?" asked the flounder. "Dear me," he said, "she wants to be like God." "Just go home, she's back in the old pigsty already."

And there they are living to this day.

> Jakob and Wilhelm Grimm, translated by Ralph Manheim
> "The Fisherman and His Wife"

I met a traveler from an antique land
Who said: Two vast and trunkless legs of stone
Stand in the desert. Near them, on the sand,
Half sunk, a shattered visage lies, whose frown,
And wrinkled lip, and sneer of cold command,

Tell that its sculptor well those passions read
Which yet survive, stamped on these lifeless things,
The hand that mocked them and the heart that fed;
And on the pedestal these words appear:
"My name is Ozymandias, king of kings:
Look on my works, ye Mighty, and despair!"
Nothing beside remains. Round the decay
Of that colossal wreck, boundless and bare
The lone and level sands stretch far away.

Percy Bysshe Shelley
"Ozymandias"

There was a proud Teapot, proud of being made of porcelain, proud of its long spout and its broad handle. It had something in front of it and behind it; the spout was in front, and the handle behind, and that was what it talked about. But it didn't mention its lid, for it was cracked and it was riveted and full of defects, and we don't talk about our defects—other people do that. The cups, the cream pitcher, the sugar bowl—in fact, the whole tea service—thought much more about the defects in the lid and talked more about it than about the sound handle and the distinguished spout. The Teapot knew this.

"I know them," it told itself. "And I also know my imperfections, and I realise that in that very knowledge is my humility and my modesty. We all have many defects, but then we also have virtues. The cups have a handle, the sugar bowl has a lid, but of course I have both, and one thing more, one thing they can never have; I have a spout, and that makes me the queen of the tea table. The sugar bowl and the cream pitcher are permitted to be serving maids of delicacies, but I am the one who gives forth, the adviser. I spread blessings abroad among thirsty mankind. Inside of me the Chinese leaves give flavor to boiling, tasteless water."

This was the way the Teapot talked in its fresh young life. It stood on the table that was prepared for tea and it was lifted up by the most delicate hand. But that most delicate hand was very awkward. The Teapot was dropped; the spout broke off, and the handle broke off; the lid is not worth talking about; enough has been said about that. The Teapot lay in a faint on the floor, while the boiling water ran out of it. It was a great shock it got, but the worst thing of all was that the others laughed at it—and not at the awkward hand.

"I'll never be able to forget that!" said the Teapot, when later on it talked to itself about its past life. "They called me an invalid, and stood me in a corner, and the next day gave me to a woman who was begging for food. I fell into poverty, and was speechless both outside and inside, but as I stood there my better life began. One is one thing and then becomes quite another. They put earth in me, and for a Teapot that's the same as being buried, but in that earth they planted a flower bulb. Who put it there and gave it to me, I don't know; but it was planted there, a substitution for the Chinese leaves and the boiling water, the broken handle and spout. And the bulb lay in the earth, inside of me, and it became my heart, my living heart, a thing I never had before. There was life in me; there were power and might; my pulse beat. The bulb put out sprouts; thoughts and feeling sprang up and burst forth into flower. I saw it, I bore it, and I forgot myself in its beauty. It is a blessing to forget oneself in others!

"It didn't thank me, it didn't even think of me—everybody admired it and praised it. It made me very happy; how much more happy it must have made it!

"One day I heard them say it deserved a better pot. They broke me in two— that really hurt—and the flower was put into a better pot; then they threw me out into the yard, where I lie as an old potsherd. But I have my memory; *that* I can never lose!"

Hans Christian Andersen
"The Teapot"

I think we have lost a lot of life's riches, and are continuing to do so, because we haven't learned the lesson of our own uniqueness. No matter how much alike we think we are, we are still different, and no matter how different we think we are, we are still alike. If you believe, as many people do, that your sameness creates your basis for trust and safety, and your differentness creates your problems, then you are using only half your resources. Everyone would like to be without problems and if you think that differentness creates your problems, you will use your energy to get rid of it. I think sameness can be comfortable but if that is all there is, in time it leads to boredom. Differentness can be a source of difficulty, but it also holds the key to a lot of locked up energy and experiences that make life exciting and fulfilling. Allow yourself to think in terms of all your parts, the ones with which you are very familiar, the ones which have not been developed and the ones which you may not even know exist. Think of each of your parts as a resource, regardless of whether it is the same or different from anyone else's or whether you consider it good or bad. Whatever you have represents new possibilities of yourself.

Virginia Satir
Your Many Faces

How do you measure success?
To laugh often and much;
To win the respect of intelligent people
and the affection of children;
To earn the appreciation of honest critics
and endure the betrayal of false friends;
To appreciate beauty;
To find the best in others;
To leave the world a bit better,
whether by a healthy child, a garden
patch, a redeemed social condition, or a job well done;
To know even one other life has breathed easier
because you have lived—
This is to have succeeded.

Ralph Waldo Emerson
"What Is Success?"

In the movie *Breaking Away* released some years ago, the story centers on a young man from Indiana who has grown up in a community and in a home where stone-cutting is the only way to make a living. He comes to a crisis in his life when he tries to decide whether to consider trying to go to college...

Everybody in his neighborhood is either a stonecutter by trade or the son or daughter of a stonecutter. Typically, the sons and daughters follow in their fathers' and mothers' career paths. It is tradition. They never go away to college. They stay close to home and cut stones.

The young man's father takes him to the university campus one day, and they stand on the front steps of the administration building.

"I cut the stones that you see placed here to build this university, Son," the father says, with his arm around his boy's shoulders. "I'm proud of that accomplishment. I think I did a good job." His son nods and they look each other in the eyes.

Then his father offers, "But I'm a cutter. And I've been watching you. You're not a cutter, and you don't have to try to be one. You can be anything you want. Just find out what you really like and what you really want, and you can be different. You can stand up and break away."

And so he does.

Denis Waitley
Being the Best

Go placidly amid the noise and haste, and remember what peace there may be in silence. As far as possible without surrender be on good terms with all persons. Speak your truth quietly and clearly; and listen to others, even the dull and ignorant; they too have their story.

Avoid loud and aggressive persons, they are vexations to the spirit. If you compare yourself with others, you may become vain and bitter; for always there will be greater and lesser persons than yourself. Enjoy your achievements as well as your plans.

Keep interested in your own career, however humble; it is a real possession in the changing fortunes of time. Exercise caution in your business affairs; for the world is full of trickery. But let this not blind you to what virtue there is; many persons strive for high ideals; and everywhere life is full of heroism.

Be yourself. Especially, do not feign affection. Neither be cynical about love; for in the face of all aridity and disenchantment it is perennial as the grass.

Take kindly the counsel of the years, gracefully surrendering the things of youth. Nurture strength of spirit to shield you in sudden misfortune. But do not distress yourself with imaginings. Many fears are born of fatigue and loneliness. Beyond a wholesome discipline, be gentle with yourself.

You are a child of the universe, no less than the trees and the stars; you have a right to be here. And whether or not it is clear to you, no doubt the universe is unfolding as it should.

Therefore be at peace with God, …and whatever your labors and aspirations, in the noisy confusion of life keep peace with your soul.

With all its sham, drudgery and broken dreams, it is still a beautiful world. Be careful. Strive to be happy.

"Desiderata"
(found in Old Saint Paul's Church, Baltimore, dated 1692)

Once, as a young man full of exuberant fancy,...I set down my inventory of earthly desirables: health, love, beauty, talent, power, riches, and fame—together with several minor ingredients of what I considered man's perfect portion.

When my inventory was completed I proudly showed it to a wise elder who had been the mentor and spiritual model of my youth...

At the corner of my friend's old eyes, I saw wrinkles of amusement gathering in a patient net. "An excellent list," he said, pondering it thoughtfully. "Well digested in content and set down in not-unreasonable order. But it appears, my young friend, that you have omitted the most important element of all. You have forgotten the one ingredient lacking which each possession becomes a hideous torment, and your list as a whole an intolerable burden."

"And what," I asked, peppering my voice with truculence, "is that missing ingredient?"

With a pencil stub he crossed out my entire schedule. Then, having demolished my adolescent dream structure at a single stroke, he wrote down three syllables: peace of mind.

"This is the gift that God reserves for His special proteges," he said. "Talent and beauty He gives to many. Wealth is commonplace, fame not rare. But peace of mind—that is His final guerdon of approval, the fondest sign of His love. He bestows it charily. Most men are never blessed with it; others wait all their lives— yes, far into advanced age—for this gift to descend upon them."

Joshua L. Liebman
Peace of Mind

When I set God at the center of my life, I realize vast freedoms and surprising spontaneities. When I center life in my own will, my freedom diminishes markedly. I live constricted and anxious.

Eugene Peterson
Traveling Light

...after some work with a colored pencil I succeeded in making my first drawing. My Drawing Number One...

I showed my masterpiece to the grown-ups, and asked them whether the drawing frightened them.

But they answered: "Frighten? Why should any one be frightened by a hat?"

My drawing was not a picture of a hat. It was a picture of a boa constrictor digesting an elephant...

Grown-ups never understand anything by themselves, and it is tiresome for children to be always and forever explaining things to them...

In the course of this life I have had a great many encounters with a great many people who have been concerned with matters of consequence. I have lived a great deal among grown-ups. I have seen them intimately, close at hand. And that hasn't much improved my opinion of them.

Whenever I met one of them who seemed to me at all clear-sighted, I tried the experiment of showing him my Drawing Number One, which I have always kept. I would try to find out, so, if this was a person of true understanding. But, whoever it was, he, or she, would always say:

"That is a hat."

Then I would never talk to that person about boa constrictors, or primeval forests, or stars. I would bring myself down to his level. I would talk to him about bridge, and golf, and politics, and neckties. And the grown-up would be greatly pleased to have met such a sensible man.

Antoine de Saint-Exupéry
The Little Prince

1—Never lose your capacity for enthusiasm.

2—Never lose your capacity for indignation.

3—Never judge people, don't type them too quickly; but in a pinch never first assume that a man is bad; first assume always that he is good and that at worst he is in the gray area between bad and good.

4—Never be impressed by wealth alone or thrown by poverty.

5—If you can't be generous when it's hard to be, you won't be when it's easy.

6—The greatest builder of confidence is the ability to do something—almost anything—well.

7—When that confidence comes, then strive for humility; you aren't as good as all that.

8—And the way to become truly useful is to seek the best that other brains have to offer. Use them to supplement your own, and be prepared to give credit to them when they have helped.

9—The greatest tragedies in world and personal events stem from misunderstandings.

ANSWER: communicate.

> Gordon Dean, former Atomic Energy Commission chairman
> "Lessons Learned" (found on the back of an envelope
> among his effects after his death in a plane crash)

When my grandmother was raising me in Stamps, Arkansas, she had a particular routine when people who were known to be whiners entered her store. Whenever she saw a known complainer coming, she would call me from whatever I was doing and say conspiratorially, "Sister, come inside. Come." Of course I would obey.

My grandmother would ask the customer, "How are you doing today, Brother Thomas?"

And the person would reply, "Not so good." There would be a distinct whine in the voice. "Not so good today, Sister Henderson. You see, it's this summer. It's this summer heat. I just hate it. Oh, I hate it so much. It just frazzles me up and frazzles me down. I just hate the heat. It's almost killing me." Then my grandmother would stand stoically, her arms folded, and mumble, "Uh-huh, uh-huh." And she would cut her eyes at me to make certain that I had heard the lamentation.

At another time a whiner would mewl, "I hate plowing. That packed-down dirt ain't got no reasoning, and mules ain't got good sense. Sure ain't. It's killing me. I can't ever seem to get done. My feet and my hands stay sore, and I get dirt in my eyes and up my nose. I just can't stand it." And my grandmother, again stoically, with her arms folded, would say, "Uh-huh, uh-huh," and then look at me and nod.

As soon as the complainer was out of the store, my grandmother would call me to stand in front of her. And then she would say the same thing she had said at least a thousand times, it seemed to me. "Sister, did you hear what Brother So-and-So or Sister Much-to-Do complained about? You heard that?" And I would nod. Mamma would continue, "Sister, there are people who went to sleep all over the world last night, poor and rich and white and black, but they will never wake again. Sister, those who expected to rise did not, their beds became their cooling boards, and their blankets became their winding sheets. And those dead folks would give anything, anything at all for just five minutes of this weather or 10 minutes of that plowing that person was grumbling about. So you watch yourself about complaining, Sister. What you're supposed to do when you don't like a thing is change it. If you can't change it, change the way you think about it. Don't complain."

It is said that persons have few teachable moments in their lives. Mamma seemed to have caught me at each one I had between the ages of three and 13. Whining is not only graceless, but can be dangerous. It can alert a brute that a victim is in the neighborhood.

Maya Angelou
Wouldn't Take Nothing for My Journey Now

The great thing, if one can, is to stop regarding all the unpleasant things as inter-ruptions of one's "own," or "real" life. The truth is of course that what one calls the interruptions are precisely one's real life—the life God is sending one day by day: What one calls one's "real life" is a phantom of one's own imagination.

C. S. Lewis
They Stand Together

A few years ago I met an old professor at the University of Notre Dame. Look-ing back on his long life of teaching, he said with a funny wrinkle in his eyes: "I have always been complaining that my work was constantly interrupted, until I slowly discovered that my interruptions were my work."

That is the great conversion in our life: to recognize and believe that the many unexpected events are not just disturbing interruptions of our projects, but the way in which God molds our hearts and prepares us for his return. Our great temptations are boredom and bitterness. When our good plans are interrupted by poor weather, our well-organized careers by illness or bad luck, our peace of mind by inner turmoil, our hope for peace by a new war, our desire for a stable government by a constant changing of the guards, and our desire for immortality by real death, we are tempted to give in to a paralyzing boredom or to strike back in destructive bitterness. But when we believe that patience can make our expectations grow, then fate can be converted into a vocation, wounds into a call for deeper understanding, and sadness into a birthplace for joy.

Henri J. Nouwen
Out of Solitude

Why do I judge my day by how much I have "accomplished"?

When I get to where I can enjoy just lying on the rug picking up lint balls I will no longer be too ambitious.

Hugh Prather
Notes to Myself

Perhaps what we need is less escape and more rest. In the contemplative and monastic traditions, there is a critical distinction between rest and escape. Rest, in the contemplative sense, is not necessarily the absence of activity. Rest involves conscious effort. To rest is to put aside; to escape is to avoid. To rest is to recognize; to escape is to deny. To rest is to retreat; to escape is to flee...One of the very best ways you will rest is when you do what you love—even when it might look like a flurry of productivity. Last night I went to a cooking class. I learned how to prepare five new pasta dishes, from perciatelli carbona with pancetta to fusilli with shrimp, roasted garlic, tomatoes, and artichoke hearts. It was great. As soon as class was over, I rushed to the grocery store to buy the ingredients I needed for tonight's meal. I didn't get home until after my normal bedtime, and yet I awoke today refreshed and excited. *I rested with activity* instead of escaping by lying on the couch and watching my favorite sitcom...

Charlie Hedges
Getting the Right Things Right

A plain Country Mouse was one day unexpectedly visited at his hole, by a fine Mouse of the town, who had formerly been his play-fellow. The honest rustic, pleased with the honour, resolved to entertain his friend as sumptuously as possible. He set before him a reserve of delicate grey pease and bacon, a dish of fine oatmeal, some parings of new cheese, and to crown all with a dessert, a remnant of a charming mellow apple. When the repast was nearly finished, the spark of the town, taking breath, said, Old Crony, give me leave to be a little free with you; how can you bear to live in this melancholy hole here, with nothing but woods, and meadows, and mountains, and rivulets about you? Do you not prefer the conversation of the world to the chirping of birds, and the splendour of the court, to the rude aspect of a wild like this? With many flowery arguments, he at last prevailed upon his country friend to accompany him to town, and about midnight they safely entered a certain great house, where there had been an entertainment the day before. Here it was the courtier's turn to entertain, and placing his guest on a rich Persian carpet, they both began to regale most deliciously, when on a sudden the noise of somebody opening the door, made them scuttle in confusion about the dining-room. The rustic in particular was ready to die with fear at the many hair-breadth escapes which followed. At last, recovering himself, Well, says he, if this be your town-life, much good may it do you. Give me my poor quiet hole again, with my homely, but comfortable grey pease.

Æsop
Fables

I am learning…that a man can live profoundly without masses of things.

Richard E. Byrd
Alone (after spending months alone in the Arctic)

I went to the woods because I wished to live deliberately, to front only the essential facts of life, and see if I could not learn what it had to teach, and not, when I came to die, discover that I had not lived. I did not wish to live what was not life, living is so dear; nor did I wish to practice resignation, unless it was quite necessary. I wanted to live deep and suck out all the marrow of life, to live so sturdily and Spartan-like as to put to rout all that was not life, to cut a broad swath and shave close, to drive life into a corner, and reduce it to its lowest terms, and, if it proved to be mean, why then to get the whole and genuine meanness of it, and publish its meanness to the world; or if it were sublime, to know it by experience, and be able to give a true account of it in my next excursion…Our life is frittered away by detail. An honest man has hardly need to count more than his ten fingers, or in extreme cases he may add his ten toes, and lump the rest. Simplicity, simplicity, simplicity! I say, let your affairs be as two or three, and not a hundred or a thousand; instead of a million count half a dozen, and keep your accounts on your thumb nail. In the midst of this chopping sea of civilized life, such are the clouds and storms and quicksands and thousand-and-one items to be allowed for, that a man has to live, if he would not founder and go to the bottom and not make his port at all, by dead reckoning, and he must be a great calculator indeed who succeeds. Simplify, simplify.

Henry David Thoreau
Walden

By examining as closely and candidly as I could the life that had come to seem to me in many ways a kind of trap or dead-end street, I discovered that it really wasn't that at all. I discovered that if you really keep your eye peeled to it and your ears open, if you really pay attention to it, even such a limited and limiting life as the one I was living on Rupert Mountain opened up onto extraordinary vistas. Taking your children to school and kissing your wife goodbye. Eating lunch with a friend. Trying to do a decent day's work. Hearing the rain patter against the window. There is no event so commonplace but that God is present within it, always hiddenly, always leaving you room to recognize him, but all the more fascinatingly because of that, all the more compellingly and hauntingly. In writing those lectures and the book they later turned into, it came to seem to me that if I were called upon to state in a few words the essence of everything I was trying to say both as a novelist and as a preacher, it would be something like this: Listen to your life. See it for the fathomless mystery it is. In the boredom and pain of it no less than in the excitement and gladness: touch, taste, smell your way to the holy and hidden heart of it because in the last analysis all moments are key moments, and life itself is grace.

Frederick Buechner
Now and Then

...forgive yourself when you are not the person you want to be. Then get out your baby picture, look at it and forgive yourself. Then get on with being who you want to be.

Bernie S. Siegel, M.D.
Foreword, *Chicken Soup for the Soul*

It was at a church service in Munich that I saw him, the former S.S. man who had stood guard at the shower room door in the processing center at Ravensbruck. He was the first of our actual jailers that I had seen since that time. And suddenly it was all there—the roomful of mocking men, the heaps of clothing, Betsie's pain-blanched face.

He came up to me as the church was emptying, beaming and bowing. "How grateful I am for your message, *Fraulein*." he said. "To think that, as you say, He has washed my sins away!"

His hand was thrust out to shake mine. And I, who had preached so often to the people in Bloemendaal the need to forgive, kept my hand at my side.

Even as the angry, vengeful thoughts boiled through me, I saw the sin of them. Jesus Christ had died for this man; was I going to ask for more? Lord Jesus, I prayed, forgive me and help me to forgive him.

I tried to smile, I struggled to raise my hand. I could not. I felt nothing, not the slightest spark of warmth or charity. And so again I breathed a silent prayer. Jesus, I cannot forgive him. Give me Your forgiveness.

As I took his hand the most incredible thing happened. From my shoulder along my arm and through my hand a current seemed to pass from me to him, while into my heart sprang a love for this stranger that almost overwhelmed me.

And so I discovered that it is not on our forgiveness any more than on our goodness that the world's healing hinges, but on His. When He tells us to love our enemies, He gives, along with the command, the love itself.

Corrie ten Boom
The Hiding Place

Speed, die when I may, I want it said of me by those who know me best,—that I have always plucked a thistle and planted a flower whenever I thought a flower would grow.

Abraham Lincoln
(upon signing the order for a condemned man's reprieve
following an emotional plea by the man's wife)

Clara Barton, the founder of the American Red Cross, was reminded one day of a vicious deed that someone had done to her years before. But she acted as if she had never heard of the incident.

"Don't you remember it?" her friend asked.

"No," came Barton's reply. "I distinctly remember forgetting it."

Luis Palau
Experiencing God's Forgiveness

When somebody you've wronged forgives you, you're spared the dull and self-diminishing throb of a guilty conscience.

When you forgive somebody who has wronged you, you're spared the dismal corrosion of bitterness and wounded pride.

For both parties, forgiveness means the freedom again to be at peace inside their own skins and to be glad in each other's presence.

Frederick Buechner
Wishful Thinking

"Listen, all of you. Love your *enemies.* Do *good* to those who *hate* you. Pray for the happiness of those who *curse* you; implore God's blessing on those who *hurt* you.

"If someone slaps you on one cheek, let him slap the other too! If someone demands your coat, give him your shirt besides. Give what you have to anyone who asks you for it; and when things are taken away from you, don't worry about getting them back. Treat others as you want them to treat you.

"Do you think you deserve credit for merely loving those who love you? Even the godless do that! And if you do good only to those who do you good—is that so wonderful? Even sinners do that much! And if you lend money only to those who can repay you, what good is that? Even the most wicked will lend to their own kind for full return!

"Love your *enemies!* Do good to them! Lend to *them!* And don't be concerned about the fact that they won't repay. Then your reward from heaven will be very great, and you will truly be acting as sons of God: for he is kind to the *unthankful* and to those who are *very wicked.*

"Try to show as much compassion as your Father does.

"Never criticize or condemn—or it will all come back on you. Go easy on others; then they will do the same for you. For if you give, you will get! Your gift will return to you in full and overflowing measure, pressed down, shaken together to make room for more, and running over. Whatever measure you use to give—large or small—will be used to measure what is given back to you."

Luke 6:27–38 (TLB)

The LORD bless you and keep you; the LORD make his face shine upon you and be gracious to you; the LORD turn his face toward you and give you peace.

Numbers 6:24-26 (NIV)

Enjoying

LIFE TO THE FULL

CHAPTER TWELVE

ENJOYING LIFE TO THE FULL

—✺—

For life is a mystery to be lived out rather than a problem to be solved.

anonymous

We hold these truths to be self-evident, that all men are created equal, that they are endowed by their Creator with certain unalienable rights, that among these are life, liberty and the pursuit of happiness.

The American Declaration of Independence,
July 4, 1776

Seize the day.

Quintus Horatius Flaccus
Odes

Today, when I awoke, I suddenly realized that this is the best day of my life, ever!

There were times when I wondered if I would make it to today; but I did! And because I did, I'm going to celebrate! Today I'm going to celebrate what an unbelievable life I have had so far; the accomplishments, the many blessings, and yes, even the hardships, because they have served to make me stronger.

I will live this day with my head held high and a happy heart. I will take time to marvel at God's seemingly simple gifts, the morning dew, the sun, the clouds, the trees, the flowers, the birds. Today, none of these miraculous creations will escape my notice.

Today I will share my excitement for life with other people. I'll make someone smile. I'll go out of my way to perform an act of kindness for someone I don't even know. Today I'll give a word of encouragement to someone who seems down. I'll pay someone a sincere compliment. I'll tell a child how special they are. And I'll tell someone I love, just how deeply I care for them and how much they mean to me.

Today is the day I quit worrying about what I don't have, and start being grateful for all the wonderful things God has already given me. I'll remember that to worry is just a waste of time, because my faith in God and His divine plan insures everything will be just fine.

And tonight, before I go to bed, I'll take a stroll outside and raise my eyes to the heavens. I will stand in awe at the beauty of the stars and the moon and the majesty of the universe and I will praise God for these magnificent treasures.

As the day ends and I lay my head down, I will thank the Almighty for the best day of my life. And I will sleep the sleep of a contented child, and yet excited with expectation, because I know tomorrow is going to be the best day of my life, ever!

Gregory M. Lousig-Nont, Ph.D.
"The Best Day of My Life"

I will drink
Life to the lees: all times I have enjoy'd
Greatly, have suffer'd greatly, both with those
That loved me, and alone.

Alfred, Lord Tennyson
"Ulysses"

Some people go skimming over the years of existence to sink gently into a placid grave, ignorant of life to the last, without ever having been made to see all it may contain.

Evan S. Connel
Mrs. Bridge

You can live on bland food so as to avoid an ulcer; drink no tea or coffee or other stimulants, in the name of health; go to bed early and stay away from night life; avoid all controversial subjects so as never to give offense; mind your own business and avoid involvement in other people's problems; spend money only on necessities and save all you can. You can still break your neck in the bathtub, and it will serve you right.

Eileen Guder

For me, thinking seems to act at times as a defense mechanism, a way of avoiding some feeling, or a way of *not* looking at the situation I am in. I believe this is especially true in social situations, where I lead with my head.

My trouble is I analyze life instead of live it.

Hugh Prather
Notes to Myself

Live all you can; it's a mistake not to. It doesn't so much matter what you do in particular, so long as you have your life. If you haven't had that what *have* you had?

Henry James
The Ambassadors

Happiness is the sense that one matters. Happiness is an abiding enthusiasm. Happiness is single-mindedness. Happiness is whole-heartedness. Happiness is a by-product. Happiness is faith.

Samuel M. Shoemaker
How You Can Find Happiness

All the world is searching for joy and happiness, but these cannot be purchased for any price in any market place, because they are virtues that come from within, and like rare jewels must be polished, for they shine brightest in the light of faith, and in the services of brotherly love.

Lucille R. Taylor
Quoted in *Relief Society Magazine*

That is happiness; to be dissolved into something complete and great.

Willa S. Cather

My Ántonia

I'm a standup comic. I was working at a radio station in New York, doing the weather as this character called June East (Mae West's long-lost sister). One day, a woman from *The Daily News* called and said she wanted to do an article on me. When she had finished interviewing me for the article, she asked, "What are you planning to do next?"

Well, at the time, there was absolutely nothing I was planning on doing next, so I asked her what she meant, stalling for time. She said she really wanted to follow my career. Here was a woman from *The Daily News* telling me she was interested in me! So I thought I'd better tell her something. What came out was, "I'm thinking about breaking the Guinness Book of World Records for Fastest-Talking Female."

The newspaper article came out the next day, and the writer had included my parting remarks about trying to break the world's Fastest-Talking Female record. At about 5:00 p.m. that afternoon, I got a call from *Larry King Live* asking me to go on the show. They wanted me to try to break the record, and they told me they would pick me up at 8:00—because they wanted me to do it *that night!*

Now, I had never heard of *Larry King Live,* and when I heard the woman say she was from the Manhattan Channel, I thought, *Hmmm, that's a porn channel, right?* But she patiently assured me that it was a national television show and that this was a one-time offer and opportunity—it was either that night or not at all.

I stared at the phone. I had a gig that night in New Jersey, but it wasn't hard to figure out which of the two engagements I'd prefer to do. I had to find a replacement for my 7:00 show, and I started calling every comic I knew. By the grace of God, I finally found one who would fill in for me, and five minutes before the deadline, I told *Larry King Live* I could make it.

Then I sat down to figure out what on earth I was going to do on the show. I called Guinness to find out how to break a fast-talking record. They told me I would have to recite something from either Shakespeare or the Bible.

Suddenly I started saying the ninety-first Psalm, a prayer of protection my mother had taught me. Shakespeare and I had never really gotten along, so I figured the Bible was my only hope. I began practicing and practicing, over and over again. I was both nervous and excited at the same time.

At 8:00, the limousine picked me up. I practiced the whole way there, and by the time I reached the New York studio, I was tongue-tied. I asked the woman in charge, "What if I don't break the record?"

"Larry doesn't care if you break it or not," she said. "He just cares that you try it on his show first." So I asked myself, *What's the worst that can happen? I'll look like a fool on national television! A minor thing,* I told myself, thinking I could live through that. And what if I broke the record?

So I decided just to give it my best shot, and I did. I broke the record, becoming the World's Fastest-Talking Female by speaking 585 words in one minute in front of a national television audience. (I broke it again two years later, with 603 words in a minute.) My career took off.

People often ask me how I did that. Or how I've managed to do many of the things I've done, like lecturing for the first time, or going on stage for the first time, or bungee jumping for the first time. I tell them I live my life by this simple philosophy: I always say yes first; then I ask, *Now, what do I have to do to accomplish that?*

Then I ask myself, *What is the worst thing that can happen if I don't succeed?* The answer is, I simply don't succeed! And what's the best thing that can happen? I succeed!

What more can life ask of you? Be yourself, and have a good time!

Fran Capo
"Just Say Yes"

Believe me! The secret of reaping the greatest fruitfulness and the greatest enjoyment from life is to live dangerously!

Friedrich Nietzsche
Die fröhliche Wissenschaft

Gather ye rosebuds while ye may,
Old Time is still a-flying;
And this same flower that smiles to-day,
To-morrow will be dying.

Robert Herrick
"To the Virgins, to Make Much of Time"

Sound, sound the clarion, fill the fife,
Throughout the sensual world proclaim,
One crowded hour of glorious life
Is worth an age without a name.

Thomas Osbert Mordaunt
"Verses Written During the War"

My father told me that God must surely have a reason for me being the way I am today. I'm beginning to believe it.

I was the kind of kid that things always worked out for. I grew up in Laguna Beach, California, and I loved surfing and sports. But at a time when most kids my age thought only of TV and the beach, I started thinking of ways I could become more independent, see the country and plan my future.

I began working at the age of 10. By the time I was 15, I worked between one to three jobs after school. I made enough money to buy a new motorcycle. I didn't even know how to ride it. But after paying cash for the bike and one year's worth of full insurance coverage, I went to parking lots and learned to ride it. After 15 minutes of figure eights, I rode home. I was 151/2, had just received my driver's permit and had bought a new motorcycle. It changed my life.

I wasn't one of those just-for-fun-weekend riders. I loved to ride. Every spare minute of every day, every chance I got, I averaged 100 miles a day on top of that bike. Sunsets and sunrises looked prettier when I enjoyed them from a winding mountain road. Even now, I can close my eyes and still feel the bike naturally beneath me, so naturally that it was a more familiar feeling than walking. As I rode, the cool wind gave me a feeling of total relaxation. While I explored the open road outside, inside I was dreaming about what I wanted my life to be.

Two years and five new motorcycles later, I ran out of roads in California. I read motorcycle magazines every night and one night, a BMW motorcycle ad caught my eye. It showed a muddy motorcycle with a duffel bag on the back parked on the side of a dirt road in front of a large "Welcome to Alaska" sign. One year later, I took a photograph of an even muddier motorcycle in front of that exact same sign. Yes, it was me! At 17 years old I made it to Alaska alone with my bike, conquering over 1,000 miles of dirt highway.

Prior to departing for my seven-week, 17,000-mile camping adventure, my friends said that I was crazy. My parents said that I should wait. Crazy? Wait? For what? Since I was a kid, I had dreamed about going across America on a motor-cycle. Something strong inside of me told me that if I didn't go on this trip now, I never would. Besides, when would I have the time? I would be starting college on a scholarship very soon, then a career, perhaps even a family some day. I didn't know if it was just to satisfy me or if in my mind I felt it would somehow trans-form me from a boy to a man. But what I did know was that for that summer, I was going on the adventure of a lifetime.

I quit all of my jobs and because I was only 17 I had my mother write a letter stating that I had her permission to go on this trip. With $1,400 in my pocket, two duffel bags, a shoe box full of maps strapped to the back of my motorcycle, a pen flashlight for protection and a lot of enthusiasm, I left for Alaska and the East Coast.

I met a lot of people, enjoyed the rugged beauty and lifestyle, ate off the open fire and thanked God every day for giving me this opportunity. Sometimes, I didn't see or hear anyone for two or three days and just rode my motorcycle in endless silence with only the wind racing around my helmet. I didn't cut my hair, I took cold showers at campgrounds when I could, and I even had several unscheduled confrontations with bears during that trip. It was the greatest adventure!

Even though I took several more trips, none can ever compare to that summer. It has always held a special place in my life. I can never go back again and explore the roads and mountains, the forests and glacial waters the same way I did back then on that trip, alone with my motorcycle. I can never make the same trip in the exact same way because at the age of 23, I was in a motorcycle accident on a street in Laguna Beach where I was hit by a drunk driver/drug dealer who left me paralyzed from the ribs down.

At the time of my accident, I was in great shape, both physically and men-tally. I was a full-time police officer, still riding my motorcycle on my days off. I was married and financially secure. I had it made. But in the space of less than a second, my whole life changed. I spent eight months in the hospital, got divorced, saw that I could not return to work in the way that I had known it and, along with learning how to deal with chronic pain and a wheelchair, I saw all the dreams I had for my future leaving my reach. Luckily for me, help and support helped new dreams to develop and be fulfilled.

When I think back to all of those trips I took, all of those roads that I traveled,

I think of how lucky I was to have been able to do that. Every time I rode, I always said to myself, "Do it now. Enjoy your surroundings, even if you're at a smoggy city intersection; enjoy life because you cannot depend on getting a second chance to be in the same place or do the same things."

After my accident, my father said that God had a reason for me being a paraplegic. I believe it. It has made me a stronger person. I returned to work as a desk officer, bought a home and married again. I also have my own consulting business and am a professional speaker. Every now and again, when things get rough, I remind myself of all the things that I have accomplished, all the things I have yet to accomplish, and my father's words.

Yes, he was right. God sure did have a reason. Most importantly, I remind myself to enjoy every moment of every day. And if you can do something, do it. Do it now!

Glenn McIntyre
"Why Wait?…Just Do It!"

Whatever you want to do, do it now. There are only so many tomorrows.

Michael Landon

There is a time for everything, and a season for every activity under heaven: a time to be born and a time to die, a time to plant and a time to uproot, a time to kill and a time to heal, a time to tear down and a time to build, a time to weep and a time to laugh, a time to mourn and a time to dance, a time to scatter stones and a time to gather them, a time to embrace and a time to refrain, a time to search and a time to give up, a time to keep and a time to throw away, a time to tear and a time to mend, a time to be silent and a time to speak, a time to love and a time to hate, a time for war and a time for peace.

What does the worker gain from his toil? I have seen the burden God has laid on men. He has made everything beautiful in its time. He has also set eternity in the hearts of men; yet they cannot fathom what God has done from beginning to end. I know that there is nothing better for men than to be happy and do good while they live. That everyone may eat and drink, and find satisfaction in all his toil—this is the gift of God. I know that everything God does will endure forever; nothing can be added to it and nothing taken from it. God does it so that men will revere him.

Ecclesiastes 3:1-14 (NIV)

Everywhere we look, the world urges us to turn on the radio or TV, to make a phone call, to see a movie. Many of us, I fear, worry that, if left alone with our thoughts and feelings, we may discover that we do not make very good company for ourselves.

James O. Freedman
Quoted in *Readers Digest*, January 1997

Don't let artificial light and city streets keep you from noticing sunsets and sun-rises, from experiencing the spring of new life and the harvest of fall.

M. Basil Pennington
A Place Apart

Climb the mountains and get their good tidings. Nature's peace will flow into you as sunshine flows into trees. The winds will blow their freshness into you, and the storms their energy, while cares will drop off like autumn leaves.

John Muir

When I was ten
how could I
have known
that a lifetime
has nothing to do
with years...

...only with time.

And that its value
isn't measured by
the important things
that happen...

...unless
smiling
with a seagull
is important.

Flavia Weedn
"A Lifetime"

All work and no play makes Jack a dull boy;
All play and no work makes Jack a mere toy.

Mother Goose

If I had my life to life over again, I'd try to make more mistakes next time. I would relax. I would limber up. I would be sillier than I have been this trip. I know of a very few things I would take seriously. I would take more trips. I would climb more mountains, swim more rivers, and watch more sunsets. I would eat more ice cream and fewer beans. I would have more actual troubles and fewer imaginary ones. You see, I am one of those people who lives prophylactically and sensibly and sanely hour after hour, day after day. Oh, I've had my moments; and if I had it to do over again, I'd have more of them. In fact, I'd try to have nothing else. Just moments, one after another, instead of living so many years ahead of each day. I have been one of those people who never go anywhere without a thermometer, a hot water bottle, a raincoat, aspirin, and a parachute. If I had to do it over again, I would go places, do things, and travel lighter than I have.

If I had my life to live over, I would ride on more merry-go-rounds—pick more daisies.

Brother Jeremiah

My heart leaps up when I behold
A rainbow in the sky;
So was it when my life began;
So is it now I am a man;
So be it when I shall grow old.
Or let me die!
The Child is father of the Man;
And I could wish my days to be
Bound each to each by natural piety.

William Wordsworth
"My Heart Leaps Up"

"My, how foolish I am!" my friend cries, suddenly alert, like a woman remembering too late she has biscuits in the oven. "You know what I've always thought?" she asks in a tone of discovery, and not smiling at me but a point beyond. "I've always thought a body would have to be sick and dying before they saw the Lord. And I imagined that when He came it would be like looking at the Baptist window: pretty as colored glass with the sun pouring through, such a shine you don't know it's getting dark. And it's been a comfort: to think of that shine taking away all the spooky feeling. But I'll wager it never happens. I'll wager at the very end a body realizes the Lord has already shown Himself. That things as they are"—her hand circles in a gesture that gathers clouds and kites and grass and Queenie pawing earth over her bone—"just what they've always seen, was seeing Him. As for me, I could leave the world with today in my eyes."

Truman Capote
A Christmas Memory

Give to me the life I love,
Let the lave go by me,
Give the jolly heaven above
And the byway nigh me.
Bed in the bush with stars to see,
Bread I dip in the river
There's the life for a man like me,
There's the life for ever.

Robert Louis Stevenson
"The Vagabond"

Celebrate the temporary
Don't wait until tomorrow
Live today…

Live in the now
With all its problems and its agonies
With its joy
And its pain…

Clyde Reid
Celebrate the Temporary

I wandered lonely as a cloud
That floats on high o'er vales and hills,
When all at once I saw a crowd,
A host, of golden daffodils,
Beside the lake, beneath the trees,
Fluttering and dancing in the breeze.

Continuous as the stars that shine
And twinkle on the milky way,
They stretched in never-ending line
Along the margin of a bay:
Ten thousand saw I at a glance,
Tossing their heads in sprightly dance.

The waves beside them danced; but they
Out-did the sparkling waves in glee;
A poet could not but be gay,
In such a jocund company;
I gazed—and gazed—but little thought
What wealth the show to me had brought:

For oft, when on my couch I lie
In vacant or in pensive mood,
They flash upon that inward eye
Which is the bliss of solitude;
And then my heart with pleasure fills,
And dances with the daffodils.

William Wordsworth
"I Wandered Lonely as a Cloud"

What is this life if, full of care,
We have no time to stand and stare?

W. H. Davies
Leisure

"To pray is to take notice of the wonder, to regain a sense of the mystery that animates all beings, the divine margin in all attainments." Prayer is "our" humble "answer" to the inconceivable surprise of living. It is all we can offer in return for the mystery by which we live. Who is worthy to be present at the constant unfolding of time? Amidst the meditation of mountains, the humility of flowers—wiser than all alphabets—clouds that die constantly for the sake of His glory, "we" are hating, hunting, hurting. Suddenly we feel ashamed for our clashes and complaints in the face of the tacit glory in nature. It is so embarrassing to live! How strange we are in the world, and how presumptuous our doings! Only one response can maintain us: gratefulness for witnessing the wonder, for the gift of our unearned right to serve, to adore, and to fulfill. It is gratefulness which makes the soul great.

Abraham Joshua Heschel
Man's Quest for God

"What I do" is literally "how I spend my time." As of this writing, in the fall of 1988, I figure in my life so far I have spent 35,000 hours eating, 30,000 hours in traffic getting from one place to another, 2,508 hours brushing my teeth, 870,000 hours just coping with odds and ends, filling out forms, mending, repairing, paying bills, getting dressed and undressed, reading papers, attending committee meetings, being sick, and all that kind of stuff. And 217,000 hours at work. There's not a whole lot left over when you get finished adding and subtracting. The good stuff has to be fitted in somewhere, or else the good stuff has to come at the very same time we do all the rest of the stuff.

Which is why I often say that I don't worry about the meaning of life—I can't handle that big stuff. What concerns me is the meaning *in* life—day by day, hour by hour, while I'm doing whatever it is that I do. What counts is not what I do, but how I think about myself while I'm doing it.

Robert Fulghum
It Was on Fire When I Lay Down on It

And today now everything will pass because it is the last day. For the last time you are seeing this rain fall and in your mind that snow, this child asleep, this cat. For the last time you are hearing this house come alive because you who are part of its life have come alive. All the unkept promises if they are ever to be kept have to be kept today.

All the unspoken words if you do not speak them today will never be spoken. The people, the ones you love and the ones who bore you to death, all the life you have in you to live with them, if you do not live it with them today will never be lived.

It is the first day because it has never been before and the last day because it will never be again. Be alive if you can all through this day today of your life. What's to be done? What's to be done?

Follow your feet. Put on the coffee. Start the orange juice, the bacon, the toast. Then go wake up your children and your wife. Think about the work of your hands…Live in the needs of the day.

Frederick Buechner
Alphabet of Grace

Could one question change the rest of your life?

It did for John Sculley.

In 1983, while standing atop a thirty-story building in New York City, Sculley, forty-two-year-old president of Pepsi Cola, didn't realize he was about to be asked a question that would change his life forever.

John Sculley was a riser who had moved through the ranks and up the ladder of success at PepsiCo faster than anyone, ever. He had joined the company in 1967, and in just seven years, at the age of thirty-four, he became president of Pepsi Cola. In 1973 his picture was on the cover of *Newsweek* magazine, and he found himself quoted regularly by all the highly regarded business journals. It would seem he had "arrived."

In the early eighties, Steve Jobs, the creative genius behind an almost unknown company called Apple Computer, approached Sculley with a radical idea. Jobs had decided that Sculley was the ideal executive to take Apple to the next level. His only problem was convincing Sculley. After several months of friendship building and unsuccessful wooing, a frustrated Jobs made his last-ditch appeal. On the penthouse floor of a New York City high-rise, Steve Jobs asked John Sculley the question that would change his life: "*John, do you want to spend the rest of your life selling sugared water, or do you want a chance to change the world?*"

Sculley was never the same. A short time later, to the shock of many, he resigned his position at Pepsi and became CEO of Apple Computer.

Charlie Hedges
Getting the Right Things Right

...if one advances confidently in the direction of his dreams, and endeavors to live the life which he has imagined, he will meet with a success unexpected in common hours...If you have built castles in the air, your work need not be lost; that is where they should be. Now put the foundations under them.

Henry David Thoreau
Walden

...Of all sad words of tongue or pen,
The saddest are these: "It might have been!"

John Greenleaf Whittier
Maud Muller

We all have moments when we feel better than our best, and we say—"I feel fit for anything; if only I could be like this always!" We are not meant to be. Those moments are moments of insight which we have to live up to when we do not feel like it. Many of us are no good for this workaday world when there is no high hour. We must bring our commonplace life up to the standard revealed in the high hour.

Never allow a feeling which was stirred in you in the high hour to evaporate. Don't put your mental feet on the mantelpiece and say—"What a marvellous state of mind to be in!" Act immediately, do something, if only because you would rather not do it. If in a prayer meeting God has shown you something to do, don't say—"I'll do it"; *do it!* Take yourself by the scruff of the neck and shake off your incarnate laziness. Laziness is always seen in cravings for the high hour; we talk about working up to a time on the mount. We have to learn to live in the grey day according to what we saw on the mount.

Don't cave in because you have been baffled once, get at it again. Burn your bridges behind you, and stand committed to God by your own act. Never revise your decisions, but see that you make your decisions in the light of the high hour.

Oswald Chambers
My Utmost for His Highest

It's an underground slogan that's spreading across the nation.

It's a crisp winter day in San Francisco. A woman in a red Honda, Christmas presents piled high in the back, drives up to the Bay Bridge toll both. "I'm paying for myself, and for the six cars behind me," she says with a smile, handing over seven commuter tickets.

One after another, the next six drivers arrive at the toll booth, dollars in hand, only to be told, "Some lady up ahead already paid your fare. Have a nice day."

The woman in the Honda, it turned out, had read something on an index card taped to a friend's refrigerator: "Practice random kindness and senseless acts of beauty." The phrase seemed to leap out at her, and she copied it down.

Judy Foreman spotted the same phrase spray painted on a warehouse wall a hundred miles from her home. When it stayed on her mind for days, she gave up and drove all the way back to copy it down. "I thought it was incredibly beautiful," she said, explaining why she's taken to writing it at the bottom of all her letters, "like a message from above."

Her husband, Frank, liked the phrase so much that he put it up on the classroom wall for his seventh-graders, one of whom was the daughter of a local columnist. The columnist put it in the paper, admitting that though she liked it, she didn't know where it came from or what it really meant.

Two days later, she heard from Anne Herbert. Tall, blond and forty, Herbert lives in Marin, one of the country's ten richest counties, where she house-sits, takes odd jobs, gets by. It was in a Sausalito restaurant that Herbert jotted the phrase down on a paper placemat, after turning it around in her mind for days.

"That's wonderful!" a man sitting nearby said, and copied it down carefully on his own placemat.

"Here's the idea," Herbert says. "Anything you think there should be more of, do it randomly."

Her own fantasies include: (1) breaking into depressing-looking schools to paint the classrooms, (2) leaving hot meals on kitchen tables in the poor part of town, (3) slipping money into a proud old woman's purse. Says Herbert, "Kindness can build on itself as much as violence can."

Now the phrase is spreading, on bumper stickers, on walls, at the bottom of letters and business cards. And as it spreads, so does a vision of guerrilla goodness.

In Portland, Oregon, a man might plunk a coin into a stranger's parking meter just in time. In Paterson, New Jersey, a dozen people with pails and mops and tulip bulbs might descend on a rundown house and clean it from top to bottom while the frail elderly owners look on, dazed and smiling. In Chicago, a teenage boy may be shoveling off a driveway when the impulse strikes...nobody's looking, he thinks, and shovels the neighbor's driveway too.

It's positive anarchy, disorder, a sweet disturbance. A women in Boston writes "Merry Christmas!" to the tellers on the back of her checks. A man in St. Louis, whose car has just been rear-ended by a young woman, waves her away, saying, "It's a scratch. Don't worry."

Senseless acts of beauty spread: A man plants daffodils along the roadway, his shirt billowing in the breeze from passing cars. In Seattle, a man appoints himself a one-man vigilante sanitation service and roams the concrete hills collecting litter in a supermarket cart. In Atlanta, a man scrubs graffiti from a green park bench.

They say you can't smile without cheering yourself up a little—likewise, you can't commit a random kindness without feeling as if your own troubles have been lightened if only because the world has become a slightly better place.

And you can't be a recipient without feeling a shock, a pleasant jolt. If you were one of those rush-hour drivers who found your bridge fare paid, who knows what you might have been inspired to do for someone else later? Wave someone on in the intersection? Smile at a tired clerk? Or something larger, greater? Like all revolutions, guerrilla goodness begins slowly, with a single act. Let it be yours.

Adair Lara
"Practice Random Kindness and Senseless Acts of Beauty"

For most of the journey, as we drove west and then west and finally south, our bus was filled with noise. We were a choir, after all, and young, and busy about ten concerts in ten days. Bus time was petcock time; we blew steam together.

But now the bus was silent. We were thoughtful and not a little frightened.

We were thirty-four bodies all together, a patchy collection of personalities, progressions, colors, classes and inclinations—though all of a single inner-city congregation and of the self-same Lord. Some were struck poetic by the Kansas sunset; others ignored it, singing songs of love in falsetto voices. Some nigh choked on the size of the Rocky Mountains and their whiteness; some stared at the heat gauge of the bus, anxious that the engine might overheat on a seven-percent grade; some ate; some slept; some played Uno and laughed; and the children did their homework, while others stayed oblivious, singing songs of love in falsetto voices.

Yet, for all our scattered concerns, our purpose was common and the same: through four states and eight cities we bore the Holy God upon our lips, his love in our voices—the Sounds of Grace, gone singing its Thanksgiving.

Only now, on the afternoon of Thanksgiving Day itself, did all our moods become one mood, and we gazed forward grimly. Tense, silent, and uncertain. Songs of love had ceased. Falsetto throats had thickened. We were scheduled to sing within the Colorado women's penitentiary.

Holy, holy, holy. Who suckered us into this?…

The auditorium was a great cement room in which all sound was as alive and clean as a guitar string. Folding chairs, a pool table, a huge wooden box (in which the piano was locked) and a little kindergarten stage.

Hollis began to set up the amplifier for his bass.

Brenda plinked at the freed piano.

There was some giggling and little humor.

Cheryl, louder than she intended, called the choir to position and to practice in its little space—

But who would listen to us? And of those who did, what would they care? Would they scorn us? Sneer in the face of our earnest offering?

Well, we were free to come and go. They weren't. That's a burdensome knowledge. We were soft as the civilized belly. These were hard, slouching and experienced. They walked like men and swore like mercenaries, with absolute, silken conviction. Yep: they could make bombs of film—and bullets out of toilet paper, for all we knew.

Cheryl raised her arms before our parti-colored choir, intending to practice a piece, to measure the sound of the place. Hollis hit a chord.

And then the stark wonder began.

Sloppy was our singing at first, but very fast and punctuated by our clapping. Nerves are an excellent upper. "Good!" shouted Cheryl as voices came together. "Good!"

She hardly saw behind her an entering band of women, hard eyes gone curious—but Hollis did. By the fourth and the sixth contingent of the inmates' entrance, hot, black Hollis was smiling like he never had in church, and his guitar had discovered a new certitude, new rhythm that flirted with the unholy, holy, holy—

It wasn't even time, yet, for the concert to begin. No introductions had been made, either by voice or music, and this was not our program. Yet the women were coming, and the practice piece drew a spattering of applause, and Cheryl was lost. By fitful habit she led the choir into another piece for practice, "Soon and very soon, we are going to meet the king." Oh, the choir swung hard and speedily against its beat, and Timmy simply hid himself in the solo, and the women laughed at our abandon, and behold: the song itself, it took us over! The nerves left us, and we too began to laugh as we sang, as though there were some huge joke afoot, and we were grateful for the freedom in our throats, and we looked, for the first time, on one another, nodding, slapping another back, singing! And the women took to clapping, some of them dancing with their faces to the floor, their shoulders hunched, and they filled the place with their constant arrival, and somewhen—no one knew when—the practice turned into an honest concert, but there was no formality to it, because we were free, don't you see, free of the restraints of propriety, free of our fears, free to be truly, truly one with these women, free (Lord, what discovery!) *in prison.*

Song after song, the women stood up and beat their palms together. And they wept, sometimes. Timmy can do that to you. And at one point the entire auditorium, choir and criminals together, joined hands and lifted those hands and rocked and sang, "Oh, How I Love Jesus."

My God, how you do break the bars! How you fling open the doors that prison and divide us! This is true, for mine eyes have seen it and my heart went out to it: You are so mighty in your mercy.

The last song sung was not ours at all. Some thirteen of the inmates demanded that we sit while they took the stage. Then, in shaky voices and in nasal Spanish, embarrassed as schoolgirls but arms around each other for support, they sang:

"De Coloris! De Coloris! The sun gives its treasures, God's light to the children.... And so must all love be of every bright color to make my heart cry."

They sang, braless and holy, so holy: "Joyfully! We will live in God's friendship because he has willed it, pouring outward the light from within, the grace of our God, his infinite love—"

They sang. And we answered, "Yes." And the mountains themselves said, "Amen."

Walter Wangerin, Jr.
Ragman and Other Cries of Faith

A certain Knight growing old, his hair fell off, and he became bald; to hide which imperfection he wore a periwig. But as he was riding out with some others a hunt-ing, a sudden gust of wind blew off the periwig, and exposed his bald pate. The company could not forbear laughing at the accident; and he himself laughed as loud as any body, saying, how was it to be expected that I could keep strange hair upon my head, when my own would not stay there?

Æsop
Fables

Tell me not, in mournful numbers,
Life is but an empty dream!
For the soul is dead that slumbers,
And things are not what they seem.

Life is real! Life is earnest!
And the grave is not its goal;
Dust thou art, to dust returnest,
Was not spoken of the soul.

Henry Wadsworth Longfellow
"A Psalm of Life"

He who bends to himself a joy
Does the winged life destroy;
But he who kisses the joy as it flies
Lives in eternity's sunrise.

William Blake
"Eternity"

...the greater part of our happiness or misery depends on our dispositions, and not on our circumstances. We carry the seeds of the one or the other about with us in our minds wherever we go.

Martha Washington
Letter to Mrs. Warren (probably Mercy Otis Warren), December 26, 1789
(regarding the death of her husband, George Washington)

Make sure that your Life is a Rare Entertainment!
It doesn't take anything drastic.
You needn't be gorgeous or wealthy or smart
Just Very Enthusiastic!

Bette Midler
"The Saga of Baby Divine"

I remember the day well. It was one of those times when everything goes right. I took a shower and fixed my hair. It went just the way I wanted it to, as it so seldom does. I pulled on my new pink sweater, giving me added color, since I need all the help I can get. I pulled on my gray slacks and my taupe heels.

I checked the mirror and thought, *Lookin' good!*

Since it was a cool Michigan day, I slipped on my gray trench coat with pink on the lapels. I was color-coded from head to toe.

When I arrived in downtown Brighton, where I intended to take care of some errands, I was surprised to find heavy traffic. Brighton is a small town, but it has a large health food store. Usually, I can park right in front and run in.

But today business was so brisk I had to park two blocks away. When your attitude is right, and it's a great day, however, inconveniences and interruptions are no big deal.

I thought, *I'll just bounce down the street in time to the sunshine.*

I got out of the car, bounced down the street, crossed the road and entered the store.

As I headed toward the back of the store, I caught my reflection in the glass doors of the refrigeration system. It reaffirmed I was lookin' good. While enjoying my mirrored self, I noticed something was following me. I turned and realized it was my panty hose!

I remembered the night before when I had done a little Wonder Woman act and taken panty hose and slacks off in one fell swoop. This morning I put on new panty hose and must have pushed the old hose through when I pulled on my slacks.

I believe they made their emergence as I bounced down the street in time to the sunshine. I remembered the truck driver who stopped his truck to let me cross. As I looked up, he was laughing, and I thought, *Oh, look! The whole world is happy today.*

So I waved. Little did I realize how much I was waving.

I assumed I had reached some amount of maturity by this time in my life, but I can honestly say that when I looked back and saw that...that...dangling participle, the thought that crossed my mind was *I am going to die!*

I knew they were my panty hose because the right foot was securely wrapped around my right ankle. I knew it was secure because I tried to shake the thing off and pretend I had picked it up in the street.

It's amazing to me that we gals buy these things in flat little packages, we wear them once, and they grow. Now I had a mammoth handful of panty hose and no place to pitch them. The shelves were crowded with groceries, and my purse was too small and full, so I stuffed them in my coat pocket. They became a protruding hump on my right hip.

I decided to never leave that store. I knew all the store owners in town, and I figured that by now they would have all their employees at the windows waiting for a return parade.

I glanced cautiously around the store and noticed it was Senior Citizens' Day. They were having their blood pressures read, so I got in line to avoid having to leave the store.

The bad news was no once noticed I didn't belong in line. The good news was I had an elevated blood pressure reading. Usually nurses take mine and say, "I'm sorry but you died two days ago." Today I registered well up the scale.

Finally I realized I'd have to leave. I slipped out the door, down the street, into my car and off for home.

All the way home I said, "I'll never tell anyone I did this, I'll never tell anyone I did this, I'LL NEVER TELL ANYONE I DID THIS!"

I made it home and got out of the car. My husband was in the yard raking.

I screamed, "Do you know what I did?!"

He was so proud to know his wife had gone through town dragging her underwear. I told him I thought we should move—to another state—in the night. He thought that was extreme and suggested instead that for a while I could walk ten feet behind him. After thinking that through, we decided it should be ten feet in front of him so he could check me out.

If you have ever done anything to embarrass yourself, you know that the more you try not to think about it, the more it comes to you in living color. As I walked through my house, the replay of what I did came to me again and again.

At last I cried out to the Lord, "You take ashes and create beauty, but can You do anything with panty hose?"

Almost immediately I realized that I had dragged a lot worse things through my life than panty hose. I dragged guilt, anger, fear and shame. I was reminded by the Lord that those were far more unattractive and distracting than my hose, for they prevented others from seeing His presence and His power in my life. I needed to resolve the pain in my past that I might live more fully today and look forward to my tomorrows.

Patsy Clairmont
God Uses Cracked Pots

A Stag drinking, saw himself in the water, and pleased with the sight, stood contemplating his shape. Ah, says he, what a glorious pair of branching horns are here, how gracefully do these antlers project over my forehead, and give an agreeable turn to my whole face; but I have such legs as really make me ashamed; they look so very long and unsightly, that I had rather have none at all. In the midst of this soliloquy, he was alarmed with the cry of a pack of hounds. Away he flies in some consternation, and bounding nimbly over the plain, threw dogs and men at a vast distance behind him. After which, taking a very thick copse, he had the ill fortune to be entangled by his horns in the branches, where he was held fast till the hounds came up and seized him. In the pangs of death, he is said to have uttered these words: Unhappy creature that I am, I am too late convinced that what I prided myself in, has been the cause of my undoing; and what I so much disliked, was the only thing that could have saved me.

Æsop
Fables

We must be joyful now. Here...within...with who we are and what we've got.

Mark Speckman, a student athlete of mine during my Azusa Pacific University coaching days, knows the truth of that statement. I vividly remember the first day he came out for football. Mark was born with no hands. We all wondered how a guy with no hands could play football. He ended up not only being our starting middle linebacker, but in his senior year he was voted all-American. He used to love it when he would get called for holding. He would milk it for all it was worth with the refs. He also played the jazz trombone, basketball, and was a

3.6 student. We now play tennis together and we look forward to playing in a doubles tournament. I sometimes tell him jokingly that we will win half our games by our opponents' staring at him with wonder. Currently he's an outstanding coach and, when we can get him, he works as a Summit [a mountaineering organization] instructor. What made the difference? He decided to make life a challenge, and to tackle it all with joy. His joy is the source of his strength.

Tim Hansel
Holy Sweat

One of the panel members was Harold Krentz, the young Harvard- and Oxford-trained attorney who was the inspiration for that moving stage and screen play *Butterflies Are Free*. Harold is blind.

And a swift and sure raconteur.

The hall rang with happy laughter when he described some trouble he and his wife had recently had with their car.

"My wife is sighted and she was driving," he began. "Sometimes we alternate. The way Kit drives, I might as well. She has been in two accidents in the last two months, which wasn't easy because we didn't have a car when she was in her second accident. Anyway, the other night we were heading home to Washington from Rockville, Maryland, in the middle of the night when Kit told me she thought something was wrong with the car. She didn't have to tell me; you could hardly breathe in the smoke that was coming out of the motor.

"'What are we going to *do?*' she asked me. Well, I suggested that we drop back thirty yards and punt. Kit didn't find that very amusing. She said, 'You're the husband, you know. You're supposed to have everything worked out.' So I told her to relax; I'd fix the car.

"Folks, I doubt if you've ever seen anything funnier than a blind mechanic. I went underneath the car...after a bit I said that the trouble was obvious; there was a hole in the hose. I didn't know where the hose was, or whether we had one, but it sounded logical to me. The next thing was to get a lift. I told her I'd hide in the bushes until she thumbed down a car, and when she did I'd jump out and hop in the car. It worked!"

The young lawyer's brow furrowed, his mood changed, and the audience hushed. He said he would like to comment on a previous speaker's expressed desire to be regarded by the able-bodied as normal.

"I'd like to amend that slightly and say we are normal," Krentz said, searching the battered room with sightless eyes. "My ambition, for example, was to become a lawyer. Now I am a lawyer. I am married to a great girl. My ambitions are to make her happy and eventually to make our kids happy when we have them, and to be a top-notch attorney. These are ambitions that are completely normal.

"The people who are handicapped, frankly, are the people who are 'normal.' The so-called 'normal' people who tend not to get as much out of life as they should, but just exist from day to day. Life for them is one big yawn. Whatever abilities I have I must develop to the fullest. Self-pity is a luxury I can't engage in. I must live life to the hilt. If any of you have seen the way I cross streets, you'll know. I wave my cane wildly over my head, repeat all the prayers I know, and run. If I'm going to be hit, I hope it will be by a Rolls-Royce.

"But, seriously, I think that the ones who have real problems to overcome are not us. We have had to fight our battles. If anything, we have developed a certain security, a certain understanding, a certain strength that people in our society should take lessons from. When we say we have something to contribute, I think it's much more than that. I think it's time people started learning from *us!*"

Bob Considine
They Rose Above It

There is another person well into the later years. For some months now she has been in uncertain health. Each morning when she awakes, she stops for a period of meditation. The phrase is the same each day: "This is the day that the Lord has made. I will rejoice and be glad in it." At night, as she turns out the light over her bed, she says it a little differently because "rejoice" and "be glad" are not very restful words. She says, "This is the night which the Lord has made. I will relax and rest in it." One day she had a fall, but managed to pull herself up without calling for help. She was quite shaken and was in much pain. She prepared herself for bed and with much discomfort was able to get in beneath the covers. As she turned out the light, she said, "This is the night which the Lord has made. I will relax and cry in it." Then she realized what she had said, and her tears were all mixed with her laughter.

Varied and rich indeed are the methods used by individuals who have discovered the strength and serenity that come from the "practice of the Presence of God."

Howard Thurman
The Inward Journey

I warmed both hands before the fire of life;
It sinks, and I am ready to depart.

Walter Savage Landor
Finis

It was a very sad day, and every heart in the house felt the deepest grief; for the youngest child, a boy of four years old, the joy and hope of his parents, was dead. Two daughters, the elder of whom was going to be confirmed, still remained: they were both good, charming girls; but the lost child always seems the dearest; and when it is youngest, and a son, it makes the trial still more heavy. The sisters mourned as young hearts can mourn, and were especially grieved at the sight of their parents' sorrow. The father's heart was bowed down, but the mother sunk completely under the deep grief. Day and night she had attended to the sick child, nursing and carrying it in her bosom, as a part of herself. She could not realize the fact that the child was dead, and must be laid in a coffin to rest in the ground. She thought God *could not* take her darling little one from her; and when it did happen notwithstanding her hopes and her belief, and there could be no more doubt on the subject, she said in her feverish agony, "God does not know it. He has hard-hearted ministering spirits on earth, who do according to their own will, and heed not a mother's prayers." Thus in her great grief she fell away from her faith in God, and dark thoughts arose in her mind respecting death and a future state. She tried to believe that man was but dust, and that with his life all existence ended. But these doubts were no support to her, nothing on which she could rest, and she sunk into the fathomless depths of despair. In her darkest hours she ceased to weep, and thought not of the young daughters who were still left to her. The tears of her husband fell on her forehead, but she took no notice of him; her thoughts were with her dead child; her whole existence seemed wrapped up in the remembrances of the little one and of every innocent word it had uttered.

The day of the little child's funeral came. For nights previously the mother had not slept, but in the morning twilight of this day she sunk from weariness into a deep sleep; in the mean time the coffin was carried into a distant room, and there nailed down, that she might not hear the blows of the hammer. When she awoke, and wanted to see her child, the husband, with tears, said, "We have closed the coffin; it was necessary to do so."

"When God is so hard to me, how can I expect men to be better?" she said with groans and tears.

The coffin was carried to the grave, and the disconsolate mother sat with her young daughters. She looked at them, but she saw them not; for her thoughts were far away from the domestic hearth. She gave herself up to her grief, and it tossed her to and fro, as the sea tosses a ship without compass or rudder. So the day of the funeral passed away, and similar days followed, of dark, wearisome pain. With tearful eyes and mournful glances, the sorrowing daughters and the afflicted husband looked upon her who would not hear their words of comfort; and, indeed, what comforting words could they speak, when they were themselves so full of grief? It seemed as if she would never again know sleep, and yet it would have been her best friend, one who would have strengthened her body and poured peace into her soul. They at last persuaded her to lie down, and then she would lie as still as if she slept.

One night, when her husband listened, as he often did, to her breathing, he quite believed that she had at length found rest and relief in sleep. He folded his arms and prayed, and soon sunk himself into healthful sleep; therefore he did not notice that his wife arose, threw on her clothes, and glided silently from the house, to go where her thoughts constantly lingered—to the grave of her child. She passed through the garden, to a path across a field that led to the churchyard. No one saw her as she walked, nor did she see any one; for her eyes were fixed upon the one object of her wanderings. It was a lovely starlight night in the beginning of September, and the air was mild and still. She entered the churchyard, and stood by the little grave, which looked like a large nosegay of fragrant flowers. She sat down, and bent her head low over the grave, as if she could see her child through the earth that covered him—her little boy, whose smile was so vividly before her, and the gentle expression of whose eyes, even on his sick-bed, she could not forget. How full of meaning that glance had been, as she leaned over him, holding in hers the pale hand which he had no longer strength to raise!

As she had sat by his little cot, so now she sat by his grave; and here she could weep freely, and her tears fell upon it.

"Thou wouldst gladly go down and be with thy child," said a voice quite close to her,—a voice that sounded so deep and clear, that it went to her heart.

She looked up, and by her side stood a man wrapped in a black cloak, with a hood closely drawn over his face; but her keen glance could distinguish the face under the hood. It was stern, yet awakened confidence, and the eyes beamed with youthful radiance.

"Down to my child," she repeated; and tones of despair and entreaty sounded in the words.

"Darest thou to follow me?" asked the form. "I am Death."

She bowed her head in token of assent. Then suddenly it appeared as if all the stars were shining with the radiance of the full moon on the many-colored flowers that decked the grave. The earth that covered it was drawn back like a floating drapery. She sunk down, and the spectre covered her with a black cloak; night closed around her, the night of death. She sank deeper than the spade of the sexton could penetrate, till the churchyard became a roof above her. Then the cloak was removed, and she found herself in a large hall, of wide-spreading dimensions, in which there was a subdued light, like twilight, reigning, and in a moment her child appeared before her, smiling, and more beautiful than ever; with a silent cry she pressed him to her heart. A glorious strain of music sounded—now distant, now near. Never had she listened to such tones as these; they came from beyond a large dark curtain which separated the regions of death from the land of eternity.

"My sweet, darling mother," she heard the child say. It was the well-known, beloved voice; and kiss followed kiss, in boundless delight. Then the child pointed to the dark curtain. "There is nothing so beautiful on earth as it is here. Mother, do you not see them all? Oh, it is happiness indeed."

But the mother saw nothing of what the child pointed out, only the dark curtain. She looked with earthly eyes, and could not see as the child saw,—he whom God has called to be with Himself. She could hear the sounds of music, but she heard not the words, *the Word* in which she was to trust.

"I can fly now, mother," said the child; "I can fly with other happy children into the presence of the Almighty. I would fain fly away now; but if you weep for me as you are weeping now, you may never see me again. And yet I would go so gladly. May I not fly away? And you will come to me soon, will you not, dear mother?"

"Oh, stay, stay!" implored the mother; "only one moment more; only once more, that I may look upon thee, and kiss thee, and press thee to my heart."

Then she kissed and fondled her child. Suddenly her name was called from above; what could it mean? her name uttered in a plaintive voice.

"Hearest thou?" said the child. "It is my father who calls thee." And in a few moments deep sighs were heard, as of children weeping. "They are my sisters," said the child. "Mother, surely you have not forgotten them."

And then she remembered those she left behind, and a great terror came over her. She looked around her at the dark night. Dim forms flitted by. She seemed to recognize some of them, as they floated through the regions of death towards the dark curtain, where they vanished. Would her husband and her daughters flit past? No; their sighs and lamentations still sounded from above; and she had nearly forgotten them, for the sake of him who was dead.

"Mother, now the bells of heaven are ringing," said the child; "mother, the sun is going to rise."

An overpowering light streamed in upon her, the child had vanished, and she was being borne upwards. All around her became cold; she lifted her head, and saw that she was lying in the churchyard, on the grave of her child. The Lord, in a dream, had been a guide to her feet and a light to her spirit. She bowed her knees, and prayed for forgiveness. She had wished to keep back a soul from its immortal flight; she had forgotten her duties towards the living who were left her. And when she had offered this prayer, her heart felt lighter. The sun burst forth, over her head a little bird carolled his song, and the church-bells sounded for the early service. Everything around her seemed holy, and her heart was chastened. She acknowledged the goodness of God, she acknowledged the duties she had to perform, and eagerly she returned home. She bent over her husband, who still slept; her warm, devoted kiss awakened him, and words of heartfelt love fell from the lips of both. Now she was gentle and strong as a wife can be; and from her lips came the words of faith: "Whatever he doeth is right and best."

Then her husband asked, "From whence hast thou all at once derived such strength and comforting faith?"

And as she kissed him and her children, she said, "It came from God, through my child in the grave."

Hans Christian Andersen
"The Child in the Grave"

That thou art happy, owe to God;
That thou continuest such, owe to thyself;
God made thee perfect, not immutable;
And good He made thee; but to persevere
He left it in thy power—ordained thy will
By nature free, not over-ruled by fate
Inextricable, or strict necessity.

John Milton
Paradise Lost

There is something sad in people running from church to church trying to get an injection of "the joy of the Lord." Joy is not found in singing a particular kind of music or in getting with the right kind of group or even in exercising the charismatic gifts of the Spirit, good as all these may be. Joy is found in obedience. When the power that is in Jesus reaches into our work and play and redeems them, there will be joy where once there was mourning. To overlook this is to miss the meaning of the Incarnation.

Richard J. Foster
Celebration of Discipline

And now, brothers, as I close this letter let me say this one more thing: Fix your thoughts on what is true and good and right. Think about things that are pure and lovely, and dwell on the fine, good things in others. Think about all you can praise God for and be glad about. Keep putting into practice all you learned from me and saw me doing, and the God of peace will be with you.

Philippians 4:8–9, TLB

At first, I saw God as my observer,
my judge,
keeping track of the things I did wrong,
so as to know whether I merited heaven
or hell when I die.
He was out there sort of like a president.
I recognized His picture when I saw it,
but I really didn't know Him.

But later on
when I met Christ,
it seemed as though life were rather like a bike ride,
but it was a tandem bike,
and I noticed that Christ
was in the back helping me pedal.

I don't know just when it was
that He suggested we change places,
but life has not been the same since.

When I had control,
I knew the way.
It was rather boring,
but predictable...
It was the shortest distance between two points.

But when He took the lead,
He knew delightful long cuts,
up mountains,
and through rocky places
at breakneck speeds,
it was all I could do to hang on!
Even though it looked like madness,
He said, "Pedal!"

I worried and was anxious
and asked,
"Where are you taking me?"
He laughed and didn't answer,
and I started to learn to trust.

I forgot my boring life
and entered into the adventure.
And when I'd say, "I'm scared,"
He'd lean back and touch my hand.

He took me to people with gifts that I needed,
gifts of healing,
acceptance
and joy.
They gave me gifts to take on my journey,
my Lord's and mine.

And we were off again.
He said, "Give the gifts away;
they're extra baggage, too much weight."
So I did,
to the people we met,
and I found that in giving I received,
and still our burden was light.

I did not trust Him,
at first,
in control of my life.
I thought He'd wreck it;
but He knows bike secrets,
knows how to make it bend to take sharp corners,
knows how to jump to clear high rocks,
knows how to fly to shorten scary passages.

And I am learning to shut up
and pedal
in the strangest places,
and I'm beginning to enjoy the view
and the cool breeze on my face
with my delightful constant companion, Jesus Christ.

And when I'm sure I just can't do any more,
He just smiles and says…"Pedal."

anonymous
"The Road of Life"

Enjoying My

RELATIONSHIP
WITH GOD

CHAPTER THIRTEEN

ENJOYING MY RELATIONSHIP WITH GOD

—◦∿◦—

The fear of the LORD is the beginning of knowledge.

Proverbs 1:7 (NIV)

If you ask me how I believe in God, how God creates himself in me, and reveals himself to me, my answer may perhaps provoke your smiles or laughter, and even scandalize you. I believe in God as I believe in my friends, because I feel the breath of his affection, feel his invisible and tangible hand drawing me, leading me, grasping me.

Miguel de Unamuno
Prosa Diversa

We worship that God Who has appointed to the natures created by Him both the beginnings and the end of their existing and moving: Who holds, knows, and disposes the causes of things; Who hath created the virtue of seeds; Who hath given to what creatures He would a rational soul, which is called mind; Who hath bestowed the faculty and use of speech; Who hath imparted the gift of fore-telling future things to whatever spirits it seemed to Him good; Who also Him-self predicts future things through whom He pleases, and through whom He will remove diseases; Who, when the human race is to be corrected and chastised by wars, regulates also the beginnings, progress, and ends of these wars; Who hath created and governs the most vehement and most violent fire of this world, in due relation and proportion to the other elements of immense nature; Who is the governor of all the waters; Who hath made the sun brightest of all material lights, and hath given him suitable power and motion; Who hath not withdrawn, even from the inhabitants of the nether world, His dominion and power; Who hath appointed to mortal natures their suitable seed and nourishment, dry or liquid; Who establishes and makes fruitful the earth; Who bountifully bestows its fruits on animals and on men; Who knows and ordains, not only principal causes, but also subsequent causes; Who hath determined for the moon her motion; Who affords ways in heaven and on earth for passage from one place to another; Who hath granted also to human minds, which He hath created, the knowledge of the various arts for the help of life and nature; Who hath appointed the union of male and female for the propagation of offspring; Who hath favoured the societies of men with the gift of terrestrial fire for the simplest and most familiar purposes, to burn on the hearth and to give light.

These are, then, the things which that most acute and most learned man Varro has laboured to distribute among the select gods, by I know not what physical interpretation, which he has got from other sources and also conjectured for himself. But these things the one true God makes and does, but as the same God—that is, as He who is wholly everywhere, included in no space, bound by no chains, mutable in no part of His being, filling heaven and earth with omnipresent power, not with a needy nature. Therefore He governs all things in such a manner as to allow them to perform and exercise their own proper movements. For although they can be nothing without Him, they are not what He is.

He does also many things through angels; but only from Himself does He beatify angels. So also, though He send angels to men for certain purposes, He does not for all that beatify men by the good inherent in the angels, but by Himself, as He does the angels themselves.

Saint Augustine
The City of God

The Being who, to me, is the real God is the one who created this majestic universe and rules it. He is the only originator, the only originator of thoughts; thoughts suggested from within, not from without. The originator of colors and all their possible combinations; of forces and the laws that govern them; of forms and shapes of all forms—man has never invented a new one. He is the only originator. He made the materials of all things; he made the laws by which, and by which only, man may combine them into the machines and other things which outside influences suggest to him. He made character—man can portray it but not "create" it, for He is the only creator. He is the perfect artisan, the perfect artist.

Mark Twain
Autobiography

Earth's crammed with heaven,
And every common bush afire with God.
Only he who sees takes off his shoes,
The rest sit round and pluck blackberries.

Elizabeth Barrett Browning
Aurora Leigh

There can be no doubt but that everything in the world, by the beauty of its order, and the evidence of a determinate and beneficial purpose which pervades it, testifies that some supreme efficient Power must have pre-existed, by which the whole was ordained for a specific end.

John Milton
A Treatise on Christian Doctrine

Laws of Nature are God's thoughts thinking themselves out in the orbits and the tides.

Charles H. Parkhurst
Sermons

We may well know that there is a God without knowing what He is. By faith we know His existence; in glory we shall know His nature.

Blaise Pascal
Pensées

Faith is the opening of all sides and every level of one's life to the divine inflow.

Martin Luther King, Jr.
Strength to Love

"I've been readen th Bible an a hunten God fer a long while—off an on—but it ain't so easy as picken up a nickel off th floor."

Harriette Arnow
The Dollmaker

What you are is God's gift to you: what you make of it is your gift to God.

Anthony Dalla Villa
Eulogy at memorial Mass for Andy Warhol

It is God that accomplishes all term to hopes,
God, who overtakes the flying eagle, outpasses the dolphin
in the sea;
who bends under his strength the man with thoughts too high.

Pindar
Odes

God, please help me to build up my faith.

Let me understand that faith is not a blind acceptance, but a certain and reasonable knowledge.

Not a gift bestowed upon favored people, but a powerful conviction achieved through serious effort.

God, guide me to people who can encourage me in my faith. (Thank you for such people.)

Lead me to books that will enlighten and enhance my faith. (Thank you for such books.)

Show me works both human and divine that prove that you do exist and love us. Open my eyes to your many wonders.

Free my cluttered and limited mind from its confusions. Release it, refresh it, widen it so that into it may flow an appreciation of your vast, shining, limitless intelligence. (Thank you for that clearing and that comprehension now.)

Help me to practice my faith, for only through practice can it grow in me. Oh God, remind me to reach you and understand you, and renew my faith through prayer.

Marjorie Holmes
I've Got to Talk to Somebody, God

God, when you thought of a pine tree,
How did you think of a star?

Angela Morgan
"God, the Artist"

To Whom It May Concern,

I want to believe in you real hard. But I don't know how. My mom does but my dad does not. How can I know for sure? Why don't you make things easier? It would be nice. Nothing special. You don't have to part the sea or nothing. Just something easy.

Like have me turn thirteen sooner.
Joan

twelve-year-old child
Quoted in *Dear God: Children's Letters to God*

God, so great an artificer in great things, is not less great in small things.

Saint Augustine
The City of God

God is in all things and in every place. There is not a place in the world in which He is not most truly present. Just as birds, wherever they fly, always meet with the air, so we, wherever we go, or wherever we are, always find God present.

Saint Francis of Sales
Sermons

I have encountered nothing on Apollo 15 or in this age of space and science that dilutes my faith in God. While I was on the moon, in fact, I felt a sense of inspiration, a feeling that someone was with me and watching over me, protecting me. There were several times when tasks seemed to be impossible—but they worked out all right every time.

Colonel James B. Irwin
New York Times, August 13, 1971

Every day is a messenger of God.

Russian proverb

I would rather be a doorkeeper in the house of my God than dwell in the tents of the wicked.

Psalm 84:10 (NIV)

The world we inhabit must have had an origin; that origin must have consisted in a cause; that cause must have been intelligent; that intelligence must have been supreme; and that supreme, which always was and is supreme, we know by the name of God.

anonymous

God, ...consisting of infinite attributes, each one of which expresses eternal and infinite essence, necessarily exists.

If this be denied, conceive, if it be possible, that God does not exist. Then it follows that His essence does not involve existence. But this is absurd. Therefore God necessarily exists.

Baruch Spinoza
Ethics

There are two kinds of people: those who say to God, "Thy will be done," and those to whom God says, "All right, then, have it your way."

C. S. Lewis
The Great Divorce

"Well, it's a good thing to trust in Providence. But I believe the Almighty likes a little cooperation now and again."

Frances Parkinson Keyes
Blue Camellia

Be strong and courageous. Do not be terrified; do not be discouraged, for the LORD your God will be with you wherever you go.

Joshua 1:9 (NIV)

He who has no friend has God.

Egyptian proverb

There isn't a certain time we should set aside to talk about God. God is part of our every waking moment.

Marva Collins
Quoted in *Message*, February 1987

Isolation has led me to reflection, reflection to doubt, doubt to a more sincere and intelligent love of God.

Marie Lenéru
Journal

The conception of God which is the most common and the most full of meaning is expressed well enough in the words: God is an absolutely perfect being. The implications, however, of these words fail to receive sufficient consideration. For instance, there are many different kinds of perfection, all of which God possesses, and each one of them pertains to him in the highest degree.

We must also know what perfection is. One thing which can surely be affirmed about it is that those forms or natures which are not susceptible of it to the highest degree, say the nature of numbers or of figures, do not permit of perfection. This is because the number which is the greatest of all (that is, the sum of all the numbers), and likewise the greatest of all figures, imply contradictions. The greatest knowledge, however, and omnipotence contain no impossibility. Consequently power and knowledge do admit of perfection, and in so far as they pertain to God they have no limits.

Whence it follows that God who possesses supreme and infinite wisdom acts in the most perfect manner not only metaphysically, but also from the moral standpoint. And with respect to our selves it can be said that the more we are enlightened and informed in regard to the works of God the more will we be disposed to find them excellent and conforming entirely to that which we might desire.

Gottfried Wilhelm Leibniz
Discourse on Metaphysics

Heaven is above all yet; there sits a judge
That no king can corrupt.

William Shakespeare
Henry VIII

Jesus is God spelling Himself out in language that man can understand.

S. D. Gordon
Quoted in *Reader's Digest,* July 1972

To believe in God is to yearn for His existence and, furthermore, it is to act as if He did exist.

Miguel de Unamuno
The Tragic Sense of Life

Almighty God
forgive me for my agnosticism;
For I shall try to keep it gentle, not cynical,
nor a bad influence.

And O!
if Thou art truly in the heavens,
accept my gratitude
for all Thy gifts
and I shall try
to fight the good fight. Amen.

John Gunther, Jr.
"Unbeliever's Prayer"

He who leaves God out of his reasoning does not know how to count.

Italian proverb

"I ought to tell you that I do not believe...do not believe in God," said Pierre, regretfully and with an effort, feeling it essential to speak the whole truth.

The mason looked intently at Pierre and smiled as a rich man with millions in hand might smile at a poor fellow who told him that he, poor man, had not the five rubles that would make him happy.

"Yes, you do not know Him, my dear sir," said the mason. "You do not know Him and that is why you are unhappy."

"Yes, yes, I am unhappy," assented Pierre. "But what am I to do?"

"You know Him not, my dear sir, and so you are very unhappy. You do not know Him, but He is here, He is in me…" pronounced the mason in a stern and tremulous voice.

He paused and sighed, evidently trying to calm himself.

"If He were not," he said quietly, "you and I would not be speaking of Him, my dear sir. Of what, of whom, are we speaking? Whom hast thou denied?" he suddenly asked with exulting austerity and authority in his voice. "Who invented Him, if He did not exist? Whence came thy conception of the existence of such an incomprehensible Being? Why didst thou, and why did the whole world, conceive the idea of the existence of such an incomprehensible Being, a Being all-powerful, eternal, and infinite in all His attributes?…"

He stopped and remained silent for a long time.

Pierre could not and did not wish to break this silence.

"He exists, but to understand Him is hard," the mason began again, looking not at Pierre but straight before him, and turning the leaves of his book with his old hands which from excitement he could not keep still. "If it were a man whose existence thou didst doubt I could bring him to thee, could take him by the hand and show him to thee. But how can I, an insignificant mortal, show His omnipotence, His infinity, and all His mercy to one who is blind, or who shuts his eyes that he may not see or understand Him and may not see or understand his own vileness and sinfulness?"

He paused again. "Who art thou? Thou dreamest that thou art wise because thou couldst utter those blasphemous words," he went on, with a somber and scornful smile. "And thou art more foolish and unreasonable than a little child, who, playing with the parts of a skillfully made watch, dares to say that, as he does not understand its use, he does not believe in the master who made it. To know Him is hard…For ages, from our forefather Adam to our own day, we labor to attain that knowledge and are still infinitely far from our aim; but in our lack of understanding we see only our weakness and His greatness…"

Leo Tolstoy
War and Peace

God will not look you over for medals, degrees or diplomas, but for scars.

Elbert Hubbard
Quoted in *Reader's Digest*, May 1960

Never forget that [God] tests his real friends more severely than the lukewarm ones.

Kathryn Hulme
The Nun's Story

Don't bargain with God.

Jewish proverb

Others try to worship things that are less than God; it may be money, or ambition, or drugs, or sex. In the end they find that they are worthless idols. To worship means to give due worth to someone or something.

Desmond Tutu
Quoted in *Jet*, September 26, 1988

We should give God the same place in our hearts that He holds in the universe.

anonymous

The LORD is my shepherd, I shall not be in want.
He makes me lie down in green pastures,
he leads me beside quiet waters, he restores my soul.
He guides me in paths of righteousness for his name's sake.
Even though I walk through the valley of the shadow of death,
I will fear no evil, for you are with me;
your rod and your staff, they comfort me.
You prepare a table before me in the presence of my enemies.
You anoint my head with oil; my cup overflows.
Surely goodness and love will follow me all the days of my life,
and I will dwell in the house of the LORD forever.

Psalm 23:1-6 (NIV)

Take a view of the works of nature, listen to the voice within, and then tell me what God hath omitted to say to your sight, your conscience, your understanding?

Jean Jacques Rousseau
Emile

We cannot always understand the ways of Almighty God—the crosses which He sends us, the sacrifices which He demands of us…But we accept with faith and resignation His holy will with no looking back to what might have been, and we are at peace.

Rose Fitzgerald Kennedy
Times to Remember

God is mightiest in power, fairest in beauty, immortal in existence, supreme in virtue; therefore, being invisible to every mortal nature, he is seen through his works themselves.

Aristotle
De Mundo

God is ever the constant foreknowing overseer, and the everpresent eternity of His sight moves in harmony with the future nature of our actions, as it dispenses rewards to the good, and punishments to the bad. Hopes are not vainly put in God, nor prayers in vain offered: if these are right, they cannot but be answered. Turn therefore from vice: ensue virtue: raise your soul to upright hopes: send up on high your prayers from this earth. If you would be honest, great is the necessity enjoined upon your goodness, since all you do is done before the eyes of an all-seeing Judge.

Anicius Manlius Severinus Boethius
Consolation of Philosophy

If every gnat that flies were an archangel, all that could but tell me that there is a God; and the poorest worm that creeps tells me that.

John Donne
Sermons

How can you expect God to speak in that gentle and inward voice which melts the soul, when you are making so much noise with your rapid reflections? Be silent and God will speak again.

François Fénelon
Spiritual Letters

Our intellect and other gifts have been given to be used for God's greater glory, but sometimes they become the very god for us. That is the saddest part: we are losing our balance when this happens. We must free ourselves to be filled by God. Even God cannot fill what is full.

Mother Teresa
Quoted in *Time*, December 29, 1975

"We saw his star at its rising and have come to do him homage" (Matthew 2:2). This is what the wise men told the inhabitants of Jerusalem upon their arrival in the Holy City. They inquired about "the newborn king of the Jews." These are the very words that we recite at the Feast of the Epiphany: the manifestation of Jesus as the Messiah, the Son of God, and the Savior to the peoples who have lived in the darkness of paganism.

The wise men, representatives of the pagan peoples, remind us of our own search for God. They perceived his presence in the wonders of creation. To find the truth, which they had only glimpsed through nature and study, they undertook a journey full of unanswered questions and great risks. Their search ended in a discovery and in an act of deep humble adoration before the infant Jesus and his mother. They offered him their precious treasures and received in return the priceless gift of Christian faith and joy.

May the wise men be our guides so that our daily walk will always have as its aim Jesus himself, the eternal Son of God and the son of Mary.

Pope John Paul II
Lift Up Your Hearts

God said to Moses, "I AM WHO I AM. This is what you are to say to the Israelites: 'I AM has sent me to you.' "

God also said to Moses, "Say to the Israelites, 'The LORD, the God of your fathers—the God of Abraham, the God of Isaac and the God of Jacob—has sent me to you.' This is my name forever, the name by which I am to be remembered from generation to generation."

Exodus 3:14-15 (NIV)

God is related to the universe, as Creator and Preserver; the laws by which He created all things are those by which He preserves them. He acts according to these rules, because He knows them; He knows them, because He made them; and He made them, because they are in relation to His wisdom and power.

Montesquieu
Spirit of Laws

I would rather walk with God in the dark than go alone in the light.

Mary Gardiner Brainard
"Not Knowing"

The visible marks of extraordinary wisdom and power appear so plainly in all the works of the creation, that a rational creature, who will but seriously reflect on them, cannot miss the discovery of a Deity. And the influence that the discovery of such a Being must necessarily have on the minds of all that have but once heard of it is so great, and carries such a weight of thought and communication with it, that it seems stranger to me that a whole nation of men should be anywhere found so brutish as to want the notion of a God, than that they shoud be without any notion of numbers, or fire.

John Locke
Concerning Human Understanding

The Almighty does nothing without reason, though the frail mind of man cannot explain the reason.

Saint Augustine
The City of God

I have lived, sir, a long time. And the longer I live, the more convincing proofs I see of this truth—that God governs in the affairs of men. And if a sparrow cannot fall on the ground without his notice, is it probable that an empire can rise without his aid?

Benjamin Franklin
Autobiography

How beautiful on the mountains are the feet of those who bring good news, who proclaim peace, who bring good tidings, who proclaim salvation, who say to Zion, "Your God reigns!"

Listen! Your watchmen lift up their voices; together they shout for joy. When the LORD returns to Zion, they will see it with their own eyes.

Isaiah 52:7-8 (NIV)

The power that holds the sky's majesty wins our worship.

Æschylus
The Libation Bearers

Certainly we must do all in our power to bring social justice, to work for peace among nations, to put down poverty. These are proper concerns of the church. But even though you give people the highest standard of living, firm laws that make social and racial justice mandatory, and assign aid by the billions to needy people, your efforts will be largely futile if greed and prejudice and hatred are still there. God alone can remove those elements from human nature…

Reverend Billy Graham
Quoted in Reader's Digest, July 1970

Our heart oft times wakes when we sleep, and God can speak to that, either by words, by proverbs, by signs and similitudes, as well as if one was awake.

John Bunyan
The Pilgrim's Progress

He Who is before the ages and on into the ages thus adorned the great things of His wisdom: nothing excessive, nothing defective, no room for any censure. How lovely are his works! All things, in twos, one against one, none lacking its opposite. He has strengthened the goods—adornment and propriety—of each and every one and established them in the best reasons, and who will be satiated seeing their glory?

Johannes Kepler
Harmonies of the World

Call on God, but row away from the rocks.

Indian proverb

Though our mind cannot conceive of God, without ascribing some worship to him, it will not be sufficient merely to apprehend that he is the only proper object of universal worship and adoration, unless we are also persuaded that he is the fountain of all good, and seek for none but in him. This I maintain, not only because he sustains the universe, as he once made it, by his infinite power, governs it by his wisdom, preserves it by his goodness, and especially reigns over the human race in righteousness and judgment, exercising a merciful forbearance, and defending them by his protection; but because there cannot be found the least particle of wisdom, light, righteousness, power, rectitude, or sincere truth which does not proceed from him, and claim him for its author.

John Calvin
Institutes of the Christian Religion

God does not die on the day when we cease to believe in a personal deity, but we die on the day when our lives cease to be illumined by the steady radiance, renewed daily, of a wonder, the source of which is beyond all reason.

Dag Hammarskjöld
Markings

It is at least as certain that God, who is a Being so perfect, is, or exists, as any demonstration of geometry can possibly be.

René Descartes
Discourse on Method

God may well be taken as a substitute for everything; but nothing can be taken as a substitute for God.

anonymous

Let me then not fail to praise my God continually, for it is his due, and it is all I can return for his many favours and great goodness to me; and let me resolve to be virtuous, that I may be happy, that I may please Him, who is delighted to see me happy.

Benjamin Franklin
Papers

God! Thou art love! I build my faith on that.

Robert Browning
Paracelsus

"I am the Alpha and the Omega," says the Lord God, "who is, and who was, and who is to come, the Almighty."

Revelation 1:8 (NIV)

We talked of the beauty of this world of God's and of the great mystery of it. Every blade of grass, every insect, ant and golden bee, all so amazingly know their path, though they have not intelligence, they bear witness to the mystery of God and continually accomplish it themselves.

Fyodor Dostoevsky
The Brothers Karamazov

Sometimes my soul feels dead. Other times tortured. Right now I feel a terrible combination of both.

I hate these times. I wish I were a simple, happy man. I know people who seem so much happier than I. Why must I go through these bouts with despair? When I do, I have trouble finding within me—or in anyone else—something that brings joy. I am utterly miserable, a terrible advertisement for Christianity. I wonder if people who read my books imagine that I can get this low.

During these times of anguish, I am genuinely afraid. I feel it right now. Is there enough left of me to continue on, to do my work, to love my family, to face life? Or have I disappeared into a cave of dark, tangled tunnels, a cold black maze that angles downward from which I will never emerge?

I worry, but not with a productive frenzy that gets me moving. My worry feels more like despair, like falling into that black hole and wondering whether the next bump will be the final one that kills me or merely one more crash against the wall before I hit bottom.

What can I do? I can't stand feeling this way. I'm no good to anyone like this. Where's God? What's he supposed to be doing? I want to move, to choose something aggressively. But a deep, angry boredom, a hopeless indifference, has robbed me of energy. I can't run, walk, or stand. At best, I seem only to shuffle along the path of least resistance, pouting more than grumbling.

But if I continue to shuffle, merely to drift with the tide, I fear losing my mind. I long to become a mature, stable, loving man, someone my wife can draw strength from and enjoy. I *must* not drift. I *must* take action.

But that's the problem. The idea of moving presupposes an energy within me capable of being harnessed. It assumes that I exist as a real, separate entity, as someone who is able to choose a direction freely and then follow it.

Taking action presumes something further—a reason to move this way and not that, a benevolent Creator behind this whole mess with a good design that I might miss if I ignore him.

To move at all, I must believe these two things: one, that I exist beneath my pain as a free person who can move, and, two, that there really is an infinitely good Person who invites me to move toward a joy that he provides.

If I believe that God is good and I am free, then I can move through the ups and downs of life with hope—there is meaning to be found. Goodness is greater than badness. There's reason for cheer.

If, however, I believe in only one or neither, then life is a hopeless tragedy, a cruel hoax, enticing me toward something it cannot provide. It becomes a mockery, laughing at me, hatefully sneering at my every effort to rise above its pointlessness—or to retreat from it. I am then left with nothing but pain, unending and unendurable.

But even as I write, I cannot help but notice two things—and I smell hope. When I speak of unbelief, I still think of final reality as more than an "it." I just spoke of "it" mocking me. But *things* aren't capable of mockery. Only *persons* are. Matter mocks no one. Matter simply is. Only persons mock. Persons mock—or love—other persons. Laughing at a strange rock formation or a silly-looking dog is entirely different from laughing at a friend. I believe God exists. And I believe I exist.

I can't get away from the idea of a personal energy outside of myself big enough to hem me in. I can think of this personal reality as good or bad, but I can't envision his (not "its") absence, his nonexistence.

Someone is there! Final reality is personal. I know it. It must be. The inconsolable longings within me, to say nothing of the intricate design of an insect, can be explained in no other way. The question then becomes: Is this Final Person good or bad?

And that question drives me to my second observation. Not only do I reflexively think of a Person beyond matter, but I also envision that Person moving toward me and feeling something for me as he comes closer.

I find that I cannot break away from a bedrock fact: *reality is defined by the interaction of two persons*, one, an infinite Person who is either good or bad; and two, me, and a community of people just like me, individuals who are free to move away from or toward the infinite Person depending on what we believe about him.

What do I believe about him? I know I exist and I know he exists. But is he good, and therefore worthy of trust and a legitimate basis of hope? Or is he bad, and am I therefore alone, abandoned to my resources to find happiness in a world that doesn't have it to give, unless I pretend I want less than I know I want.

When I push matters that far, I discover within me a strangely unshakable conviction that this Ultimate Person is, in fact, the God of the Bible, the God revealed in Jesus Christ, someone thoroughly good, relentlessly moral, unstoppably powerful, unimaginably loving, and determined to display his highest virtues by making me extremely happy.

If I make myself ask why I believe God is good, why the Supreme Being is not bad, my attention goes quickly to my thirst for beauty: the beauty of love, the beauty of order, the beauty of joy. I know the lust for beauty is within me—I can't get away from it. And I know it is a *good* lust, one that I can deny but never eliminate. If beauty has no source, I don't know how to explain my desire for it.

I find myself being brought to a foundation that I cannot fall beneath. There is a God and he is good. And I am alive as a person with the capacity to trust him or turn away from him.

Now I can see the final reality of a relational encounter between God and me for what it really is. The question to ask is not, "What will I do with God?" but rather, "What will he do with me, someone who refuses to trust his goodness?"

The moment I ask that question with the urgency it deserves, something happens. It is then that I catch a glimpse of God's blazing glory. What has he done with me? He accepts me! He loves me! That glimpse gives me a taste of him, and I know that he is good beyond every imagination.

He sees my rebellion, my refusal to trust him, my determination to build my city here. He also sees how easily my feeble desire to do what is good is overwhelmed by stronger desires for bad things. And still he loves me! He feels compassion toward me! He wants me for a friend!

As I ponder the relationship between God and me—one that he has arranged—I sense the stirrings of hope. I see light. The cave is still black, but I am no longer falling more deeply into it. Through no power of mine, I feel myself being lifted out of it. I find myself walking in a meadow blooming with wild flowers, moving toward a stream of clear water, then lying down beside it on a grassy bank.

The sun is shining, warming my body, while a gentle breeze keeps me from becoming uncomfortably hot. And I am aware of the sheer joy of being alive. I seem to be resting and moving at the same time, resting in Christ and moving toward him, farther and farther away from the black hole that so recently had been my prison. And I think I shall never fall into that hole again.

Then something happens, perhaps small, perhaps big. A filling falls out of a tooth. I receive disturbing news about someone I love. I struggle to maintain perspective, but it slips away. I tell myself that God is still good, that I can trust him, but the reality is gone. In an instant, the grassy bank disappears, and I am again plummeting into darkness. Again my soul feels dead, tortured, alive only with pain and doubt.

The cycle repeats itself, this time with lower lows and higher highs. I'm pressed again to return to my foundations: Is God really good? Do I believe it? Am I alive with the power to pursue him? Is he still there? Will he let me find him? I become more aware of the importance of trusting him, of resting in his goodness, of choosing against sin.

Sometimes I wish I could settle for merely engaging pleasantly with life, brushing my teeth, paying my bills, and correcting my slice off the tee. But the pursuit of God requires more.

The more I see the real issues of life, the more I have no choice but to move toward spiritual greatness or spiritual failure, toward powerful depth or bland impotence. I long to become a man of God, to know Christ well enough for him to be recognizable in me through my moody, fickle weirdness. I want him; sometimes I want him more than life itself. I must seek him with all my heart; only then will he let me find him. And only if I find him will I know the joy of living.

Lord, another glimpse, please!

Larry Crabb
Finding God

I would rather live in a world where my life is surrounded by mystery than live in a world so small that my mind could comprehend it.

Harry Emerson Fosdick
Riverside Sermons

In his holy flirtation with the world, God occasionally drops a handkerchief. These handkerchiefs are called saints.

Frederick Buechner
Wishful Thinking

All things change, creeds and philosophies and outward systems—but God remains!

Mary Augusta Ward
Robert Elsmer

God is a highest conception, not to be explained in terms of other things, but explainable only by exploring more and more profoundly the conception itself.

Sören Kierkegaard
Concluding Unscientific Postscript

There is nothing on earth that does not show either the wretchedness of man, or the mercy of God; either the weakness of man without God, or the strength of man with God.

Blaise Pascal
Pensées

He drooped and fell away from himself for a moment; then lifting his face to them again, showed a deep joy in his eyes, as he cried out with a heavenly enthusiasm,—"But oh! shipmates! on the starboard hand of every woe, there is a sure delight; and higher the top of that delight, than the bottom of the woe is deep. Is not the main-truck higher than the kelson is low? Delight is to him—a far, far upward, and inward delight—who against the proud gods and commodores of this earth, ever stands forth his own inexorable self. Delight is to him whose strong arms yet support him, when the ship of this base treacherous world has gone down beneath him. Delight is to him, who gives no quarter in the truth, and kills, burns, and destroys all sin though he pluck it out from under the robes of Senators and Judges. Delight,—top-gallant delight is to him, who acknowledges no law or lord, but the Lord his God, and is only a patriot to heaven. Delight is to him, whom all the waves of the billows of the seas of the boisterous mob can never shake from this sure Keel of the Ages. And eternal delight and deliciousness will be his, who coming to lay him down, can say with his final breath—O Father!—chiefly known to me by Thy rod—mortal or immortal, here I die. I have striven to be Thine, more than to be this world's, or mine own. Yet this is nothing; I leave eternity to Thee; for what is man that he should live out the lifetime of his God?"

He said no more, but slowly waving a benediction, covered his face with his hands, and so remained, kneeling, till all the people had departed, and he was left alone in the place.

Herman Melville
Moby-Dick

The world around us is the mighty volume wherein God hath declared himself. Human languages and characters are different in different nations. And those of one nation are not understood by the rest. But the book of nature is written in an universal character, which every man may read in his own language.

John Wesley
Letters

God is himself in no interval nor extension of place, but in his immutable, preeminent all-possibility is both within everything, because all things are in him, and without everything because he transcends all things.

Saint Augustine
On the Trinity

We should find God in what we do know, not in what we don't; not in outstanding problems, but in those we have already solved.

Dietrich Bonhoeffer
Letters and Papers from Prison

You have not measured your fingers with God's, therefore you cannot know what is in store.

Lithuanian proverb

God is waiting eagerly to respond with new strength to each little act of self-control, small disciplines of prayer, feeble searching after him. And his children shall be filled if they will only hunger and thirst after what he offers.

Richard Holloway
Beyond Belief

We are meant to be addicted to God, but we develop secondary addictions that temporarily appear to fix our problem.

Edward M. Berckman
Living Church, February 15, 1987

God is our refuge and strength, an ever-present help in trouble.

Psalm 46:1 (NIV)

When God's hand is bent to strike, "it is a fearful thing to fall into the hands of the living God"; but to fall out of the hands of the living God is a horror beyond our expression, beyond our imagination. That God should let my soul fall out of his hand into a bottomless pit and roll an unremovable stone upon it and leave it to that which it finds there (and it shall find that there which it never imagined till it came thither) and never think more of that soul, never have more to do with it; that of that providence of God that studies the life of every weed and worm and ant and spider and toad and viper there should never, never any beam flow out upon me; that that God who looked upon me when I was nothing and called me when I was not, as though I had been, out of the womb and depth of darkness, will not look upon me now, when though a miserable and a banished and a damned creature, yet I am his creature still; that that God who hath often looked upon me in my foulest uncleanness and when I had shut out the eye of the day, the sun, and the eye of the night, the taper, and the eyes of all the world with curtains and windows and doors, did yet see me and see me in mercy by making me see that he saw me and sometimes brought me to a present remorse and (for that time) to a forbearing of that sin, should so turn himself from me to his glorious saints and angels as that no saint nor angel nor Christ Jesus himself should ever pray him to look towards me, never remember him that such a soul there is; that that God who hath so often said to my soul, *Quare morieris?* why wilt thou die? and so often sworn to my soul, *Vivit Dominus,* as the Lord liveth, I would not have thee die but live, will neither let me die nor let me live, but die an everlasting life and live an everlasting death; that that God who, when he could not get into me by standing and knocking, by his ordinary means of entering, by his word, his mercies, hath applied his judgments and hath shaked the house, this body, with agues and palsies, and set this house on fire with fevers and calentures, and frighted the master of the house, my soul, with horrors and heavy apprehensions and so made an entrance into me; that that God should frustrate all his own purposes and practices upon me and leave me and cast me away as though I had cost him nothing; that this God at last should let this soul go away as a smoke, as a vapor, as a bubble; and that then this soul cannot be a smoke, a vapor, nor a bubble, but must lie in darkness as long as the Lord of light is light itself, and never spark of that light reach to my soul; what Tophet is not paradise, what brimstone is not amber, what gnashing is not a comfort, what gnawing of the worm is not a tickling, what torment is not a marriage bed to this damnation, to be secluded eternally, eternally, eternally from the sight of God?

John Donne
Sermon LXXVI

God reveals Himself—the Creator of the world—an author!

Johan Georg Hamann
Journal

To me it seems as if when God conceived the world, that was Poetry; He formed it, and that was Sculpture; He colored it, and that was Painting; He peopled it with living beings, and that was the grand, divine, eternal Drama.

Charlotte Saunders Cushman
Quoted in Charlotte Cushman

Sir, my concern is not whether God is on our side; my great concern is to be on God's side, for God is always right.

Abraham Lincoln
Reply to a deputation of Southerners

Curiosity, or the love of knowledge of causes, draws a man from the consideration of the effect, to seek the cause; and again, the cause of that cause; till of necessity he must come to this thought at last, that there is some cause whereof there is no former cause, but is eternal; which is it men call God.

Thomas Hobbes
Leviathan

No eye has seen, no ear has heard, no mind has conceived what God has prepared for those who love him.

1 Corinthians 2:9 (NIV)

A God all mercy is a God unjust.

Edward Young
Night Thoughts

The world is charged with the grandeur of God.

Gerard Manley Hopkins
God's Grandeur

God, give us grace to accept with serenity the things that cannot be changed, courage to change the things which should be changed and the wisdom to distinguish the one from the other.

Reinhold Niebuhr
Part of a sermon

Though God's attributes are equal, yet his mercy is more attractive and pleasing in our eyes than his justice.

Miguel de Cervantes
Don Quixote

To whom turn I but to thee, the ineffable Name?
Builder and maker, thou, of houses not made with hands!
What, have fear of change from thee who are ever the same?
Doubt that thy power can fill the heart that thy power expands?
There shall never be one lost good! What was, shall live as before;
The evil is null, is naught, is silence implying sound;
What was good shall be good, with, for evil, so much good more;
On the earth the broken arcs; in the heaven a perfect round.

Robert Browning
Abt Vogler

The beginning! but where is the beginning? You know that the beginning is God.
Edgar Allan Poe
Mesmeric Revelation

There is no unbelief;
Whoever plants a seed beneath the sod
And waits to see it push away the clod,
He trusts in God.

Elizabeth York Case
"There Is No Unbelief"

It is as certain that there is a God, as that the opposite angles made by the intersection of two straight lines are equal. There was never any rational creature that set himself sincerely to examine the truth of these propositions that could fail to assent to them; though yet it be past doubt that there are many men, who, having not applied their thoughts that way, are ignorant both of the one and the other.

John Locke
Concerning Human Understanding

I sometimes think that the analogy of a poet and his work—say Shakespeare and his plays—is the most helpful in forming an idea of the relation of God to the world.

William Ralph Inge
God and the Astronomers

The eternal God is your refuge, and underneath are the everlasting arms.

Deuteronomy 33:27 (NIV)

I raised my eyes aloft, and I beheld the scattered chapters of the Universe gathered and bound into a single book by the austere and tender hand of God.

Dante
The Divine Comedy

And I smiled to think God's greatness flowed
around our incompleteness—
Round our restlessness, His rest.

Elizabeth Barrett Browning
"Rhyme of the Duchess May"

After reading the entire Gospel of Luke for the first time, a post-Valley girl said: "Wow! Like Jesus has this totally intense thing for ragamuffins."

The young lady is onto something.

Jesus spent a disproportionate amount of time with people described in the gospels as: the poor, the blind, the lame, the lepers, the hungry, sinners, prostitutes, tax collectors, the persecuted, the downtrodden, the captives, those possessed by unclean spirits, all who labor and are heavy burdened, the rabble who know nothing of the law, the crowds, the little ones, the least, the last, and the lost sheep of the house of Israel.

In short, Jesus hung out with ragamuffins.

Obviously his love for failures and nobodies was not an exclusive love—that would merely substitute one class prejudice for another. He related with warmth and compassion to the middle and upper classes not because of their family connections, financial clout, intelligence, or Social Register status but because they, too, were God's children. While the term *poor* in the gospel includes the economically deprived and embraces all the oppressed who are dependent upon the mercy of others, it extends to all who rely entirely upon the mercy of God and accept the gospel of grace—the poor in spirit (Matthew 5:3).

Brennan Manning
The Ragamuffin Gospel

It is the great God himself who drives away the flies from a tailless cow.

Yoruba proverb

God is where He was.

English proverb

I believe in God the Father Almighty because wherever I have looked, through all that I see around me, I see the trace of an intelligent mind, and because in natural laws, and especially in the laws which govern the social relations of men, I see, not merely the proofs of intelligence, but the proofs of beneficence.

Henry George
Speech

God has been replaced, as he has all over the West, with respectability and air conditioning.

Le Roi Jones
Home

Where there is faith, where there is need, there is the True God ready to clasp the hands that stretch out seeking for him into the darkness behind the ivory and gold.

H. G. Wells
God the Invisible King

So Moses thought, "I will go over and see this strange sight—why the bush does not burn up."

When the LORD saw that he had gone over to look, God called to him from within the bush, "Moses! Moses!"

And Moses said, "Here I am."

"Do not come any closer," God said. "Take off your sandals, for the place where you are standing is holy ground." Then he said, "I am the God of your father, the God of Abraham, the God of Isaac and the God of Jacob." At this, Moses hid his face, because he was afraid to look at God.

Exodus 3:3-6 (NIV)

Good Will...good Christian, come a little way with me, and I will teach thee about the way thou must go. Look before thee; dost thou see this narrow way? THAT is the way thou must go. It was cast up by the Patriarchs, Prophets, Christ, and his Apostles; and it is as straight as a Rule can make it: This is the way thou must go.

But said Christian, *Is there no turnings nor windings by which a Stranger may lose the way?*

Good Will. Yes, there are many ways *but* down upon this; and they are crooked, and wide: But *thus* thou may'st distinguish the right from the wrong, *That* only being straight and narrow.

John Bunyan
The Pilgrim's Progress

The Christian religion...teaches men these two truths; that there is a God whom men can know, and that there is a corruption in their nature which renders them unworthy of Him. It is equally important to men to know both these points; and it is equally dangerous for man to know God without knowing his own wretchedness, and to know his own wretchedness without knowing the Redeemer who can free him from it. The knowledge of only one of these points gives rise either to the pride of philosophers, who have known God, and not their own wretchedness, or to the despair of atheists, who know their own wretchedness, but not the Redeemer.

And, as it is alike necessary to man to know these two points, so is it alike merciful of God to have made us know them. The Christian religion does this; it is in this that it consists.

Let us herein examine the order of the world and see if all things do not tend to establish these two chief points of this religion: Jesus Christ is the end of all, and the centre to which all tends. Whoever knows Him knows the reason of everything.

Those who fall into error err only through failure to see one of these two things. We can, then, have an excellent knowledge of God without that of our own wretchedness and of our own wretchedness without that of God. But we cannot know Jesus Christ without knowing at the same time both God and our own wretchedness.

Therefore I shall not undertake here to prove by natural reasons either the existence of God, or the Trinity, or the immortality of the soul, or anything of that nature; not only because I should not feel myself sufficiently able to find in nature arguments to convince hardened atheists, but also because such knowledge without Jesus Christ is useless and barren. Though a man should be convinced that numerical proportions are immaterial truths, eternal and dependent on a first truth, in which they subsist and which is called God, I should not think him far advanced towards his own salvation.

The God of Christians is not a God who is simply the author of mathematical truths, or of the order of the elements; that is the view of heathens and Epicureans. He is not merely a God who exercises His providence over the life and fortunes of men, to bestow on those who worship Him a long and happy life. That was the portion of the Jews. But the God of Abraham, the God of Isaac, the God of Jacob, the God of Christians, is a God of love and of comfort, a God who fills the soul and heart of those whom He possesses, a God who makes them conscious of their inward wretchedness, and His infinite mercy, who unites Himself to their inmost soul, who fills it with humility and joy, with confidence and love, who renders them incapable of any other end than Himself.

All who seek God without Jesus Christ, and who rest in nature, either find no light to satisfy them, or come to form for themselves a means of knowing God and serving Him without a mediator. Thereby they fall either into atheism, or into deism, two things which the Christian religion abhors almost equally.

Without Jesus Christ the world would not exist; for it should needs be either that it would be destroyed or be a hell.

If the world existed to instruct man of God, His divinity would shine through every part in it in an indisputable manner; but as it exists only by Jesus Christ, and for Jesus Christ, and to teach men both their corruption and their redemption, all displays the proofs of these two truths.

All appearance indicates neither a total exclusion nor a manifest presence of divinity, but the presence of a God who hides Himself. Everything bears this character.

Blaise Pascal
Pensées

No one has the capacity to judge God. We are drops in that limitless ocean of mercy.

Mohandas K. Gandhi
Non-Violence in Peace and War

I could prove God statistically. Take the human body alone—the chance that all the functions of the individual would just happen is a statistical monstrosity.

George Gallup
Quoted in *Reader's Digest*, October 1943

Our Lord God is an endless being without changing, almighty without failing, sovereign wisdom, light, soothness without error or darkness; sovereign goodness, love, peace, and sweetness.

Walter Hilton
The Song of Angels

A sense of Diety is inscribed on every heart.

John Calvin

The first contrivance of those very artificial parts of animals, the eyes, ears, brain, muscles, heart, lungs, midriff, glands, larynx, hands, wings, swimming bladders, natural spectacles, and other organs of sense and motion; and the instinct of brutes and insects can be the effect of nothing else than the wisdom and skill of a powerful, everliving agent, who being in all places, is more able by His will to move the bodies within His boundless uniform sensorium, and thereby to form and reform the parts of the Universe, than we are by our will to move the parts of our own bodies. And yet we are not to consider the world as the body of God, or the several parts thereof as the parts of God. He is a uniform Being, void of organs, members or parts, and they are his creatures subordinate to him, and subservient to His will; and He is no more the soul of them than the soul of man is the soul of the species of things carried through the organs of sense into the place of its sensation, where it perceives them by means of its immediate presence, without the intervention of any third thing. The organs of sense are not for enabling the soul to perceive the species of things in its sensorium, but only for conveying them thither; and God has no need of such organs, He being everywhere present to the things themselves.

Isaac Newton
Optics

God never shuts one door but He opens another.

Irish proverb

The way of God is complex, he is hard for us to predict.
He moves the pieces and they come somehow into a kind of order.

Euripides
Helen

When all thy mercies, O my God,
My rising soul surveys,
Transported with the view I'm lost,
In wonder, love and praise.

Joseph Addison
"With All Thy Mercies"

Let nothing disturb thee,
Nothing affright thee;
All things are passing;
God never changeth;
Patient endurance
Attaineth to all things;
Who God possesseth
In nothing is wanting;
Alone God sufficeth.

Henry Wadsworth Longfellow
Santa Teresa's Bookmark

I can't understand what must be in a man's mind if he doesn't feel seriously that
there is a God when he sees the sun rise. It must at times occur to him that there
are eternal things, or else he must push his face into the dirt like a sow. For it's
incredible that they [the planets] be observed to move without inquiring whether
there isn't somebody who moves them.

Martin Luther
Table Talk

Heaven and earth and all that is in them tell me wherever I look that I should love You, and they cease not to tell it to all men, so that there is no excuse for them. *For You will have mercy on whom You will have mercy, and You will show mercy to whom You will show mercy:* otherwise heaven and earth cry their praise of You to deaf ears.

But what is it that I love when I love You? Not the beauty of any bodily thing, nor the order of seasons, nor the brightness of light that rejoices the eye, nor the sweet melodies of all songs, nor the sweet fragrance of flowers and ointments and spices: not manna nor honey, not the limbs that carnal love embraces. None of these things do I love in loving my God. Yet in a sense I do love light and melody and fragrance and food and embrace when I love my God—the light and the voice and the fragrance and the food and embrace in the soul, when that light shines upon my soul which no place can contain, that voice sounds which no time can take from me, I breathe that fragrance which no wind scatters, I eat the food which is not lessened by eating, and I lie in the embrace which satiety never comes to sunder. This it is that I love, when I love my God.

Saint Augustine
Confessions

Dear God,
　　Could you change the taste of asparagus?
　　Everything else is OK.
Love,
Fred

nine-year-old child
Quoted in *Dear God: Children's Letters to God*

The best thing is to go from nature's God down to nature; and if you once get to nature's God, and believe him, and love him, it is surprising how easy it is to hear music in the waves, and songs in the wild whisperings of the winds; to see God everywhere in the stones, in the rocks, in the rippling brooks, and hear him everywhere, in the lowing of cattle, in the rolling of thunder, and in the fury of tempests.

Charles Haddon Spurgeon
Sermons

The immediate person thinks and imagines that when he prays, the important thing, the thing he must concentrate upon, is that *God should hear* what HE *is praying for.* And yet in the true, eternal sense it is just the reverse: the true relation in prayer is not when God hears what is prayed for, but when *the person praying* continues to pray until he is *the one who hears*, who hears what God wills. The immediate person, therefore, uses many words and, therefore, makes demands in his prayer; the true man of prayer only *attends*.

Sören Kierkegaard
Journals

When we pray, we link ourselves with the inexhaustible power that spins the universe. We ask that a part of this power be apportioned to our needs. Even in asking, our human deficiencies are filled and we arise strengthened and repaired.

Dr. Alexis Carrel
Quoted in *Reader's Digest,* March 1941

Father Zossima. Young man, be not forgetful of prayer. Every time you pray, if your prayer is sincere, there will be new feeling and new meaning in it, which will give you fresh courage, and you will understand that prayer is an education.

Fyodor Dostoevsky
The Brothers Karamazov

If a good God made the world why has it gone wrong? And for many years I simply refused to listen to the Christian answers to this question, because I kept on feeling "whatever you say, and however clever your arguments are, isn't it much simpler and easier to say that the world was not made by any intelligent power? Aren't all your arguments simply a complicated attempt to avoid the obvious?" But then that threw me back into another difficulty.

My argument against God was that the universe seemed so cruel and unjust. But how had I got this idea of *just* and *unjust?* A man does not call a line crooked unless he has some idea of a straight line. What was I comparing this universe with when I called it unjust? If the whole show was bad and senseless from A to Z, so to speak, why did I, who was supposed to be part of the show, find myself in such violent reaction against it? A man feels wet when he falls into water, because man is not a water animal: a fish would not feel wet. Of course I could have given up my idea of justice by saying it was nothing but a private idea of my own. But if I did that, then my argument against God collapsed too—for the argument depended on saying that the world was really unjust, not simply that it did not happen to please my private fancies. Thus in the very act of trying to prove that God did not exist—in other words, that the whole of reality was sense- less—I found I was forced to assume that one part of reality—namely my idea of justice—was full of sense. Consequently atheism turns out to be too simple. If the whole universe has no meaning, we should never have found out that it has no meaning: just as, if there were no light in the universe and therefore no creatures with eyes, we should never know it was dark. *Dark* would be without meaning.

C. S. Lewis

Mere Christianity

The heavens declare the glory of God; the skies proclaim the work of his hands.

Day after day they pour forth speech; night after night they display knowl- edge.

There is no speech or language where their voice is not heard.

Their voice goes out into all the earth, their words to the ends of the world,

In the heavens he has pitched a tent for the sun, which is like a bridegroom coming forth from his pavilion, like a champion rejoicing to run his course.

It rises at one end of the heavens and makes its circuit to the other; nothing is hidden from its heat.

The law of the LORD is perfect, reviving the soul.

The statutes of the LORD are trustworthy, making wise the simple.

The precepts of the LORD are right, giving joy to the heart.

The commands of the LORD are radiant, giving light to the eyes.

The fear of the LORD is pure, enduring forever.

The ordinances of the LORD are sure and altogether righteous.

They are more precious than gold, than much pure gold; they are sweeter than honey, than honey from the comb.

By them is your servant warned; in keeping them there is great reward.

Who can discern his errors? Forgive my hidden faults.

Keep your servant also from willful sins; may they not rule over me.

Then will I be blameless, innocent of great transgression.

May the words of my mouth and the meditation of my heart be pleasing in your sight, O LORD, my Rock and my Redeemer.

Psalm 19:1-14 (NIV)

Thee Father first they [the angel choir] sung Omnipotent,
Immutable, Immortal, Infinite,
Eternal King; thee Author of all being,
Fountain of Light, thy self invisible
Amidst the glorious brightness where thou sit'st
Thron'd inaccessible, but when thou shad'st
The full blaze of thy beams, and through a cloud
Drawn round about thee like a radiant Shrine,
Dark with excessive bright thy skirts appeer,
Yet dazle Heav'n, that brightest Seraphim
Approach not, but with both wings veil their eyes.

John Milton
Paradise Lost

With God, go over the sea—without Him, not over the threshold.

Russian proverb

God is the perfect poet,
Who in his person acts his own creations.

Robert Browning
Paracelsus

Earth with her thousand voices, praises God.

Samuel Taylor Coleridge
Hymn before Sunrise in the Vale of Chamouni

God is light; in him there is no darkness at all.

1 John 1:5 (NIV)

We live inside this unbelievable cosmos, inside our unbelievable bodies—everything so perfect, everything so in tune. I got to think God had a hand in it…There's got to be something greater than us.

Ray Charles
Brother Ray

As puppets are to men, and dolls to children, so is man's workmanship to God's: we are the picture, he the reality.

William Penn
Some Fruits of Solitude

God tempers the cold to the shorn lamb.

Henri Estienne
Premises

If God is for us, who can be against us?

Romans 8:31 (NIV)

Only That which made us, meant us to be mightier by and by,
Set the sphere of all the boundless Heavens within the human eye,

Sent the shadow of Himself, the boundless, through the human soul;
Boundless inward, in the atom, boundless outward, in the whole.

Alfred, Lord Tennyson
"That Which Made Us"

If I go up to the heavens, you [God] are there; if I make my bed in the depths, you are there.

Psalm 139:8 (NIV)

The world is God's journal wherein he writes his thoughts and traces his tastes.

Henry Ward Beecher
Sermons

We pay God honor and reverence, not for His sake (because He is of Himself full of glory to which no creature can add anything), but for our own sake, because by the very fact that we revere and honor God, our mind is subjected to Him; wherein its perfection consists, since a thing is perfected by being subjected to its superior.

Saint Thomas Aquinas
Summa Theologica

[Jesus said] "I and the Father are one."

John 10:30 (NIV)

He wraps himself in light as with a garment; he stretches out the heavens like a tent and lays the beams of his upper chambers on their waters. He makes the clouds his chariot and rides on the wings of the wind. He makes winds his messengers, flames of fire his servants.

Psalm 104:2-4 (NIV)

What...is my God, what but the Lord God? *For who is Lord but the Lord, or Who is God but our God?* O Thou, the greatest and the best, mightiest, almighty, most merciful and most just, utterly hidden and utterly present, most beautiful and most strong, abiding yet mysterious, suffering no change and changing all things: never new, never old, making all things new, *bringing age upon the proud and they know it not;* ever in action, ever at rest, gathering all things to Thee and needing none; sustaining and fulfilling and protecting, creating and nourishing and making perfect; ever seeking though lacking nothing.

Saint Augustine
Confessions

A hasty kind of reasoning may hold that praying is an unprofitable act, because a man's prayer does not really change the Unchangeable; but even if this in the process of time were desired, might not changeable man come easily to regret that he had changed God? The true kind of reasoning is therefore the only desirable kind as well; prayer does not change God, but changes him who prays.

Sören Kierkegaard
Works of Love

Jesus answered, "I am the way and the truth and the life. No one comes to the Father except through me."

John 14:6 (NIV)

God's gifts put man's best dreams to shame.

Elizabeth Barrett Browning
Sonnets from the Portuguese

Sing to the Lord a new song; sing to the Lord, all the earth.
Sing to the Lord, praise his name; proclaim his salvation day after day.
Declare his glory among the nations, his marvelous deeds among all peoples.
For great is the Lord and most worthy of praise; he is to be feared above all
gods.
For all the gods of the nations are idols, but the Lord made the heavens.
Splendor and majesty are before him; strength and glory are in his sanctuary.
Ascribe to the Lord, O families of nations, ascribe to the Lord glory and
strength.
Ascribe to the Lord the glory due his name; bring an offering and come into
his courts.
Worship the Lord in the splendor of his holiness; tremble before him, all the
earth.
Say among the nations, "The Lord reigns." The world is firmly established, it
cannot be moved; he will judge the peoples with equity.
Let the heavens rejoice, let the earth be glad; let the sea resound, and all that
is in it; let the fields be jubilant, and everything in them.
Then all the trees of the forest will sing for joy; they will sing before the Lord,
for he comes, he comes to judge the earth.
He will judge the world in righteousness and the peoples in his truth.

Psalm 96:1-13 (NIV)

If thou knowest God, thou knowest that everything is possible for God to do.

Callimachus
Fragmenta Incertae

God's transcendent power is not so much displayed in the vastness of the heavens, or the luster of the stars, or the orderly arrangement of the universe or his perpetual watching over it, as in his condescension to our weak nature. We marvel at the way the sublime entered a state of lowliness.

> Saint Gregory of Nyssa
> *Address on Religious Instruction*

I am trying here to prevent anyone saying the really foolish thing that people often say about Him: "I'm ready to accept Jesus as a great moral teacher, but I don't accept His claim to be God." That is the one thing we must not say. A man who was merely a man and said the sort of things Jesus said would not be a great moral teacher. He would either be a lunatic—on a level with the man who says he is a poached egg—or else he would be the Devil of Hell. You must make your choice. Either this man was, and is, the Son of God: or else a madman or something worse. You can shut Him up for a fool, you can spit at Him and kill Him as a demon; or you can fall at His feet and call Him Lord and God. But let us not come with any patronizing nonsense about His being a great human teacher. He has not left that open to us. He did not intend to.

> C. S. Lewis
> *Mere Christianity*

For God so loved the world that he gave his one and only Son, that whoever believes in him shall not perish but have eternal life. For God did not send his Son into the world to condemn the world, but to save the world through him.

> John 3:16–17 (NIV)

Growing

OLDER

CHAPTER FOURTEEN

GROWING OLDER

—⟋⟍—

To know how to grow old is the master-work of wisdom, and one of the most difficult chapters in the great art of living.

Henri Frédéric Amiel
Journal Intime

Everyone faces at all times two fateful possibilities; one is to grow older, the other not.

anonymous

...old age is like a plane flying through a storm. Once you're aboard, there's nothing you can do. You can't stop the plane, you can't stop the storm, you can't stop time. So one might as well accept it calmly, wisely.

Golda Meir
Quoted in *Le'Europeo*

Aging seems to be the only available way to live a long time.

Daniel-François-Esprit Auber
Dictionnaire Encyclopédique

"Madame, if you live, you will grow old."

Kathleen Winsor
Forever Amber

As newer comers crowd the fore,
We drop behind—
We who have laboured long and sore
Times out of mind,
And keen are yet, must not regret
To drop behind.

Thomas Hardy
The Superseded

It's later than you think—everything is farther away now than it used to be. It's twice as far to the corner—and they added a hill. I notice I've given up running for the bus—it leaves faster than it used to. It seems to me they are making steps steeper than in the old days, and have you noticed the smaller print they use in the newspapers? There is no sense asking anyone to read aloud...everyone speaks in such a low voice I can scarcely hear them. Material in dresses is so skimpy, especially around the hips. It's all but impossible to reach my shoe laces. Even people are changing—they are much younger than they used to be when I was their age. On the other hand, people my age are much older than I. I ran into an old classmate the other day, and she had aged so much she didn't remember me. I got to thinking about the poor thing while I was combing my hair this morning, and I glanced in the mirror at my reflection, and, confound it, they don't make mirrors like they used to either.

anonymous

Sweet and of their nature vacant are the days I spend—
Quiet as a plough laid by at the furrow's end.

Katharine Bradley
"Old Age"

When one gets old one is so thankful to be quiet.

Augusta, Duchess of Saxe-Coburg-Saalfeld
Diary entry, December 19, 1817

When you're old, everything you do is sort of a miracle.

Millicent Fenwick
Quoted on "Sixty Minutes," CBS-TV, February 1, 1981

You know you're getting old when your back starts going out more than you do.

Phyllis Diller
Quoted in Earl Wilson's "Broadway" column,
September 8, 1978

...I saw my wrinkles in their wrinkles. You know, one looks at herself in the mirror every morning, and she doesn't see the difference, she doesn't realize that she is aging. But then she finds a friend who was young with her, and the friend isn't young anymore, and all of a sudden, like a slap on her eyes, she remembers that she, too, isn't young anymore.

Ingrid Bergman
Quoted in *The Egotists*

You know you're getting older when...
- everything hurts and what doesn't hurt doesn't work.
- you feel like the night after when you haven't been anywhere.
- you get winded playing checkers.
- your children begin to look middle-aged.
- your broad mind and narrow waist have traded places.
- you know all the answers, but nobody asks you the questions.

anonymous

Few people know how to be old.

François de La Rochefoucauld
Maximes

An elder is a person who is still growing, still a learner, still with potential and whose life continues to have within it promise for, and connection to, the future. An elder is still in pursuit of happiness, joy, and pleasure, and her or his birthright to these remains intact. Moreover, an elder is a person who deserves respect and honor and whose work it is to synthesize wisdom from long life experience and formulate this into a legacy for future generations.

Zalman Schachter-Shalomi and Ronald S. Miller
Age-ing to Sage-ing

I have passed from the positive to the negative side of life, when we begin to take in sail; when we want less and not more; when the hunger for new scenes and new worlds to conquer is diminishing; when the inclination not to stir beyond one's own chimney corner is fast growing upon us.

John Burroughs
Journal entry, January 30, 1900

If I cannot work or rise from my chair or my bed, love remains to me; I can pray.

Father Congreve

Man arrives as a novice at each age of his life.

Nicholas Chamfort
Caractères et anecdotes

The contented older person is very much aware of his importance to his family and his community. He can look back on the achievements of his lifetime with a sense of pride, and he has satisfaction and a feeling of continuity as he sees younger members of his family carrying on his work. His sense of his own secure place in his community is extended and enhanced with every new birth in his family, for he sees his line and everything he holds valuable thus being perpetuated into the future.

Above all, the well-adjusted elder is active. His daily life is filled with occupations that he feels to be purposeful and useful and that are appreciated as being so by members of his family and community. On festive occasions celebrated by his family or acquaintances his manner reflects his satisfaction with his life. Yet for all his strong feelings of closeness and identity with his family he maintains a spirit of independence, and he prefers to attend to his own chores rather than to be aided with them.

In talking to his grandchildren he will tell them of the past. To his own children he will talk of the present. With his contemporaries he will discuss the future, since life is still ahead for him and he has plans for the future that thoughts of his possible demise do not disturb. Many a contented older man, looking out of a window of a home he expects to pass on to future generations of his family, has decided to improve the view from it by planting a tree that he knows he will never see come to full growth, but he enjoys the prospect of it in his mind, as he knows his posterity will see it.

Dr. Doris Jonas and Dr. David Jonas
Young Till We Die

I miss being needed.
Once the whole family depended on me.
I was the breadwinner.
Only I didn't win the bread, I worked hard and earned it.
When I picked up my paycheck, I was proud.
I didn't mind that it went for the family.
I was proud to buy shoes, a Flexible Flyer sled, a college education.
I was needed at work.
In the community.
At home.
To build and haul.
To serve on committees.
To decide things. To help people out.
Sometimes I'd get exasperated and say, Does the whole world have to lean
    on me?
Now I wish somebody would.
The trouble is, now that I'm old, people have no idea what I'm good for.
Well, neither do I.
But I can find out.
Maybe to be needed, a man doesn't always have to be doing something.
He can just be there. Like a star. A fixed point. For others to take their bear-
    ings from.

Elise Maclay
"I Miss Being Needed"

Old age is no such uncomfortable thing, if one gives oneself up to it with a good grace, and don't drag it about "To midnight dances and the public show."

Horace Walpole
Letter to the Countess of Ailesbury

If we have not achieved our early dreams, we must either find new ones or see what we can salvage from the old. If we have accomplished what we set out to do in our youth, then we need not weep like Alexander the Great that we have no more worlds to conquer. There is clearly much left to be done, and whatever else we are going to do, we had better get on with it.

Rosalynn Smith Carter
Something to Gain

The mark of the immature man is that he wants to die nobly for a cause, while the mark of the mature man is that he wants to live humbly for one.

Wilhelm Stekel
Quoted in *The Catcher in the Rye*

Give me a staff of honour for mine age,
But not a sceptre to control the world.

William Shakespeare
Titus Andronicus

And if I should live to be
The last leaf upon the tree
In the spring,
Let them smile, as I do now,
At the old forsaken bough
Where I cling.

Oliver Wendell Holmes
"The Last Leaf"

The course of life is fixed, and nature admits of its being run but in one way, and only once; and to each part of our life there is something specially seasonable; so that the feebleness of children, as well as the high spirit of youth, the soberness of maturer years, and the ripe wisdom of old age—all have a certain natural advantage which should be secured in its proper season.

Marcus Tullius Cicero
Old Age

You know you're getting older when...
- you look forward to a dull evening.
- you turn out the light for economic reasons rather than romantic ones.
- you sit in a rocking chair and can't get it going.
- your knees buckle and your belt won't.
- you're 17 around the neck, 42 around the waist, 96 around the golf course.

anonymous

We age inevitably:
The old joys fade and are gone:
And at last comes equanimity and the flame burning clear.

James Oppenheim
"New Year's Eve"

Those pleasures [of growing old] include some that younger people find hard to appreciate. One is simply sitting still, like a snake on a sun-warmed stone, with a delicious feeling of indolence that was seldom attained in earlier years. A leaf flutters down; a cloud moves by inches across the horizon. At such moments the older person, completely relaxed, has become a part of nature—and a living part, with blood coursing through his veins. The future does not exist for him. He thinks, if he thinks at all, that life for younger persons is still a battle royal of each against each, but that now he has nothing more to win or lose. He is not so much above as outside the battle, as if he had assumed the uniform of some small neutral country.

Malcolm Cowley
The View From 80

There are compensations for growing older. One is the realization that to be sporting isn't at all necessary. It is a great relief to reach this stage of wisdom.

Cornelia Otis Skinner
Dithers and Jitters

Manhood in the Christian life is a better thing than boyhood, because it is a riper thing; and old age ought to be a brighter and a calmer, and a more serene thing than manhood.

F. W. Robertson
Sermons

Tho' much is taken, much abides; and tho'
We are not now that strength which in old days
Moved earth and heaven; that which we are, we are—
One equal temper of heroic hearts,
Made weak by time and fate, but strong in will
To strive, to seek, to find, and not to yield.

Alfred, Lord Tennyson
"Ulysses"

The woman who has a gift for old age is the woman who delights in comfort. If warmth is known as the blessing it is, if your bed, your bath, your best-liked food and drink are regarded as fresh delights, then you know how to thrive when old. If you get the things you like on the simplest possible terms, serve yourself lightly, efficiently and calmly, all is almost well.

Florida Scott-Maxwell
The Measure of My Days

So Life's year begins and closes;
Days, though short'ning, still can shine;
What though youth gave love and roses,
Age still leaves us friends and wine.

Thomas Moore
"Spring and Autumn"

You must live long in order to see much.

> Miguel de Cervantes
> *Don Quixote*

Ah well, perhaps one has to be very old before one learns how to be amused rather than shocked.

> Pearl S. Buck
> China, Past and Present

The touch of flame—the illuminating fire—the loftiest look at last...
The calmer sight—the golden setting, clear and broad:...
The points of view, the situations whence we scan...
The lights indeed from them—old age's lambent peaks.

> Walt Whitman
> *Old Age's Lambent Peaks*

Certainly old age has a great sense of calm and freedom; when the passions relax their hold, then, as Sophocles says, you have escaped from the control not of one master, but of many.

> Plato
> *Republic*

I am profoundly grateful to old age, which has increased my eagerness for conversation and taken away that for food and drink.

> Marcus Tullius Cicero
> *De Senectute*

[Age] has weathered the perilous capes and shoals in the sea whereon we sail, and the chief evil of life is taken away in removing the grounds of fear...At every stage we lose a foe.

> Ralph Waldo Emerson
> *Society and Solitude: Old Age*

The sun looks brighter…as the evening of life draws near.

Sarah Alden Ripley
Quoted in *Notable American Women*

> The tree of deepest root is found
> Least willing still to quit the ground:
> 'Twas therefore said by ancient sages,
> That love of life increased with years
> So much that in our later stages
> When pain grows sharp and sickness rages,
> The greatest love of life appears.

Hector Lynch Piozzi
"Three Warnings"

It's been said that as we get older, we don't regret the things that we did do, but only those things that we failed or forgot to do. How many of those wonderful, brief capsules of time do I miss each day, I wonder?…

At times I grow embarrassed when I realize how deaf I am to life's symphony, for if God speaks to us anywhere, I think it is in our daily lives. I wonder how much of God's grace I experience…and how much I'm capable of experiencing…

I don't know how much string is left on my ball of twine. There are no guarantees as to how long any of us will live, but I know full well that I would rather make my days count than merely count my days. I want to live each one of them as close to the core of life as possible, experiencing as much of God and my family and friends as I am capable. Since life is inevitably too short, for all of us, I know full well that I want to enjoy it as much as I can, no matter what the circumstances are.

Tim Hansel
You Gotta Keep Dancin'

I love everything that's old: old friends, old times, old manners, old books, old wine.

Oliver Goldsmith
She Stoops to Conquer

Age is not all decay; it is the ripening, the swelling, of the fresh life within, that withers and bursts the husk.

> George Macdonald
> *The Marquis of Lossie*

Women sit or move to and fro, some old, some young,
The young are beautiful—but the old are more beautiful than the young.

> Walt Whitman
> "Beautiful Women"

To be seventy years young is sometimes far more cheerful and hopeful than to be forty years old.

> Oliver Wendell Holmes
> Letter to Julia Ward Howe on her 70th birthday,
> May 27, 1889

The old age of an eagle is better than the youth of a sparrow.

> Greek proverb

In seventy or eighty years, a man may have a deep gust of the world; know what it is, what it can afford, and what 'tis to have been a man.

> Sir Thomas Browne
> *Christian Morals*

Old age, especially when crowned with honor, enjoys an authority which is of more value than all the sensual pleasures of youth.

> Marcus Tullius Cicero
> *De Senectute*

And he died in a good old age, full of days, riches, and honour.

> 1 Chronicles 29:28

Old age and the wear of time teach many things.

> Sophocles
> *Tyro*

For true it is, age has great advantage;
experience and wisdom come with age;
Men may the old out-run, but not out-wit.

> Geoffrey Chaucer
> *Canterbury Tales*

For in all the world there are no people so piteous and forlorn as those who are forced to eat the bitter bread of dependency in their old age, and find how steep are the stairs of another man's house.

> Dorothy Dix
> *Dorothy Dix, Her Book*

Each generation imagines itself to be more intelligent than the one that went before it, and wiser than the one that comes after it.

> George Orwell

'Tis the defect of age to rail at the pleasures of youth.

> Susannah Centlivre
> *The Basset-Table*

The young man who has not wept is a savage, and the old man who will not laugh is a fool.

> George Santayana
> *Dialogues in Limbo*

The arrogance of age must submit to be taught by youth.

> Edmund Burke
> Letter to Fanny Burney

Nothing so dates a man as to decry the younger generation.

> Adlai E. Stevenson
> Speech, University of Wisconsin, Madison,
> October 8, 1952

Unusual irritability, which leads to quarrels, shortens life.

Alexander A. Bogomoletz
The Prolongation of Life

We grow old as soon as we cease to love and trust.

Louise Honorine de Choiseul
Quoted in *Portraits of Women*

In this country, some people start being miserable about growing old while they are still young.

Margaret Mead
Quoted in *Family Circle*, July 26, 1977

Nothing is more dishonorable than an old man, heavy with years, who has no other evidence of having lived long except his age.

Lucius Annaeus Seneca
De Tranquillitate

Old age is no excuse for copping out. Each of us can find ways in which to make a difference.

Eda LeShan
It's Better to Be Over the Hill Than Under It

We grow old more through indolence, than through age.

Christina of Sweden
Maxims

Shall I tremble at a gray hair...

Dorothy Dow
Time and Love

"Old Cary Grant fine. How you?"

Cary Grant
(replying to a telegram sent to his agent
inquiring: "How old Cary Grant?")

It is so comic to hear oneself called old, even at ninety I suppose!

Alice James
The Diary of Alice James

You'll understand later that one keeps on forgetting old age up to the very brink of the grave.

Sidonie-Gabrielle Colette
My Mother's House

How true is it, yet how consistent…that while we all desire to live long, we have all a horror of being old!

Fanny Burney
Cecelia

I have always felt that a woman has the right to treat the subject of her age with ambiguity until, perhaps, she passes into the realm of over ninety. Then it is better she be candid with herself and with the world.

Helena Rubenstein
My Life for Beauty

Whenever a man's friends begin to compliment him about looking young, he may be sure that they think he is growing old.

Washington Irving
Bracebridge Hall

A diplomat is a man who always remembers a woman's birthday but never remembers her age.

Robert Frost

For never any man was yet so old
But hoped his life one winter more might hold.

Sir John Denham
"Of Old Age"

At sixteen I was stupid, confused, insecure and indecisive. At twenty-five I was wise, self-confident, prepossessing and assertive. At forty-five I am stupid, confused, insecure and indecisive. Who would have supposed that maturity is only a short break in adolescence?

Jules Feiffer
Quoted in *The Observer*, February 3, 1974

How old would you be if you didn't know how old you was?

Leroy (Satchel) Paige
Quoted in the *New York Times*, June 8, 1984

"Age" is the acceptance of a term of years. But maturity is the glory of years.

Martha Graham
Quoted in the *Christian Science Monitor*,
May 25, 1979

It is not years that make souls grow old, but having nothing to love, nothing to hope for.

Father Congreve

...planting trees is a fine metaphor for what to do about getting old. Instead of sitting and wringing our hands because so much of our lives is behind us, we need to think creatively about what we can do for the future. And in this ailing world the opportunities are endless. A wonderful cure for "the old-age blues" is to ask: "What can I do for future generations?" It would be impossible to run out of possibilities during the rest of our lives.

Eda LeShan
It's Better to Be Over the Hill Than Under It

I prefer to forget both pairs of glasses and pass my declining years saluting strange women and grandfather clocks.

Ogden Nash
Peekaboo, I Almost See You

A man is not old until regrets take the place of dreams.

John Barrymore
Quoted in *Good Night, Sweet Prince*

In a time when an American man's life expectancy was 33, Benjamin Franklin, that most civilized of beings, lived to be 84.

His life in Colonial America was hard. He survived blistering summers and punishing winters. Traveling, which he did as much as any man of his time, was physically debilitating. A trip from Boston to Philadelphia took three difficult days of coach travel. Even the distance from Philadelphia to New York occupied a long day. His many trips abroad were wearing. To London and return, to Paris and return, again and again, each journey lasting from five to seven weeks.

The range of his interests and activities is impressive, even to the modern man. Printer, publisher, author, humorist, statesman, scientist, inventor, innovator (adult education, life insurance, *The Saturday Evening Post,* the Franklin stove), ambassador, signer of the Declaration of Independence.

At 80, Franklin invented the flexible catheter, experimented with treatment of paralysis by electricity, and did significant work on lead poisoning. He also concerned himself with the alleviation of gout, insomnia, fever, deafness, the common cold, infection from dead bodies, and the death rate of infants.

Further, at about this time, he became increasingly irritated by the deterioration of his eyes. He thought it a nuisance to have to use two pairs of glasses: one for distance, another for reading. Many had been similarly bothered. But Benjamin Franklin invented bifocal lenses.

He once remarked that all want to live long but that none want to be old.

One of the advantages of *this* century is the growing recognition not only that senior citizens should not be discarded but that they can be valuable resources.

Certain of Franklin's biographers have marveled at his longevity in the face of the range of his activities and its correlative expenditure of energy. They miss the point. Franklin's life span was achieved not in *spite* of this vivacity, but *because* of it. Active people learn in time that it is the functions of their existence which generate energy.

The battery of an unused automobile that stands in a garage for several weeks will almost invariably run down. The running car charges its battery.

Energy in physics and in nature is generated by action, by movement: a windmill, a waterfall, a dynamo—whatever is the opposite of stagnation...

In many respects, man is a machine. Franklin—the scientist, the philosopher—understood this. He lived by rules, by maxims. He organized his time frugally, meting out the hours with care and consideration...

"Don't waste time," he once said. "That's the stuff life's made of."...

It can be argued that Benjamin Franklin was a phenomenon, a genius,...and that ordinary mortals cannot aspire to the emulation of such a giant. But they can and should. The great men and women are the ones who surpass the standards, who expand human possibility.

Consider what Helen Keller, setting an example, has done for generations of blind or deaf children and their parents; what Franklin Roosevelt did to inspire thousands upon thousands of the handicapped.

Certainly we should all attempt to imitate Franklin—that "harmonious human multitude"—and even dream of besting him. We shall probably fail, but in the attempt, in the struggle, we may produce the energy and create the excitement that make life at any age worth living.

Garson Kanin
It Takes a Long Time to Become Young

...he who began a good work in you will carry it on to completion until the day of Christ Jesus.

Philippians 1:6 (NIV)

Grave was the man in years, in looks, in word,
His locks were gray, yet was his courage green.

Torquato Tasso
"Jerusalem Delivered"

The older I get, the more wisdom I find in the ancient rule of taking first things first—a process which often reduces the most complex human problems to manageable proportions.

Dwight D. Eisenhower
Quoted in *The Reader's Digest*, December 1963

To me, old age is always fifteen years older than I am.

Bernard M. Baruch
(upon observing his 85th birthday, in 1955)

Old age isn't so bad when you consider the alternative.

Maurice Chevalier
Quoted in the *New York Times*, October 9, 1960

If I were running in the stadium, ought I to slacken my pace when approaching the goal? Ought I not rather to put on speed?

Diogenes Laertius
Diogenes

In 1989 Robin Williams starred in a fascinating motion picture titled *Dead Poets Society*. Williams played the role of John Keating, a new literature instructor in a prestigious (i.e., stuffy) northeastern boys academy.

But this teacher was like a pair of neon orange running shoes at a black-tie affair. To him, life was to be lived with creative passion, not lock-step mediocrity. So Keating dedicated himself to helping his students discover and achieve their life's potential.

On the first day of class, the new teacher took his students into the foyer, where the walls were filled with photographs of the classes of boys who had graduated decades before. Like those boys in Keating's class, each of the hundreds of boys in the photographs had once been young and carefree. Each had thought he would live forever. But now they were all gone...deceased...mere memories on the wall of a classroom building.

As Keating's students gaped at one photograph after another of young men who had thought they would live forever, they began to realize that they, too, would someday be gone from this earth, that life was just a brief moment of eternity. Their mouths hung open in wonder as their teacher stood behind them and whispered:

Seize the day...make your lives extraordinary.

...the words burned a place in my memory. Seize the day...make your lives extraordinary.

Much as we would like to think we'll live forever, the truth is that we spend just a few short years on earth. One New Testament writer described human life as "vapor." The psalmist wrote to God, "You speak, and man turns back to dust...We glide along the tides of time as swiftly as a racing river, and vanish as quickly as a dream" (Psalm 90:3, 5-6, TLB).

Take a moment to imagine that you are age ninety, looking back over the years of your life...Do you have any regrets?

Dan Benson
Man Talk

That in my age as cheerful I might be
As the green winter of the Holly Tree.

Robert Southey
"The Holly Tree"

Age...is a matter of feeling, not of years.

George William Curtis
Prue and I

I am at present in such health and such spirits, that when I recollect I am an old woman, I am astonished.

Catherine Clive
The Life of Mrs. Catherine Clive

One is as old as one's heart.

Alfred d'Houdetot
Age

The vanished hours can ne'er come back again,
Still may the old their youthful joys retain;
The past may yet within our memory live,
And courage vigor to the old may give.

Leonora Christina
Memoirs of Leonora Christina

We who are old know that age is more than a disability. It is an intense and varied experience, almost beyond our capacity at times, but something to be carried high. If it is a long defeat it is also a victory, meaningful for the initiates of time, if not for those who have come less far.

Florida Scott-Maxwell
The Measure of My Days

Character contributes to beauty. It fortifies a woman as her youth fades. A mode of conduct, a standard of courage, discipline, fortitude and integrity can do a great deal to make a woman beautiful.

Jacqueline Bisset
Quoted in the *Los Angeles Times*, May 16, 1974

Old age approaches, an awful specter of loneliness to those who have never found joy in being alone.

Dorothy Thompson
The Courage to Be Happy

With age, we become responsible for what's in our heads—the character of the memories there, the music we are familiar with, the storehouse of books we have read, the people whom we can call, the scenery we know and love. Our memories become our dreams.

Edward Hoagland
Quoted in *Harper's*, January 1991

We do not necessarily improve with age: for better or worse we become more like ourselves.

Peter Hall
Quoted in *The Observer*, January 24, 1988

To have lived long does not necessarily imply the gathering of much wisdom and experience. A man who has pedaled twenty-five thousand miles on a stationary bicycle has not circled the globe. He has only garnered weariness.

Paul Eldridge
Horns of Glass

Teach us to number our days aright, that we may gain a heart of wisdom.

Psalm 90:12 (NIV)

...my lot is not at all such a dark one. I have lived as my convictions have prompted me; I could not do otherwise; therefore I await what is in store for me with a clear conscience.

Sofia Perovskaya
Letter to her mother

Old age takes away from us what we have inherited and gives us what we have earned.

Gerald Brenan
Thoughts in a Dry Season

If you want to be a dear old lady at seventy, you should start early, say about seventeen.

Maude Royden

He that would pass the latter part of life with honour and decency, must, when he is young, consider that he shall one day be old; and remember, when he is old, that he has once been young.

Samuel Johnson
Rambler No. 50

You are old, Father William, the young man cried,
The few locks which are left you are gray;
You are hale, Father William, a hearty old man,
Now tell me the reason, I pray.
In the days of my youth, Father William replied,
I remember'd that youth would fly fast,
And abused not my health and my vigour at first,
That I never might need them at last.

Robert Southey
The Old Man's Comforts

I don't believe one grows older. I think that what happens early on in life is that at a certain age one stands still and stagnates.

T. S. Eliot
Quoted in the *New York Times*, September 21, 1958

They used to say that a woman is as old as she looks and a man is as old as he feels. I believe that a person is as old as his habits.

Gelett Burgess
Look Eleven Years Younger

Inside me is a scared teenager, a proud college graduate, a thrilled young bride, and an exhausted mother of an infant. Inside me too are the roles I still have—daughter, mother, sister, wife, writer. And now joining this club there is "Grandma," and writer about aging, and student of new aches and pains, and keeper of the flame of memory for those many I have loved and who have now died.

The shock of changing roles isn't so overwhelming if we keep careful track of all the other roles. When I hear "Grandma" I know that little girl can never see me as a little girl or a young woman, but *I* can remember. "Grandma" becomes everything I have ever been, with a new addition—a terrific role to be savored fully.

Eda LeShan
It's Better to Be Over the Hill Than Under It

You end up as you deserve. In old age, you must put up with the face, the friends, the health and the children you have earned.

Fay Weldon
Praxis

I [Socrates] replied: There is nothing which for my part I like better, Cephalus, than conversing with aged men; for I regard them as travellers who have gone a journey which I too may have to go, and of whom I ought to enquire, whether the way is smooth and easy, or rugged and difficult. And this is a question which I should like to ask of you who have arrived at that time which the poets call the "threshold of old age"—Is life harder towards the end, or what report do you give of it?

I will tell you, Socrates, he said, what my own feeling is. Men of my age flock together; we are birds of a feather, as the old proverb says; and at our meetings the tale of my acquaintance commonly is—I cannot eat, I cannot drink; the pleasures of youth and love are fled away: there was a good time once, but now that is gone, and life is no longer life. Some complain of the slights which are put upon them by relations and they will tell you sadly of how many evils their old age is the cause. But to me, Socrates, these complainers seem to blame that which is not really in fault. For if old age were the cause, I too being old, and every other old man, would have felt as they do. But this is not my own experience, nor that of others whom I have known. How well I remember the aged poet Sophocles, when in answer to the question, How does love suit with age, Sophocles—are you still the man you were? Peace, he replied: most gladly have I escaped the thing of which you speak; I feel as if I had escaped from a mad and furious master. His words have often occurred to my mind since, and they seem as good to me now as at the time when he uttered them. For certainly old age has a great sense of calm and freedom; when the passions relax their hold, then, as Sophocles says, we are freed from the grasp not of one mad master only, but of many. The truth is, Socrates, that these regrets, and also the complaints about relations, are to be attributed to the same cause, which is not old age, but men's characters and tempers; for he who is of a calm and happy nature will hardly feel the pressure of age, but to him who is of an opposite disposition youth and age are equally a burden.

Plato
Republic

Gray hair is a crown of splendor; it is attained by a righteous life.

Proverbs 16:31 (NIV)

The course of my long life hath reached at last,
In fragile bark o'er a tempestuous sea,
The common harbor, where must rendered be,
Account of all the actions of the past.

Henry Wadsworth Longfellow
"Old Age"

Old age is the verdict of life.

Amelia Barr
All the Days of My Life

The true way to render age vigorous is to prolong the youth of the mind.

Mortimer Collins
The Village Comedy

Youth is the time for the adventures of the body, but age for the triumphs of the mind.

Logan Pearsall Smith
On Reading Shakespeare

The essence of age is intellect.

Ralph Waldo Emerson
Society and Solitude: Old Age

To be interested in the changing seasons is, in this middling zone, a happier state of mind than to be hopelessly in love with spring.

George Santayana
Little Essays

The sentimentalist ages far more quickly than the person who loves his work and enjoys new challenges.

Lily Langtry
Quoted in the *New York Sun*, 1906

It is always in season for the old to learn.

Æschylus
Fragments

If you rest, you rust.

Helen Hayes
Quoted in the *Washington Post*, May 7, 1990

The brain is the organ of longevity.

George Alban Sacher
Perspectives in Experimental Gerontology

Never too late to learn.

proverb

Better is a poor and a wise child than an old and foolish king, who will no more be admonished.

Ecclesiastes 4:13

But I grow old ever learning many things.

Solon
Quoted in Plutarch's *Lives*

It is too late! Ah, nothing is too late
Till the tired heart shall cease to palpitate.
Cato learned Greek at eighty; Sophocles
Wrote his grand Œdipus, and Simonides
Bore off the prize of verse from his compeers,
When each had numbered more than four-score years,...
Chaucer, at Woodstock with the nightingales,
At sixty wrote the Canterbury Tales;
Goethe at Weimar, toiling to the last,
Completed Faust when eighty years were past.
These are indeed exceptions; but they show
How far the gulf-stream of our youth may flow
Into the arctic regions of our lives...
For age is opportunity no less
Than youth itself, though in another dress,
And as the evening twilight fades away
The sky is filled with stars, invisible by day.

Henry Wadsworth Longfellow
"Morituri Salutamus"

I promise to keep on living as though I expected to live forever. Nobody grows old by merely living a number of years. People grow old only by deserting their ideals. Years may wrinkle the skin, but to give up interest wrinkles the soul.

General Douglas MacArthur
Address at the dedication of the MacArthur Monument,
Los Angeles, January 26, 1955

Nor can the snow, which now cold Age does shed
Upon thy reverend head,
Quench or allay the noble fires within.

Abraham Cowley
"To Mr. Hobs"

The fact is that old age is respectable just as long as it asserts itself, maintains its proper rights, and is not enslaved to any one. For as I admire a young man who has something of the old man in him, so do I an old one who has something of a young man. The man who aims at this may possibly become old in body—in mind he never will.

Marcus Tullius Cicero
Old Age

Call him not old whose visionary brain
Holds o'er the past its undivided reign.
For him in vain the envious seasons roll
Who bears eternal summer in his soul.

Oliver Wendell Holmes
"The Old Player"

I am still learning.

Michelangelo
His motto

You know, by the time you reach my age, you've made plenty of mistakes if you've lived your life properly.

Ronald Reagan
Quoted in *The Observer*, March 8, 1987

The great affairs of life are not performed by physical strength, or activity, or nimbleness of body, but by deliberation, character, expression of opinion. Of these old age is not only not deprived, but, as a rule, has them in a greater degree.

Marcus Tullius Cicero
Old Age

Old places and old persons in their turn, when spirit dwells in them, have an intrinsic vitality of which youth is incapable; precisely the balance and wisdom that comes from long perspectives and broad foundations.

George Santayana
My Host the World

A man bowed with age, and wise with untold wisdom.

Homer
Odyssey

The latter part of a wise man's life is taken up in curing the follies, prejudices, and false opinions he had contracted in the former.

Jonathan Swift
Thoughts on Various Subjects

Miss not the discourse of the elders.

Apocrypha: Ecclesiasticus 8:9

"Age ain't nothin' but a number." But age is other things, too. It is wisdom, if one has lived one's life properly. It is experience and knowledge. And it is getting to know all the ways the world turns, so that if you cannot turn the world the way you want, you can at least get out of the way so you won't get run over.

Miriam Makeba
Makeba: My Story

In youth we learn; in age we understand.

> Marie von Ebner Eschenbach
> *The Two Countesses*

Rashness is a quality of the budding-time of youth, prudence of the harvest-time of old age.

> Marcus Tullius Cicero
> *De Senectute*

As you are old and reverend, you should be wise.

> William Shakespeare
> *King Lear*

Then welcome Age and fear not sorrow;
. Today's no better than tomorrow...
I know we grow more lovely
Growing wise.

> Alice Corbin
> "Two Voices"

With the ancient is wisdom; and in length of days understanding.

> Job 12:12

It is sobering to consider that when Mozart was my age he had already been dead for a year.

> Tom Lehrer
> Quoted in *An Encyclopedia of Quotations about Music*

A man that is young in years may be old in hours, if he have lost no time.

> Francis Bacon
> *Essays of Youth and Age*

The man who views the world at 50 the same as he did at 20 has wasted 30 years of his life.

> Muhammad Ali

Father Time is not always a hard parent, and, though he tarried for none of his children, often lays his hand lightly on those who have used him well.

Charles Dickens
Barnaby Rudge

This I know without being told,
'Tis time to live as I grow old.
'Tis time short pleasures now to take,
Of little Life the best to make,
And manage wisely the last stake.

Abraham Cowley
"Age"

What's a man's age? He must hurry more, that's all;
Cram in a day what his youth took a year to hold.

Robert Browning
"The Flight of the Duchess"

One wastes so much time, one is so prodigal of life, at twenty! Our days of winter count for double. That is the compensation of the old.

George Sand
Correspondence

For the past eighty years I have started each day in the same manner. It is not a mechanical routine but something essential to my daily life. I go to the piano, and I play two preludes and fugues of Bach. I cannot think of doing otherwise. It is a sort of benediction on the house. But that is not its only meaning for me. It is a rediscovery of the world which I have the joy of being a part. It fills me with awareness of the wonder of life, with a feeling of the incredible marvel of being a human being. The music is never the same for me, never. Each day it is something new, fantastic and unbelievable.

Pablo Casals

Whenever I feel myself inferior to everything about me, threatened by my own mediocrity, frightened by the discovery that a muscle is losing its strength, a desire its power, or a pin the keen edge of its bite, I can still hold up my head and say to myself:…"Let me not forget that I am the daughter of a woman who bent her head, trembling, between the blades of a cactus, her wrinkled face full of ecstasy over the promise of a flower, a woman who herself never ceased to flower, untiringly, during three quarters of a century."

Sidonie-Gabrielle Colette
Break of Day

Laura was blooming still, had made the best
Of time, and time return'd the compliment.

George Gordon, Lord Byron
"Beppo"

The dear old ladies whose cheeks are pink
In spite of the years of winter's chill,
Are like the Autumn leaves, I think,
A little crumpled, but lovely still.

Jane Screven Heyward
"Autumn Leaves"

As a white candle in a holy place,
So is the beauty of an aged face.

Joseph Campbell
"The Old Woman"

To me, fair friend, you never can be old,
For as you were when first your eye I eyed,
Such seems your beauty still.

William Shakespeare
"Sonnet 104"

I shall grow old, but never lose life's zest,
Because the road's last turn will be the best.

Henry van Dyke
"The Zest of Life"

Life is most delightful when it is on the downward slope...Let us cherish and love old age; for it is full of pleasure, if one knows how to use it...The best morsel is reserved to the last.

Lucius Annaeus Seneca
Epistulae ad Lucilium

You know you're getting older when...
- you just can't stand people who are intolerant.
- you burn the midnight oil until 9 p.m.
- your pacemaker raises the garage door when you see a pretty girl go by.
- the little gray-haired lady you help across the street is your wife.
- you have too much room in the house and not enough in the medicine closet.
- dialing long distance wears you out.

anonymous

Youth, large, lusty, loving—youth full of grace, force, fascination,
    Do you know that Old Age may come after you with equal grace, force, fascination?

Walt Whitman
Youth, Day, Old Age and Night

Grow old along with me!
The best is yet to be,
The last of life, for which the first was made:
Our times are in his hand
Who saith, "A whole I planned,
youth shows but half; trust God: see all,
Nor be afraid!"

Robert Browning
"Rabbi Ben Ezra"

He had become enveloped in the Indian Summer of the soul.

O. Henry
The Indian Summer of Dry Valley Johnson

What I wish for myself and for all of us is to feel until the very end of life that each day is a gift of time and possibility, and to fill each day with less self-criticism and more self-knowledge, fewer grievances about age and more gratitude for life, more time and the wisdom to enjoy it.

Letty Cottin Pegrebin
Getting Over Getting Older

Nobody loves life like an old man.

Sophocles
Acrisius

...his eye was not dim, nor his natural force abated.

Deuteronomy 34:7

Spring still makes spring in the mind
When sixty years are told;
Love makes anew this throbbing heart,
And we are never old.
Over the winter glaciers
I see the summer glow,
And through the wild-piled snowdrift,
The warm rosebuds below.

Ralph Waldo Emerson
"The World-Soul"

There's many a good tune played on an old fiddle.

proverb

Of earthly blessing age is not the least,
Serene its twilight sky, the journey past;
Like that rare draught at Cana's marriage feast,
Life's best wine is the last.

Frances E. Pope
"The End of the Road"

More are men's ends mark'd than their lives before:
The setting sun, and music at the close,
As the last taste of sweets, is sweetest last,
Writ in remembrance more than things long past.

William Shakespeare
Richard II

When you have loved as she has loved you grow old beautifully.

W. Somerset Maugham
The Circle

Though summer goes, remember
The harvest fields;
The color-work of autumn
And what it yields.

Frederick Herbert Adler
"To One Who Fears Old Age"

No Spring nor Summer Beauty hath such grace
As I have seen in one Autumnal face.

John Donne
"Elegies"

I think of age as a great universalizing force. It's the only thing we all have in common. It doesn't begin when you collect your social security benefits. Aging begins with the moment of birth, and it ends only when life itself has ended. Life is a continuum; only we—in our stupidity and blindness—have chopped it up into little pieces and kept all those little pieces separate.

Maggie Kuhn

What the retired need...isn't 'leisure,' it's occupation...Two weeks is about the ideal length of time to retire.

Alex Comfort
A Good Age

I have an understandable reluctance to pay much attention to the passage of time, and a certain animosity toward those who assume that if one is in his seventies he must have been a high school buddy of Abraham Lincoln.

Fred de Cordova
Johnny Came Lately

It is charming to totter into vogue.

Horace Walpole
Letter to G. A. Selwyn, 1765

There is a wicked inclination in most people to suppose an old man decayed in his intellects. If a young or middle-aged man, when leaving a company, does not recollect where he laid his hat, it is nothing; but if the same inattention is discovered in an old man, people will shrug up their shoulders, and say, 'His memory is going.'

Samuel Johnson
Quoted in *The Life of Samuel Johnson*

When somebody says to me—which they do like every five years—"How does it feel to be over the hill," my response is, "I'm just heading up the mountain."

Joan Baez
Quoted in *Rolling Stone,* 1983

Being seventy is not a sin.

Golda Meir
Quoted in *Reader's Digest,* July 1971

What we must build in this country—among all our people—is a new attitude toward old age; an attitude which insists that there can be no retirement from living, no retirement from responsibility, and no retirement from citizenship.

Richard M. Nixon
June 25, 1971

Which of you is going to step up and put me out to pasture?

John Wayne
(to Congressional Committee on Aging, 1977)

A medical revolution has extended the life of our elder citizens without providing the dignity and security those later years deserve.

John F. Kennedy
Acceptance speech, Democratic National Convention,
Los Angeles, July 15, 1960

Life is precious to the old person. He is not interested merely in thoughts of yesterday's good life and tomorrow's path to the grave. He does not want his later years to be a sentence of solitary confinement in society. Nor does he want them to be a death watch.

Dr. David Allman
Speech, "The Brotherhood of Healing," National Conference
of Christians and Jews, February 12, 1958

I live a day at a time. Each day I look for a kernel of excitement. In the morning, I say: "What is my exciting thing for today?" Then, I do the day. Don't ask me about tomorrow.

Barbara Jordan
Quoted in *Parade*, February 16, 1986

Get up at five, have lunch at nine,
Supper at five, retire at nine.
And you will live to ninety-nine.

anonymous

Avoid fried meats which angry up the blood. If your stomach disputes you, lie down and pacify it with cool thoughts. Keep the juices flowing by jangling around gently as you move. Go very light on the vices, such as carrying on in society. The social ramble ain't restful. Avoid running at all times. Don't look back. Someone might be gaining on you.

Leroy (Satchel) Paige
Quoted in *Collier's*, June 13, 1953

Pick the right grandparents, don't eat or drink too much, be circumspect in all things, and take a two-mile walk every morning before breakfast.

Harry S. Truman
Prescription for reaching the age of 80,
May 8, 1964

It don't do
to wake up
quick...

Marie Evans
"The Alarm Clock"

Keep breathing.

Sophie Tucker
Anniversary Speech, January 13, 1964

People who fear they're going to die young because they're sick so much should take a look at Mabel Taylor's health record. She has survived three separate bouts of cancer: a radical mastectomy at 25, thyroidectomy at 35, and removal of a 7-inch section of colon at 94. She had a compound ankle fracture at 80 that would not bind until a metal screw was inserted. She once had rheumatism so bad that she couldn't comb her own hair.

Genetics has not done her any favors either: neither of her parents lived to be old. What's more, her tendency toward illnesses goes back to early childhood. She had such a serious case of quinsy as a little girl that she was taken out of school for 13 weeks and cured only after her mother wrapped a sock soaked in turpentine and lard around her neck. Her chronic sore throats continued into adulthood and once threatened to become rheumatic fever.

"I was sickly in my younger days. I wasn't strong, but I always had to work."

It's not surprising that, when asked how she got so old, Mabel Taylor says, "I don't know. My prayers are mostly prayers of thanksgiving."

Jim Heynen
One Hundred Over 100
(written when Mabel Taylor was 106 years old)

Old age and sickness bring out the essential characteristics of a man.

Felix Frankfurter
Felix Frankfurter Reminisces

For my eightieth year warns me to pack up my baggage before I leave life.

Marcus Terentius Varro
De Re Rustica

The riders in a race do not stop short when they reach the goal. There is a little finishing canter before coming to a standstill. There is time to hear the kind voice of friends and to say to one's self: "The work is done."

Oliver Wendell Holmes
Radio address on his 90th birthday,
March 8, 1931

I stand upon the summit of my years;
Behind, the toil, the camp, the march, the strife,
The wandering and the desert; vast, afar,
Beyond this weary way, behold! the Sea!

Joseph Brownlee Brown
"Thalatta! Thalatta!"

So mays't thou live till, like ripe fruit, thou drop
Into thy mother's lap, or be with ease
Gather'd, not harshly pluck'd, for death mature:
This is old age.

John Milton
Paradise Lost

But an old age serene and bright,
And lovely as a Lapland night,
Shall lead thee to thy grave.

William Wordsworth
"To a Young Lady"

The robe of flesh wears thin, and with the years God shines through all things.

John Buchan
The Wise Years

Youth having passed, there is nothing to lose but memory. Cherishing the past without regrets and viewing the future without misgiving, we wait, then, for the nightfall when one may rest and call it a life.

George E. Macdonald
Fifty Years of Free-Thought

And not by eastern windows only,
When daylight comes, comes in the light;
In front, the sun climbs slow, how slowly,
But westward, look, the land is bright.

Arthur Hugh Clough
"Say Not the Struggle Nought Availeth"

So we saunter toward the Holy Land, till one day the sun shall shine more brightly than ever he has done, shall perchance shine into our minds and hearts, and light up our whole lives with a great awakening light, as warm and serene and golden as on a bank-side in autumn.

Henry David Thoreau
Thoreau on Man and Nature

...the time has come for my departure. I have fought the good fight, I have finished the race, I have kept the faith. Now there is in store for me the crown of righteousness, which the Lord, the righteous Judge, will award to me on that day—and not only to me, but also to all who have longed for his appearing.

2 Timothy 4:6-8 (NIV)

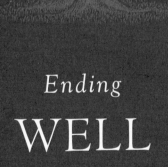

Ending

WELL

CHAPTER FIFTEEN

ENDING WELL

All mankind is of one author, and is one volume; when one man dies, one chapter is not torn out of the book, but translated into a better language; and every chapter must be so translated; God employs several translators; some pieces are translated by age, some by sickness, some by war, some by justice; but God's hand is in every translation, and his hand shall bind up all our scattered leaves again for that library where every book shall lie open to one another.

John Donne
Devotions

Mozart died at thirty-six. Raphael at practically the same age. Byron was only a little older. But each of them had accomplished his mission perfectly, and it was time for them to go so that others might still have something left to do in a world created to last a long while.

Johann Wolfgang von Goethe
Conversations with Eckermann

Death is sometimes a punishment, sometimes a gift, to many it has come as a favor.

Lucius Annaeus Seneca
Hercules Oetaeus

The great Mrs. Churchill was no more...Goldsmith tells us that when lovely woman stoops to folly, she has nothing to do but die; and when she stoops to be disagreeable, it is equally to be recommended as a clearer of ill fame. Mrs. Churchill, after being disliked at least twenty-five years, was now spoken of with compassionate allowances.

Jane Austen
Emma

To live in hearts we leave
Is not to die.

Thomas Campbell
"Hallowed Ground"

Death, kind Nature's signal of retreat.

Samuel Johnson
The Vanity of Human Wishes

It is a thing that every one suffers, even persons of the lowest resolution, of the meanest virtue, of no breeding, of no discourse. Take away but the pomps of death, the disguises and solemn bugbears, the tinsel, and the actings by candle-light, and proper and fantastic ceremonies, the minstrels and the noise-makers, the women and the weepers, the swoonings and the shriekings, the nurses and the physicians, the dark room and the ministers, the kindred and the watchers; and then to die is easy, ready and quitted from its troublesome circumstances. It is the same harmless thing that a poor shepherd suffered yesterday, or a maid-servant today; and at the same time in which you die, in that very night a thousand creatures die with you, some wise men, and many fools; and the wisdom of the first will not quit him, and the folly of the latter does not make him unable to die.

Of all the evils of the world which are reproached with an evil character, death is the most innocent of its accusation. For when it is present, it hurts nobody; and when it is absent, it is indeed troublesome, but the trouble is owning to our fears, not the affrighting and mistaken object: and besides this, if it were an evil, it is so transient, that it passes like the instant or undiscerned portion of the present time; and either it is past, or it is not yet; for just when it is, no man hath reason to complain of so insensible, so sudden, so undiscerned a change.

Jeremy Taylor
Holy Dying

As the door of life, by the gate of breath,
There are worse things waiting for men than death.

Algernon Charles Swinburne
The Triumph of Time

Death, like life, is an affair of being more frightened than hurt.

Samuel Butler
Erewhon

Behold, I shew you a mystery; We shall not all sleep; but we shall all be changed, In a moment, in the twinkling of an eye, at the last trump: for the trumpet shall sound, and the dead shall be raised incorruptible, and we shall be changed. For this corruptible must put on incorruption, and this mortal must put on immortality. So when this corruptible shall have put on incorruption, and this mortal shall have put on immortality, then shall be brought to pass the saying that is written, Death is swallowed up in victory. O death, where is thy sting? O grave, where is thy victory? The sting of death is sin; and the strength of sin is the law. But thanks be to God, which giveth us the victory through our Lord Jesus Christ. Therefore, my beloved brethren, be ye steadfast, unmoveable, always abounding in the work of the Lord, forasmuch as ye know that your labour is not in vain in the Lord.

1 Corinthians 15:51-58

Our last garment is made without pockets.

Italian proverb

The Bible tells us, and tells us clearly, that by the death of Jesus Christ on a cross, death itself has been conquered, its bitter sting has been removed, and in a day yet to be, it will be destroyed.

Joseph Bayly

They rest from their labours.

> Burial of the Dead
> *The Book of Common Prayer*

Sunset and evening star,
And one clear call for me!
And may there be no moaning of the bar.
When I put out to sea.

> Alfred, Lord Tennyson
> "Crossing the Bar"

Death is a camel that lies down at every door.

> Persian proverb

His time was come; he ran his race;
We hope he's in a better place.

> Jonathan Swift
> *On the Death of Dr. Swift*

Neither the sun nor death can be looked at steadily.

> François de La Rochefoucauld
> *Maximes*

Cowards die many times before their deaths;
The valiant never taste of death but once.
Of all the wonders that I yet have heard,
It seems to me most strange that men should fear,
Seeing that death, a necessary end,
Will come when it will come.

> William Shakespeare
> *Julius Caesar*

It is as natural to die as to be born.

> Francis Bacon
> *Essays*

The soldier is convinced that a certain interval of time, capable of being indefinitely prolonged, will be allowed him before the bullet finds him, the thief before he is taken, men in general before they have to die.

Marcel Proust
Remembrance of Things Past

The sense of death is most in apprehension,
And the poor beetle that we tread upon,
In corporal sufferance finds a pang as great
As when a giant dies.

William Shakespeare
Measure for Measure

Death takes away the commonplace of life.

Alexander Smith
Dreamthorp

Death is like a fisherman who catches fish in his net and leaves them for a while in the water; the fish is still swimming but the net is around him, and the fisherman will draw him up—when he thinks fit.

Ivan Turgenev
On the Eve

Christ has changed death. Although death is an enemy, "The last enemy that will be abolished" (1 Corinthians 15:26), it is also a friend. To the Corinthians Paul said, "Therefore, being always of good courage, and knowing that while we are at home in the body we are absent from the Lord—for we walk by faith, not by sight—we are of good courage, I say, and prefer rather to be absent from the body and to be at home with the Lord" (2 Corinthians 5:6-8). The same thought was expressed in his letter to the Philippians: "But I am hard-pressed from both directions, having the desire to depart and be with Christ, for that is very much better" (Philippians 1:23).

Death for the believer is no longer just death. It is sleep. When we die, we fall asleep in Jesus, laying aside this house of clay for a little while. Death means going to be with Jesus—which is far better. Like sleep, death for us is temporary and has its awakening.

Christ controls death. "I have the keys of death and Hades." Think of it. The devil doesn't have the keys to his own house! The keys are a symbol of authority, of control, of possession and government. As terrible as it is, death is not allowed to run rampant without control. Nothing happens by chance. All history lies in the elective purpose of God. Even death is in the hands of God. It moves only at the permissive will of heaven.

Christ holds the key to the door of death, and no man enters it unless Christ uses the key and opens it.

Christ conquered death. "I was dead, and behold, I am alive forevermore." Death for the Christian isn't permanent or final. Death will not hold our bodies forever. Christ died and survived the grave and because He lives we shall live also. Christ shares His victory with us.

Ron Dunn
Will God Heal Me?

All men think all men mortal but themselves.

Edward Young
Night Thoughts

I have asked for death. Begged for it. Prayed for it. Then the worst thing can't be death.

Archibald MacLeish
JB

As men, we are all equal in the presence of death.

Publilius Syrus
Moral Sayings

God is favorable to those whom he makes to die by degrees; 'tis the only benefit of old age. The last death will be so much the less painful: it will kill but a quarter of a man or but half a one at most.

Michel Eyquem de Montaigne
Essays

What man is he that liveth, and shall not see death? Shall he deliver his soul from the hand of the grave?

Psalm 89:48

God himself took a day to rest in, and a good man's grave is his Sabbath.

John Donne
Sermons

The body of Benjamin Franklin, Printer,
like the covering of an old book, its contents
torn out and stripped of its lettering and gilding,
lies here, food for worms;
But the work shall not be lost,
it will (as he believed) appear once more,
in a new and more elegant edition,
revised, and corrected by the Author.

Benjamin Franklin's epitaph

Precious in the sight of the Lord is the death of his saints.

Psalm 116:15

I believe that there are certain doors that only illness can open. There is a certain state of health that does not allow us to understand everything; and perhaps illness shuts us off from certain truths; but health shuts us off just as effectively from others, or turns us away from them so that we are not concerned with them.

André Gide
The Journals of André Gide

Do not seek death. Death will find you. But seek the road which makes death a fulfillment.

Dag Hammarskjöld
Markings

And knowing that his existence here is limited, a man's workings have reference to others rather than to himself, and thereby into his nature comes a new influx of nobility. If a man plants a tree, he knows that other hands than his will gather the fruit; and when he plants it, he thinks quite as much of those other hands as of his own. Thus to the poet there is the dearer life after life; and posterity's single laurel leaf is valued more than a multitude of contemporary bays. Even the man immersed in money-making does not make money so much for himself as for those who may come after him.

Alexander Smith
Dreamthorp

There is only one way to be prepared for death: to be sated. In the soul, in the heart, in the spirit…To the brim.

Henry de Montherlant
"Explicit Mysterium"

But in the visions of the night of the 18th…I saw with my spiritual eyes, a hand who plainly pointed out to me and said, "Desire not to live a few years; for it won't be granted to thee; but thee may be spared a little time longer; so thee may try to be in readiness against…thy appointed time to die." Ever since the above night, I have set my whole heart to study how to get in readiness and to strive to have my past sinful life pardoned so I may be at peace with my maker before I die and go hence and am seen of man no more in this world of trouble.

Samuel Cole David
"Diary"

O they tell me of a King in His beauty there,
And they tell me that mine eyes shall behold,
Where He sits on the throne that is whiter than snow,
In the city that is made of gold.

O the land of cloudless day,
O the land of an unclouded day;
O they tell me of a home where no storm clouds rise,
O they tell me of an unclouded day.

Reverend J. K. Alwood
"The Unclouded Day"

Thou shalt come to thy grave in a full age, like as a shock of corn cometh in his season.

Job 5:26

Here was a man who now for the first time found himself looking into the eyes of death—who was passing through one of those rare moments of experience when we feel the truth of a commonplace, which is as different from what we call knowing it, as the vision of waters upon the earth is different from the delirious vision of the water which cannot be had to cool the burning tongue. When the commonplace 'We must all die' transforms itself suddenly into the acute consciousness 'I must die—and soon', then death grapples us, and his fingers are cruel; afterwards, he may come to fold us in his arms as our mother did, and our last moment of dim earthly discerning may be like the first.

George Eliot
Middlemarch

Live while you live, then die and be done with it.

John Gunther
Quoted in *Death Be Not Proud*

Sickness is the mother of modesty, putteth us in mind of our mortality; and when we are in the full career of worldy pomp and jollity, she pulleth us by the ear, and maketh us know ourselves.

Robert Burton
The Anatomy of Death

And they came to a place which was named Gethsemane: and he saith to his disciples, Sit ye here, while I shall pray. And he taketh with him Peter and James and John, and he began to be sore amazed, and to be very heavy; And saith unto them, My soul is exceeding sorrowful unto death: tarry ye here, and watch.

Mark 14:34

If you are a parent, perhaps the most wrenching aspect of your dying is leaving behind your younger child or children—your toddler, elementary-schooler, or teen. Someone else will rear them to adulthood, not you. How can you explain that to them? Since their birth, you have protected them from all harm. How can you protect them from your absence?…

When your child knows you're seriously ill, and your illness begins to affect your daily life, reassure him that it's not his fault. Sometimes a child believes a parent got sick because he got mad at her and even wishes she'd die. He needs to understand that his thoughts can't cause things to happen.

Also, if you have been fighting with your spouse, or are separated or divorced, let your child know the estranged spouse is not to blame. He'll be needing that parent even more in the future.

Most important, you want to ensure that your child will have a stable environment, that someone will be caring for him when you're gone. Assure him of this, and see that he spends plenty of time with that person and in the place where he'll be (for example, an ex-spouse's home). In this way, you help smooth the transition.

It's a lot to ask, I know. You're going through your own personal agonies—physical, mental, emotional, perhaps spiritual. But it's an act of love, and love is a marvelous painkiller.

Patricia Weenolsen, Ph.D.
The Art of Dying

Death has to be waiting at the end of the ride before you truly see the earth, and feel your heart, and love the world.

Jean Anouilh
The Lark

Since I am coming to that holy room,
Where, with thy quire of Saints for evermore,
I shall be made thy music; as I come
I tune the Instrument here at the door,
And what I must do then, think here before.

John Donne
"Hymn to God my God, in my Sickness"

And being found in fashion as a man, he humbled himself, and became obedient unto death, even the death of the cross.

Philippians 2:8

Mythologizing is no surprise, of course, except that it begins immediately, from the moment I walk up to the hospital's front desk, ready to hear she has a broken this or that, and hear instead, in tones of reassurance, that she still has a pulse. I am not allowed to see her because her spleen needs to be sewn back together, and her left leg is broken, and her left lung is punctured and collapsed, all of which are "small potatoes" next to the head injury.

I sit down on the plastic chair against the wall.

Okay, I'll just wait here; I'll be over here. But while I'm waiting could you tell me, please, what did she look like when I just saw her, less than an hour ago, when she said good-bye and left for work? And what did we do yesterday, minute by minute? And how will I dare to tell her this story: "I already felt myself beginning to forget your face, if you can believe that."...

Then I am brought to a wall phone to make the calls; her mother, her sister, Conna, my own mother way down south. "She's been...it doesn't look..." They fracture like actresses. She, the fact of her, has become, as though by practiced shift, a huge and cloudy notion, a sudden, aggressive brainteaser in too many pieces.

I am still on the phone when they wheel her down the hall past me. She is going to the next ambulance and forty miles away to Burlington, where the head wound can best be treated. She has been stabilized and given seven pints of blood, so I've learned.

This is the last time I will ever see her. She comes out of foggy storyland and then—zip—goes back into storyland, wheeled off through doors that fly automatically open. But for ten or fifteen seconds, here she is, visiting in the air by me, though not pausing. Yes, I could drop the phone and run over, close the distance of perhaps eight feet, make them stop the gurney while I touch her and say words to her, that whole routine. But I'm just looking, thank you. Her face is round and pale, head wound hidden on the other side, eyes closed, hair just as we left it. Somehow, somehow, I can relax. She is so much smaller and cleaner and simpler and...fresher than her implications. I take refuge in how she's really no more difficult to understand than a hurt squirrel lying there. And it's pure oxygen to have to think, only, Aw, the poor little thing.

Christopher Noël
In the Unlikely Event of a Water Landing

Let us endeavour so to live that when we come to die even the undertaker will be sorry.

Mark Twain
Pudd'nhead Wilson's Calendar

For this God is our God for ever and ever: he will be our guide even unto death.

Psalm 48:14

One phenomenon in terminal illness that can cause hurt and misunderstanding is the seeming *withdrawal* of the patient from loved ones. There appears to be a touch-me-not attitude or an invisible wall that cannot or will not be discussed by the ill person. This withdrawing is often misinterpreted as rejection.

Realize that withdrawal is a form of introspection and/or pre-death grieving. Accept the fact that a person who is terminally ill *must* go through this period in order to find the answers to his or her conditions of mind, body and spirit, and you will find that after withdrawal passes, he/she will be better able to cope with the everyday process of living until the end.

It seems cruel and mysterious that a loved one would withdraw from you when your time together is most precious, but think of it as a period when he or she is packing for a journey and needs time to gather up the loose ends of life. Your understanding, assurance, and constancy will make it easier for him or her to pass through this phase of illness. Your misunderstanding of this withdrawal will add to the guilts and frustrations of the process and can ultimately prolong the distance between you. Be patient. Accept.

Norma S. Upson
When Someone You Love Is Dying

Have you come to the Red Sea place in your life
Where, in spite of all you can do,
There is no way out, there is no way back,
There is no other way but through?

Annie Johnson Flint
"At the Place of the Sea"

The LORD is my shepherd; I shall not want. He maketh me to lie down in green pastures: he leadeth me beside the still waters. He restoreth my soul: he leadeth me in the paths of righteousness for his name's sake. Yea, though I walk through the valley of the shadow of death, I will fear no evil: for thou art with me; thy rod and thy staff they comfort me. Thou preparest a table before me in the presence of mine enemies: thou anointest my head with oil; my cup runneth over. Surely goodness and mercy shall follow me all the days of my life: and I will dwell in the house of the LORD for ever.

Psalm 23:4

Any man's death diminishes me, because I am involved in mankind; and there-fore never send to know for whom the bell tolls; it tolls for thee.

John Donne
Devotions

Too often, in the presence of a dying person, the approach of death is never men-tioned. Conversation is sanitized and the end itself, whatever it is the end of, is treated as some awful obscenity. Even friends who knew that Karyl was totally aware of her condition, filled their conversation with such empty platitudes as, "You're looking better," or "You'll lick this thing yet." They did not seem to real-ize that, having accepted her death and owned it, she did not want or need to be dragged back to life with empty promises. She was ready for the next adventure, the next stage in her journey. That is what she wanted to talk about and to dwell on.

Herbert and Kay Kramer
Conversations at Midnight

The years seem to rush by now, and I think of death as a fast-approaching end of a journey—double and treble reason for loving as well as working while it is day.

George Eliot
*George Eliot's Life as Related
in Her Letters and Journals*

Softly and tenderly Jesus is calling,
Calling for you and for me;
See, on the portals He's waiting and watching,
Watching for you and for me.
Come home, come home,
Ye who are weary, come home;
Softly and tenderly, Jesus is calling,
Calling, O sinner, come Home!

Will L. Thompson
"Softly and Tenderly"

The letters were swimming before Steavens's eyes. Was it possible that these men did not understand, that the palm on the coffin meant nothing to them? The very name of their town would have remained for ever buried in the postal guide had it not been now and again mentioned in the world in connection with Harvey Merrick's. He remembered what his master had said to him on the day of his death, after the congestion of both lungs had shut off any probability of recovery, and the sculptor had asked his pupil to send his body home. "It's not a pleasant place to be lying while the world is moving and doing and bettering," he had said with a feeble smile, "but it rather seems as though we ought to go back to the place we came from, in the end. The townspeople will come in for a look at me; and after they have had their say, I shan't have much to fear from the judgment of God!"

Willa S. Cather
The Sculptor's Funeral

And there at Venice gave
His body to that pleasant country's earth,
And his pure soul into his captain Christ,
Under whose colours he had fought so long.

William Shakespeare
Richard II

God's finger touched him, and he slept.

Alfred, Lord Tennyson
"In Memoriam"

As the last bell struck, a peculiar sweet smile shone over his face, and he lifted up his head a little, and quickly said, "Adsum!" and fell back. It was the word we used at school, when names were called; and lo, he, whose heart was as that of a little child, had answered to his name, and stood in the presence of The Master.

William Makepeace Thackeray
The Newcomes

Then with no fiery, throbbing pain,
No cold gradations of decay,
Death broke at once the vital chain,
And freed his soul the nearest way.

Samuel Johnson
On the Death of Dr. Robert Levet

Our very hopes belied our fears,
Our fears our hopes belied—
We thought her dying when she slept.
And sleeping when she died.

For when the morn came dim and sad—
And chill with early showers,
Her quiet eyelids clos'd—she had
Another morn than ours.

Thomas Hood
"The Death-Bed"

...as I have discovered, passionate grief does not link us with the dead but cuts us off from them. This becomes clearer and clearer. It is just at those moments when I feel least sorrow—getting into my morning bath is one of them—that H. rushes upon my mind in her full reality, her otherness. Not, as in my worst moments, all foreshortened and patheticized and solemnized by miseries, but as she is in her own right. This is good and tonic.

C. S. Lewis
A Grief Observed

One cannot live with the dead; either we die with them or we make them live again.

Louis Martin-Chauffier
L'Homme et la bête

When all is said and done, the pain of mourning is a horrible thing, but it is the only door through which healing can begin. Initial pain includes acute emotional and often physical distress. It includes tears and helplessness, and fear and anger and guilt, all of which can be so intense that a mourner may need to stop his world to endure, to act "crazy" for a time in order to remain sane…

   To help a friend through the crazies one needs simply to *let him be crazy*. He might not mention why he is doing what he is doing, or even that he is doing it at all. But if he has called on you or allowed you to be with him to talk or cry, and then suddenly ceases to call, give him room. He may be grave-sitting, or talking to the dead person, or looking at albums, or lying in bed holding his pillow with a blouse of the dead person wrapped around it, or otherwise acting out the crazies. He may not want you to know that, not for a long time, if ever. Don't pry or make him feel guilty or abnormal; he is fighting for his sanity.

Nina Herrmann Donnelley
I Never Know What to Say

The righteous perisheth, and no man layeth it to heart: and merciful men are taken away, none considering that the righteous is taken away from the evil to come. He shall enter into peace: they shall rest in their beds, each one walking in his uprightness.

Isaiah 57:1-2

It is well known that mourners often get the illness which led to the death of a close person. Habits and interests of the deceased may be taken over indiscriminately…A hitherto rather dull wife whose witty husband had died surprised herself and all around her by her newly acquired gift of repartee. She tried to explain this by saying alternately, 'I have to do it for him now' or, 'It isn't really me, he speaks out of me' (like a ventriloquist). This same woman, partner in a very good, loving marriage, told me that she had always been amused by her husband's patient peeling of the top of his boiled egg, while she used to cut it off. 'Now,' she said, 'I just cannot bring myself to cut the top off, I have to peel it off patiently.'

Lily Pincus
Death and the Family

He who has gone, so we but cherish his memory, abides with us, more potent, nay, more present, than the living man.

Antoine de Saint-Exupéry
The Wisdom of the Sands

The finer the nature, and the higher the level at which it seeks to live, the lower in grief it not only sinks but dives: it goes to weep with beggars and mountebanks, for these make the shame of being unhappy less.

Elizabeth Bowen
The Death of the Heart

Grief should be the Instructor of the wise;
Sorrow is Knowledge.

George Gordon, Lord Byron
Manfred

Sorrow makes us all children again.

Ralph Waldo Emerson
Journals

Especially concentrate on the children. Listen to them. Celebrate them. They may have deep feelings that will be overlooked if you focus on yourself. Getting out Christmas tree ornaments one by one and decorating the tree can be a draining emotional experience when you are grieving. The temptation may be great to "forget it." But consider the importance of the Christmas tree and gifts to the children. A friend or relative will likely be more than happy to decorate your tree and help with purchasing and wrapping gifts if you cannot.

Janice Harris Lord
No Time for Goodbyes

There is something pleasurable in calm remembrance of a past sorrow.

Marcus Tullius Cicero
Ad Familiares

Melancholy and remorse form the deep leaden keel which enables us to sail into the wind of reality.

Cyril Connolly
The Unquiet Grave

I measure every Grief I meet
With narrow, probing Eyes—
I wonder if It weights like Mine—
Or has an Easier size.

Emily Dickinson
"I measure every grief I meet"

Sadness flies on the wings of the morning and out of the heart of darkness comes the light.

Jean Giraudoux
The Madwoman of Chaillot

Learn weeping, and thou shalt gain laughing.

George Herbert
Jacula Prudentum

I am so happy in Jesus,
Captivity's Captor is He;
Angels rejoice when a soul's saved,
Some day we like Him shall be,
Sorrow and joy have the same Lord,
Valley of shadows shall sing;
Death has its life, its door opens in heaven
Eternally, Christ is King.

Charles R. Scoville
"Christ Is King"

Death is a thing of grandeur. It brings instantly into being a whole new network of relations between you and the ideas, the desires, the habits of the man now dead. It is a rearrangement of the world.

Antoine de Saint-Exupéry
Flight to Arras

Great grief is a divine and terrible radiance which transfigures the wretched.

Victor Hugo
Les Misérables

"I am the first and the last," Jesus said. He is present at the beginning and at the end. He is there at the moment of birth and the moment of death. He is there when we set out on our Christian journey and He is there when we finish our course.

When the kings of the earth sleep in the dust of the ground and their power has vanished like a wisp of smoke, when all the enduring monuments of the world have turned into the mists that the morning sun drives away, when all the great men of the earth lie silent in their graves, Jesus will still be here.

It was the *known* presence of Jesus that calmed the apostle's heart. Christ does not say to us, "Fear not, here is a million dollars," or "Fear not, here is a miracle drug." He says, "Fear not, *it is I.*" Jesus' presence always banished fear, and it still does...

Jesus said, "I will never desert you, nor will I ever forsake you" (Hebrews 13:5).

The one constant in the believer's life is the presence of Jesus. Teilhard de Chardin was right when he said, "Joy is not the absence of pain but the presence of God."

Ron Dunn
Will God Heal Me?

When a man or woman loves to brood over a sorrow and takes care to keep it green in their memory, you may be sure it is no longer a pain to them.

Jerome K. Jerome
The Idle Thoughts of an Idle Fellow

While grief is fresh, every attempt to divert only irritates.

Samuel Johnson
Quoted in *The Life of Samuel Johnson*

Grief can't be shared. Everyone carries it alone, his own burden, his own way.

Anne Morrow Lindbergh
Dearly Beloved

Physical suffering apart, not a single sorrow exists that can touch us except through our thoughts.

Maurice Maeterlinck
Wisdom and Destiny

Do Your Mourning Now
- Don't postpone, deny, cover or run from your pain. Be with it. Now.
- Everything else can wait. An emotional wound requires the same priority treatment as a physical wound. Set time aside to mourn.
- The sooner you allow yourself to be with your pain, the sooner it will pass. The only way *out* is *through*.
- When you resist mourning, you interfere with the body's natural stages of recovery.
- If you postpone the healing process, grief can return months—even years—later to haunt you.
- Feel the fear, pain, desolation, anger. It's essential to the healing process.
- You are alive. You will survive.

Melba Colgrove, Harold Bloomfield, and Peter McWilliams
How to Survive the Loss of a Love

There is in this world in which everything wears out, everything perishes, one thing that crumbles into dust, that destroys itself still more completely, leaving behind still fewer traces of itself than Beauty: namely Grief.

Marcel Proust
Remembrance of Things Past:
The Sweet Cheat Gone

Why not leave their private sorrows to people? Is sorrow not, one asks, the only thing in the world people really possess?

Vladimir Nabokov
Pnin

For the wages of sin is death, but the free gift of God is eternal life through Jesus Christ our Lord.

Romans 6:23 (TLB)

Sorrows remembered sweeten present joy.

Robert Pollok
The Course of Time

Sorrow breaks seasons and reposing hours,
Makes the night morning and the noontide night.

William Shakespeare
Richard III

We wasters of sorrows!
How we stare away into sad endurance beyond them,
trying to foresee their end! Whereas they are nothing else
than our winter foliage,
our sombre evergreen, *one*
of the seasons of our interior year.

Rainer Maria Rilke
Duino Elegies

Sorrow is one of the vibrations that prove the fact of living.

Antoine de Saint-Exupéry
Wind, Sand, and Stars

Every one can master a grief but he that has it.

William Shakespeare
Much Ado About Nothing

When people fall in deep distress, their native sense departs.

Sophocles
Antigone

He that conceals his grief finds no remedy for it.

Turkish proverb

Father...Father...the letter glittered in the criss-cross light as I read the rest. Nollie had no details, not how or where he had died, not even where he was buried.

Footsteps were passing on the coconut matting. I ran to the door and pressed my face to the closed pass-through. "Please! Oh please!"

The steps stopped. The shelf dropped open. "What's the matter?"

"Please! I've had bad news—oh please, don't go away!"

"Wait a minute." The footsteps retreated, then returned with a jangle of keys. The cell door opened.

"Here." The young woman handed me a pill with a glass of water. "It's a seda-tive."

"This letter just came," I explained. "It says that my father—it says my father has died."

The girl stared at me. "Your father!" she said in astonished tones.

I realized how very old and decrepit I must look to this young person. She stood in the doorway a while, obviously embarrassed at my tears. "Whatever hap-pens," she said at last, "you brought it on yourself by breaking the laws!"

Dear Jesus, I whispered as the door slammed and her footsteps died away, how foolish of me to have called for human help when You are here. To think that Father sees You now, face to face! To think that he and Mama are together again, walking those bright streets...

I pulled the cot from the wall and below the calendar scratched another date.

March 9, 1944. Father. Released.

Corrie ten Boom
The Hiding Place

Where there is sorrow there is holy ground.

Oscar Wilde
De Profundis

In my Father's house are many mansions: if it were not so, I would have told you. I go to prepare a place for you. And if I go and prepare a place for you, I will come again, and receive you unto myself; that where I am, there ye may be also.

John 14:2-3

It is better to drink of deep griefs than to taste shallow pleasures.

William Hazlitt
Characteristics

A man's sorrow runs uphill; true it is difficult for him to bear, but it is also difficult for him to keep.

Djuna Barnes
Nightwood

First: nothing can make up for the absence of someone whom we love, and it would be wrong to try to find a substitute; we must simply hold out and see it through. That sounds very hard at first, but at the same time it is a great consolation, for the gap, as long as it remains unfilled, preserves the bonds between us. It is nonsense to say that God fills the gap; he doesn't fill it, but on the contrary, he keeps it empty and so helps us to keep alive our former communion with each other, even at the cost of pain.

Secondly: the dearer and richer our memories, the more difficult the separation. But gratitude changes the pangs of memory into a tranquil joy. The beauties of the past are borne, not as a thorn in the flesh, but as previous gifts in themselves. We must take care not to wallow in our memories or hand ourselves over to them, just as we do not gaze all the time at a valuable present, but only at special times, and apart from these keep it simply as a hidden treasure that is ours for certain. In this way the past gives us lasting joy and strength.

Dietrich Bonhoeffer
letter to Eberhard Bethge from Tegel Military Prison

Happiness is beneficial for the body, but it is grief that develops the powers of the mind.

Marcel Proust
Remembrance of Things Past: The Past Recaptured

A deep distress hath humanised my Soul.

William Wordsworth
"Elegiac Stanzas"

Grief drives men into habits of serious reflection, sharpens the understanding and softens the heart.

John Adams
letter to Thomas Jefferson

There is not any advantage to be won from grim lamentation.

Homer
Iliad

Winter is come and gone,
But grief returns with the revolving year.

Percy Bysshe Shelley
Adonais

For I reckon that the sufferings of this present time are not worthy to be compared with the glory which shall be revealed in us.

Romans 8:18

The funeral is the first major event of the mourner's life without the deceased. More than an unhappy gathering, more than a formalized farewell, the funeral is the pivot between before and after. Like other rituals, it is a rite of passage that provides a framework for change. At the funeral, if at no other time, the awesome passage from life to death is seriously addressed. The funeral is a ceremony of separation that provides an opportunity to express strong feelings, to be recognized and comforted as a mourner, to say farewell with structure, solemnity, and support, and to realign ourselves with the community of mourners—the living. For all those reasons, the funeral or memorial service can help enormously in the process of grieving.

Candy Lightner and Nancy Hathaway
Giving Sorrow Words

Sorrow is better than laughter: for by the sadness of the countenance the heart is made better.

Ecclesiastes 7:3

A man's dying is more the survivors' affair than his own.

Thomas Mann
The Magic Mountain

Take this sorrow to thy heart, and make it a part of thee, and it shall nourish thee till thou art strong again.

Henry Wadsworth Longfellow
Hyperion

Verily, verily, I say unto you, He that heareth my word, and believeth on him that sent me, hath everlasting life, and shall not come into condemnation; but is passed from death unto life.

John 5:24

Now we face a paradox: on the one hand nothing in the world is more precious than one single human person; on the other hand nothing in the world is more squandered, more exposed to all kinds of dangers, than the human being—and this condition must be. What is the meaning of this paradox? It is perfectly clear. We have here a sign that man knows very well that death is not an end, but a beginning. He knows very well, in the secret depths of his own being, that he can run all risks, spend his life and scatter his possessions here below, because he is immortal. The chant of the Christian liturgy before the body of the deceased is significant: Life is changed, life is not taken away.

Jacques Maritain
"Man's Destiny in Eternity"

I have good hope that there is something after death.

Plato
Phaedo

And the twelve gates were twelve pearls; every several gate was of one pearl: and the street of the city was pure gold, as it were transparent glass. And I saw no temple therein: for the Lord God Almighty and the Lamb are the temple of it. And the city had no need of the sun, neither the moon, to shine in it: for the glory of God did lighten it, and the Lamb is the light thereof.

Revelation 21:21-23

If you are thinking you might get bored or tired after being in Heaven for a while...don't worry! Try to imagine something with me. Imagine you are a little bird who lives in a tiny cage made of rusty metal. And inside your cage you have a food dish, and a little mirror, and a tiny perch to swing on.

Then one day some kind person takes your cage to a big, beautiful forest. The forest is splashed with sunlight. Proud, towering trees cover the hills and valleys as far as you can see. There are gushing waterfalls, and bushes drooping with purple berries, and fruit trees, and carpets of wild flowers, and a wide blue sky to fly in. And besides all these things, there are millions of other little birds...hopping from one green limb to another and eating their fill and raising their little families and singing their hearts out all through the day.

Now, little bird, can you imagine wanting to stay in your cage? Can you imagine saying, "Oh please don't let me go. I will miss my cage. I will miss my little food dish with seeds in it. I will miss my plastic mirror and my tiny little perch. I might get bored in that big forest."

That would be silly, wouldn't it? And it's just as silly to think we might run out of things to do in Heaven!

Larry Libby
Someday Heaven

Our Creator would never have made such lovely days, and have given us the deep hearts to enjoy them, unless we were meant to be immortal.

Nathaniel Hawthorne
Mosses from an Old Manse

For I am persuaded, that neither death, nor life, nor angels, nor principalities, nor powers, nor things present, nor things to come, nor height, nor depth, nor any other creature, shall be able to separate us from the love of God, which is in Christ Jesus our Lord.

Romans 8:38-39

Death, be not proud, though some have called thee
Mighty and dreadful, for thou art not so;
For those whom thou think'st thou dost overthrow
Die not, poor Death; not yet canst thou kill me.
From rest and sleep, which but thy pictures be,
Much pleasure; then from thee much more must flow;
And soonest our best men with thee do go—
Rest of their bones and souls' delivery!
Thou'rt slave to fate, chance, kings, and desperate men,
And does with poison, war, and sickness dwell;
And poppy or charms can make us sleep as well
And better than thy stroke. Why swell'st thou then?
One short sleep past, we wake eternally,
And Death shall be no more: Death, thou shalt die.

John Donne
"Death, Be Not Proud"

And this is the record, that God hath given to us eternal life, and this life is in his Son. He that hath the Son hath life; and he that hath not the Son of God hath not life. These things have I written unto you that believe on the name of the Son of God; that ye may know that ye have eternal life, and that ye may believe on the name of the Son of God.

1 John 5:11-13

Death is the veil which those who live call life:
They sleep, and it is lifted.

Percy Bysshe Shelley
Prometheus Unbound

What reason do atheists have to say that one cannot rise from the dead? Which is the more difficult, to be born or to be reborn? That that which has never existed should exist, or that that which has existed should exist again? Is it more difficult to come into being than to return to it? Custom makes the one seem easy, absence of custom makes the other seem impossible: a vulgar way of judging!

Blaise Pascal
Pensées

And I give unto them eternal life; and they shall never perish, neither shall any man pluck them out of my hand.

John 10:28

There we shall be with seraphims and cherubims, creatures that will dazzle your eyes to look on them. There, also, we shall meet with thousands and thousands that have gone before us to that place; none of them are hurtful, but loving and holy, every one walking in the sight of God, and standing in his presence with acceptance for ever; in a word, there we shall see the elders with their golden crowns, there we shall see the holy virgins with golden harps; there we shall see men, that by the world were cut in pieces, burnt in flames, eaten of beasts, drowned in the seas, for the love that they bear to the Lord of the place; all well, and clothed with immortality as with a garment.

John Bunyan
The Pilgrim's Progress

And God shall wipe away all tears from their eyes; and there shall be no more death, neither sorrow, nor crying, neither shall there be any more pain: for the former things are passed away.

Revelation 21:4

We're all homesick.

A pastor once counseled a homeless man who claimed to be homesick. "But you have no home," the pastor declared. "How can you be homesick?"

The street dweller responded, "I'm homesick for the home I never had."

If you've never met Christ, I'm sure you're looking for the home you've never had. The Spirit calls to you from eternity, "Do you want a home here?" All you need do is answer, "Yes, Lord. Prepare a place for me, too."

If you've known the Lord but have wandered, you might be wondering if your room at home is still available. It is. As soon as you turn your heart toward home, the Father will see you from a distance and run to meet you.

If you are walking daily in God's grace, perhaps you're wondering if there's more. There sure is. You have a far better place prepared for you. You just haven't had the privilege of moving in there yet.

Jesus' invitation to childhood again may mean getting homesick for Heaven. But that's OK. Your Father won't leave you here forever. In the meantime, I suggest you call home often.

Alan D. Wright
A Chance at Childhood Again

Lives again our glorious King...
Where, O death, is now thy sting?...
Dying once, He all doth save...
Where thy victory, O grave?...

Love's redeeming work is done...
Fought the fight, the battle won...
Death in vain forbids Him rise...
Christ has opened Paradise...

Soar we now, where Christ has led...
Foll'wing our exalted Head...
Made like Him, like Him we rise...
Ours the cross, the grave, the skies. Alleluia!

Charles Wesley
"Christ the Lord Is Risen Today"

As I have experienced the deaths of three of my sons, God has become my Comforter. He is always available to me; He doesn't judge me or rebuke me for admitting that I hurt. God has experienced sorrow. He, in fact, was a bereaved parent, because He, too, had a Son who suffered and died. But the exciting news is God's

Son didn't stay dead. He conquered death for each of us so that we can have the hope of spending eternity with Him in heaven. We also can have the hope of seeing our loved ones again.

I have vivid memories of a special night when Nate was five years old. I was tucking him into bed and he seemed restless and unable to settle down. I asked him if there was a problem. He squirmed a little and then said, "I'm not sure I've invited Jesus into my heart."

I asked him why he wanted to invite Jesus into his life. "Because I've done some wrong things, and I want to make sure I'll go to heaven."

I listened as Nathan prayed and asked Jesus to come into his heart and live with him. After that there was no doubt in Nate's mind. He referred to the event often. As he grew, we saw the effect of the decision in his desire to study God's Word and in his submissive attitude toward us and toward God. How thankful I am I can look back on that evening and have confidence I will see Nate again.

"And now, dear brothers, I want you to know what happens to a Christian when he dies so that when it happens, you will not be full of sorrow, as those who are who have no hope. For since we believe that Jesus died and then came back to life again, we can also believe that when Jesus returns, God will bring back with him all the Christians who have died" (1 Thessalonians 4:13-14, TLB).

Marilyn Willett Heavilin
Roses in December

We feel and know that we are eternal.

Baruch Spinoza
Ethics

Many people have asked me to tell them about heaven and the afterlife. I sometimes smile because I do not know any more than they do. Yet when one young man asked if I looked forward to being united with God and all those who have gone before me, I made a connection to an old memory.

The first time I traveled with my mother and sister to my parents' homeland of Tonadico di Primiero in Northern Italy, I felt as if I had been there before. After years of looking through my mother's photo albums, I knew the mountains, the land, the houses, the people. As soon as we entered the valley, I said, "I know this place. I am home." Somehow I think crossing from this life into life eternal will be similar. I will be home.

Joseph Cardinal Bernardin
The Gift of Peace

And he said unto Jesus, Lord, remember me when thou comest into thy kingdom. And Jesus said unto him, Verily I say unto thee, Today shalt thou be with me in paradise.

Luke 23:42-43

I'll be home soon. My plane is nearing San Antonio. I can feel the nose of the jet dipping downward. I can see the flight attendants getting ready. Denalyn is somewhere in the parking lot, parking the car and hustling the girls toward the terminal.

I'll be home soon. The plane will land. I'll walk down that ramp and hear my name and see their faces. I'll be home soon.

You'll be home soon, too. You may not have noticed it, but you are closer to home than ever before. Each moment is a step taken. Each breath is a page turned. Each day is a mile marked, a mountain climbed. You are closer to home than you've ever been.

Before you know it, your appointed arrival time will come; you'll descend the ramp and enter the City.

You'll see faces that are waiting for you. You'll hear your name spoken by those who love you. And, maybe, just maybe—in the back, behind the crowds—the One who would rather die than live without you will remove his pierced hands from his heavenly robe and...applaud.

Max Lucado
The Applause of Heaven

When we've been there ten thousand years,
Bright shining as the sun,
We've no less days to sing God's praise
Than when we first begun.

John Newton
"Amazing Grace"

Acknowledgments

Every effort has been made to provide accurate source attribution for selections in this volume. Should any attribution be found to be incorrect, the publisher welcomes written documentation supporting correction for subsequent printings. For material not in the public domain, selection was made according to generally accepted fair-use standards and practices. The publisher gratefully acknowledges the cooperation of the following publishers and individuals for their permission to excerpt longer selections; credits have been worded as directed by those copyright holders. Requests to reprint any selections should be directed to the original sources.

CHAPTER ONE
HANDLING ADVERSITY

They Rose Above It by Bob Considine. Copyright © 1977 by Millie Considine as Executive of the Estate of Bob Considine. Used by permission of Doubleday, a division of Bantam Doubleday Dell Publishing Group, Inc.

Joni Eareckson Tada, *Secret Strength*, used by permission of Multnomah Publishers, Inc., Sisters, Oregon.

Maggie Bedrosian, "No Road Too Steep," as printed in the book *Life Is More Than Your To-Do List: Blending Success & Satisfaction* (Maryland: BCI Press, 1995). Used by permission.

Jennifer Rosenfeld with Alison Lambert, "No Hair Day," from *Chicken Soup for the Woman's Soul* (New York: Health Communications, Inc., 1996), pp. 105-107. Used by permission.

Joni Eareckson Tada, *Glorious Intruder*, used by permission of Multnomah Publishers, Inc., Sisters, Oregon.

John Wayne Schlatter, "The Finest Steel Gets Sent Through the Hottest Furnace," (California: John Wayne Schlatter, 1995). Used by permission. John Wayne Schlatter is a motivational speaker and can be reached at P. O. Box 577, Cypress, CA, 90630.

Philip Gulley, *Front Porch Tales*, used by permission of Multnomah Publishers, Inc., Sisters, Oregon.

D. James Kennedy and Jerry Newcombe, *New Every Morning*, used by permission of Multnomah Publishers, Inc., Sisters, Oregon.

"The Man in the Water," 1/25/82. © 1982 Time, Inc. Reprinted by permission.

Lilly Walters, "Why Do These Things Have to Happen?" Used by permission.

Ron Dunn, *Will God Heal Me?* used by permission of Multnomah Publishers, Inc., Sisters, Oregon.

Normal Is Just a Setting on Your Dryer by Patsy Clairmont and published by Focus on the Family. Copyright © 1993, Patsy Clairmont. All rights reserved. International copyright secured. Used by permission.

CHAPTER TWO
SUCCEEDING WITH MY MONEY

Dan Benson, *21 Days to Financial Freedom* (Grand Rapids, Michigan: Zondervan Publishing House, 1998). Used by permission.

Straight Talk on Money, reprinted with the permission of Simon & Schuster, copyright ©1993 by Ken and Daria Dolan.

Cornelius P. McCarthy, *The Under 40 Financial Planning Guide: From Graduation to Your First House* (California: Merritt Publishing, 1996), pp. 7-8. Used by permission.

Ken and Daria Dolan, *Straight Talk on Money* (New York: Simon & Schuster, 1993), pp. 50-51.

Cornelius P. McCarthy, *The Under 40 Financial Planning Guide: From Graduation to Your First House* (California: Merritt Publishing, 1996), pp. 111-112. Used by permission.

CHAPTER THREE
SUCCEEDING AT MY WORK

Joni Eareckson Tada, *Glorious Intruder,* used by permission of Multnomah Publishers, Inc., Sisters, Oregon.

Alan D. Wright, *A Chance at Childhood Again,* used by permission of Multnomah Publishers, Inc., Sisters, Oregon.

Charlie Hedges, *Getting the Right Things Right,* used by permission of Multnomah Publishers, Inc., Sisters, Oregon.

Jane Ellen Ibur, "If Only" from the book *If I Had a Hammer: Women's Work in Poetry, Fiction, and Photographs,* edited by Sandra Martz (California, Papier-Mache Press, 1990), pp. 37-38. Used by permission.

Virginia Rudasill Mortenson, "Hideaway Inn" from the book *If I Had a Hammer: Women's Work in Poetry, Fiction, and Photographs,* edited by Sandra Martz (California, Papier-Mache Press, 1990), pp. 169-176. Used by permission.

CHAPTER FOUR
COPING WITH LIFE'S HURTS

D. James Kennedy and Jerry Newcombe, *New Every Morning,* used by permission of Multnomah Publishers, Inc., Sisters, Oregon.

Robert H. Schuller, *Life's Not Fair, but God Is Good* (Tennessee: Thomas-Nelson,

1991), pp. 81-84. Used by permission.

Christopher Nolan, *Under the Eye of the Clock: The Life Story of Christopher Nolan* (England, Weidenfeld and Nicolson Publishers, 1987), pp. 37-38. Used by permission.

Ron Mehl, *The Cure for a Troubled Heart,* used by permission of Multnomah Publishers, Inc., Sisters, Oregon.

Melba Colgrove, Ph.D., Harold H. Bloomfield, M.D., & Peter McWilliams, *How to Survive the Loss of a Love* (California, Prelude Press, 1991), p. 16. Used by permission.

CHAPTER FIVE
LEARNING TO LOVE

A. E. Housman, "More Poems," from *The Collected Poems of A. E. Housman* (New York: Henry Holt & Company, Inc., 1965), p. 198. Used by permission.

John M. Drescher, *Meditations for the Newly Married* (Pennsylvania: Herald Press, 1969), pp. 61-62. Used by permission.

Rabbit Hill by Robert Lawson. Copyright © 1944 by Robert Lawson. Renewed copyright © 1971 by John W. Boyd. Used by permission of Viking Penguin, a division of Penguin Books USA Inc.

Leo F. Buscaglia, Ph.D., *Born for Love: Reflections on Loving* (New Jersey: SLACK, Incorporated, 1992), p. 124. Used by permission.

Leo Buscaglia, Ph.D., *Living, Loving & Learning* (New Jersey, copyright © 1982 by Leo Buscaglia, Inc.), p. 207. Used by permission.

Random Acts of Kindness by The Editors of Conari Press, copyright © 1993 by Conari Press, reprinted by permission from Conari Press.

C. S. Lewis, *Mere Christianity* (London, England: HarperCollins, Ltd., 1943), p. 116.

CHAPTER SIX
ENJOYING A GOOD MARRIAGE

Dale V. Atkins and Meris Powell, *From the Heart: Men and Women Write Their Private Thoughts About Their Married Lives* (New York: Henry Holt and Company, Inc., 1994), pp. 10-12.

Mike Mason, *The Mystery of Marriage,* used by permission of Multnomah Publishers, Inc., Sisters, Oregon.

Gene Perret, "Please, Don't Ask Me That!" (New York: as published in the January 1997 issue of *Good Housekeeping* Magazine). Used by permission.

So You're Getting Married by H. Norman Wright. © Copyright 1985. Gospel Light/Regal Books, Ventura, CA 93003. Used by permission.

Love & Marriage by Bill Cosby. Copyright © 1989 by Bill Cosby. Used by permission of Doubleday, a division of Bantam Doubleday Dell Publishing Group, Inc.

Marriage Made in Heaven copyright © 1983 by Jhan Robbins reprinted by permission of The Putnam Publishing Group.

Dale V. Atkins and Meris Powell, *From the Heart: Men and Women Write Their Private Thoughts About Their Married Lives* (New York: Henry Holt and Company, Inc., 1994), pp. 196-200.

O. Henry, "The Gift of the Magi" from *The Best Short Stories of O. Henry* (New York: Doubleday & Company, Inc., 1994), pp. 1-7.

From This Day Forward by Louise DeGrave. Copyright © 1981 by Louise DeGrave. By permission of Little, Brown and Company.

Chapter Seven
Being a Good Parent

God Uses Cracked Pots by Patsy Clairmont and published by Focus on the Family. Copyright © 1991, Patsy Clairmont. All rights reserved. International copyright secured. Used by permission.

Marilyn Heavilin, *Becoming a Woman of Honor,* pp. 137-38. Used by permission.

Gary and Anne Marie Ezzo, *Reaching the Heart of Your Teen,* used by permission of Multnomah Publishers, Inc., Sisters, Oregon.

Kent Nerburn, *Letters to My Son: Reflections on Becoming a Man* (California: New World Library, 1993), pp. 67-74. Used by permission.

Kevin Huggins, *Parenting Adolescents* (Colorado: NavPress, 1989), pp. 191-192. Used by permission.

Philip Gulley, *Front Porch Tales,* used by permission of Multnomah Publishers, Inc., Sisters, Oregon.

Chapter Eight
Being a Good Friend

Stu Weber, *Locking Arms,* used by permission of Multnomah Publishers, Inc., Sisters, Oregon.

"Little Acts of Kindness…," from *Simple Wisdom* by Kathleen Mahoney. Copyright © 1993 by Kathleen Mahoney; photographs copyright © 1993 by Lilo Raymond. Used by permission of Viking Penguin, a division of Penguin Books USA Inc.

Somewhere a Master by Elie Wiesel, translated by Marion Wiesel. Copyright © 1982 by Elirion Associates, Inc. Reprinted with the permission of Simon & Schuster.

Joseph Bayly, as quoted in *Acts of Love* by David Jeremiah, used by permission of Multnomah Publishers, Inc., Sisters, Oregon.

Philip Gulley, *Front Porch Tales,* used by permission of Multnomah Publishers, Inc., Sisters, Oregon.

CHAPTER NINE
BEING A GOOD CITIZEN

The Tightwad Gazette: Promoting Thrift as a Viable Alternative Lifestyle by Amy Dacyczyn. Copyright © 1992 (New York, Random House, Inc.). Used by permission.

The abridged version of *The Tailor of Gloucester* by Beatrix Potter. Copyright © Frederick Warne & Co., 1903. Reproduced by kind permission of Frederick Warne & Co.

Cry, the Beloved Country by Alan Paton. Copyright 1948 by Alan Paton; copyright renewed © 1976 by Alan Paton. Reprinted with the permission of Scribner, a Division of Simon & Schuster.

B. White, *Sleeping at the Starlite Motel* (pages 43-46). © 1995 Bailey White. Reprinted by permission of Addison-Wesley Longman Inc.

Max Lucado, *No Wonder They Call Him the Savior*, used by permission of Multnomah Publishers, Inc., Sisters, Oregon.

CHAPTER TEN
SAYING AND DOING THE RIGHT THING

Philip Gulley, *Front Porch Tales*, used by permission of Multnomah Publishers, Inc., Sisters, Oregon.

Alan D. Wright, *A Chance at Childhood Again*, used by permission of Multnomah Publishers, Inc., Sisters, Oregon.

Howard Thurman, "Deep Is the Hunger," *Disciplines for the Inner Life*, by Bob Benson and Michael W. Benson (Thomas Nelson Publishers, © October 1989, Nashville, TN), pp. 269-270. Used by permission.

Charlie Hedges, *Getting the Right Things Right*, used by permission of Multnomah Publishers, Inc., Sisters, Oregon.

The excerpt from *The Education of Little Tree* by Forrest Carter, published by The University of New Mexico Press, is reprinted by arrangement with Eleanor Friede Books Inc. © 1976 by Forrest Carter. All rights reserved.

Dan Clark, "Just in Time," *Chicken Soup for the Woman's Soul* (Utah: Dan Clark, 1996), pp. 14-15.

Plain Speaking: An Oral Biography of Harry S. Truman by Merle Miller, copyright 1973, 1974. Published by arrangement with The Berkley Publishing Group.

CHAPTER ELEVEN
FINDING PEACE AND FULFILLMENT

Joni Eareckson Tada, *Glorious Intruder*, used by permission of Multnomah Publishers, Inc., Sisters, Oregon.

Robert Frost, "The Road Not Taken" from *The Collected Poems, Complete and Unabridged*, edited by Edward Connery Lathem (New York; Henry Holt & Company, Inc., 1969), p. 105. Used by permission.

Chérie Carter-Scott, "The Rules for Being Human," from *Chicken Soup for the Soul* (Florida: Health Communications, Inc., 1993), pp. 81-82. Used by permission.

Virginia Satir, "My Declaration of Self-Esteem" used with permission of AVANTA The Virginia Satir Network, 2104 S.W. 152nd Street, Suite 2, Burien, WA 98166. All rights reserved.

"The Fisherman and His Wife" from *Grimm's Tales For Young And Old* by Jakob and Wilhelm Grimm. Copyright © 1977 by Ralph Manheim. Used by permission of Doubleday, a division of Bantam Doubleday Dell Publishing Group, Inc.

Gordon Dean, "Lessons Learned," from *They Rose Above It* by Bob Considine. Copyright © 1977 by Millie Considine as Executive of the Estate of Bob Considine. Used by permission of Doubleday, a division of Bantam Doubleday Dell Publishing Group, Inc.

Wouldn't Take Nothin' for My Journey Now by Maya Angelou. Copyright © 1993 by Maya Angelou. Reprinted by permission of Random House, Inc. and Maya Angelou, "Whiners," from *Wouldn't Take Nothin' for My Journey Now* (London: Virago Press, 1993). Used by permission.

Charlie Hedges, *Getting the Right Things Right*, used by permission of Multnomah Publishers, Inc., Sisters, Oregon.

Corrie ten Boom with John and Elizabeth Sherrill, *The Hiding Place*. Chosen Books, Inc., Chappaqua, NY, 1971, p. 238. Used by permission.

CHAPTER TWELVE
ENJOYING LIFE TO THE FULL

Gregory M. Lousig-Nont, Ph.D., "The Best Day of My Life" (Nevada: Gregory Lousig-Nont, Ph.D., 1995). Used by permission.

Fran Capo, "Just Say Yes" (New York: Fran Capo, 1996). Used by permission.

Glenn McIntyre, "Why Wait?...Just Do It!" (Glenn B. McIntyre, McIntyre & Associates).

Charlie Hedges, *Getting the Right Things Right*, used by permission of Multnomah Publishers, Inc., Sisters, Oregon.

My Utmost for His Highest by Oswald Chambers. Copyright © 1935 by Dodd, Mead & Co., renewed © 1963 by the Oswald Chambers Publications Assn. Ltd., and is issued by permission of Discovery House Publishers, Box 3566, Grand Rapids, MI 49501. All rights reserved.

Adair Lara, "Practice Random Kindness and Senseless Acts of Beauty" (California: 1991). Used by permission. Author of "At Adair's House, More Columns From America's Favorite Former Single Mom" (Chronicle Books).

"The Body Of Christ—Set Free" from *Ragman and Other Cries of Faith* by Walter J. Wangerin. Copyright © 1984 by Walter Wangerin, Jr. Reprinted by permission of Harper-Collins Publishers, Inc.

God Uses Cracked Pots by Patsy Clairmont and published by Focus on the Family. Copyright © 1991, Patsy Clairmont. All rights reserved. International copyright secured. Used by permission.

They Rose Above It by Bob Considine. Copyright © 1977 by Millie Considine as Executive of the Estate of Bob Considine. Used by permission of Doubleday, a division of Bantam Doubleday Dell Publishing Group, Inc.

CHAPTER THIRTEEN
ENJOYING MY RELATIONSHIP WITH GOD

I've Got to Talk to Somebody, God by Marjorie Holmes. Copyright 1968, 1969 by Marjorie Holmes Mighell. Used by permission of Doubleday, a division of Bantam Doubleday Dell Publishing Group, Inc.

David Heller, *Dear God: Children's Letters to God*, Doubleday, 1987.

"Unbeliever's Prayer" from *Death Be Not Proud* by John Gunther. Copyright 1949 by John Gunther. Copyright renewed 1976 by Jane Perry Gunther. Reprinted by permission of HarperCollins Publishers, Inc.

Pope John Paul II, "January 9—Our Search for God," from *Lift Up Your Hearts* (Italy: Edizioni Piemme S.P.A., 1995), p. 18.

Finding God by Dr. Larry Crabb, Jr. Copyright © 1993 by Lawrence J. Crabb, Jr., Ph.D., P.A., dba, Institute of Biblical Counseling. Used by permission of Zondervan Publishing House.

David Heller, *Dear God: Children's Letters to God*, Doubleday, 1987.

C. S. Lewis, *Mere Christianity* (London, England: HarperCollins, Ltd., 1943), pp. 45-46.

C. S. Lewis, *Mere Christianity* (London, England: HarperCollins, Ltd., 1943), pp. 55-56.

CHAPTER FOURTEEN
GROWING OLDER

Elise Maclay, "I Miss Being Needed" from *Green Winter* (New York: Henry Holt & Company, Inc., 1977), p. 17. Used by permission.

Young Till We Die by Dr. Doris Jonas and Dr. David Jonas. Copyright © 1973 by Davidor, Ltd. Reprinted by permission of The Putnam Publishing Group.

Garson Kanin, *It Takes a Long Time to Become Young*, copyright © 1978, T. F. T. Corporation (New York), pp. 59, 61, 65. Used by permission.

CHAPTER FIFTEEN
ENDING WELL

Ron Dunn, *Will God Heal Me?* used by permission of Multnomah Publishers, Inc., Sisters, Oregon.

In the Unlikely Event of a Water Landing by Christopher Noël. Copyright © 1996 by Christopher Noël. Reprinted by permission of Times Books, a division of Random House, Inc.

Alan D. Wright, *A Chance at Childhood Again,* used by permission of Multnomah Publishers, Inc., Sisters, Oregon.

Marilyn Heavilin, *Roses in December,* pp. 102-103. Used by permission.

Index